The Forked Flame

The Forked Flame

a study of D. H. LAWRENCE

by

H. M. Daleski

The University of Wisconsin Press

Published 1987

The University of Wisconsin Press
114 North Murray Street
Madison, Wisconsin 53715

The University of Wisconsin Press, Ltd.
1 Gower Street
London WC1E 6HA, England

First Wisconsin printing
Originally published in 1965 by Faber and Faber Limited
and Northwestern University Press

Printed in the United States of America

Library of Congress Cataloging-in-Publication Data

Daleski, H. M. (Hillel Matthew), 1926–
The forked flame.
Includes bibliographical references and index.
1. Lawrence, D. H. (David Herbert), 1885–1932—
Criticism and interpretation. I. Title.
PR6023.A93Z6235 1987   823'.912   87-6005
ISBN 0-299-11410-4
ISBN 0-299-11414-7 (pbk.)

So I believe in the little flame between us. For me now, it's the only thing in the world. . . . It's my Pentecost, the forked flame between me and you.

Mellors to Connie, *Lady Chatterley's Lover*

A man who is well balanced between male and female, in his own nature, is, as a rule, happy, easy to mate, easy to satisfy, and content to exist. It is only a disproportion, or a dissatisfaction, which makes the man struggle into articulation.

D. H. Lawrence: 'Study of Thomas Hardy'

Contents

A Retrospective Note

ONE CANNOT STEP TWICE, Heraclitus has told us, into the same river—
and by the same token one could not write the same book twice. The
critical river has certainly flowed to some purpose since *The Forked Flame*
was first published more than twenty years ago; and if I were writing
the book today, I am aware how different it would be in many of its
particulars as a result both of the ongoing critical debate and the
scholarly work that has been done in the interim. At the same time,
since the book offers a view of Lawrence that is based, in its theoretical
presuppositions, on his own writings, and in its supporting demonstration, on a close analysis of the texts discussed, this view—for what
it's worth—seems to me to retain its own general validity; and on re-
reading the book, it was pleasant to find that I can still endorse its
argument. But it is not only rivers that flow on. We too are not what
we were; and I am even more strongly aware, in the light of my own
continued engagement with Lawrence over the years, of what I would
want to do differently if I were writing the book today.

One of the main problems I was initially confronted with was my selection of texts. I wished both to present an overall view of Lawrence's development and to offer detailed readings of the works analyzed. In order to avoid ending up with a book of inordinate length, this meant concentrating on texts which were presented as representative of stages in the line of development. To that end I chose *Sons and Lovers* as representative of what I called "the first period"; and though I still value this novel highly, I now very much regret that the choice entailed the omission of *The White Peacock*, which I summarily dismissed as "immature work." It is no doubt immature in its clumsy handling of its first-person narrative and in its evasive treatment of the relationship of Cyril Beardsall and Emily Saxton, but it also has real power and seems to me today a considerable achievement. Nor is its achievement merely a matter of its striking descriptions of nature, a feature that has long been recognized and acclaimed. It also offers ample evidence of some of Lawrence's characteristic strengths as a novelist, his profound apprehension of character and his ability to render this by means of symbolic action—as in the chapter entitled "The Scent of Blood," which provides a foretaste of the fine and justly famous animal scenes in *Women in Love*. Furthermore, I now think that *The White Peacock* would on several counts have made a better starting point than *Sons and Lovers* for the particular matter I wished to pursue; and were I writing today, I would risk the additional length entailed by its inclusion as a text.

My revaluation of the *The White Peacock* was dependent on a change of focus. Once I ceased to view George Saxton as the protagonist of the novel, it was possible to locate its centre in Lettie Beardsall and to do justice to both the nature of its organization and the complexity of her presentation. She is Lawrence's first major character, and it is significant that she is torn between what he was later to define as the male and female principles, embodying such inner conflict in a prototypical form. Lettie is very much a woman with a mind, placing a high value on things of the intellect; at the same time she has an abundant physical vitality, showing a real capacity for living "in the blood." Her inability to reconcile these two sides of her nature is dramatized in her denial of one or the other half of her self in her relationships with George Saxton and Leslie Tempest, as also in her continued veering between the two men as what has been repressed in her seeks expression. Her conflict may also be thought of as one between what Lawrence (in a 1915 letter) calls "blood-consciousness" and "mental consciousness," terms that are vividly concretized in the novel. This formulation highlights the continuity of Lawrence's concerns throughout his career as a novelist, for it is essentially the same as that in which *Lady Chatterley's Lover* figures (in a 1928 letter) as a novel of "the phallic Consciousness versus the mental-spiritual Consciousness." *The White Peacock* is a first novel that not only repays careful attention in its own right but also epitomizes the extent to which Lawrence's end is in his beginning.

Lawrence's beginning as a novelist was conditioned by his own personal circumstances, in a manner that I described; but it was also rooted in the literary tradition he inherited, which I do not think I paid sufficient attention to. Lawrence, it seems to me now, comes straight out of George Eliot, not Hardy, as is commonly supposed, Hardy's influence being of significance at a later stage, from the time of the "Study of Thomas Hardy" (1914). A further reason for wishing I had begun with *The White Peacock* is the opportunity this would have provided for establishing the crucial nature of George Eliot's influence. That influence is everywhere apparent in it, to a degree that Lawrence's first novel may well be regarded as his rewriting of *The Mill on the Floss.* Jessie Chambers recounts that Lawrence explicitly stated he was using George Eliot as a model when he began to write *The White Peacock,* and her memoir abounds with references by Lawrence to the earlier novelist and to *The Mill on the Floss* and his "favourite heroine," Maggie Tulliver. In this novel Lawrence found a structural pattern which he could use to express his own deepest intuitions: namely, the kind of love triangle which presents the two men to whom the heroine is attracted as opposites and as embodying opposed tendencies within the heroine herself. The nature of the self-division of the heroine is thus concretized in the opposition between the two lovers as it is also externalized in her attraction to both men. It is a pattern that Lawrence used not only in *The White Peacock* but also in *Lady Chatterley's Lover* and, allowing for a hero rather than a heroine as protagonist, in *Sons and Lovers* as well. But in following George Eliot, Lawrence may be said to have found himself, for *The White Peacock* marks the beginning of his lifelong search for a means of reconciling the opposed principles exemplified in it.

It also seems to me today that *Aaron's Rod* does not warrant the kind of detailed attention I gave it. Reference certainly needs to be made to it as introducing "the third period," but I think this could have been confined to a short account of the relationship of Aaron and Lilly and of Lilly's doctrine of power. Instead I would today use *The Ladybird* tales as the text which most effectively represents Lawrence at this stage of his career. "The Ladybird," "The Fox," and "The Captain's Doll" are among Lawrence's finest tales, and a discussion of them would have gone some way to paying a necessary tribute to his work as a writer of short fiction. At the same time these tales dramatize what Lilly pontificates about, the necessity to replace the love-mode by the power-mode. In adumbrating a new kind of relationship between men and women in these tales, Lawrence also hints at the need for a kind of sexual submission on the part of the woman that becomes explicit only in *The Plumed Serpent. The Ladybird* volume thus leads more directly to *The Plumed Serpent* than does *Aaron's Rod*, and it also prepares us for the extreme lengths to which Lawrence drove himself at this period. These are not suddenly manifest in *The Plumed Serpent*; they are clearly apparent too in these tales—in his justification of murder in "The Fox," for instance.

If I started this retrospect by stating that I stand by the general argument of *The Forked Flame*, it seems to me fitting that I should end it by affirming how over the years Lawrence has retained a supreme interest for me. It is not only that now, toward the end of the century, he clearly stands out, together with James Joyce, as one of the two greatest novelists of the age. On me he has had the kind of personal impact I have not experienced in my work on any other writer; and if in this book I tried to shape his development, it is salutary to know just how much he has shaped me.

Jerusalem   H. M. D.
October 1986

Preface

In this study I have undertaken a detailed critical analysis of representative novels in order to trace the development of D. H. Lawrence as a novelist. I have approached the novels by way of the ideas that are formulated in Lawrence's expository writings, and particularly by way of one of the central statements of his beliefs, the 'Study of Thomas Hardy'. The most striking feature of Lawrence's *Weltanschauung* is its dualism; and in the essay on Hardy Lawrence sets out his concept of duality in terms of the 'male' and 'female' principles, insisting that all creativity is dependent on the fruitful interaction of the two principles. It is my contention that Lawrence, though believing intensely in himself as a male, was fundamentally identified with the female principle as he himself defines it in the essay on Hardy. The consequent breach in his nature made it imperative for him to try to reconcile the opposed elements within himself, and I have viewed his work as a lifelong attempt to effect such a reconciliation.

I do not for a moment wish to suggest that my account of the conflict in Lawrence between the male and female elements in his nature serves to 'explain' him in any comprehensive sense. Genius is always too large and complex to be reducible to any single explanation. I do claim, however, that this conflict was the psychological motive force of his 'struggle into articulation', and that an analysis of the artistic expression of the conflict both reveals the continuity of Lawrence's preoccupations as a novelist and suggests the reasons for some sharp changes in direction. I believe, furthermore, that an awareness of this conflict is often of help in interpreting Lawrence's symbolism, and thus in illuminating crucial but obscure passages in the novels.

'If you divide the human psyche into two halves', wrote Lawrence, 'one half will be white, the other black. It's the division itself which is pernicious. The swing to one extreme causes the swing to the other.'[1] I think that some such movement may be discerned in the novels. I have tried to follow this movement, putting my emphasis on the important novels and only dealing with what seems to me to be inferior work in so far as this is necessary to mark the line of development.

From a consideration of their themes, the major novels may be divided into four groups corresponding to four distinct periods in Lawrence's writing life. In the first period he tries to assimilate the experiences of his youth, and particularly to resolve the problems associated with his relationships with his father and mother and with the women whom he loved before he met his wife. These relationships, I believe, left him with an abiding sense of duality. *The White Peacock*, like most first novels, is interesting for the indications it gives of themes which are to be fully developed later, but it is immature work. *The Trespasser*, Lawrence's second novel, is I should say the worst book he wrote. I have not, therefore, discussed either of these novels. They both lead up to the completely realized vision of *Sons and Lovers*, which I have treated as the representative work of this period.

In the second period Lawrence attempts to create the 'supreme art', which will reconcile the 'law of the woman' and the 'law of the man'.[2] I think that most critics today would agree that *The Rainbow* and *Women in Love*, the two novels of this period, are his greatest achievement, and I have given them the prominence they deserve.

[1] Review of *Solitaria* by V. V. Rozanov, *Phoenix: The Posthumous Papers of D. H. Lawrence*, ed. Edward D. McDonald (London, 1936), p. 370.
[2] The phrases are from the Hardy essay. The passage in which they occur is quoted in full in Chap. 1—see pp. 31–32 below.

In the third period Lawrence's interest in the relations between man and woman is subordinated to a concern with the themes of male friendship and leadership in the world of men. He is primarily concerned, that is to say, with the 'law of the man', and in this regard he slowly moves to an extreme position. In the novels of this period he may be said to be writing against his own deepest sympathies, and, in comparison with *The Rainbow* and *Women in Love*, there is a significant decline in creative achievement. I wanted to record this decline and to try to establish its cause, but I did not wish to emphasize it unduly. Accordingly, I have discussed only the first and last novels of this period, taking these to be sufficiently representative of the weakness of Lawrence's work at this time.

The Lost Girl was published between *Women in Love* and *Aaron's Rod*, but chiefly no doubt because of the circumstances of its composition, it is clearly out of the main line of development. (It was begun in 1912, but the MS was left in Germany in 1914, and it was only in 1920 that Lawrence was able to recover it and to resume work on it. It was thus 'three parts done' before the war[1] – before, that is, the major work of *The Rainbow* and *Women in Love* was completed.) I have therefore treated *Aaron's Rod* as the first novel of the third period, and though I do not consider it a good book, it is of interest both because it announces the new theme of leadership and because it discloses Lawrence's changed attitude to his art. In *The Plumed Serpent*, the last novel of this period, Lawrence drives the leadership theme to what he himself ultimately recognizes is a repugnant conclusion. I have not discussed *Kangaroo* because, though Lawrence tries in it to test his ideas of male friendship and of leadership by applying them to a particular political situation, his tentative treatment of the themes exhibits all the weaknesses of *Aaron's Rod* and little of the power of *The Plumed Serpent*. I have also omitted *The Boy in the Bush* (which, like *Kangaroo*, is set in Australia) since it is a work of collaboration and it would be difficult, to say the least, to determine the extent of Lawrence's contribution to it.

'The swing to one extreme causes the swing to the other': *Lady Chatterley's Lover*, the only novel of the fourth period, testifies to the truth of Lawrence's remark. The book is an implicit vindication of the female principle as this is defined in the Hardy essay, and in it Lawrence moves away from leadership to 'tenderness', firmly opposing the 'phallic consciousness' to the 'mental consciousness'. *Lady Chatterley's Lover*, in my view, falls just short of the larger achievement of

[1] *The Letters of D. H. Lawrence*, ed. Aldous Huxley (London, 1956), p. 488.

the two novels of the second period, but it is a most impressive work, and I have given it detailed consideration.

Concerning the method I have employed: I have tried to pin my analysis of the novels to the text, and I have therefore made lavish use of quotation. The quotations are meant to serve a double purpose. First and foremost, they are offered as a check on the criticism. In accordance with Lawrence's own injunction, my procedure has been to trust the tale, not the artist; and a reader, it seems to me, can do no less than willingly submit himself to a similar restriction, that of trusting the artist, not the critic. I hope there is no unsubstantiated judgement in this book; a reading may well be disputed, but the grounds for the interpretation should not be found obscure. Second, the fullness of the quotations has enabled me to dispense with synopses of the action. A knowledge of the novels is assumed, but the quotations should enable a reader without such knowledge to follow the main line of the action in each instance. Moreover, as Percy Lubbock long ago remarked, the image of a book we have read 'escapes and evades us like a cloud'; the quotations, I hope, will be accepted as solid ground even by those familiar with Lawrence.

I am deeply aware how much I owe to the work of others in the field of Lawrence studies. I wish to pay tribute, above all, to the work of F. R. Leavis. I also wish to record my special indebtedness to the criticism of Mark Spilka, Graham Hough, and Mark Schorer; and to the biographies of Harry T. Moore and Edward Nehls. Julian Moynahan's *The Deed of Life*, an excellent recent study of Lawrence, appeared after my own work was completed, but I profited greatly from his previously published essay on *Lady Chatterley's Lover*.

I am also glad to acknowledge a large personal indebtedness. My principal debts are to three friends and colleagues: to Professor Adam Mendilow, who commented with great acumen on the typescript and showed me how it could be improved in many ways; to Dr Ruth Nevo, who coupled rigorous, discerning criticism and encouragement, and whose guidance in regard to a crucial issue saved me from despair; and to Professor Dorothea Krook, who bore with me in long, inestimably helpful discussions and deftly pointed out the vague and the clumsy in the typescript. I am also grateful to Professor Lawrance Thompson of Princeton University for his many valuable suggestions. My thanks are due to several of my students, whose challenges forced me to amendments.

This book is based on material which was submitted in vastly different form to The Hebrew University as a doctoral dissertation. I am grateful to the Anglo-Jewish Association of London for a grant in 1957 which enabled me to spend a year in England; and to Professor David Daiches, then of Jesus College, Cambridge, for help given at that time. I am indebted to the Israeli Mifal Hapayis for a grant which covered the costs of typing.

Chapter 1, 'The Duality of Lawrence', has appeared in different form as an essay in *Modern Fiction Studies*; I wish to thank the Editor for permission to use this material. I also wish to thank Messrs William Heinemann Ltd for permission to print the quotations from Lawrence's works.

The Hebrew University   H.M.D.
Jerusalem

1 The Tiger and the Lamb: The Duality of Lawrence

IN THE FOREWORD TO *Fantasia of the Unconscious* LAWRENCE CLAIMS that his 'pseudo-philosophy' is 'deduced from the novels and poems, not the reverse', and he goes on to say that 'the novels and poems are pure passionate experience. These "pollyanalytics" are inferences made afterwards, from the experience.'[1] It is tempting to accept this claim at its face value. To do so would ensure that critical attention is directed primarily to Lawrence's imaginative writing, as it should be; and we are only too aware of the sort of misrepresentation to which Lawrence has been subjected by critics who insist on regarding him as a prophet or 'pseudo-philosopher'. Nevertheless, I am inclined to think it is not the whole truth. Lawrence's 'pollyanalytics' are not only *a posteriori*; in the *Fantasia*, published in 1922, he was indeed concerned to give systematic expression to some of the insights gained in the writing of *The Rainbow* (1915) and *Women in Love* (1920), but it is clear that in that work he was equally preoccupied with the ideas he was to develop in

[1] London, 1931, pp. 10–11.

the novels from *Aaron's Rod* (1922) to *The Plumed Serpent* (1926). The *Fantasia* was written while he was at work on *Aaron's Rod*, and I think it is justifiable to regard it as an exploration of the new as much as a consolidation of the old.

There is other, even more striking evidence that the ideas contained in Lawrence's expository writing of any given period tend to be coeval with their imaginative formulation, and often to precede it. Lawrence's polemical correspondence with Bertrand Russell in 1915, for instance, marks the beginning of his preoccupation with the question of leadership; it was several years before he returned to this subject, first in parts of the essay 'The Education of the People',[1] and then in the novels of the third phase. Again, the 'Study of Thomas Hardy'[2] was written while Lawrence was at work on *The Rainbow*, and it deals explicitly with problems which arise both in that novel and in *Women in Love*.

What I am suggesting, then, is that it is wise to regard the expository writings not as laboratory reports on experiments successfully concluded but as signposts to a road which is finally travelled only in the art. In those writings Lawrence clearly did not use the precise instruments of a philosopher, and it was only by embodying his ideas in the 'pure passionate experience' of his art that he could hope to establish their validity. But the *a priori* theories were consistently modified by the artistic experience, which in turn led to further formulations. The result, as far as Lawrence's major creative work is concerned—I assume it is agreed that the novels are his main achievement and that, though the poems and stories may illuminate facets of the experience recorded there, they are of less importance—is a series of novels remarkable for their constant and organic development. I believe that some of the early essays provide us with a key to this development, and that the novels may therefore be best approached by way of Lawrence's ideas. I am aware, however, that a theory of a writer's development bears the same relation to criticism as Lawrence's 'pollyanalytics' to his art: it is only detailed *literary* criticism which can make the theory meaningful.

[1] Published in *Phoenix* (1936), but written in 1918. See *Letters*, p. 459.
[2] Published in *Phoenix*, but begun in September 1914. See *Letters*, p. 208.

II

A central feature of Lawrence's thought is its dualism. Lawrence both proclaimed his own duality – 'I know I am compound of two waves . . . I am framed in the struggle and embrace of the two opposite waves of darkness and of light'[1] – and asserted that 'everything that exists, even a stone, has two sides to its nature'.[2] We are not surprised, therefore, to find that his interpretation of the large movement of history should be expressed in these terms:

'We must never forget that mankind lives by a twofold motive: the motive of peace and increase, and the motive of contest and martial triumph. As soon as the appetite for martial adventure and triumph in conflict is satisfied, the appetite for peace and increase manifests itself, and *vice versa*. It seems a law of life.'[3]

Similarly, Lawrence detects in 'nearly all great novelists' a dichotomy of a 'didactic purpose . . . directly opposite to their passional inspiration'.[4] He also distinguishes between the Old and New Testaments in terms of the Holy Spirit which manifests itself both as a Dove (the New Testament) and as an Eagle,[5] and maintains that Christianity itself is dual, being both a 'religion of the strong, [that teaches] renunciation and love', and a 'religion of the weak, [that teaches] down with the strong and the powerful, and let the poor be glorified'.[6]

I do not wish to suggest that Lawrence invariably clamped diverse generalizations into the vice of a dualistic thesis. Statements such as those I have just quoted were rather the natural ambience of a constant position, and in the expository writings which deal specifically with his theory of duality he is for the most part content to make his point metaphorically or symbolically. That is to say, duality is viewed as an all-pervading principle, but no attempt is made to demonstrate or argue the intuition systematically. Instead, the opposed forces are seen symbolically, in terms of the dark and the light, the eagle and the

---

[1] 'The Crown', *Reflections on the Death of a Porcupine* (Philadelphia, 1925), p. 24.

[2] '. . . Love Was Once a Little Boy', *Reflections*, p. 183.

[3] *Movements in European History*, pseud. Lawrence H. Davison (London, 1921), p. 306.

[4] 'The Novel', *Reflections*, p. 105. See too *Studies in Classic American Literature* (New York, 1923), *passim*.

[5] *Twilight in Italy* (London, 1916), p. 29.

[6] *Apocalypse* (London, 1932), p. 18.

dove, the tiger and the lamb, or the lion and the unicorn. What is insisted on, however, time and again, is both the fact of opposition and the necessity for its existence, to the point indeed of turning the conflict itself into a *raison d'être*: '[The lion and the unicorn] would both cease to be, if either of them really won in the fight [for the crown] which is their sole reason for existing';[1] and 'Homer was wrong in saying, "Would that strife might pass away from among gods and men!" He did not see that he was praying for the destruction of the universe; for in the tension of opposites all things have their being.'[2] It is this concept of the tension of opposites and the relation which Lawrence wishes to see established between the contending forces that have a direct bearing on his art.

It is not easy to describe the nature of the relation precisely since Lawrence expresses his intuitions symbolically. 'Phoenix, Crown, Rainbow, Plumed Serpent', writes Henry Miller, 'all . . . centre about the same obsessive idea: *the resolution of two opposites in the form of a mystery*'.[3] The selection of symbols is illuminating, but the word 'resolution', in so far as it implies a dissolution of the opposites, is misleading. The end product *is* a mystery–it is a unified whole created out of discordant elements–but what distinguishes Lawrence's position from most dualist philosophies is his insistence that the contending forces must retain their separate identities. The new whole which is created by establishing a relation between the opposites is not a fusing of the two into one but a complementing of the one by the other; and the

---

[1] 'The Crown', *Reflections*, p. 3. Cf. Blake in 'The Marriage of Heaven and Hell': 'Without contraries is no progression. Attraction and Repulsion, Reason and Energy, Love and Hate, are necessary to Human existence.' F. R. Leavis was the first, in this respect, to point out the 'significant parallel' between Lawrence's thought and that of Blake; see 'D. H. Lawrence', *For Continuity* (Cambridge, 1933), pp. 111–13.

[2] 'Notes for *Birds, Beasts and Flowers*', *Phoenix*, p. 67. Cf. 'War, then, is the father and king of all things, in the world as in human society; and Homer's wish that strife might cease was really a prayer for the destruction of the world.' John Burnet, *Early Greek Philosophy* (London, 1920), p. 164. Though Lawrence was interested in Burnet as early as 1916–see Edward Nehls, *D. H. Lawrence: A Composite Biography*, Vol. I (Madison, 1957), p. 402–there is no evidence that he had read *Early Greek Philosophy* when he first formulated his theory of duality in works such as *Twilight in Italy* and the 'Study of Thomas Hardy'. I am inclined to believe that Lawrence's dualistic outlook was primarily the result of his own early experience–see p. 73 below– and that he turned later to the Greek philosophers for confirmation of his ideas.

[3] 'Creative Death', *The Wisdom of the Heart* (London, 1947), p. 10.

relation itself is the only absolute Lawrence is prepared to acknowledge:

'It is past the time to cease seeking one Infinite, ignoring, striving to eliminate the other. The Infinite is twofold, the Father and the Son, the Dark and the Light, the Senses and the Mind, the Soul and the Spirit, the self and the not-self, the Eagle and the Dove, the Tiger and the Lamb. The consummation of man is twofold, in the Self and in Selflessness. By great retrogression back to the source of darkness in me, the Self, deep in the senses, I arrive at the Original, Creative Infinite. By projection forth from myself, by the elimination of my absolute sensual self, I arrive at the Ultimate Infinite, Oneness in the Spirit. They are two Infinites, twofold approach to God. And man must know both.

'But he must never confuse them. They are eternally separate. The lion shall never lie down with the lamb. The lion eternally shall devour the lamb, the lamb eternally shall be devoured. Man knows the great consummation in the flesh, the sensual ecstasy, and that is eternal. Also the spiritual ecstasy of unanimity, that is eternal. But the two are separate and never to be confused. To neutralise the one with the other is unthinkable, an abomination. . . .

'The two Infinites, negative and positive, they are always related, but they are never identical. They are always opposite, but there exists a relation between them. This is the Holy Ghost of the Christian Trinity. . . . That which I may never deny, and which I have denied, is the Holy Ghost which relates the dual Infinites into One Whole, which relates and keeps distinct the dual nature of God. To say that the two are one, this is the inadmissible lie. The Two are related, by the intervention of the Third, into a Oneness.

'. . . There are two opposite ways to consummation. But that which relates them, like the base of the triangle, this is the constant, the Absolute, this makes the Ultimate Whole. . . .'[1]

Lawrence's reference in this passage to the Holy Ghost is an instance of his transvaluation of Christian terminology; I shall have occasion later to discuss his highly personal view of Judaism. The point to register, however, is not his theological inexactitude, for he is clearly assigning his own poetic value to the Holy Ghost 'figure', but the analogical suggestiveness of the allusion. The Hebraic-Christian tradition provides him with a rich source of imagery for his private religion, and he exploits the emotional power of the tradition while using it for

[1] *Twilight in Italy*, pp. 80–2.

his own purposes–as in 'The Man Who Died', which is a superb example of this procedure. In the quoted passage, Lawrence is really concerned with the relation between the opposing forces within the individual psyche; the reference to the Holy Ghost as the reconciler between the Father and the Son, viewed as opposites, both illuminates Lawrence's concept of an absolute (the unified self) and sanctifies it. What he is insisting on is that the individual is required not only to recognize his dual nature but, on due occasion, to go as far as he can towards either extremity: it is the ever-present acceptance, however, of a relation between the two extremes which, like the base of the triangle, establishes a unity, prevents derangement, and, so to speak, keeps the forces in line. There is an interesting similarity, in this respect, between Lawrence's views and those of E. M. Forster. Forster's terms are different–he writes of the monk and the beast and of the mystic and the businessman–but he, too, insists on the need for relation between the opposed parts and on the necessity for 'continuous excursions' into the opposed 'realms'. It is particularly striking that he, too, should choose the rainbow (he talks of 'the rainbow bridge that should connect the prose in us with the passion') to symbolize the sort of connection he wishes to see established.[1] Lawrence's theory of polarity (the two extremes are negative and positive) may also be compared, as Graham Hough has suggested,[2] with Jung's concept of integration. Certainly Lawrence maintains that the full acceptance of duality results in a state of more intense and purer being:

'Because we are both these, because we are lambs, frail and exposed, because we are lions furious and devouring, because we are both and have the courage to be both, in our separate hour, therefore we transcend both, we pass into a beyond, we are roses of perfect consummation.'[3]

Lawrence views relationship between individuals in much the same way. I have avoided using the word 'balance' to describe what is really a recurring movement from one extreme to the other of forces within the individual, but it aptly suggests the counterpoise which Lawrence believes to be necessary in personal relations. Where the relationship is that between a man and a woman, there is a double reconciliation of opposites, for the man and the woman are required not only to

[1] *Howards End* (London, 1947), pp. 183–4, 192. The 'sermon' is attributed to Margaret, but it is clearly representative of Forster's own thought.
[2] *The Dark Sun* (London, 1956), p. 230.
[3] 'The Reality of Peace', *Phoenix*, p. 690.

meet as opposites but, as we have seen, to reconcile the opposing qualities within themselves. The relationship is envisaged as a meeting on equal terms of two people who have themselves achieved full individuality and transcend their duality in the balance that is attained between them:

'If it is to be life then it is fifty per cent. me, fifty per cent. thee: and the third thing, the spark, which springs from out of the balance, is timeless. Jesus, who saw it a bit vaguely, called it the Holy Ghost.

'Between man and woman, fifty per cent. man and fifty per cent. woman: then the pure spark. Either this, or less than nothing.'[1]

The duality of male and female is central to Lawrence's dualism and requires separate consideration. Lawrence's major pronouncement on this subject is to be found in the 'Study of Thomas Hardy' (1914).[2] His starting-point is the assertion that the duality of all life is manifested in two opposing wills which must be brought into true relation:

'So life consists in the dual form of the Will-to-Motion and the Will-to-Inertia, and everything we see and know and are is the resultant of these two Wills. . . .

'Since there is never to be found a perfect balance or accord of the two Wills, but always one triumphs over the other, in life, according to our knowledge, so must the human effort be always to recover balance, to symbolize and so to possess that which is missing. Which is the religious effort of Man.

...

'The dual Will we call the Will-to-Motion and the Will-to-Inertia. These cause the whole of life, from the ebb and flow of a wave, to the stable equilibrium of the whole universe, from birth and being and knowledge to death and decay and forgetfulness. And the Will-to-Motion we call the male will or spirit, the Will-to-Inertia the female. . . .'[3]

Lawrence cautiously states that 'the division into male and female is arbitrary, for the purpose of thought', since 'motion and rest are the same, when seen completely';[4] but in fact the two wills serve as a pair

[1] 'Him with His Tail in His Mouth', *Reflections*, p. 141.
[2] Cf. 'I am just finishing a book, supposed to be on Thomas Hardy, but in reality a sort of Confessions of my Heart. I wonder if ever it will come out. . . .' Letter to Amy Lowell (November 1914), S. Foster Damon, *Amy Lowell: A Chronicle* (New York, 1935), p. 279.
[3] 'Study of Thomas Hardy', *Phoenix*, pp. 447–8.
[4] *Ibid.*, p. 448.

of primary attributes in his formulation of the male and female principles:

'The goal of the male impulse is the announcement of motion, endless motion, endless diversity, endless change. The goal of the female impulse is the announcement of infinite oneness, of infinite stability. When the two are working in combination, as they must in life, there is, as it were, a dual motion, centrifugal for the male, fleeing abroad, away from the centre, outward to infinite vibration, and centripetal for the female, fleeing in to the eternal centre of rest. A combination of the two movements produces a sum of motion and stability at once, satisfying. But in life there tends always to be more of one than the other. . . .'[1]

The dualism of Will-to-Motion and Will-to-Inertia is subsumed within that of the more comprehensive principles of Love and Law:

'The two great conceptions, of Law and of Knowledge or Love, are not diverse and accidental, but complementary. They are, in a way, contradictions each of the other. But they are complementary. They are the Fixed Absolute, the Geometric Absolute, and they are the radiant Absolute, the Unthinkable Absolute of pure, free motion. They are the perfect Stability, and they are the perfect Mobility. They are the fixed condition of our being, and they are the transcendent condition of knowledge in us. They are our Soul, and our Spirit, they are our Feelings, and our Mind. They are our Body and our Brain. They are Two-in-One.

'And everything that has ever been produced has been produced by the combined activity of the two, in humanity, by the combined activity of soul and spirit. When the two are acting together, then Life is produced, then Life, or Utterance, Something, is *created*. And nothing is or can be created save by combined effort of the two principles, Law and Love.

. . .

'Now the principle of the Law is found strongest in Woman, and the principle of Love in Man. . . .

'Man and woman are, roughly, the embodiment of Love and the Law: they are the two complementary parts. . . .'[2]

In this passage it is not the thought which is difficult but the terminology which is confusing. If, however, we shed conventional associations of the words 'Law' and 'Love', we find that the two principles are adequately defined by the context. Law is the natural law of the body,

[1] *Ibid.*, p. 457. [2] *Ibid.*, pp. 513–14.

Love is the counter-movement of the spirit, and the distinction pointed to is one between a condition of being and a condition of knowing. Inherently Lawrence is making the old distinction between the flesh and the spirit;[1] but his idiosyncratic terminology is a measure of his rebellion against the Christian implications of this division. His reaction against the traditional denigration of the flesh is strikingly emphasized by his collocation of Soul and Law in opposition to Spirit and Love. 'Soul', it would seem, is apprehended as the consciousness of the body; and by associating it with the flesh, Lawrence is attempting to give the body full value. True blessedness, for Lawrence, is not to be attained by the flight of the soul from the flesh to the spirit but by the 'combined activity' of Soul and Spirit viewed as opposites which complement each other. The coming together of the two principles of Law and Love implicitly constitutes a third principle, a creative principle, which operates most obviously in the sexual union of man and woman, the embodiments respectively of Love and Law. Love and Law, therefore, are the complementary principles not only of life itself but of all creation, and indeed Lawrence insists that the sex act is productive of more than progeny:

'This is the desire of every man, that his movement, the manner of his walk, and the supremest effort of his mind, shall be the pulsation outwards from stimulus received in the sex, in the sexual act, that the woman of his body shall be the begetter of his whole life, that she, in her female spirit, shall beget in him his idea, his motion, himself. When a man shall look at the work of his hands, that has succeeded, and shall know that it was begotten in him by the woman of his body, then he shall know what fundamental happiness is. Just as when a woman shall look at her child, that was begotten in her by the man of her spirit, she shall know what it is to be happy, fundamentally....'[2]

When Lawrence applies his theory of the principles of Law and Love to the relationships of men and women, as he does in his analysis of *Tess of the d'Urbervilles* and *Jude the Obscure*, the theory leads to the insights of a profound critical intelligence. When he forces the theory on to alien material, however, he is reduced to using it as a blunt and bludgeoning instrument. In the following passage, for instance, Law and Love are viewed as historical forces:

'It seems as if the history of humanity were divided into two epochs:

[1] Cf. 'Most fascinating in all artists is this antinomy between Law and Love, between the Flesh and the Spirit, between the Father and the Son.' *Ibid.*, p. 476.
[2] *Ibid.*, pp. 444–5.

the Epoch of the Law and the Epoch of Love. It seems as though humanity, during the time of its activity on earth, has made two great efforts:
the effort to appreciate the Law and the effort to overcome the Law in
Love. And in both efforts it has succeeded. It has reached and proved
the Two Complementary Absolutes, the Absolute of the Father, of
the Law, of Nature, and the Absolute of the Son, of Love, of Knowledge. What remains is to reconcile the two.'[1]

The generalization Lawrence makes here is so broad and so vague that
I assume historians would dismiss it out of hand. And indeed the
passage has the effect of confusing the otherwise consistent exposition
of the principles of Law and Love. Since Christ is the historical exemplar of Love, it would appear that the two epochs can be thought of as
roughly equivalent to the pre-Christian and Christian eras. Consequently we are required to regard all non-Christian civilizations as
being preponderantly representative of the principle of Law, a proceeding which illuminates neither the civilizations nor the principle.

The references in the passage quoted above to the Father and to the
Son give some indication of the way in which the two principles are
also wedded to theology. God the Father is the God of the Jews,
'the God of the body, the rudimentary God of physical laws and
physical functions';[2] the Father is the divine manifestation of the
female principle of Law: '... in the God of the Ancient Jew, the female
has triumphed. That which was born of Woman, that is indeed the
God of the Old Testament.'[3] The New Testament, on the other hand,
is 'the great assertion of the Male', and the Son is the divine manifestation of the male principle of Love. Christ is viewed as having risen
'from the suppressed male spirit of Judea', to live 'the male life utterly
apart from woman'. Consequently the body of Christ, 'that of Him
which was Woman', had to be put to death 'to testify that He was
Spirit, that He was Male, that He was Man, without any womanly
part'.[4] Lawrence, indeed, finds in the Christian conception of the
Trinity an analogue of his own mystical apprehension of the interaction of the male and female principles: the Father and the Son are
brought together in one Godhead by the Holy Ghost, in a union
analogous to that which he wishes to see established between man and
woman.[5] The Holy Ghost is 'the pure spark' which 'springs from out

---

[1] *Ibid.*, p. 510.   [2] *Ibid.*, p. 450.   [3] *Ibid.*, pp. 451–2.   [4] *Ibid.*, p. 452.
[5] G. Wilson Knight, in another connection, makes the same distinction as Lawrence in regard to the persons of the Trinity: 'Dionysus is an effeminate God,
Apollo a figure of masculine beauty.... In the Christian scheme, God the Father

of the balance' between man and woman as well as between the Father and the Son.[1]

If the analogy itself entails a radical simplification of Judaism and Christianity, the elaboration of one of its distinctions between the Father and the Son actually leads Lawrence to ascribe a quality to man which is as properly attributable to woman. It is necessary to clarify this point, for it is of considerable consequence in the novels. Lawrence asserts that woman, 'the fountain of all flesh', is 'obsessed by the one-ness of things', whereas man is 'ever keenly aware of the multiplicity of things, and their diversity'.[2] In the framework of Lawrence's formu-lation of male and female qualities this distinction is unobjectionable; but when he relates it to his conception of the Father and the Son, his argument leads him into self-contradiction. Jewish monism, the in-sistence that there is 'but One Being', is viewed as further evidence of the female character of Judaism, whereas the male conception of 'manifold Being' is manifested in Christ, who said 'Thou shalt love thy neighbour as thyself' and thus made 'the great utterance against Monism', for the command means 'Thou shalt recognize thy neigh-bour's distinction from thyself, and allow his separate being . . .'[3] Consequently, man embodies 'the desire to single out one thing from another, to reduce each thing to its intrinsic self by process of elimina-tion',[4] and the male principle, it seems, becomes not only Multiplicity and Diversity but also Singleness, Intrinsic Selfhood, Distinct Identity:

'The senses, sensation, sensuousness, these things which are incon-trovertibly Me, these are my God, these belong to God, said Job. And he persisted, and he was right. They issue from God on the female side.

'But Christ came with His contradiction: That which is Not-Me, that is God. All is God, except that which I know immediately as Myself. First I must lose Myself, then I find God. Ye must be born again.

'Unto what must man be born again? Unto knowledge of his own separate existence, as in Woman he is conscious of his own incorporate existence. Man must be born unto knowledge of his own distinct identity, as in woman he was born to knowledge of his identification with the Whole. . . .'[5]

is Dionysian; God the Son, especially at the transfiguration–for the Apollonian is visionary–Apollonian; and the Holy Spirit . . . the poetic fusion . . .' *The Mutual Flame* (London, 1955), p. 27.

[1] See p. 24 above.   [2] 'Study of Thomas Hardy', *Phoenix*, p. 451.
[3] *Ibid.*, p. 452.   [4] *Ibid.*, p. 451.   [5] *Ibid.*, p. 453.

When Lawrence deals with the relation of man and woman, however, Singleness–the ostensibly male quality–is viewed as a product of the *union* of male and female. In the sex act man and woman, equally, find themselves and are transcended:

'In Love, in the act of love, that which is mixed in me becomes pure, that which is female in me is given to the female, that which is male in her draws into me, I am complete, I am pure male, she is pure female; we rejoice in contact perfect and naked and clear, singled out unto ourselves, and given the surpassing freedom. No longer we see through a glass, darkly. For she is she, and I am I, and, clasped together with her, I know how perfectly she is not me, how perfectly I am not her, how utterly we are two, the light and the darkness, and how infinitely and eternally not-to-be-comprehended by either of us is the surpassing One we make. Yet of this One, this incomprehensible, we have an inkling that satisfies us.'[1]

If the man whom Lawrence identifies with Christ is a creature of abstraction, the man he writes of in this passage is the man he knows in the flesh. His mystical intuitions of the nature of being effectively negate his theological extrapolations; and that the abstraction is not to be trusted is sufficiently indicated by the ease with which it is abandoned:

'[Tess] knows she is herself incontrovertibly, and she knows that other people are not herself. This is a very rare quality, even in a woman. And in a civilization so unequal, it is almost a weakness.

'Tess never tries to alter or to change anybody, neither to alter nor to change nor to divert. What another person decides, that is his decision. She respects utterly the other's right to be. She is herself always.

'But the others do not respect her right to be. Alec d'Urberville sees her as the embodied fulfilment of his own desire: something, that is, belonging to him. She cannot, in his conception, exist apart from him nor have any being apart from his being. For she is the embodiment of his desire.

'This is very natural and common in men, this attitude to the world. . . .'[2]

The inconsistency of the argument, however, should not lead us into the error of reversing Lawrence's statement, of regarding Singleness and Distinct Identity as characteristic female qualities. They are qualities, it seems, which cannot usefully be classified under either

[1] *Ibid.*, p. 468.　　　　[2] *Ibid.*, p. 483.

the male or female principles because they in fact belong to both.

In the Hardy essay Lawrence is not otherwise inconsistent in his discussion of the attributes of male and female, but the scattered multiplication of instances tends to be confusing. I have therefore abstracted the qualities which are enumerated and present them in the following table:

Male	*Female*
Movement	Stability
Change	Immutability
Activity	Permanence
Time	Eternality[1]
Will-to-Motion	Will-to-Inertia[2]
Registers Relationships	Occupied in Self-Feeling
Refusal of Sensation	Submission to Sensation
Multiplicity and Diversity	Oneness[3]
Knowledge	Feeling[4]
Love	Law
Spirit	Flesh
God the Son	God the Father[5]
Service of Some Idea	Full Life in the Body
Doing	Being[6]
Self-Subordination	Self-Establishment[7]
Utterance	Gratification in the Senses[8]
Abstraction	
Public Good	Enjoyment through the Senses[9]
Community	
Mental Clarity	Sensation[10]
Consciousness	Instinct[11]
Spirit	Soul
Mind	Senses
Consciousness	Feelings[12]
Knowledge	Nature[13]
Condition of Knowledge	Condition of Being
Brain	Body[14]
Stalk	Root

[1] *Ibid.*, p. 446. [2] *Ibid.*, p. 448. [3] *Ibid.*, p. 451. [4] *Ibid.*, p. 455.
[5] *Ibid.*, p. 476. [6] *Ibid.*, p. 481. [7] *Ibid.*, pp. 483, 485. [8] *Ibid.*, p. 484.
[9] *Ibid.*, p. 487. [10] *Ibid.*, p. 498. [11] *Ibid.*, p. 501. [12] *Ibid.*, p. 509.
[13] *Ibid.*, p. 510. [14] *Ibid.*, p. 513.

Male   Female
Light   Darkness
Movement towards Discovery   Movement towards the Origin[1]

It is unlikely that psychologists would find these distinctions acceptable; but this is not the point at issue. The classification serves as a useful index to Lawrence's thought, and there are several inferences which can be drawn from it. In the first place, it seems clear that the male-female duality is at the heart of his dualistic beliefs. Graham Hough firmly denies this: 'The Male-Female opposition is an instance of this duality [i.e., 'dual reality'] but only an instance; and Lawrence is not constructing the world on the model of sexual duality. The Father, for example, is on the same side as the female.'[2] That the Father is an instance of the female principle is admittedly paradoxical but not by itself inconsistent; indeed, it may be argued that this is an indication of the extent to which Lawrence does construct the world on the model of male-female duality. The male-female opposition is not merely an instance of a dual reality but its underlying principle: Lawrence explicitly asserts that 'everything that is, is either male or female or both, whether it be clouds or sunshine or hills or trees or a fallen feather from a bird . . .'[3] The opposition is not only a paradigm on which Lawrence bases a large number of his beliefs about life; it is fundamental to all creativeness: 'In life, then, no new thing has ever arisen, or can arise, save out of the impulse of the male upon the female, the female upon the male. The interaction of the male and the female spirit begot the wheel, the plough, and the first utterance that was made on the face of the earth.'[4]

Second, Lawrence formulates his conception of art in terms of male and female. We cannot afford to ignore the purpose which, even if only tacitly avowed, is central to his work:

'It needs that a man shall know the natural law of his own being, then that he shall seek out the law of the female, with which to join himself as complement. He must know that he is half, and the woman is the other half: that they are two, but that they are two-in-one.

'He must with reverence submit to the law of himself: and he must with suffering and joy know and submit to the law of the woman: and he must know that they two together are one within the Great Law, reconciled within the Great Peace. Out of this final knowledge shall

---

[1] *Ibid.*, p. 514.   [2] *The Dark Sun*, p. 225.
[3] 'Study of Thomas Hardy', *Phoenix*, p. 446.   [4] *Ibid.*, p. 444.

come his supreme art. There shall be the art which recognizes and utters his own law; there shall be the art which recognizes his own and also the law of the woman, his neighbour, utters the glad embraces and the struggle between them, and the submission of one; there shall be the art which knows the struggle between the two conflicting laws, and knows the final reconciliation, where both are equal, two in one, complete. This is the supreme art, which yet remains to be done. Some men have attempted it, and left us the results of efforts. But it remains to be fully done.'[1]

Third, it is important to recognize the relation between the male and female principles and the disposition of conflicting forces within the individual psyche. It is here that we find a significant discrepancy between Lawrence's views in the 'Study of Thomas Hardy' (1914) and in *Fantasia of the Unconscious* (1922). In the former, his position is consistent with his general dualistic viewpoint: 'For every man comprises male and female in his being, the male always struggling for predominance. A woman likewise consists in male and female, with female predominant.'[2] 'Male' and 'female', therefore, can be regarded as roughly equivalent to the various pairs of opposites to which Lawrence refers in the description of individual duality already quoted,[3] and a coherent personality would then be one in which male and female elements are reconciled. Man's creativeness, moreover, would appear to be dependent not only on the stimulus received in his contact with woman but also on the fruitful interaction of male and female elements within himself.[4]

Early on in the *Fantasia*, Lawrence's view of individual duality is consistent with that advanced in the Hardy essay:

'. . . considering man at his best, he is at the start faced with the great problem. At the very start he has to undertake his tripartite being, the mother within him, the father within him, and the Holy Ghost,

---

[1] *Ibid.*, pp. 515–16.   [2] *Ibid.*, p. 481.   [3] See p. 22 above.
[4] See the passage from the Hardy essay quoted on p. 25 above. G. Wilson Knight takes a similar view of the creative process: 'That the creative artist should be pre-eminently bisexual is, of course, natural enough, since such creation demands continually a kind of sexual intercourse within the personality. . . . Our argument raises a host of disquieting problems and risks plunging us into a morass of contradictions, but our aim is, really, very simple and very obvious. I suggest a certain blend, a synthesis of the masculine and feminine principles, to be recorded and announced by poetry, as such . . .' *Christ and Nietzsche* (London, 1948), pp. 124–5. Cf. too Virginia Woolf, *A Room of One's Own* (London, 1946), pp. 147–8.

the self which he is supposed to consummate, and which mostly he doesn't.'[1]

Later, however, there is a radical change of view:

'A child is either male or female; in the whole of its psyche and physique is either male or female. Every single living cell is either male or female, and will remain either male or female as long as life lasts. And every single cell in every male child is male, and every cell in every female child is female. The talk about a third sex, or about the indeterminate sex, is just to pervert the issue.

'Biologically, it is true, the rudimentary formation of both sexes is found in every individual. That doesn't mean that every individual is a bit of both, or either, *ad lib. . . .*'[2]

This discrepancy is radical indeed, and has to be accounted for. I suggest that it can best be explained in terms of a deep split in Lawrence himself. Ernest Jones writes: 'When the attraction exercised by the mother is excessive it may exert a controlling influence over the boy's later destiny. . . . The maternal influence may . . . manifest itself by imparting a strikingly tender feminine side to the later character.'[3] This statement would seem to have at least a *prima facie* relevance to the development of the author of *Sons and Lovers*. I believe that Lawrence initially made a strenuous effort to reconcile the male and female elements in himself, but that he was more strongly feminine than masculine and that he was unable to effect such a reconciliation. I suggest, furthermore, that his insistence in the *Fantasia* on an absolute degree of masculinity is evidence of an extreme reaction, a refusal even to acknowledge the existence of feminine components in his make-up. 'The individual psyche divided against itself', said Lawrence, 'divides the world against itself'.[4] That there are valid grounds for believing that Lawrence was divided against himself I shall now try to show.

The more elementary biographical evidences have to be considered along with the rest. The members of Lawrence's family appear to have been agreed that as a youth he was somewhat 'effeminate':

'Bert usually preferred the company of girls. He detested football and cricket, and I don't remember him taking part in them. But he had a genius for inventing games, especially indoors.'[5]

'[Lawrence's] older brother George, with whom he quarrelled in

[1] p. 26. [2] *Ibid.*, p. 86. [3] *Hamlet and Oedipus* (New York, 1954), pp. 87–8.
[4] *Psychoanalysis and the Unconscious* (London, 1923), p. 106.
[5] Ada Lawrence and G. Stuart Gelder, *The Early Life of D. H. Lawrence* (London, 1932), pp. 29–30.

later life, remembered him affectionately as a child: "Oh, Bert was a grand little lad–he was always delicate–it was a source of grief to him that he wasn't able to enter the boys' games–he used to gather the girls together to go blackberrying–he was so delicate that I've carried him on my shoulder for miles. We all petted and spoiled him from the time he was born–my mother poured her very soul into him." [1]

William Hopkin, an Eastwood friend of Lawrence's, confirms this impression. Harry T. Moore reports him as saying:

'"I well remember the day when I was passing the school as the scholars were leaving for their dinner. [Lawrence] was walking between two girls, and a number of Breach boys walked behind him, monotonously chanting, 'Dicky Dicky Denches plays with the wenches.' That charge branded him as effeminate–the local term is 'mardarse'. Bert's chin was in the air as though he cared not a jot, but his eyes were full of anger and mortification." [2]

J. D. Chambers, the younger brother of Jessie Chambers (Lawrence's boyhood friend and the original of Miriam of *Sons and Lovers*), bluntly states what a number of Lawrence's contemporaries felt about him: 'As a matter of fact Lawrence was a woman in a man's skin. . . .' [3] In the various memoirs of Lawrence there are frequent references to his interest, in adult life, in what Olive Moore calls 'the housewifely virtues, the love of cooking, scrubbing, sewing, and the making of clothes'; [4] and in this connection it is perhaps not entirely trivial to

[1] Harry T. Moore, *The Intelligent Heart* (London, 1955), p. 9.
[2] *Ibid.*, p. 19. Cf. the testimony of Mabel Collishaw, J. E. Hobbs, and Ernest Wilson in Edward Nehls, *D. H. Lawrence*, I, 30, 33, 542 respectively; of May Holbrook in Edward Nehls, *D. H. Lawrence*, Vol. III (Madison, 1959), pp. 565–6, 580; and of George H. Neville, 'The Early Days of D. H. Lawrence', *The London Mercury*, 23 (March 1931), 477.
[3] Letter to Edward Nehls, *D. H. Lawrence*, I, 548. Cf. the views of Albert Limb and Stanley Hocking, *ibid.*, pp. 32, 367 respectively; of May Eva Gawler, in Edward Nehls, *D. H. Lawrence*, Vol. II (Madison, 1958), p. 134; of Trigant Burrow, in Edward Nehls, III, 148; and of Frederick Carter, *D. H. Lawrence and the Body Mystical* (London, 1932), p. 9.
[4] 'Further Reflections on the Death of a Porcupine', *The Apple Is Bitten Again: Self Portrait* (London, n.d.), p. 161. Cf. Cecil Gray, *Musical Chairs* (London, 1948), p. 126; Mark Schorer, 'Two Houses, Two Ways: The Florentine Villas of Lewis and Lawrence, Respectively', *New World Writing*, 4 (October 1953), 152–3; Eleanor Farjeon, 'Springtime with D. H. Lawrence', *The London Magazine* 2 (April 1955), 50; Hilda Cotterell and Cecily Minchin, in Edward Nehls, I, 455, 464 respectively; Rosalind Popham, in Nehls, II, 5; William Gerhardi, Angelo Ravagli, Barbara Barr, and Raul Mirenda, in Nehls, III, 12, 17–18, 24, 61 respectively.

mention his beard–which he remarked on in a letter to Catherine Carswell: 'Oh, by the way, I was seedy and have grown a beard. I think I look hideous, but it is so warm and complete, and such a clothing to one's nakedness, that I like it and shall keep it.'[1] The sum of these suggestions is indeed a thin caricature, not a portrait; and, taken alone, the imputation of effeminacy is not worth serious consideration. But the imputation has a larger context, and as such it may serve as a hint.

There is no need of outside testimony in regard to Lawrence's fundamental identification with the female principle. We have only to scan the table on pp. 30–1 to recognize this; for there is little doubt that Lawrence's sympathies are with the qualities ranged under the female. Although his effort is to reconcile the two principles, his stress is on the value of the female, on 'being', not 'doing':

'What is it that really matters? For the poppy, that the poppy disclose its red: for the cabbage, that it run up into weakly fiery flower: for Dido, that she be Dido, that she become herself, and die as fate will have it. Seed and fruit and produce, these are only a minor aim: children and good works are a minor aim. Work, in its ordinary meaning, and all effort for the public good, these are labour of self-preservation, they are only means to the end. The final aim is the flower, the fluttering, singing nucleus which is a bird in spring, the magical spurt of being which is a hare all explosive with fulness of self, in the moonlight; the real passage of a man down the road, no sham, no shadow, no counterfeit, whose eyes shine blue with his own reality, as he moves amongst things free as they are, a being; the flitting under a lamp of a woman incontrovertible, distinct from everything and from everybody, as one who is herself, of whom Christ said, "to them that have shall be given".'[2]

The male principle is almost exactly coextensive with all that Lawrence spent most of his life fighting against: abstraction, idealism, what he called, generically, the 'mental consciousness'; and conversely (and of course paradoxically), the female principle comes close to subsuming what he termed the 'phallic consciousness', which he fiercely espoused. This perverse alignment could only result in a split, for he believed intensely in himself as a male.

---

[1] *The Savage Pilgrimage* (London, 1932), p. 27. Lawrence also wrote to Amy Lowell: 'But I've been seedy, and I've grown a red beard, behind which I shall take as much cover henceforth as I can, like a creature under a bush.' S. Foster Damon, *Amy Lowell*, pp. 271–2.
[2] 'Study of Thomas Hardy', *Phoenix*, p. 403.

I think Lawrence provides us with a clue to the understanding of this inner division in the following passage:

'We are divided in ourselves, against ourselves. And that is the meaning of the cross symbol. . . .

'Nowadays men do hate the idea of dualism. It's no good, dual we are. The Cross. If we accept the symbol, then, virtually, we accept the fact. We are divided against ourselves. . . .

'You can't get away from this.

'Blood-consciousness overwhelms, obliterates, and annuls mind-consciousness.

'Mind-consciousness extinguishes blood-consciousness, and consumes the blood.

'We are all of us conscious in both ways. And the two ways are antagonistic in us. . . .

'My father hated books, hated the sight of anyone reading or writing.

'My mother hated the thought that any of her sons should be condemned to manual labour. Her sons must have something higher than that.

'She won. But she died first.

'He laughs longest who laughs last.'[1]

The dualism adumbrated here is familiar; what is interesting is that it is referred to not in terms of polarity but of division, and what is significant is that Lawrence's father and mother should appear to be unnecessarily dragged into the discussion. His father is identified, incompletely in this context but indisputably, with blood-consciousness, which is a property of the female principle; his mother, in turn, is identified with mind-consciousness, a property of the male principle. Lawrence's reference to his father and mother is, I suspect, not arbitrary but an unconscious revelation of the cause of his own identification with the female principle. There is further evidence that his mother and father embodied qualities which he classified under the male and female principles respectively, and I suggest that his passionate advocacy of the 'phallic consciousness' is a measure of his ultimate repudiation of his mother and identification with his father.

Sons and Lovers is the best source to turn to for substantiation of this claim, and in my analysis of the novel I shall deal with this question, but for the moment I should prefer to keep the implicit artistic for-

[1] *Studies in Classic American Literature*, pp. 123–5.

mulations separate and to draw on more explicit statements. In the
following quotations I think it fair to assume that Lawrence has his
mother and father in mind when he talks of the colliers and their
wives:

'Now the colliers had also an instinct of beauty. The colliers' wives
had not. The colliers were deeply alive, instinctively. But they had no
daytime ambition, and no daytime intellect. They avoided, really, the
rational aspect of life. They preferred to take life instinctively and
intuitively. . . .'[1]

'My mother's generation was the first generation of working-class
mothers to become really self-conscious. . . . The woman freed herself
at least mentally and spiritually from the husband's domination, and
then she became that great institution, that character-forming power,
the mother of my generation. I am sure the character of nine-tenths
of the men of my generation was formed by the mother: the character
of the daughters too.

'And what sort of characters? Well, the woman of my mother's
generation was in reaction against the ordinary high-handed, obstinate husband who went off to the pub to enjoy himself and to waste
the bit of money that was so precious to the family. The woman felt
herself the higher moral being: and justly, as far as economic morality
goes. She therefore assumed the major responsibility for the family,
and the husband let her. So she proceeded to mould a generation.'[2]

Both Jessie and May Chambers give us a direct impression of Lawrence's parents:

'Mrs Lawrence occupied a remarkable position in her family. She
ruled by a sort of divine right of motherhood, the priestess rather than
the mother. Her prestige was unchallenged; it would have seemed
like sacrilege to question her authority. I wondered often what was
the secret of her power, and came to the conclusion that it lay in her
unassailable belief in her own rightness.'[3]

'Only on very rare occasions did I see the father in Chapel. He looked
handsome in a rugged way: black curly hair and beard streaked
slightly with silver: blue eyes smiling kindly in a rugged face, glancing
over the congregation with a friendly air; well-built and strong in
figure; and a genial manner. By comparison the mother appeared

[1] 'Nottingham and the Mining Countryside', *Phoenix*, p. 136.
[2] '[Autobiographical Fragment]', *Phoenix*, p. 818.
[3] 'E.T.' (Jessie Chambers), *D. H. Lawrence: A Personal Record* (London, 1935),
p. 138.

bitter, disillusioned, and austere. Her attire was black, as I recall it.'[1]
Lawrence's father and mother are differentiated in terms which are
by now familiar. And his reaction against his mother is marked. There
is a hint of this in the ironic conclusion to the passage quoted from
Studies in Classic American Literature; it is plainly evident in 'The Education
of the People':

'Would God a she-wolf had suckled me, and stood over me with her
paps, and kicked me back into a rocky corner when she'd had enough
of me. It might have made a man of me.

'But it's no use sighing. Romulus and Remus had all the luck. We
see now why they bred a great, great race: because they had no mother:
a race of men. Christians have no fathers: only these ogling woman-
worshipping saints, and the self-conscious friction of exalted mothers.'[2]
With *Sons and Lovers* in mind, we may also note Lawrence's assertion that
'it is despicable for any one parent to accept a child's sympathy against
the other parent. And the one who *received* the sympathy is always
more contemptible than the one who is hated.'[3] Just how much he
'hated' his father is debatable: certainly, in later life, he tended to
admire him. Barbara Barr, Frieda's daughter by her first marriage,
reports that in 1926 Lawrence sometimes talked to her of his childhood, 'proudly saying that there had been more life and richness in it
than in any middleclass child's home. . . . Lawrence had formerly
hated his drunken father, but at this time had swung in sympathy
towards him, away from his mother.'[4]

III

I propose, then, to discuss Lawrence's development as a novelist in
terms of the self-division I have described. Before I turn to the novels,
however, I think it worth adding that his characteristic preoccupation
with sexual relations is also connected with this inner conflict.

Lawrence's interest in sexual relations is twofold. On one level, the
sex act is a tangible manifestation of the Holy Ghost; that is to say, in

[1] May (Chambers) Holbrook, memoir in Nehls, III, 554.
[2] *Phoenix*, p. 632.
[3] *Fantasia of the Unconscious*, p. 86.
[4] Memoir in Nehls, III, 22. Similar confessions are reported by Achsah Brewster
(see Chap. 2, p. 42 below) and by Rhys Davies, 'D. H. Lawrence in Bandol', *Horizon*,
2 (October 1940), 197.

the act man and woman are brought more closely than in any other way into a pure relation, both spiritual and physical, and are transcended in a consummation which, uniting both male and female, is greater than either and provides the stimulus for creative self-fulfilment. It is a consummation, indeed, which epitomizes the sort of unity Lawrence sought in a dualistic universe.

On a personal level, however, the act had a deeper significance for him. Just what it meant is perhaps best understood by considering his dualistic conception of love:

'But the love between a man and a woman, when it is whole, is dual. It is the melting into pure communion, and it is the friction of sheer sensuality, both. In pure communion I become whole in love. And in pure, fierce passion of sensuality I am burned into essentiality. I am driven from the matrix into sheer separate distinction. I become my single self, inviolable and unique, as the gems were perhaps once driven into themselves out of the confusion of earths. The woman and I, we are the confusion of earths. Then in the fire of their [our?] extreme sensual love, in the friction of intense, destructive flames, I am destroyed and reduced to her essential otherness. It is a destructive fire, the profane love. But it is the only fire that will purify us into singleness, fuse us from the chaos into our own gem-like separateness of being.

'All whole love between man and woman is thus dual, a love which is the motion of melting, fusing together into oneness, and a love which is the intense, frictional, and sensual gratification of being burnt down, burnt apart into separate clarity of being, unthinkable otherness and separateness. . . .

'There must be two in one, always two in one—the sweet love of communion and the fierce, proud love of sensual fulfilment, both together in one love. And then we are like a rose. We surpass even love, love is encompassed and surpassed. We are two who have a pure connexion. We are two, isolated like gems in our unthinkable otherness. But the rose contains and transcends us, we are one rose, beyond.'[1]

The sex act, therefore, is a union but not a fusion of man and woman; on the contrary, it is the means, the only means, whereby the man is forced to become pure male and the woman pure female. Female elements in the man are, for the moment, in abeyance; he is 'destroyed and reduced' to the essential otherness of the woman. The sex

[1] 'Love', *Phoenix*, pp. 154–5.

act, in other words, is the means by which Lawrence can resolve the conflict in himself between male and female.

Lawrence's conception of love as a social force is an extension of his account of love between man and woman:

'The Christian love, the brotherly love, this is always sacred. I love my neighbour as myself. . . .

'But, alas! however much I may be the microcosm, the exemplar of brotherly love, there is in me this necessity to separate and distinguish myself into gem-like singleness, distinct and apart from all the rest, proud as a lion, isolated as a star. This is a necessity within me. And as this necessity is unfulfilled, it becomes stronger and stronger and it becomes dominant.

'. . . We are bewildered, dazed. In the name of brotherly love we rush into stupendous blind activities of brotherly hate. We are made mad by the split, the duality in ourselves. . . .

'There must be brotherly love, a wholeness of humanity. But there must also be pure, separate individuality, separate and proud as a lion or a hawk. There must be both. In the duality lies fulfilment. Man must act in concert with man, creatively and happily. This is greatest happiness. But man must also act separately and distinctly, apart from every other man, single and self-responsible and proud with un-quenchable pride, moving for himself without reference to his neigh-bour. These two movements are opposite, yet they do not negate each other. We have understanding. And if we understand, then we balance perfectly between the two motions, we are single, isolated individuals, we are a great concordant humanity, both, and then the rose of perfection transcends us, the rose of the world which has never yet blossomed, but which will blossom from us when we begin to understand both sides and to live in both directions, freely and without fear, following the inmost desires of our body and spirit, which arrive to us out of the unknown.'[1]

The duality referred to in this passage is clearly of a similar nature to that defined in the description of love between a man and a woman: man's movement towards his fellows in brotherly love is similar to his 'melting into pure communion' with the woman, and his move-ment back to self, to isolated individuality, is analogous to the 'clarity of being' to which he attains in 'fierce passion of sensuality'. The differ-ence between brotherly love and sexual love, of course, is that in the sphere of social relations there is no catalyst equivalent to the sex act

[1] *Ibid.*, pp. 155–6.

to bring the contrary impulses into a harmoniously liberating relation. It is not surprising that it proves difficult to 'balance perfectly between the two motions', as can be seen in the novels of the leadership phase, particularly *Kangaroo*. For the same reason it is not easy to achieve such a balance in the personal relations of man and man. And even in the relations of man and woman the sex act, as Lawrence shows time and again in the novels, may fail to yield the mystic rose. The attempt to transcend the duality is, indeed, one of the central issues in Lawrence's work from *The Rainbow* onwards. I hesitate to talk of male and female impulses in this connection, for 'singleness', one of the terms of the duality as Lawrence states it, is not amenable to such classification.[1] An implied male-female dualism is, however, persistently present. The dual love between a man and a woman is 'the melting into pure communion' and 'the friction of sheer sensuality': here, plainly, is an instance of a male-female opposition. In brotherly love man 'acts in concert with man' though he must also be able to 'move for himself without reference to his neighbour': if he is able to do both he 'understands both sides' and so follows 'the inmost desires of his body and spirit'. It seems to me that the duality may also be stated in terms of Communion, Relationship, and Self-Subordination as opposed to Being, Self-Feeling, and Self-Establishment;[2] and when the duality is not transcended, when there is a bitter consciousness of a 'split' within the self, we may assume it is because the male and female princiˡᵉˢ are not reconciled but remain oppugnant.

[1]See pp. 28–30 above.   [2] See the table on pp. 30–1 above.

2 The Release: The First Period

Sons and Lovers

'A [CEYLONESE] WORKMAN WAS ARRANGING A SCREEN ON THE verandah where we were seated. He was alert; with sure, graceful movement and fine head; his dark eyes flashing; his features regular; the beard clipped in an elegant line. Lawrence pensively watched him, announcing that he resembled his father–the same clean-cut and exuberant spirit, a true pagan. He added that he had not done justice to his father in *Sons and Lovers*, and felt like rewriting it. When children they had accepted the dictum of their mother that their father was a drunkard, therefore was contemptible, but that as Lawrence had grown older he had come to see him in a different light; to see his unquenchable fire and relish for living. Now [i.e., in 1922] he blamed his mother for her self-righteousness, her invulnerable Christian virtue within which she was entrenched. She had brought down terrible scenes of vituperation upon their heads from which she might have protected them. . . .'[1]

[1] Earl and Achsah Brewster, *D. H. Lawrence: Reminiscences and Correspondence* (London,

If we object that *Sons and Lovers*, though avowedly an autobiographical novel,[1] has a validity which is independent of the real life on which it is based, we are nevertheless aware that Lawrence's reservations do point to a weakness in the book. Justice is not done to 'the early married life of the Morels'. In effect, however, the weakness is only marginal. The weight of hostile comment which Lawrence directs against Morel is balanced by the unconscious sympathy with which he is presented dramatically, while the overt celebration of Mrs Morel is challenged by the harshness of the character in action. The artist, it would seem, penetrated to the truth which the son subsequently thought he had not seen, for the impression which Mr and Mrs Morel in fact make is not notably different from that which Lawrence had of his father and mother in later life.

Lawrence's conscious attitude to Mr and Mrs Morel is typified by the extreme statements he makes about them. We are told that Mrs Morel, for instance, 'was one of those naturally exquisite people who can walk in mud without dirtying their shoes' (p. 152), but Morel is said to be 'an outsider. He had denied the God in him' (p. 82).[2] That Lawrence was of the Devil's party without knowing it, however, is suggested by the effect of one of the early scenes between the Morels:

'At half-past eleven her husband came. His cheeks were very red and very shiny above his black moustache. His head nodded slightly. He was pleased with himself.

' "Oh! Oh! waitin' for me, lass? I've bin 'elpin' Anthony, an' what's think he's gen me? Nowt b'r a lousy hae'f-crown, an' that's ivry penny–"

' "He thinks you've made the rest up in beer," she said shortly.

' "An' I 'aven't–that I 'aven't. You b'lieve me, I've 'ad very little this day, I have an' all." His voice went tender. "Here, an' I browt thee a bit o' brandysnap, an' a coconut for th' children." He laid the gingerbread and the coconut, a hairy object, on the table. "Nay, tha niver said thankyer for nowt i' thy life, did ter?"

'As a compromise, she picked up the coconut and shook it, to see if it had any milk.

1934), p. 254. Cf. Frieda Lawrence: 'In after years he said: "I would write a different *Sons and Lovers* now; my mother was wrong, and I thought she was absolutely right." ' *Not I, But the Wind* . . . (London, 1935), p. 52.   [1] See *Letters*, p. 85.
[2] Throughout this book page references to Lawrence's novels are to Penguins, in which the novels are most readily available.

' "It's a good 'un, you may back yer life o' that. I got it fra' Bill
Hodgkisson. 'Bill,' I says, 'tha non wants them three nuts, does ter?
Arena ter for gi'ein' me one for my bit of a lad an' wench?' 'I ham,
Walter, my lad,' 'e says; 'ta'e which on 'em ter's a mind.' An' so I
took one, an' thanked 'im. I didn't like ter shake it afore 'is eyes, but
'e says, 'Tha'd better ma'e sure it's a good un, Walt.' An' so, yer see,
I knowed it was. He's a nice chap, is Bill Hodgkisson, 'e's a nice
chap!"

' "A man will part with anything so long as he's drunk, and you're
drunk along with him," said Mrs Morel.

' "Eh, tha mucky little 'ussy, who's drunk, I sh'd like ter know?"
said Morel. He was extraordinarily pleased with himself, because of
his day's helping to wait in the Moon and Stars. He chattered on.

'Mrs Morel, very tired, and sick of his babble, went to bed as quickly
as possible, while he raked the fire' (p. 14).

The difference between the Morels is epitomized in the way they react
to the gift of the coconut. Despite his roughness, Morel has a natural
delicacy which prevents him from shaking the coconut in front of Bill
Hodgkisson, though he is tempted to do so; but Mrs Morel, who
usually regulates her conduct according to standards of formal pro-
priety, is unfailingly graceless to her husband. Her shaking of the
coconut, moreover, exemplifies her hard, cold materialism which
makes her view the miner's drinking as a financial, as well as a moral,
tragedy. At the same time – and it is this rich comprehensiveness which
distinguishes Lawrence's writing in *Sons and Lovers* – her querulousness is
provoked by her husband's having left her to her own devices on the
day of the wakes. In the clash of temperament which explodes in the
violent quarrels to which this scene is a prelude there is justification
on both sides.

The scene is also representative in a way apparently not realized by
Lawrence: Morel's warmth and exuberance emerge plainly from it,
and there is in it more than a hint of Mrs Morel's martyred self-
righteousness. This view of the Morels corresponds to that given of
Lawrence's parents in *A Collier's Friday Night*, the posthumous play
which preceded *Sons and Lovers* by several years, and in 'Adolf' and 'Rex',
two sketches roughly contemporaneous with the novel. What differ-
entiates the presentation of the Morels from that of the parents in the
other work, however, is the author's interpolative antagonism in *Sons
and Lovers* towards the father. In 'Rex', for example, the father is said to
have an 'amiable but to us heartless voice' when he shouts at the

children's newly acquired pet.[1] The phrase is clumsy but it makes an effectively moderating qualification.

Such qualifications, where they are to be found in *Sons and Lovers*, are speedily offset by fierce damning. Lawrence's attitude to Morel is indeed close to that which Blake believed Milton held towards Satan; both writers are not only unconsciously sympathetic to the hated figures but hasten to correct explicitly any unfortunately favourable impressions which the characters may make:

'Both [William and Annie] hushed into silence as they heard the approaching thud of their father's stockinged feet, and shrank as he entered. Yet he was usually indulgent to them.

'Morel made the meal alone, brutally. He ate and drank more noisily than he had need. No one spoke to him. The family life withdrew, shrank away, and became hushed as he entered. But he cared no longer about his alienation.

'Immediately he had finished tea he rose with alacrity to go out. It was this alacrity, this haste to be gone, which so sickened Mrs Morel. As she heard him sousing heartily in cold water, heard the eager scratch of the steel comb on the side of the bowl, as he wetted his hair, she closed her eyes in disgust. As he bent over, lacing his boots, there was a certain vulgar gusto in his movement that divided him from the reserved, watchful rest of the family. He always ran away from the battle with himself. Even in his own heart's privacy, he excused himself, saying, "If she hadn't said so-and-so, it would never have happened. She asked for what she's got." The children waited in restraint during his preparations. When he had gone, they sighed with relief.

'He closed the door behind him, and was glad. It was a rainy evening. The Palmerston would be the cosier. . . .

' "What shollt ha'e, Walter?" cried a voice, as soon as Morel appeared in the doorway.

' "Oh, Jim, my lad, wheriver has thee sprung frae?"

'The men made a seat for him, and took him in warmly. He was glad. In a minute or two they had thawed all responsibility out of him, all shame, all trouble, and he was clear as a bell for a jolly night' (pp. 56–7).

This passage is a clear example of the battle which the son wages against the artist in the early part of the book. Indeed the divergence between the two views provided of Morel is so great that the passage

[1] *Phoenix*, p. 15.

is subject to mutually contradictory readings. On the one hand, once the token qualification is made by the allusion to Morel's usual indulgence to the children, the eye that sees him is consistently hostile. He eats 'brutally' and his natural gusto is 'vulgar'; then he ignominiously runs away from the battle with himself, taking refuge in drink. The description might have a certain validity–for it refers to Morel's behaviour after one of the worst incidents between him and his wife which culminates in his throwing a drawer at her–were it not for the fact that the eye that hardens on Morel sees the rest of the scene so clearly. As a result we see that Morel *does* care about his alienation and that his brutal eating is in fact a protest against it; that his gusto is only vulgar because it is not shared by 'the reserved, watchful rest of the family'; that he runs away not so much from himself as from his wife's disgust and his children's shrinking; and that what the warmth of the Palmerston 'thaws' out of him (the word is significant) is as much the icy disdain of his family as 'all responsibility . . . all shame, all trouble'.

It is, therefore, Lawrence's interpretative commentary on the relationship of the Morels that fails; his dramatic presentation of them never falters. The high quality of the dramatic achievement is evident, for instance, in the description of the Morels' quarrel which precedes the passage just quoted:

'He leaned on the table with one hand, and with the other jerked at the table drawer to get a knife to cut bread. The drawer stuck because he pulled sideways. In a temper he dragged it, so that it flew out bodily, and spoons, forks, knives, a hundred metallic things, splashed with a clatter and a clang upon the brick floor. The baby gave a little convulsed start.

' "What are you doing, clumsy, drunken fool?" the mother cried.

' "Then tha should get the flamin' thing thysen. Tha should get up, like other women have to, an' wait on a man."

' "Wait on you–wait on you?" she cried. "Yes, I see myself."

' "Yis, an' I'll learn thee tha's got to. Wait on *me*, yes, tha sh'lt wait on me–"

' "Never, milord. I'd wait on a dog at the door first."

' "What–what?"

'He was trying to fit in the drawer. At her last speech he turned round. His face was crimson, his eyes bloodshot. He stared at her one silent second in threat.

' "P-h!" she went quickly, in contempt.

'He jerked at the drawer in his excitement. It fell, cut sharply on his shin, and on the reflex he flung it at her' (pp. 52-3).

In this passage the subtle complexity of life itself is rendered with a rich immediacy. The class difference between the Morels, which manifests itself here in the altercation over the duties of a working-class woman, is only a facet of their temperamental hostility. The hostility is there, lying dormant but charged, and like a booby trap it is ready to explode at the slightest touch. The explosion, when it comes, is timed to a nicety. It is the convulsed start of the baby in her arms as well as the clatter of the dropped cutlery that rouses Mrs Morel. Forgetting her earlier resolution to 'say nothing' to her husband 'whatever time he comes', she releases her pent-up envy and irritation in a venomous scorn which Morel cannot hope to match other than by arrogantly asserting his rights. And it is as much her final 'p-h' of contempt as the reflex reaction to pain that makes him fling the drawer at her. Morel is of course factually responsible for the attack on his wife, but it is forcefully suggested that moral responsibility for the clash is Mrs Morel's; it is she who goads him into fury. Yet in the scene in which Morel takes himself off to the Palmerston it is implied that blame for the incident attaches to him alone. It is very much as if Lawrence shirks the conclusions of his own art.

Lawrence is equivocal too in his apportionment of blame for the failure of the marriage as a whole:

'Paul looked at his father's thick, brownish hands all scarred, with broken nails, rubbing the fine smoothness of his sides, and the incongruity struck him. It seemed strange they were the same flesh.

' "I suppose," he said to his father, "you had a good figure once."

' "Eh!" exclaimed the miner, glancing round, startled and timid, like a child.

' "He had," exclaimed Mrs Morel, "if he didn't hurtle himself up as if he was trying to get in the smallest space he could."

' "Me!" exclaimed Morel–"me a good figure! I wor niver much more n'r a skeleton."

' "Man!" cried his wife, "don't be such a pulamiter!"

' "Strewth!" he said. "Tha's niver knowed me but what I looked as if I wor goin' off in a rapid decline."

'She sat and laughed.

' "You've had a constitution like iron," she said, "and never a man had a better start, if it was body that counted. You should have seen him as a young man," she cried suddenly to Paul, drawing herself up to imitate her husband's once handsome bearing.

'Morel watched her shyly. He saw again the passion she had had for him. It blazed upon her for a moment. He was shy, rather scared, and humble. Yet again he felt his old glow. And then immediately he felt the ruin he had made during these years . . .' (p. 243).

What the book plainly shows, time and again, is that the Morels are – at the least – equally responsible for the failure of their marriage; and yet Morel is here presented as feeling that the ruin is of his making. Indeed, if ultimate responsibility for the ruin must be fixed, then on the objective evidence offered by the book it is Mrs Morel who has the most to answer for. The moment of rare marital harmony depicted in the passage illuminates the nature of her responsibility. Body counts for more than she realizes, and through failing to make the most of Morel's physical glow, she has forfeited not only the lovable husband that he is here shown to be but her own transfiguring blaze of passion, which for a moment lights her up in middle age. Earlier in the book Paul sees his mother looking 'brave and rich with life, but as if she had been done out of her rights. It hurt the boy keenly, this feeling about her that she had never had her life's fulfilment' (p. 85): it is she who has done herself out of her rights, and it is a mark of Lawrence's ambivalent handling of the Morels that he is fully aware of this:

'She still had her high moral sense, inherited from generations of Puritans. It was now a religious instinct, and she was almost a fanatic with him, because she loved him, or had loved him. If he sinned, she tortured him. If he drank, and lied, was often a poltroon, sometimes a knave, she wielded the lash unmercifully.

'The pity was, she was too much his opposite. She could not be content with the little he might be; she would have him the much that he ought to be. So, in seeking to make him nobler than he could be, she destroyed him. She injured and hurt and scarred herself, but she lost none of her worth. She also had the children' (pp. 25–6).

'Tortured' and 'destroyed' are strong words, and 'but she lost none of her worth' is an equivocal reservation. It is clear what Mrs Morel has lost, and it is to make up for it that she turns possessively, and as relentlessly as she ruined her husband, to her sons.

II

Lawrence's portrayal of Paul's relations with his father and mother has none of the distortion which weakens his representation of the marriage. To the extent that he is to be identified with Paul, he made it clear that the portrayal, among other things, was a deliberate self-purgation: 'I felt you had gone off from me a bit, because of *Sons and Lovers*', he wrote to a friend. 'But one sheds one's sicknesses in books – repeats and presents again one's emotions, to be master of them.'[1] From the outset he has a clear understanding of the nature of Paul's love for his mother and his hatred of his father.

Paul is early overwhelmed by the unnatural love which his mother fosters in him. When he is a young boy she accepts the flowers which he brings her like 'a woman accepting a love-token' (p. 88); on the day that he goes for his interview at Jordan's she is gay with him, 'like a sweetheart' (p. 116), and they walk through the streets of Nottingham 'feeling the excitement of lovers having an adventure together' (p. 117); and, eventually, everything he does is 'for her' – 'the two shared lives' (p. 144). As far as Paul's relations with his father are concerned, the boy is from infancy united with his mother against him. When Morel cuts his wife's forehead open with the drawer which he flings at her, it is Paul whom she is holding on her lap, and as she averts her face from Morel's stumbling concern, blood from the wound drips on to the baby's hair; Morel is sure that it soaks through to the scalp (p. 54). This additional, if symbolic, tie of blood which Paul shares with his mother in her withdrawal from Morel is set over and against his more matter-of-fact connection with his father. As he grows up Paul is convinced of his hatred for his father:

'Paul hated his father. As a boy he had a fervent private religion.

' "Make him stop drinking," he prayed every night. "Lord, let my father die," he prayed very often. "Let him not be killed at pit," he prayed when, after tea, the father did not come home from work' (p. 79).

This is a delightful example of childish inconsequence; it is also, despite the initial affirmation, indicative of Paul's ambivalence towards his father.

That Lawrence knows what is behind Paul's excessive feelings of love and hate is asserted by one of the subtlest scenes in the book:

[1] Letter to A. W. McLeod (October 1913), *Letters*, p. 150.

'He had taken off his collar and tie, and rose, bare-throated, to go to bed. As he stooped to kiss his mother, she threw her arms round his neck, hid her face on his shoulder, and cried, in a whimpering voice, so unlike her own that he writhed in agony:

' "I can't bear it. I could let another woman–but not her. She'd leave me no room, not a bit of room–"

'And immediately he hated Miriam bitterly.

' "And I've never–you know, Paul–I've never had a husband–not really–"

'He stroked his mother's hair, and his mouth was on her throat.

' "And she exults so in taking you from me–she's not like ordinary girls."

' "Well, I don't love her, Mother," he murmured, bowing his head and hiding his eyes on her shoulder in misery. His mother kissed him a long, fervent kiss.

' "My boy!" she said, in a voice trembling with passionate love.

'Without knowing, he gently stroked her face.

' "There," said his mother, "now go to bed. You'll be *so* tired in the morning." As she was speaking she heard her husband coming. "There's your father–now go." Suddenly she looked at him almost as if in fear. "Perhaps I'm selfish. If you want her, take her, my boy" ' (pp. 261–2).

Mrs Morel is pathetic in her jealousy of Miriam, but if Miriam is not like an ordinary girl she herself hardly behaves like an ordinary mother. Under the painful stimulus of her complaints about her husband, the love between mother and son takes on a dangerously erotic character. And Mrs Morel is at least partially aware of what she is doing: with the approach of her husband she realizes, with a sudden feeling of guilt, how she has compromised her son. But her recantation is of little avail in the face of Paul's aroused passion for her. His passion seeks an outlet, and balked in the direction it would take, it turns viciously on his father. When Morel comes in, he takes a pie which Mrs Morel has specially bought for Paul, and on being challenged by her, he flings it into the fire. He too is ready for violence, for he has not mistaken the import of the scene which meets him:

'Paul started to his feet.

' "Waste your own stuff!" he cried.

' "What–what!" suddenly shouted Morel, jumping up and clenching his fist. "I'll show yer, yer young jockey!"

' "All right!" said Paul viciously, putting his head on one side. "Show me!"

'He would at that moment dearly have loved to have a smack at something. Morel was half crouching, fists up, ready to spring. The young man stood, smiling with his lips.

' "Ussha!" hissed the father, swiping round with a great stroke just past his son's face. He dared not, even though so close, really touch the young man, but swerved an inch away.

' "Right!" said Paul, his eyes upon the side of his father's mouth, where in another instant his fist would have hit. He ached for that stroke. But he heard a faint moan from behind. His mother was deadly pale, and dark at the mouth . . .' (p. 263).

Paul desists, ostensibly for the sake of his mother, but within the wider context of the book as a whole it is significant that neither father nor son can actually bring himself to strike the other. Their enmity is real enough but it is the surface enmity of an unhealthy rivalry rather than that of a deep-seated personal antagonism:

' "Can you go to bed, Mother?"

' "Yes, I'll come."

' "Sleep with Annie, Mother, not with him."

' "No. I'll sleep in my own bed" '

' "Don't sleep with him, Mother."

' "I'll sleep in my own bed" ' (p. 264).

The clash between Paul and Morel is of course a striking example of an oedipal situation, and indeed on publication the book was treated as a *locus classicus* by early English Freudians.[1] 'Yes', Frieda wrote to Frederick J. Hoffman, 'Lawrence knew about Freud before he wrote the final draft of *Sons and Lovers*,' but I am inclined to accept Hoffman's conclusion that 'it is doubtful . . . that the revision of *Sons and Lovers* was more than superficially affected by Lawrence's introduction to psychoanalysis'.[2] At that time Lawrence's knowledge of Freudian theory was derived at second-hand from Frieda, and she probably did no more than confirm his intuitive apprehension of the nature of Paul's relations with his parents. Nor does the book betray any signs of artificial grafting.

---

[1] Cf. John Middleton Murry: '. . . it had been discovered that in *Sons and Lovers* Lawrence had independently arrived at the main conclusions of the psycho-analysts, and the English followers of Freud came to see him.' *Reminiscences of D. H. Lawrence* (London, 1933), p. 39.

[2] *Freudianism and the Literary Mind* (Baton Rouge, Louisiana, 1945), p. 153.

The sort of penetrative understanding which is at work behind the organization of the scene I have just discussed informs countless incidents in the book. There is, for instance, the scene when Paul is ill as a young boy:

'On retiring to bed, the father would come into the sick-room. He was always very gentle if anyone were ill. But he disturbed the atmosphere for the boy.

' "Are ter asleep, my darlin'?" Morel asked softly.

' "No; is my mother comin'?"

' "She's just finishin' foldin' the clothes. Do you want anything?" Morel rarely "thee'd" his son.

' "I don't want nothing. But how long will she be?"

' "Not long, my duckie."

' The father waited undecidedly on the hearthrug for a moment or two. He felt his son did not want him. . . .

'He loitered about indefinitely. The boy began to get feverish with irritation. His father's presence seemed to aggravate all his sick impatience. At last Morel, after having stood looking at his son awhile, said softly:

' "Good-night, my darling."

' "Good-night," Paul replied, turning round in relief to be alone.

'Paul loved to sleep with his mother. Sleep is still most perfect, in spite of hygienists, when it is shared with a beloved. The warmth, the security and peace of soul, the utter comfort from the touch of the other, knits the sleep, so that it takes the body and soul completely in its healing. Paul lay against her and slept, and got better; whilst she, always a bad sleeper, fell later on into a profound sleep that seemed to give her faith' (pp. 86–7).

Morel, it is seen, does not have to be provocative to be rejected. Paul's rebuffing of his father's warm gentleness and kindliness is only understandable in terms of the inbred family situation; and indeed, as the concluding paragraph makes clear, the conflict between father and son which manifests itself later in an apparent readiness to come to blows is incipient here. At this stage Paul's childish desire to sleep with his mother is presented simply and naturally as a longing for maternal warmth and security, but later developments are anticipated in the ambiguous phraseology of the paragraph. We are reminded of Lawrence's claim in the well-known letter to Edward Garnett that the development of the book 'is slow, like growth'.[1] It is only by slow

[1] Letter dated 14 November, 1912, *Letters*, p. 77.

stages that Paul's incestuous love for his mother expresses itself in the
frankly passionate kisses of his manhood: first, there is the seemingly
childlike innocence of the foregoing scene; then there is the more
open ambiguity of his attitude as a youth. Paul is sixteen when he falls
seriously ill. It is a cruel irony that the love which then makes him
desperately assert his will to live should later prove to be so deathly
in its effects:

'Paul was very ill. His mother lay in bed at nights with him; they
could not afford a nurse. He grew worse, and the crisis approached.
One night he tossed into consciousness in the ghastly, sickly feeling of
dissolution, when all the cells in the body seem in intense irritability
to be breaking down, and consciousness makes a last flare of struggle,
like madness.

' "I s'll die, mother!" he cried, heaving for breath on the pillow.

'She lifted him up, crying in a small voice:

' "Oh, my son–my son!"

' That brought him to. He realized her. His whole will rose up and
arrested him. He put his head on her breast, and took ease of her for
love' (p. 175).

The immediate effect of Mrs Morel's poisonously possessive love for
Paul is her implacable hostility to Miriam. From the moment she senses
his interest in the girl she tries to fight her off:

'Always when he went with Miriam, and it grew rather late, he
knew his mother was fretting and getting angry about him–why, he
could not understand. As he went into the house, flinging down his
cap, his mother looked up at the clock. . . .

' "She must be wonderfully fascinating, that you can't get away
from her, but must go trailing eight miles at this time of night."

'He was hurt between the past glamour with Miriam and the
knowledge that his mother fretted. He had meant not to say anything,
to refuse to answer. But he could not harden his heart to ignore his
mother.

' "I *do* like to talk to her," he answered irritably.

' "Is there nobody else to talk to?"

' "You wouldn't say anything if I went with Edgar."

' "You know I should. You know, whoever you went with, I should
say it was too far for you to go trailing, late at night, when you've
been to Nottingham. Besides"–her voice suddenly flashed into anger
and contempt–"it is disgusting–bits of lads and girls courting" '
(pp. 199-200).

Paul's inability to understand Mrs Morel's antagonism to Miriam is, at this stage of the narrative, bound up with his own repressions. Struggling as he is with his complex emotions towards his mother, it is hardly surprising he should fail to realize that her jealousy is almost nakedly sexual. The real reason for her annoyance is casually phrased as an afterthought, but her sudden violent employment of the word 'disgusting' and the illogical asperity of the comment itself are sure guides to her feeling. It is seldom, however, that the serpent in the garden slithers out of the undergrowth in this way; Mrs Morel effectively rationalizes her dislike of Miriam:

' "She exults–she exults as she carries him off from me," Mrs Morel cried in her heart when Paul had gone. "She's not like an ordinary woman, who can leave me my share in him. She wants to absorb him. She wants to draw him out and absorb him till there is nothing left of him, even for himself. He will never be a man on his own feet–she will suck him up." So the mother sat, and battled and brooded bitterly' (p. 237).

It is a further indication of Lawrence's comprehensive view–I have already referred in this respect to his treatment of the Morel marriage –that Mrs Morel's criticism of Miriam should be just; but, as R. P. Draper has pointed out,[1] she does not perceive its application to herself. It is she who is preventing Paul from being a man on his own feet, and though she is not as hostile to Clara as to Miriam, her carping at his attachment to the married woman is parallel to her interference in his relationship with the girl. Her approval of her son's women is always irremediably conditional: ' "You know I should be *glad* [at your association with Clara]"', she tells Paul, ' "if she weren't a married woman" ' (p. 383).

Since Paul cannot but agree with his mother's objections to Miriam, it is her attitude to Clara which finally makes him aware of her possessive jealousy. Mrs Morel, asking more of Paul than he can give, relentlessly holding him back, plays the same part as the 'beggar-woman' of 'End of Another Home Holiday':

> *While ever at my side,*
> *Frail and sad, with grey, bowed head,*
> *The beggar-woman, the yearning-eyed*
> *Inexorable love goes lagging.*[2]

[1] 'D. H. Lawrence on Mother-Love', *Essays in Criticism*, 8 (July 1958), 287.
[2] *The Complete Poems of D. H. Lawrence* (London, 1957), I, 39.

separatorThe Release: The First Period 55

Eventually Paul comes to realize that his mother is defrauding him of life:

'Then sometimes he hated her, and pulled at her bondage. His life wanted to free itself of her. It was like a circle where life turned back on itself, and got no farther. She bore him, loved him, kept him, and his love turned back into her, so that he could not be free to go forward with his own life, really love another woman . . .' (p. 420).

And from pulling at her bondage it is but a short step to a scarcely disguised wish for her death:

' "And as for wanting to marry," said his mother, "there's plenty of time yet."

' "But no, mother. I even love Clara, and I did Miriam; but to *give* myself to them in marriage I couldn't. I couldn't belong to them. They seem to want *me*, and I can't ever give it them."

' "You haven't met the right woman."

' "And I never shall meet the right woman while you live," he said' (p. 427).

These two passages alone, quite apart from the circumstances of Mrs Morel's death which I shall discuss in a moment, should suffice to refute the criticism that in *Sons and Lovers* Lawrence capitulates to his mother. This misreading of the book derives, it would seem, from an uncritical acceptance of Jessie Chambers' verdict: 'His mother conquered indeed, but the vanquished one was her son. In *Sons and Lovers* Lawrence handed his mother the laurels of victory.'[1] In her wake the froth gathers: '. . . at the same time that the book condemns the mother it justifies her';[2] '. . . the story of Paul Morel . . . was to be his mother's justification and apotheosis';[3] '. . . hence the distortion he made in the presentation of Miriam in his great novel, in order that the mother might triumph';[4] '. . . Lawrence was unable to detach himself from the mother whom he celebrates as heroine or to achieve the impersonality that the most personal art requires';[5] 'Lawrence tells us that Paul "fought against his mother almost as he fought against Miriam" (Chapter IX). But this statement we may disregard, for the

footnotes[1] *A Personal Record*, p. 202.

[2] Mark Schorer, 'Technique as Discovery', *Forms of Modern Fiction*, ed. William Van O'Connor (Minneapolis, 1948), p. 19.

[3] Helen Corke, *D. H. Lawrence's 'Princess': A Memory of Jessie Chambers* (Thames Ditton, Surrey, 1951), p. 13.

[4] A. L. Rowse, *The English Past* (London, 1951), p. 230.

[5] William York Tindall, *Forces in Modern British Literature, 1885–1956* (New York, 1956), pp. 222–3.

evidence of the novel gives it the lie. He did not fight against his mother; he grew in bondage and until her death in bondage he remained.'[1] It is necessary to clarify this assumption of the mother's triumph, for it underlies the even more widely accepted view that the Miriam section of the book (which remains to be discussed) is both false and a failure. Mrs Morel does have a limited triumph, in so far as Paul does not marry while she lives, but then his failure to do so is only partially attributable to her; it has as much to do with Miriam and Clara. The extent, moreover, to which Paul himself, because of his mother's influence, is to blame for the failure is fully and frankly indicated, as the two passages quoted above should make abundantly clear. And the so-called 'justification' of Mrs Morel is a matter not of approbation but of truly creative presentment of character, whereby the motivating circumstances of her overpowering love for Paul are sympathetically portrayed. They may even be shown as extenuating circumstances, but that her influence is crippling–it is the theme of the book–is quite unambiguous. If it is crippling, however, it is not paralysing–as Jessie Chambers apparently believed. Paul makes his own stand for life.

There is, significantly, an image associated with the idea of crippling in the poem 'Monologue of a Mother':

> *Strange he is, my son, for whom I have waited like a lover;*
> …
> *Like a thin white bird blown out of the northern seas,*
> *Like a bird from the far north blown with a broken wing*
> *Into our sooty garden, he drags and beats*
> *Along the fence perpetually, seeking release*
> *From me, from the hand of my love which creeps up, needing*
> *His happiness, while he in displeasure retreats.*[2]

Like the son in the poem and like the bird with a broken wing, Paul also seeks release; and it is surely an Empsonian ambiguity that the chapter which describes the painful suffering and death of Mrs Morel should be entitled 'The Release'.

Any interpretation of *Sons and Lovers* must finally centre on this chapter, and so it is perhaps as well first to marshal the facts. Mrs Morel is stricken with cancer and her long-drawn-out suffering is so acute that Paul wishes she would die (p. 472). Weeks pass and he

---

[1] Eliseo Vivas, *D. H. Lawrence: The Failure and the Triumph of Art* (Evanston, 1960), p. 183.
[2] *Poems*, I, 19.

begins to dilute her milk so that it will not nourish her (p. 476).
Finally, Paul decides to end her misery by giving her an overdose of
morphia:
'That evening he got all the morphia pills there were, and took
them downstairs. Carefully he crushed them to powder.
' "What are you doing?" said Annie.
' "I s'll put 'em in her night milk."
'Then they both laughed together like two conspiring children.
On top of all their horror flickered this little sanity' (p. 479).
Mrs Morel lasts through the night, and Paul wonders whether her
'horrible breathing' will stop if he piles 'heavy clothes on top of her'
(p. 483). She dies the next morning.

Clearly, on one level, Paul's killing of his mother is a mercy-killing.
His agony at her suffering is poignantly described, and when she is
dead he can only helplessly wish that she were alive again:
'She lay like a maiden asleep. . . . She would wake up. She would lift
her eyelids. She was with him still. He bent and kissed her passionately. But there was coldness against his mouth. He bit his lip with
horror. Looking at her, he felt he could never, never let her go. No!
He stroked the hair from her temples. That, too, was cold. He saw the
mouth so dumb and wondering at the hurt. Then he crouched on
the floor, whispering to her:
' "Mother, mother!" ' (pp. 485–6).
But, on a deeper level, the killing and the desire to smother his
mother have a significance which he is not aware of consciously. I
think we must concur with Anthony West and Graham Hough that
Paul's killing of his mother represents, symbolically, both a repudiation of what she stands for[1] and a decisive act of self-liberation,[2] as
does his turning towards the city at the end of the book:
'But no, he would not give in. Turning sharply, he walked towards
the city's gold phosphorescence. His fists were shut, his mouth set
fast. He would not take that direction, to the darkness, to follow her.
He walked towards the faintly humming, glowing town, quickly.'
I believe that a close textual analysis of the passage, quoted above,
which describes the preparation of the death-draught, reveals further significances of the killing. It will be recalled that, when
Paul tells Annie that he intends to give Mrs Morel the morphia, 'they
both laughed together', and that their laughter is described as the

[1] Anthony West, *D. H. Lawrence* (London, 1950), pp. 14, 115.
[2] Graham Hough, pp. 51–2.

flickering of a 'little sanity': it suggests, then, not only the tension they feel and their instinctive ('sane') need for some relief from their oppressive horror, but also the sanity–in defiance of established law–which the mercy-killing represents. They are also said, however, to laugh 'like two conspiring children'. Taken together with the fact that Paul replies to Annie's question in the dialect of his youth, the simile, I think, points back to an earlier and apparently irrelevant incident which illuminates the meaning of Paul's killing of his mother.

The only childhood 'conspiracy' in which Paul and Annie can be said to engage occurs when he decides to burn her doll, which he has accidentally smashed. The 'flickering' of Paul's 'sanity', it seems, should ultimately be related to the flames in which the doll is 'sacrificed':

' "You couldn't tell it was there, mother; you couldn't tell it was there," he repeated over and over. So long as Annie wept for the doll he sat helpless with misery. Her grief wore itself out. She forgave her brother–he was so much upset. But a day or two afterwards she was shocked.

' "Let's make a sacrifice of Arabella," he said. "Let's burn her."

'She was horrified, yet rather fascinated. She wanted to see what the boy would do. He made an altar of bricks, pulled some of the shavings out of Arabella's body, put the waxen fragments into the hollow face, poured on a little paraffin, and set the whole thing alight. He watched with wicked satisfaction the drops of wax melt off the broken forehead of Arabella, and drop like sweat into the flame. So long as the stupid big doll burned he rejoiced in silence. At the end he poked among the embers with a stick, fished out the arms and legs, all blackened, and smashed them under stones.

' "That's the sacrifice of Missis Arabella," he said. "An' I'm glad there's nothing left of her."

'Which disturbed Annie inwardly, although she could say nothing. He seemed to hate the doll so intensely, because he had broken it' (pp. 75–6).

Child psychologists, I imagine, would find the symbolism of this burning of the doll familiar. The 'wicked satisfaction' which Paul derives from his violent and compulsive destruction of the doll is surely not unrelated to the fact that he calls the 'big' doll 'Missis' Arabella and that the melted wax of its forehead drops 'like sweat' into the flame. But I am not so much concerned with the burning of the doll as an expression of a childhood wish to destroy the mother as with its relation to the actual killing which takes place later. First, we might note, in passing, the analogy between Paul's smashing of the arms and legs of the doll after the burning and his urge to smother his mother after she has already taken the morphia. Second, he hates and destroys the doll 'because he [has] broken it'; in other words, the 'sacrifice' represents some sort of expiation[1]–as, in a measure, the killing is an unconscious purgation of the feelings of guilt which his ambiguous relationship with his mother has necessarily involved. Third, the burning of the doll seems to represent a childish but resolute refusal to sacrifice himself to it. In the same way, the killing, in one of its complex meanings, is a decisive protest against the self-sacrifice which subjection to his mother has entailed:

'And he came back to her. And in his soul was a feeling of the satisfaction of self-sacrifice because he was faithful to her. She loved him first; he loved her first. And yet it was not enough. His new young life, so strong and imperious, was urged towards something else. It made him mad with restlessness . . .' (p. 273).

Indeed, the pernicious effect of self-sacrifice is an insistent theme in the novel. Mrs Morel's married life is almost wholly self-sacrificial, involving as it does unwilling service of her husband, and despite her possessive love for Paul, abnegation of self for the sake of her children. In fact her self-sacrifice borders, masochistically, on the self-destructive:

' "Are you sure it's a tumour?" [Paul asked Dr Ansell] ."Why did Dr Jameson in Nottingham never find out anything about it? She's been going to him for weeks, and he's treated her for heart and indigestion."

' "Mrs Morel never told Dr Jameson about the lump," said the doctor' (p. 452).

Mrs Morel is the embodiment of a principle which Lawrence fought against all his life, and in refusing to sacrifice himself to her, Paul repudiates a great deal of what she stands for. Nor is Paul's fight against self-sacrifice confined to his relations with his mother; it is also at the

---

[1] In this respect the ritualistic burning is a more obvious example of what C. L. Barber, in relation to Hal's rejection of Falstaff, calls 'a nonlogical process of purification by sacrifice': 'Hal's final expulsion of Falstaff appears . . . to carry out an impersonal pattern, not merely political but ritual in character. After the guilty reign of Bolingbroke, the prince is making a fresh start as the new king. At a level beneath the moral notions of a personal reform, we can see a nonlogical process of purification by sacrifice–the sacrifice of Falstaff.' 'Saturnalia in the Henriad', *Shakespeare: Modern Essays in Criticism*, ed. Leonard F. Dean (New York, 1957), p. 176.

heart of his conflict with Miriam. It is perhaps significant that, of all
the major characters, Walter Morel is the only one who doggedly
pursues his own way, neither sacrificing himself for others nor expecting that they should sacrifice themselves for him.

Sons and Lovers, then, forcefully suggests Paul's ultimate rejection of
his mother; it also implies his unconscious identification with his
father. As far as his father is concerned, there are no dramatic manifestations of feeling comparable to his killing of his mother and his
turning towards the town at the end of the book, but his identification
with him is none the less unmistakable. It shows itself, for instance, in
his unconscious imitation of his father's mannerisms – when Morel
greets Clara she sees 'Paul's manner of bowing and shaking hands'
(p. 392) – and, more explicitly, in his reflections on class:

‘ “You know,” he said to his mother, “I don't want to belong to the
well-to-do middle class. I like my common people best. I belong to
the common people.”

‘ “But if anyone else said so, my son, wouldn't you be in a tear.
You know you consider yourself equal to any gentleman.”

‘ “In myself,” he answered, “not in my class or my education or my
manners. But in myself I am.”

‘ “Very well, then. Then why talk about the common people?”

‘ “Because – the difference between people isn't in their class, but in
themselves. Only from the middle classes one gets ideas, and from the
common people – life itself, warmth. You feel their hates and loves.”

‘ “It's all very well, my boy. But, then, why don't you go and talk
to your father's pals?”

‘ “But they're rather different.”

‘ “Not at all. They're the common people. After all, whom do you
mix with now – among the common people? Those that exchange
ideas, like the middle classes. The rest don't interest you.”

‘ “But – there's the life –”

‘ “I don't believe there's a jot more life from Miriam than you could
get from any educated girl – say Miss Moreton. It is *you* who are snob-
bish about class” ’ (pp. 313–14).

Paul's ideas about class, it may be remarked, are a rough statement of
the sort of clash which is dramatized in *Lady Chatterley's Lover*; they also
point to the way in which he is drawn to his father. There is of course
a lot in what Mrs Morel says, and Paul finds it difficult to define his
feelings and to explain his reluctance to associate with his 'father's
pals', but if he could bring himself to own it, it is clearly his father –

and not Miriam, as Mrs Morel jealously and falsely supposes – who is the prototype of his image of the 'common people' (to whom he feels he belongs) and who embodies the vitality and exuberance and warmth which evoke his deepest sympathies. And despite his antipathy towards his father, he recognizes what it is that Morel has given his wife: the 'real, real flame of feeling' which he tells Miriam his mother has experienced 'through' his father (p. 386) is simply an alternative phrase for 'life itself, warmth', for that quality which he tries to convince his mother the working class possesses.

I think it is fair to assume that the depiction of Paul's relations with his mother and father is a reliable guide to the nature of Lawrence's feelings about his own parents. Certainly there is wide agreement about his unconscious identification with his father in real life and in the work which follows *Sons and Lovers*. And Lawrence himself, though he phrases the affirmation obliquely, attests the vital nature of the bond which existed between him and his father:

'. . . if the large parent mother-germ still lives and acts vividly and mysteriously in the great fused nucleus of your solar plexus, does the smaller, brilliant male-spark that derived from your father act any less vividly? By no means. It is different – it is less ostensible. It may be even in magnitude smaller. But it may be even more vivid, even more intrinsic. So beware how you deny the father-quick of yourself. You may be denying the most intrinsic quick of all.'[1]

It is also instructive, I think, to compare the following two passages, the first from *Sons and Lovers*, the second from a letter written a few months after the completion of the novel:

'Gertrude Coppard had watched [Morel], fascinated. He was so full of colour and animation, his voice ran so easily into comic grotesque, he was so ready and so pleasant with everybody. Her own father had a rich fund of humour, but it was satiric. This man's was different: soft, non-intellectual, warm, a kind of gambolling.

'She herself was opposite. She had a curious, receptive mind, which found much pleasure and amusement in listening to other folk. She was clever in leading folk on to talk. She loved ideas, and was considered very intellectual. What she liked most of all was an argument on religion or philosophy or politics with some educated man. . . .

'She was a puritan, like her father, high-minded, and really stern. Therefore the dusky, golden softness of this man's sensuous flame of life, that flowed off his flesh like the flame from a candle, not baffled

---

[1] *Fantasia of the Unconscious*, p. 24.

and gripped into incandescence by thought and spirit as her life was, seemed to her something wonderful, beyond her' (pp. 17-18).

'I conceive a man's body as a kind of flame, like a candle flame, forever upright and yet flowing: and the intellect is just the light that is shed on to the things around. And I am not so much concerned with the things around–which is really mind–but with the mystery of the flame forever flowing, coming God knows how from out of practically nowhere, and being *itself*, whatever there is around it, that it lights up. . . .'[1]

The recurrence of the striking candle flame image, with its suggestion of glowing warmth and mysterious being, signifies yet again a link between what Lawrence's father was (I think it is safe, at this stage, to identify the characters with their prototypes in real life) and what he himself was most concerned with. And it was not to his mother alone, we sense, that what the miner was 'seemed something wonderful'. But there are other implications to the passage quoted from the novel. What it vividly suggests is the strength of the impulse by which the young couple are attracted to their opposites, and the opposition described is so radical that it clearly must have had an important influence on Lawrence himself. Indeed Diana Trilling declares that, 'identifying himself now with the one parent, now with the other, Lawrence tried throughout his life to understand and to reconstitute in his own person their unhappy marriage';[2] and Richard Rees follows her in believing that Lawrence's 'attempt to balance the scale [of values represented by his parents] was to be an important part of his life's work'.[3] The views of these critics link up, at one point, with those advanced in Chapter 1 of this discussion, but the difference between us is precisely that which I wish to pursue in the analysis of Lawrence's development subsequent to the writing of *Sons and Lovers*. This seminal novel suggests the personal significance of Lawrence's formulation some two years later (in the Hardy essay) of the male and female principles. A comparison between the table in Chapter 1 and the passage describing the meeting of his father and mother indicates that, in terms of that formulation, it is the decidedly male father who represents the *female* principle and the mother the *male*. (It is noticeable, even, that the '*golden* softness' of the miner's 'sensuous *flame* of life' is

---

[1] Letter to Ernest Collings (January 1913), *Letters*, p. 94.

[2] 'Lawrence: Creator and Dissenter', *The Saturday Review of Literature*, 29 (December 7, 1946), 18.

[3] *Brave Men: A Study of D. H. Lawrence and Simone Weil* (London, 1958), p. 42

'*dusky*'.) Lawrence's formulation of the female principle as a complement of the male principle may therefore be viewed as an attempt to
give full weight to qualities which his father embodied and which
were underrated in his own home.[1] Indeed the value accorded the
female principle is a measure of his liberation from his mother's
dominance. But the fact that his father is associated with the female
principle and his mother with the male is also suggestive of the cause
of the breach in his own nature. It is this breach which made it imperative for him to try to reconcile the opposing qualities within
himself. The novels after *Sons and Lovers* are a record of this struggle and
of the violent negations it engendered.

III

If Lawrence's reaction against his mother was the fundamental cause
of his hostility towards much of what he characterized as the male
principle, Helen Corke, Louie Burrows, and Jessie Chambers were con-
tributory factors in his repudiation of 'idealism' and 'spirituality'.[2] Of
these young women Jessie Chambers was the most decisive influence
and, as Miriam in *Sons and Lovers*, Lawrence prepared for her both a
grave and a monument. But if he dug her grave it does not necessarily
follow that he betrayed her. The charge has to be faced, however, for
it has been made the basis of a considerable body of accusatory criticism.

[1] Cf. 'Who is [Angel Clare], that he shall be pure male, and deny the existence of
the female? This is the question the Creator asks of him. Is then the male the
exclusive whole of life?–is he even the higher or supreme part of life? Angel
Clare thinks so: as Christ thought.

'Yet it is not so, as even Angel Clare must find out. Life, that is Two-in-One,
Male and Female. Nor is either part greater than the other.

'. . . [Angel Clare] had no idea that there was such a thing as positive Woman, as
the Female, another great living Principle counterbalancing his own male principle. He conceived of the world as consisting of the One, the Male Principle.'
'Study of Thomas Hardy', *Phoenix*, p. 485.

[2] Helena, the heroine of Lawrence's second novel, *The Trespasser*, was based on Helen
Corke. Lawrence deals directly with his relationship with her in a number of
poems (addressed to Helen) which were written at about the same time as *The
Trespasser*. See *Poems*, I, 64, 78, 100, 102, 140. Louie Burrows does not appear in any
of the novels of this time, but Lawrence was engaged to her. The disappointment
he experienced in his relationship with her finds bitter expression in 'The Hands
of the Betrothed', and the conflict between them erupts in 'Snap-Dragon', one of
the most powerful of the early poems. See *Poems*, I, 108, 114.

As was perhaps only to be expected, the cry of betrayal was first uttered by Jessie Chambers herself:

'As the sheets of manuscript came rapidly to me I was bewildered and dismayed at [the] treatment [of Miriam]. I began to perceive that I had set Lawrence a task far beyond his strength. In my confidence I had not doubted that he would work out the problem with integrity. But he burked the real issue. It was his old inability to face his problem squarely. His mother had to be supreme, and for the sake of that supremacy every disloyalty was permissible.'[1]

I quote, too, what I think is a representative example of the way in which her judgement has been followed by critics:

'. . . as we now know, there is a fundamental falsity in [the history of Paul's relations with the two women, Miriam and Clara]. The moving reminiscences of E.T., Lawrence's real-life Miriam, have now made it clear that not only did he use his novel to give himself imaginatively the sexual gratification he could not find in life, but he refused to face the truth of his difficulty when he insisted on placing the blame for his failure upon the girl rather than on his mother, where it belonged.'[2]

In passing, we may remark the egoism of Jessie Chambers' attitude and the unwarranted assumption to which it gives rise–Lawrence was not writing the novel as a task set by her–but I am more concerned with the fallacies inherent in Edward Wagenknecht's argument. In the first place it is not clear on what basis Jessie's word is automatically accepted as better than Lawrence's. Though we can understand her charge of 'disloyalty', the following extract from a letter suggests that Lawrence did not falsify the history of his relations with her:

'I see Frieda has written a defence of me against Miriam–or Jessie, whatever she shall be called. It's all very well for Miss Chambers to be spiritual–perhaps she can bring it off–I can't. She bottled me up till I was going to burst. But as long as the cork sat tight (herself the cork) there was spiritual calm. When the cork was blown out, and Mr

---

[1] *A Personal Record*, p. 201. Cf. too her letter to Helen Corke which runs in part: 'The "Miriam" part of the novel is a slander–a fearful treachery. . . .' Helen Corke, *D. H. Lawrence's 'Princess'*, p. 33.

[2] Edward Wagenknecht, *Cavalcade of the English Novel* (New York, 1943), pp. 495–6. Cf. Nathan A. Scott, Jr.: '[Lawrence] cannot endure the ultimate truth of his personal history, and so he begins to misrepresent the facts. He seeks, for instance, to represent Miriam as the one who is really at fault in her relationship with Paul; it is she who shrinks from the sexual mystery; it is she who is frigid.' *Rehearsals of Discomposure* (London, 1952), pp. 138–9.

Lawrence foamed, Miriam said "This yeastiness I disown: it was not so in my day." God bless her, she always looked down on me–spiritually. But it hurt when she sent a letter of mine back: quite an inoffensive letter, I think. And look, she is bitterly ashamed of having had me–as if I had dragged her spiritual plumage in the mud. Call that love! Ah well.'[1]

Moreover, in regard to Jessie's assertion that the Clara episode 'had no foundation in fact',[2] Harry T. Moore's researches have established–it seems to me conclusively–that the episode was based at least in part on an actual experience.[3] Lawrence's 'imaginative sexual gratification', therefore, was decidedly not imaginary. But that is hardly important. What should be noticed is Wagenknecht's confusion of art and life. If there is a 'fundamental falsity' in the novel, then the critics who take this line should be able to point to the falsity in the text, but this they signally fail to do. There is, no doubt, the unsubstantiated claim that Lawrence places the blame for 'his' failure on Miriam rather than on his mother, but this is simply not true. The extent to which Paul, as a result of his mother's influence, is to blame for the failure of his relationship with Miriam is fully and frankly acknowledged. I have already drawn attention to two passages in which such acknowledgement is made,[4] and they are by no means isolated instances. The plan of the book entails Paul's slowly growing recognition of his own inadequacy and there are numerous references to it, varying from direct commentary: 'He was afraid of her love for him. It was too good for him, and he was inadequate. His own love was at fault, not hers' (p. 255), to explicit admission: ' "I can only give friendship–" [said Paul], "it's all I'm capable of–it's a flaw in my make-up. The thing overbalances to one side–I hate a toppling balance. Let us have done" ' (p. 271).[5]

---

[1] *The Collected Letters of D. H. Lawrence*, ed. Harry T. Moore (London, 1962), I, 199. Henceforth I shall use the short titles *Letters* and *Collected Letters* to refer to the Huxley and Moore editions respectively. The title of the latter edition is a misnomer, for Moore has reprinted only about three-quarters of the letters contained in the Huxley edition and merely a selection of the numerous letters published elsewhere. Consequently, as a reviewer in *The Times Literary Supplement* of 27 April 1962 has remarked, 'it is still necessary to search among more than a dozen books to find Lawrence's letters', and there is now clearly a need for a comprehensive collection.

[2] *A Personal Record*, p. 202.

[3] See *The Intelligent Heart*, pp. 93, 95.

[4] See p. 55 above.

[5] See too, for instance, pp. 188, 194, 204, 210, 238, 298–9.

A more recent critic, apparently in reaction against Jessie Chambers and those who follow her, has swung to the other extreme. Mark Spilka finds that 'the chief "split" between Paul and Miriam comes from the abstract nature of their love, and not from the mother's hold upon the young man's soul. And the final responsibility for this split belongs with Miriam';[1] but this is surely to underestimate the central importance of Mrs Morel and the extent of Paul's own difficulties. The relationship fails because of fatal hindrances on both sides –even if Mark Schorer finds this objectionable:

'The central section of the novel is shot through with alternate statements as to the source of the difficulty: Paul is unable to love Miriam wholly and Miriam can love only his spirit. These contradictions appear sometimes within single paragraphs, and the point of view is never adequately objectified and sustained to tell us which is true.'[2]

The truth which Lawrence presents is, apparently, more inclusive than critics seem willing to admit, and if it is not of the black and white variety that does not mean to say that he is contradicting himself. I hope that in my discussion of Paul's relations with his mother I have sufficiently indicated the nature of the barrier which prevents him from loving Miriam; I shall therefore endeavour to show that, as far as Miriam is concerned, the point of view is not only adequately objectified but that–whatever happened in real life–the way in which she fails Paul is convincingly demonstrated.

Miriam gives Paul, at the crucial stage of his development, much-needed intellectual stimulation–she is 'the threshing-floor on which he [threshes] out all his beliefs' (p. 279)–but what she gives in this way is vitiated by her 'sucking of his soul':

'He felt that she wanted the soul out of his body, and not him. All his strength and energy she drew into herself through some channel which united them. She did not want to meet him, so that there were two of them, man and woman together. She wanted to draw all of him into her. It urged him to an intensity like madness, which fascinated him, as drug-taking might' (p. 239).

The comparison with drug-taking suggests the debilitating nature of the relationship: Paul comes to crave Miriam's stimulation but it is artificially restricted and lacks a healthy physical counterbalance to its dizzy intensity. From the outset sexual conflict is implicit in their relations, and even though Paul is at times satisfied by the pleasure

[1] *The Love Ethic of D. H. Lawrence* (Bloomington, 1957), p. 66.
[2] 'Technique as Discovery', *loc. cit.*, p. 19.

Miriam gives him, there is a clear indication that it is unlikely to prove adequate ultimately:

'Then he began to talk about the design. There was for him the most intense pleasure in talking about his work to Miriam. All his passion, all his wild blood, went into this intercourse with her, when he talked and conceived his work. She brought forth to him his imaginations. She did not understand, any more than a woman understands when she conceives a child in her womb. But this was life for her and for him' (p. 249).

The couple's contrasted attitudes to sex are neatly symmetrical. Paul's complicated feelings spring from his mother's passionate love for him, which he reciprocates; Miriam's stem from her religious indoctrination by her mother, whom she imitates. Mrs Leivers is a woman who '[exalts] everything–even a bit of housework–to the plane of a religious trust' (p. 182), and her influence on her daughter is far-reaching. It results, for one thing, in the unnaturally high pitch at which Miriam habitually lives, and it is her emotional intensity that so often irritates Paul–though, in this respect, he no doubt dislikes in her a quality he distrusts in himself. The lovers are too like one another ever to be wholly at ease. Mrs Leivers' influence accounts, too, for Miriam's shrinking from sex. At the crisis of her relations with Paul she says, 'Mother said to me, "There is one thing in marriage that is always dreadful, but you have to bear it." And I believed it' (p. 355). The combined effect of animadversions such as this and of inculcated concepts of 'purity' is to distort her view of life. Though she lives in close contact with 'the continual business of birth and of begetting which goes on upon every farm', for instance, her blood is 'chastened almost to disgust of the faintest suggestion of such intercourse' (p. 201). Her inhibition also expresses itself in a physical timidity: she dreads chickens pecking maize from her hand–as Helena in *The Trespasser* shrinks from an anemone closing over her finger–and she feels that the very notion that she might 'want' Paul, as her sister suggests, is a 'disgrace' (p. 212). He instinctively divines and resents the willed deflection of her feelings which makes her lavish love on her younger brother in his presence (p. 190) or '[sip] . . . flowers with fervid kisses' (p. 267). The sort of relationship she consequently forces on Paul is indicated in the following passage:

'She wanted to show him a certain wild-rose bush she had discovered. . . . Almost passionately she wanted to be with him when he stood before the flowers. They were going to have a communion together–something that thrilled her, something holy. He was walking beside her in silence. They were very near to each other. She trembled, and he listened, vaguely anxious. . . .

'Paul and Miriam stood close together, silent, and watched. Point after point the steady roses shone out to them, seeming to kindle something in their souls. The dusk came like smoke around, and still did not put out the roses.

'Paul looked into Miriam's eyes. She was pale and expectant with wonder, her lips were parted, and her dark eyes lay open to him. His look seemed to travel down into her. Her soul quivered. It was the communion she wanted. He turned aside, as if pained. . . . She lifted her hand impulsively to the flowers; she went forward and touched them in worship.

' "Let us go," he said.

'There was a cool scent of ivory roses–a white, virgin scent. Something made him feel anxious and imprisoned. The two walked in silence.

' "Till Sunday," he said quietly, and left her; and she walked home slowly, feeling her soul satisfied with the holiness of the night. He stumbled down the path. And as soon as he was out of the wood, in the free open meadow, where he could breathe, he started to run as fast as he could. It was like a delicious delirium in his veins' (pp. 197–9).

The passage is effective in the way it draws together several motives. It shows how Miriam manœuvres Paul into an intimacy which is not only irreproachable and would have her mother's sanction but also feeds and satisfies her own religious longings. At the same time, however–and Lawrence is expert at suggesting feelings which Paul is only dimly aware of–the *double entendre* of Paul's look in response to Miriam's eyes and his compulsive breaking into a run when he leaves her are expressive of the frustration to which she subjects him. She turns the wood into a church for herself but into a prison for him.

A short symbolic scene, which precedes the climactic revelation of the division between Paul and Miriam, testifies–*pace* Mark Schorer–to Lawrence's objective presentment of the conflict:

'There was a great crop of cherries at the farm. . . . Paul climbed high in the tree, above the scarlet roofs of the buildings. The wind, moaning steadily, made the whole tree rock with a subtle, thrilling motion that stirred the blood. The young man, perched insecurely in the slender branches, rocked till he felt slightly drunk, reached down the boughs where the scarlet beady cherries hung thick underneath, and tore off handful after handful of the sleek, cool-fleshed fruit. Cherries touched his ears and his neck as he stretched forward, their chill finger-tips sending a flash down his blood. All shades of red, from a golden vermilion to a rich crimson, glowed and met his eyes under a darkness of leaves. . . .

'Miriam came out wondering.

' "Oh!" Paul heard her mellow voice call, "isn't it wonderful?"

'He looked down. There was a faint gold glimmer on her face, that looked very soft, turned up to him.

' "How high you are!" she said.

'Beside her, on the rhubarb leaves, were four dead birds, thieves that had been shot. Paul saw some cherry-stones hanging quite bleached, like skeletons, picked clear of flesh. He looked down again to Miriam' (pp. 347–8).

The scene takes place immediately before the lovers have intercourse for the first time, and its juxtaposition of Paul and Miriam and the birds and the cherry-stones implies the deathly nature of their relationship; despite the lush fruitfulness of the scene the suggestion of death is insistent. Paul's blood is stirred as he tears off the 'cool-fleshed' cherries, but in so far as the fruit-picking is a symbolic anticipation of the intercourse with Miriam which follows it, he is as much a thief as the four dead birds that lie at her feet. In his struggle to achieve self-knowledge he has by this time more or less divined the nature of the impediment which, on his side, prevents him from responding physically to Miriam, but though his reaction is characteristic it is self-defeating. Determining to force his way through his difficulties, he is compelled to force her too. Miriam has her own strong inhibitions to contend with, and, prior to this scene, though he browbeats her into compliance with his wishes, he succeeds in extracting from her only a reluctant intellectual consent to what he wants. Paul is, to that extent, a robber-bird. But Miriam is at least equally to blame that the intercourse which follows proves to be a 'picking clear of flesh' which reveals the skeleton beneath. Her reaction to his mechanical proposal is also characteristic, but the very terms in which she agrees to it foredoom the attempt to failure: 'There was something divine in it; then she would submit, religiously, to the sacrifice' (p. 347). The sacrifice, when it comes, is one in which she feels 'something of horror'; and afterwards, though Paul is 'physically at rest', he realizes 'that she had not been with him all the time, that her soul had stood apart, in a sort of horror' (p. 350). Paul's physical release is symbolically marked by a downfall of rain, but the 'dead pine-leaves' on which he lays his face emphasize the emotional sterility of the encounter. Their further attempts are no more successful. The look at the back of Miriam's eyes is like that of 'a creature awaiting immolation', and though Paul spends a week with her at her grandmother's cottage, 'there remained afterwards always the sense of failure and of death' (p. 354).

Miriam's sacrificial submission to sex is at once the crux and the climax of her relationship with Paul. And like Mrs Morel, who does not tell the doctor about the lump in her side, she too is masochistically self-destructive in her self-sacrifice, for it is she who deliberately provokes Paul's affair with Clara (p. 280). She does so, ostensibly, to 'test' him, but that she can regard his going to Clara as equivalent to his going to an inn for a glass of whisky (p. 387) is yet another indication of her incomprehension of the significance of the sex act. If Paul fails to break down her frigidity, she, in her anguished martyrdom, fails as decisively to liberate him:

> Since the fire has failed in me,
> What man will stoop in your flesh to plough
> The shrieking cross? [1]

In rejecting her, therefore, Paul not only acknowledges the impossibility of a satisfactory relationship with her, but refuses either to sacrifice himself to her or to allow her to continue to sacrifice herself to him. Miriam and Mrs Morel fight each other for Paul, but in the end they represent the same destructively sapping force. His abandonment of Miriam is accordingly as positive an action as his repudiation of his mother, and it is motivated by a similar desire not to deny his own life:

'He felt, in leaving her, he was defrauding her of life. But he knew that, in staying, stifling the inner, desperate man, he was denying his own life. And he did not hope to give life to her by denying his own' (p. 508).

Paul's relationship with Clara is the obverse of that with Miriam. It serves, therefore, not only as a structural balance (structurally, it is, in addition, both a parallel to William's relationship with Gyp and a means of linking Paul's workaday life at Jordan's with the emotional

---

[1] 'Last Words to Miriam', *Poems*, I, 95. Miriam is seen as a sacrificial victim in other poems which deal with her; see, for instance, 'Lightning', p. 37, and 'Scent of Irises', p. 70.

conflicts on which the book is based) but as a harsh confirmation of Mrs Morel's power over her son. While she lives, Mrs Morel holds her son's soul, and if Miriam tries to snatch it away from her, it remains far beyond Clara's grasp. Paul is attracted to Clara of course precisely because she is so different from Miriam, but though Clara satisfies his physical needs for a time, she does not give him the fulfilment he is seeking:

'She toiled to his side. Arriving there, she looked at him heavily, dumbly, and laid her head on his shoulder. He held her fast as he looked round. They were safe enough from all but the small, lonely cows over the river. He sunk his mouth on her throat, where he felt her heavy pulse beat under his lips. Everything was perfectly still. There was nothing in the afternoon but themselves.

'When she arose, he, looking on the ground all the time, saw suddenly sprinkled on the black wet beech-roots many scarlet carnation petals, like splashed drops of blood; and red, small splashes fell from her bosom, streaming down her dress to her feet.

' "Your flowers are smashed," he said.

'She looked at him heavily as she put back her hair. Suddenly he put his finger-tips on her cheek.

' "Why dost look so heavy?" he reproached her.

'She smiled sadly, as if she felt alone in herself. He caressed her cheek with his fingers, and kissed her.

' "Nay!" he said. "Never thee bother!" ' (p. 379).

Mark Spilka finds that the flowers (which Paul has bought Clara before they make love for the first time) 'give benediction to their union' and states that 'the smashing works both ways . . . for this is the "baptism of fire in passion" which Paul has been seeking. Here too is the first sign of the vision of love which Lawrence would develop, in time, to full and confident expression as an ethic of renewal.'[1] I am not sure what he means by the smashing working both ways, but it seems to me that his reading of the scene ignores its emotional overtones. The scarlet petals, it should be remembered, are 'like splashed drops of blood' and splash, like blood, from Clara's bosom; they are, I should say, an emotional equivalent of the bleached cherry-stones, which hang like skeletons, rather than a sign of renewal. They are, that is to say, a similar intimation of the likely failure of the relationship, and what they point to is its exclusively carnal nature. Clara smiles sadly, we notice, 'as if she felt alone in herself', and indeed from

[1] *The Love Ethic*, p. 54.

the outset she resents the impersonality of Paul's attitude to her. Nor is it exactly 'a baptism of fire in passion' that Paul is seeking. He wants that, even desires it urgently after his failure with Miriam, but what he is searching for–and finds neither with Miriam nor Clara–is the more lasting satisfaction of a union both of soul and body. And as the affair with Clara takes its course, Paul comes to realize that passion alone is not enough: 'it was not she who could keep his soul steady' (p. 431).

Before he breaks with Clara, Paul tries to assure himself that he loves her, but it is a heavily qualified love: ' "Sometimes, when I see her just as *the woman*, I love her, mother; but then, when she talks and criticizes, I often don't listen to her" ' (p. 426)–and 'in the daytime he [forgets] her a good deal' (p. 427). It is only a matter of time before the fire consumes itself and he begins to 'feel imprisoned' in her presence. In the end, the effect she has on him is not dissimilar to the feeling of suffocation he has when he is with Miriam.

It is Paul, we feel, who is largely at fault with Clara, but she fails him too–and in a way that relates her failure to that of Miriam:

'She caught him passionately to her, pressed his head down on her breast with her hand. She could not bear the suffering in his voice. She was afraid in her soul. He might have anything of her–anything; but she did not want to *know*. She felt she could not bear it. She wanted him to be soothed upon her–soothed. She stood clasping him and caressing him, and he was something unknown to her–something almost uncanny. She wanted to soothe him into forgetfulness.

'And soon the struggle went down in his soul, and he forgot. But then Clara was not there for him, only a woman, warm, something he loved and almost worshipped, there in the dark. But it was not Clara, and she submitted to him. The naked hunger and inevitability of his loving her, something strong and blind and ruthless in its primitiveness, made the hour almost terrible to her. She knew how stark and alone he was, and she felt it was great that he came to her; and she took him simply because his need was bigger either than her or him, and her soul was still within her. She did this for him in his need even if he left her, for she loved him' (pp. 429–30).

Middleton Murry has shrewdly remarked that 'at the crucial moment, we cannot distinguish between Clara and Miriam', but then he is concerned to show that 'this man . . . has no business with sex at all'.[1] The resemblance between Clara and Miriam indicates, rather, how

[1] D. H. Lawrence: *Son of Woman* (London, 1931), p. 36.

Clara, in her submission, fails Paul. If Miriam is unable to respond to him sexually, Clara can cope only with his physical need of her: she is always 'only a woman' to him and she gives up trying to comprehend him; she does 'not want to *know*'. Both women ineffectually attempt to 'soothe' him by sacrificing themselves. But it is against just this sort of self-sacrifice that Paul pits himself, and, finally, he engineers Clara's return to her husband. Dawes, it becomes evident, is more receptive to her pity: 'She wanted now to be self-sacrificial. . . . So she kneeled to Dawes, and it gave him a subtle pleasure' (p. 466).

Both Miriam and Clara, therefore, are vital to Paul's development; Miriam is his intellectual threshing-floor and Clara is his sexual testing ground. But what they give him is not sufficient. 'We are creatures of two halves', Lawrence wrote later, 'spiritual and sensual – and each half is as important as the other. Any relation based on the one half – say the delicate spiritual half alone – *inevitably* brings revulsion and betrayal. It is halfness, or partness, which causes Judas.'[1] It is wholeness, not partness, that Paul seeks, but because of his own relationship with his mother and the nature of the women he loves this is denied him. *Sons and Lovers* is Lawrence's *Portrait of the Artist as a Young Man*; but where Stephen Dedalus, in order to preserve his independence, has to reject church and state as well as his family, Paul, in the end, rejects the three women who threaten to stifle him. Joyce battled with church and state from the outset; Lawrence moved from the particular to the general, and his rejection of his mother and of Miriam came to involve, as Henry Miller has pointed out, a rejection of 'the whole white world doomed by its idealism, as he saw it'.[2]

Viewed in the light of Lawrence's future development, however, the ultimate significance of *Sons and Lovers* is that it was a catharsis. It liberated him from the immediate involvements of his young manhood and left him free to develop both as a man and as a writer. But the struggle recorded in the novel left its mark on him and influenced the future course of his thinking. Among other things, it left him with an abiding sense of duality, and in the expository writings which followed, he made an attempt to formulate the philosophy to which this apprehension gave rise. In his fiction he set himself the task of seeking the 'Holy Ghost' in a dualistic universe. This, in *The Rainbow* and *Women in Love*, is characteristically expressed as an attempt to balance the male and female principles.

[1] Letter to Dorothy Brett, 1925, *Letters*, pp. 626–7.
[2] 'Shadowy Monomania', *Sunday after the War* (London, 1945), p. 249.

3. Two in One : The Second Period

(A) *The Rainbow*

'I THINK THE ONLY RE-SOURCING OF ART, REVIVIFYING IT, IS TO MAKE it more the joint work of man and woman. I think *the* one thing to do, is for men to have courage to draw nearer to women, expose themselves to them, and be altered by them: and for women to accept and admit men. That is the start–by bringing themselves together, men and women–revealing themselves each to the other, gaining great blind knowledge and suffering and joy, which it will take a big further lapse of civilisation to exploit and work out. Because the source of all life and knowledge is in man and woman, and the source of all living is in the interchange and the meeting and mingling of these two: man-life and woman-life, man-knowledge and woman-knowledge, man-being and woman-being.'[1]

This extract from a letter, written shortly before Lawrence began

[1] Letter to A. W. McLeod (June 1914), *Letters*, p. 196.

74

Two in One: The Second Period 75

the final rewriting of *The Rainbow*,[1] serves to define the major interests of that work. It should be read together with the passage, quoted in full in Chapter 1,[2] in which he postulates a 'supreme art' which 'knows the struggle between the two conflicting laws' of man and woman, and which 'knows the final reconciliation, where both are equal, two in one, complete'. *The Rainbow*, it is clear, is meant to be more than a psychological or sociological study of marriage; it is the first stage in an attempt to discover the necessary conditions for a meaningful life, and since man and woman are the source of all vital knowledge, it is in the various possibilities of relationship between them that the conditions are to be sought. But marriage, as Lawrence envisages it, is not merely a conjunction of 'man-being' and 'woman-being'; it entails a radical clash of the two opposed modes of being. Where the conflict results in equipoise, there is true marriage and a basis for individual fulfilment. Like trees that are rooted in earth and rise to their own green florescence, man and woman embrace in marriage and grow into themselves. This presupposes, however, that there is a self to develop, and Lawrence's effort is directed at exploring not only failures and consummations in marriage but frustrations and achievements of true being. The one, it is seen, is dependent on the other.

It is these concerns which shape the structure of the novel. Lawrence deals with three generations in order to discover what is constant in the lives of men and women. He is interested not so much in the interaction of the generations, though this interest is by no means ignored, as in the complexities of being which recur afresh for each generation. Consequently, in so far as *The Rainbow* is a family chronicle, it is not held together by the tight links of a conventionally well-constructed plot. Its organizing principle, as F. R. Leavis has acutely pointed out, is rhythmic: a 'movement that, by recurrence along with newness, brings continually a significant recall of what has gone before'.[3] It is no accident that the opening pages of the novel–those pages which have so often been appreciatively quoted as evidence of the power of Lawrence's prose (I shall refer to them again in another connection)–should pulsate with so insistent a rhythm. The opening

[1] Lawrence had worked on material which was to become *The Rainbow* and *Women in Love* from December 1912. In December 1914 he reported that he had done about a hundred pages of the final draft of *The Rainbow* (*Letters*, p. 212). The novel was completed in March 1915 and published in the same year.
[2] See pp. 31–2 above.
[3] *D. H. Lawrence: Novelist* (London, 1955), p. 122.

strikingly emphasizes the cyclical movement of the seasons, conveying the sense of a life lived in harmony with them; it also points
to the rhythmic unfolding of life in the three generations of Brangwens of whom the book treats.

The nature of Lawrence's thematic interests led him to further
technical innovations. Conventional characterization of the sort employed in nineteenth-century novels or, for that matter, in *Sons and
Lovers*, was felt to be inadequate as a means of rendering 'man-being'
and 'woman-being', of rendering, that is to say, unconscious or only
dimly conscious psychic states:

'... that which is physic–non-human, in humanity, is more interesting to me than the old-fashioned human element–which causes one
to conceive a character in a certain moral scheme and make him
consistent. The certain moral scheme is what I object to. . . . I don't
so much care about what the woman *feels*–in the ordinary usage of
the word. That presumes an *ego* to feel with. I only care about what
the woman *is*–what she IS–inhumanly, physiologically, materially–
according to the use of the word: but for me, what she *is* as a phenom-
enon (or as representing some greater, inhuman will), instead of
what she feels according to the human conception. . . . You mustn't
look in my novel for the old stable *ego* of the character. There is
another *ego*, according to whose action the individual is unrecognisable, and passes through, as it were, allotropic states which it needs
a deeper sense than any we've been used to exercise, to discover are
states of the same single radically unchanged element. (Like as diamond and coal are the same pure single element of carbon. The
ordinary novel would trace the history of the diamond–but I say,
"Diamond, what! This is carbon." And my diamond might be coal or
soot, and my theme is carbon.)'[1]

This, of course, is only a theoretical statement, and in places there is
an imprecision of language attributable to the informality of the occasion–if the individual were really 'unrecognisable', the novel would be
strained to bursting point–but it does illuminate Lawrence's practice
in *The Rainbow*. The abandonment of the 'certain moral scheme' means

[1] Letter to Edward Garnett (June 1914), *Letters*, pp. 197–8. It is interesting to compare this statement with Paul Morel's account of his aims as a painter. He tells
Miriam that there is 'scarcely any shadow' in his work: 'it's more shimmery, as if
I'd painted the shimmering protoplasm in the leaves and everywhere, and not
the stiffness of the shape. That seems dead to me. Only this shimmeriness is the
real living. The shape is a dead crust. The shimmer is inside really.' *Sons and Lovers*,
p. 166.

that a character is judged not by social or ethical criteria but by the degree to which he is true to his deepest being, to the 'carbon' of his nature. The conception of character as a series of 'allotropic states' is based, it seems to me, on profound psychological truth: we have to learn to assent, without demanding a moral or rational causeway between the two, that the Ursula who can vow to give herself in understanding love to the children she teaches is acceptably the same Ursula who 'annihilates' Skrebensky in the moonlight. The conception springs, indeed, from Lawrence's apprehension of the co-existence of the tiger and the lamb in the individual psyche.

Lawrence's choice of 'carbon' as his theme posed a considerable technical problem. How was he, in fact, to present 'man-being' or 'woman-being'? An associational patterning of thought, such as was then being developed (though unknown to him) by James Joyce, would clearly have been unsuitable for the expression of undefined feelings at the deepest levels of consciousness. What Lawrence did was to evolve the stream of half-consciousness; that is to say, acting as an impersonal but articulate intermediary, he gave form and definition to what were really the non-rational, intuitional responses of his characters. I quote a representative instance–the description of Tom Brangwen on his wedding night:

'And Brangwen stood beside her, giving his hearty handshake to his friends, receiving their regard gratefully, glad of their attention. His heart was tormented within him, he did not try to smile. The time of his trial and his admittance, his Gethsemane and his Triumphal Entry in one, had come now.

'Behind her, there was so much unknown to him. When he approached her, he came to such a terrible painful unknown. How could he embrace it and fathom it? How could he close his arms round all this darkness and hold it to his breast and give himself to it? What might not happen to him? If he stretched and strained for ever he would never be able to grasp it all, and to yield himself naked out of his own hands into the unknown power! How could a man be strong enough to take her, put his arms round her and have her, and be sure he could conquer this awful unknown next his heart? What was it then that she was, to which he must also deliver himself up, and which at the same time he must embrace, contain?

'He was to be her husband. It was established so. And he wanted it more than he wanted life, or anything. She stood beside him in her silk dress, looking at him strangely, so that a certain terror, horror took possession of him, because she was strange and impending and he had no choice. He could not bear to meet her look from under her strange, thick brows.

' "Is it late?" she said.

'He looked at his watch.

' "No–half-past eleven," he said. And he made an excuse to go into the kitchen, leaving her standing in the room among the disorder and the drinking-glasses' (p. 58).

This passage reveals the strength of Lawrence's method. What he does well, and with great originality, is to evoke the emotional reality which finds expression only in Tom's apparently innocuous withdrawal to the kitchen. We realize as we read, moreover, that this is a reality of which Tom himself is only half-conscious; he does not so much think these thoughts as incoherently feel them. And the suggestion of ceaseless activity at this level of consciousness is so insistent that Lydia's remark implies more than a desire to know the time. The force of Lawrence's imaginative penetration, then, enables him to delineate an area of life of which we ourselves are only half-aware.

But the method has its weaknesses. First, it necessitates a distension of language. Edwin Muir has remarked that 'the instincts are only concerned, so far as we know, with absolutes. They recognize only things like life and its opposite.'[1] Consequently Lawrence is compelled, as in the above passage, to use words like 'terror' and 'horror' and metaphors like 'his Gethsemane and his Triumphal Entry' in order to suggest equivalents for the obscure feelings he is describing. The terms employed do succeed in evoking our recognition of the strength of these feelings, but then, lamentably, they fight a constant rearguard action against the force of associations related to altogether different–but more usual–contexts. The thronging insistence of the feelings is also conveyed by means of repetition, but though this is effective in an isolated passage, it becomes a limitation, stylistically, the more clamorously it manifests itself as a stock technical device.

Second, it is difficult to depict the evanescent moments of being that Lawrence is concerned with in terms of action. There are many scenes in which he surmounts this difficulty triumphantly, but I feel that in the novel as a whole there is not a sufficient number of dramatic correlatives; that is to say, too frequently there are sections of descriptive analysis that are not embodied in the sort of corroborative

[1] 'D. H. Lawrence', *Transition* (London, 1926), p. 57.

action that is also ultimately revelatory. Lawrence himself was well aware of the drawbacks of such a method, which he suggestively described as 'exhaustive':

'I shall go on now to the end of the book. It will not take me long. Then I will go over it all again, and I shall be very glad to hear *all* you have to say. But if this, the second half, also disappoints you, I will, when I come to the end, leave this book altogether. Then I should propose to write a story with a plot, and to abandon the exhaustive method entirely–write pure object and story.'[1]

In the event Lawrence did not turn to writing 'pure object and story', but *Women in Love*, which is a further elaboration of the themes of *The Rainbow*, gives evidence of a radical modification of method, of an attempt to subdue the exhaustive to the dramatic.

II

The opening pages of *The Rainbow* are not only an impassioned prose poem designed to evoke the traditional way of life at the Marsh Farm, nor do they only point to the rhythmic principle underlying the organization of the novel; they are a concentrated, introductory statement of theme. The description of the seasons, for instance, is couched in terms which make it clear that the activity of nature is both a reflection and an affirmation of the fundamental desires of men and women–the desires that Lawrence is to depict:

'But heaven and earth was teeming around them, and how should this cease? They felt the rush of the sap in spring, they knew the wave which cannot halt, but every year throws forward the seed to begetting, and, falling back, leaves the young-born on the earth. They knew the intercourse between heaven and earth, sunshine drawn into the breast and bowels, the rain sucked up in the daytime, nakedness that comes under the wind in autumn, showing the birds' nests no longer worth hiding. Their life and interrelations were such; feeling the pulse and body of the soil, that opened to their furrow for the grain, and became smooth and supple after their ploughing, and clung to their feet with a weight that pulled like desire, lying hard and unresponsive when the crops were to be shorn away . . .' (pp.7–8). The last sentence of this passage describes the relationship that is established between the Brangwen forebears and the earth; it is also

[1] Letter to Edward Garnett (January 1914), *Letters*, p. 178.

a concise analogue of the sort of responses both Tom and Will encounter in their sexual relations with Lydia and Anna.

The imagery of the passage, which reflects Lawrence's conviction that 'everything that is, is either male or female or both',[1] also suggests that it is desirable to read *The Rainbow* with the Hardy essay in mind:[2] the essay draws our attention to significances which are central to Lawrence's purpose, though they have not generally been appreciated. The opening description continues, in part:

'. . . the limbs and the body of the men were impregnated with the day, cattle and earth and vegetation and the sky, the men sat by the fire and their brains were inert, as their blood flowed heavy with the accumulation from the living day.

'The women were different. On them too was the drowse of blood-intimacy, calves sucking and hens running together in droves, and young geese palpitating in the hand while the food was pushed down their throttle. But the women looked out from the heated, blind intercourse of farm-life, to the spoken world beyond. They were aware of the lips and the mind of the world speaking and giving utterance, they heard the sound in the distance, and they strained to listen.

'It was enough for the men, that the earth heaved and opened its furrows to them . . . So much warmth and generating and pain and death did they know in their blood, earth and sky and beast and green plants, so much exchange and interchange they had with these, that they lived full and surcharged, their senses full fed, their faces always turned to the heat of the blood, staring into the sun, dazed with looking towards the source of generation, unable to turn round.

'But the woman wanted another form of life than this, something that was not blood-intimacy. Her house faced out from the farm-buildings and fields, looked out to the road and the village with church and Hall and the world beyond. She stood to see the far-off world of cities and governments and the active scope of man, the magic land to her, where secrets were made known and desires fulfilled. She faced outwards to where men moved dominant and creative, having turned their back on the pulsing heat of creation, and with this behind them, were set out to discover what was beyond, to enlarge their own scope and range and freedom; whereas the

[1] See Chap. 1, p. 31 above.
[2] Lawrence began the essay in September 1914 (*Letters*, p. 208), that is to say, at about the time he began the final draft of *The Rainbow*.

Brangwen men faced inwards to the teeming life of creation, which poured unresolved into their veins' (pp. 8–9).

F. R. Leavis adduces this passage as evidence of how absurd it is to think of Lawrence as 'the prophet of the Dark Gods', for it shows that 'the life of "blood-intimacy"' is seen as 'something to be transcended'.[1] It also suggests, I believe, that the long line of Brangwen men have failed to realize their 'man-being'. With their brains inert, they have failed to turn 'the accumulation from the living day' to account, to go beyond 'the pulsing heat of creation' onward to utterance and 'the active scope of man'. In other words, the disposition of the Brangwen men is essentially female.[2] In consequence the Brangwen women are not fulfilled; their yearnings for the outside world are only vicariously satisfied. Instead of a living interchange with their husbands, instead of their husbands being the reckless voyagers into the unknown who come back to them and complete them, it is the people of the Hall who provide them with 'their own Odyssey', who bring 'Penelope and Ulysses before them' (p. 11). Graham Hough comments on the unfulfilled aspirations of the Brangwen women, but then he complains that the theme 'apparently announced' at the beginning of the novel disconcertingly 'disappears' and 'we are concerned with Tom Brangwen's marriage to a Polish lady'.[3] It seems to me, however, that if the significance of the opening pages is taken, we are in fact prepared for the development of Lawrence's theme. The highest kind of married fulfilment is dependent on both the man and the woman extending their being to the utmost, on their reconciling, that is to say, their male and female components (as these are defined in the Hardy essay), and as a result of the tension between these components, on their transcending the limitations of either. And what is true of the individual struggle for fullness of being is true of the effort

---

[1] *D. H. Lawrence: Novelist*, p. 99. Despite the clear purport of the passage and despite Leavis's insistence, Lawrence's views in the matter are still misunderstood. S. L. Goldberg, for instance, suggests that 'the Brangwens' life' is desiderated as 'the image of a human norm'. '*The Rainbow*: Fiddle-Bow and Sand', *Essays in Criticism*, 11 (October 1961), 420.

[2] Cf. 'In every creature, the mobility, the law of change, is found exemplified in the male; the stability, the conservatism, is found in the female. In woman man finds his root and establishment. In man woman finds her exfoliation and florescence. The woman grows downwards, like a root, towards the centre and the darkness and the origin. The man grows upwards, like the stalk, towards discovery and light and utterance.' 'Study of Thomas Hardy', *Phoenix*, p. 515.

[3] *The Dark Sun*, p. 60.

of both man and woman to come together in marriage. Only Ursula, as we shall see, succeeds in becoming a genuine individual in this sense, and she, in *The Rainbow* at any rate, does not find a man who can match and complete her achievement. It is the men, as the opening pages emphasize, that have the longest road to travel.

After the suggestion of the settled continuity of life on the Marsh Farm, it should also be noted that Lawrence begins his actual chronicle by referring to the momentous changes which take place in the valley. For the previous generations of Brangwen men the twin supports of life have been the church and the land:

'Whenever one of the Brangwens in the fields lifted his head from his work, he saw the church-tower at Ilkeston in the empty sky. So that as he turned again to the horizontal land, he was aware of something standing above him and beyond him in the distance' (p. 7). But, 'about 1840', a canal is built 'across the meadows of the Marsh Farm' to connect the 'newly-opened collieries of the Erewash Valley'. As a result the Marsh is 'shut off' from Ilkeston (and the church-tower), and when a colliery is sunk on the other side of the canal and the Midland Railway comes down the valley, the 'invasion' is complete (pp. 11–12). For the Brangwens the 'something' that stands above and beyond them in the distance is now vaguely menacing:

'As they drove home from town, the farmers of the land met the blackened colliers trooping from the pit-mouth. As they gathered the harvest, the west wind brought a faint, sulphurous smell of pit-refuse burning. As they pulled the turnips in November, the sharp clink-clink-clink-clink-clink of empty trucks shunting on the line, vibrated in their hearts with the fact of other activity going on beyond them' (p. 13).

The ugly fact of the growth of industrialism is not directly alluded to again until three generations have passed and Ursula is a young woman, but it is a fundamental concern of the novel. The life of the individual is organically connected not only with the universe in which he lives but with the life of his fellows, and it is not coincidence that Lawrence begins his account of the childhood of Tom Brangwen in the eighteen-forties. It is in relation to the establishment of the collieries near the Marsh that we are tacitly asked to note, in Tom, a deviation from the traditional attitudes and responses to life of the Brangwen men. Furthermore, such a deviation necessitates an adjustment of the old relation between men and women. *The Rainbow*, indeed, marks the beginning of a search for a *new* relation–a search which, in terms of the defined interests of the two novels, is theoretically brought to a successful conclusion in *Women in Love* but which remained the impetus behind Lawrence's work till the end of his life.

Tom is at once both like his male ancestors and different from them. He has the same sort of nature: when he is at school his 'feelings' are said to be more 'discriminating' than those of the other boys, and he is 'more sensuously developed, more refined in instinct than they', but when it comes to 'mental things' he is a 'fool' (p. 16). As he grows up he feels that, like the earlier Brangwens, he too is held to the Marsh by a 'very strong root', but he is not turned inward in the drowse of blood-intimacy to the same extent as they. When, after an escapade with a girl, he meets 'her own man' who turns out to be a fine-mannered foreigner, his dissatisfactions with the life he knows are sharply focused. Unlike the Brangwen women, imaginative participation in the life of others is not sufficient to reconcile him to a more circumscribed life for himself. He '[baulks] the mean enclosure of reality, [standing] stubbornly like a bull at a gate, refusing to re-enter the well-known round of his own life' (p. 26), and he decides that there is nothing in the world of Cossethay and Ilkeston that he wants. What he wants is 'an intimacy with fine-textured, subtle-mannered people such as the foreigner at Matlock, and . . . the satisfaction of a voluptuous woman' (p. 25). These desires give promise of being simultaneously fulfilled when he woos and wins the Polish lady, Lydia Lensky.

Tom's marriage to Lydia, judged by the values implied in the opening section of the book, represents both a substantial achievement and an ultimate limitation. It marks a break with the old Brangwen inertness – 'That's her', says Tom when he sees Lydia for the first time – and, symbolically, it is an attempt to establish contact with the world outside the Marsh Farm and Cossethay: 'It was to him a profound satisfaction that she was a foreigner' (p. 32). That is to say, the marriage represents Tom's movement towards the unknown, and, when Lydia agrees to marry him, the emotional consummation of the marriage is presented in terms of his rebirth:

'He turned and looked for a chair, and keeping her still in his arms, sat down with her close to him, to his breast. Then, for a few seconds, he went utterly to sleep, asleep and sealed in the darkest sleep, utter, extreme oblivion.

'From which he came to gradually, always holding her warm and close upon him, and she as utterly silent as he, involved in the same oblivion, the fecund darkness.

'He returned gradually, but newly created, as after a gestation, a new birth, in the womb of darkness. Aerial and light everything was, new as a morning, fresh and newly-begun . . .' (p. 46).

But the marriage represents a limitation of Tom's development in that it is not the beginning of a further quest into the unknown, into the man's world of action and utterance and discovery, but the end. Nor does he come to Lydia as a man who has achieved fullness of being in his own right: however much he argues that he is 'good enough by himself', that he is a man who can stand alone, 'he must, in the starry multiplicity of the night humble himself, and admit and know that without her he [is] nothing' (p. 41). F. R. Leavis considers that Tom is 'the full complex human psyche, with all its potentialities',[1] but I think we are intended to regard him as essentially a creature of the dark, as a man who aspires towards the light–who aspires, that is to say, to realize his 'man-being'–but who cannot, unaided, incorporate the light in a unified self. That, I take it, is the symbolic force of the scene in which Tom, about to propose to Lydia, stands in the darkness outside her home, watching her for a long time through the lighted window before he enters the kitchen–as the play of light and darkness in the following passage and the phrase 'invasion from the night' suggest:

' "Good-evening," he said. "I'll just come in a minute."

'A change went quickly over her face; she was unprepared. She looked down at him as he stood in the light from the window, holding the daffodils, the darkness behind. In his black clothes she again did not know him. She was almost afraid.

'But he was already stepping on to the threshold, and closing the door behind him. She turned into the kitchen, startled out of herself by this invasion from the night. He took off his hat, and came towards her. Then he stood in the light, in his black clothes and his black stock, hat in one hand and yellow flowers in the other. She stood away, at his mercy, snatched out of herself. She did not know him, only she knew he was a man come for her. She could only see the dark-clad man's figure standing there upon her, and the gripped fist of flowers. She could not see the face and the living eyes' (p. 44).

Lydia, too, is strikingly different from the traditional Brangwen women. It is not merely that she is a lady and a foreigner; she repre-

[1] *D. H. Lawrence: Novelist*, p. 114.

sents a new conception of 'woman-being'. Unlike the Brangwen women, who only 'looked out' to the 'spoken world beyond', who 'stood to see the far-off world of cities and governments and the active scope of man', Lydia has herself been part of that world–and she recoils from it. To the end of her life she resents the fact that her first husband, a Polish surgeon and revolutionary, simply 'incorporated her in his ideas as if she were not a person herself, as if she were just his aide-de-camp, or part of his baggage, or one among his surgical appliances'. Looking back on her first marriage, she realizes that to Lensky she existed only as 'one of the baser or material conditions necessary for his welfare in prosecuting his ideas, of nationalism, of liberty, of science', but when his work failed and he believed that 'everything had failed' and 'stiffened, and died', she rebelled: 'The individual effort might fail, but not the human joy. She belonged to the human joy' (pp. 256–8). Bereaved of her husband, she experiences a sort of living death, in which for a long time she remains 'blotted safely away from living', but her responsiveness to the tenacious existence of some snowdrops which she watches is a prelude to her own spiritual rebirth: she moves 'outside the enclosure of darkness' (pp. 53–4). It is Tom who is the fertilizing influence in her regeneration. When she meets him, 'the stranger who [is] not a gentleman yet who [insists] on coming into her life', the 'pain of a new birth in herself [strings] all her veins to a new form. She would have to begin again, to find a new being, a new form, to respond to that blind, insistent figure standing over against her' (p. 40).

The coming together of Tom and Lydia, then, is the occasion for a limited but perceptible movement towards something like true male-female polarity as envisaged in the Hardy essay. Lydia is awakened through Tom to a life of the senses; she represents for Tom a vital connection with the unknown. But because Tom is not sufficiently a 'man'–in the sense previously defined–because he both yearns for the unknown and is afraid of it, their relationship is strained.

The fact that Tom attaches a special, extra-personal significance to his relationship with Lydia is the cause of their initial marital dissension. When they '[have] their hour', it is true, he '[buries] himself in the depths of her in an inexhaustible exploration', but for the most part he resents their difference of background the more acutely he realizes that even physically Lydia remains beyond him, that he cannot bring her, the unknown, into a personal relationship with himself: '. . . when they went to bed, he knew that he had nothing to do

with her. She was back in her childhood, he was a peasant, a serf, a
servant, a lover, a paramour, a shadow, a nothing. . . . And gradually
he grew into a raging fury against her' (p. 62). But, at the same time,
the fierceness of his desire for her is unappeasable just because the
only contact he can make with her strangeness is physical. Consequently, when she turns away from him during the months of her
pregnancy, 'his existence [is] annulled' (p. 64); and even after the birth
of their child, when she '[comes] to him again, with the same lifting
of her mouth as had driven him almost mad with trammelled passion
at first', her passion dies down before his and he has to 'begin the bitter
lesson, to abate himself, to take less than he wanted' (pp. 82–3). His
dissatisfaction leads him to turn to Anna for 'her sympathy and her
love' until soon they are 'like lovers, father and child' (p. 64); and it
shows itself in a renewed longing to 'clamber out' of the mud of his
own existence to the sort of 'visionary polite world' he encounters
when he visits his brother's mistress. Though he tries to allay his
disquiet, he feels 'a prisoner, sitting safe and easy and unadventurous' (p. 91) at the Marsh.

What Lawrence does, then, in his portrayal of the marriage is to assert
his own characteristic belief in the inevitability, even in the necessity,
of conflict between man and wife, and at the same time to indicate
that the intensity of the struggle between Tom and Lydia is due to
the special nature of the demands he makes on her. After they have
been married for about two years, however, their difficulties are suddenly resolved. The passage which describes the cessation of their
conflict is long and obscure, but it is centrally important:

' "My dear!" she said. He knew she spoke a foreign language.

'The fear was like bliss in his heart. He looked down. Her face was
shining, her eyes were full of light, she was awful. He suffered from the
compulsion to her. She was the awful unknown. He bent down to her,
suffering, unable to let go, unable to let himself go, yet drawn, driven.
She was now the transfigured, she was wonderful, beyond him. He
wanted to go. But he could not as yet kiss her. He was himself apart.
Easiest he could kiss her feet. But he was too ashamed for the actual
deed, which were like an affront. She waited for him to meet her,
not to bow before her and serve her. She wanted his active participation, not his submission. She put her fingers on him. And it was
torture to him, that he must give himself to her actively, participate in
her, that he must meet and embrace and know her, who was other
than himself. There was that in him which shrank from yielding to

her, resisted the relaxing towards her, opposed the mingling with her, even whilst he most desired it. He was afraid, he wanted to save himself.

'There were a few moments of stillness. Then gradually, the tension, the withholding relaxed in him, and he began to flow towards her. She was beyond him, the unattainable. But he let go his hold on himself, he relinquished himself, and knew the subterranean force of his desire to come to her, to be with her, to mingle with her, losing himself to find her, to find himself in her. He began to approach her, to draw near.

'His blood beat up in waves of desire. He wanted to come to her, to meet her. She was there, if he could reach her. The reality of her who was just beyond him absorbed him. Blind and destroyed, he pressed forward, nearer, nearer, to receive the consummation of himself, be received within the darkness which should swallow him and yield him up to himself. If he could come really within the blazing kernel of darkness, if really he could be destroyed, burnt away till he lit with her in one consummation, that were supreme, supreme.

'Their coming together now, after two years of married life, was much more wonderful to them than it had been before. It was the entry into another circle of existence, it was the baptism to another life, it was the complete confirmation.

...

'Anna's soul was put at peace between them. She looked from one to the other, and she saw them established to her safety, and she was free. She played between the pillar of fire and the pillar of cloud in confidence, having the assurance on her right hand and the assurance on her left. She was no longer called upon to uphold with her childish might the broken end of the arch. Her father and her mother now met to the span of the heavens, and she, the child, was free to play in the space beneath, between' (pp. 94–5, 97).

The subtle distinctions drawn in this passage make it difficult to follow how it is that Tom suddenly ceases to be 'the broken end of the arch', but in terms of the foregoing discussion I think the change in him is registered convincingly. When Lydia appeals to him, the blissful fear he feels is of 'the awful unknown', and his 'compulsion to her' is his obsessive desire to seize hold of 'the beyond' through her, to subdue the unknown to the known–in the flesh. But, after two years of marriage, the knowledge that the unknown cannot be conquered in this way, that she will always remain 'other than himself' is 'torture' to him. The decisive change comes with his sudden acceptance of her 'otherness', with his recognition that she is 'beyond him', and 'unattainable', not to be subdued. When he finally 'relinquishes himself', he lets go of a self that is accustomed to seeking its own expansion through her and that is consequently denied satisfaction. He also lets go of a self that '[opposes] the mingling with her', that is tightly clenched in a desire 'to save himself', to preserve his own distinct identity. But paradoxically, and the phraseology is suggestive of a mystical illumination, the moment he 'loses' himself, the moment he overcomes his fear and willingly allows the intact self to be 'destroyed', he 'finds himself in her'. Lawrence, indeed, here shows how the opposed desires to preserve the self and to yield to the beloved can be reconciled; this resolution of the problem, however, is one that (for reasons which I will discuss in the course of this study) he fails to maintain, and it is only after long years that he rediscovers it in *Lady Chatterley's Lover*.

In the newness of his revelation Tom is absorbed by 'the reality of her who [is] just beyond him'; that is to say, for the first time she becomes a woman to him – she is no longer 'the beyond' who happens to be a woman, but a woman who is the beyond. We remember the accusation that Lydia makes just prior to the passage quoted: 'You come to me as if it was for nothing, as if I was nothing there. When Paul came to me, I *was* something to him – a woman, I was. To you I am nothing – it is like cattle – or nothing –' (p. 94). Their coming together, then, is the result of Tom's religious submission to the sexual mystery – their union is both a 'baptism' and a 'confirmation' – and it is a submission that involves his final acceptance of the unknown as the unknown, to be met with through Lydia but not to be ravaged. Tom, moreover, not only 'loses' himself to find himself and to find her as a woman; it is also justifiable, I think, to regard this as the moment that Lydia, with his help, begins to find *herself*: many years later, when he is dead, she reflects that she loved him for having 'given her being . . . She was very glad she had come to her own self. She was grateful to Brangwen' (pp. 258–9).

In the last paragraph of the quoted passage the rainbow symbol is used to suggest the nature of the relationship that is finally established between Tom and Lydia. The rainbow is one of many symbols that Lawrence employs to convey his sense of unity in a dualistic universe: uniting heaven and earth (and we remember 'the intercourse between heaven and earth' that figures so prominently in the opening pages of the novel), in a meeting of sun and water, it is the 'two in one'.

As John Middleton Murry has pointed out, it has the same meaning as the crown which relates the lion and the unicorn as a 'symbol of their unity in division', or as the Holy Ghost which relates the dual nature of God.[1] As applied to Tom and Lydia, it suggests their achievement of an abiding relationship in which the differences between man and woman are not eliminated but are supplely tensed in a balance of responsive forces. But this, according to Lawrence's views, is surely no more than a *sine qua non* of marriage, a reduction of the rainbow to its minimal symbolic sense. The analogy between the rainbow and symbols such as the crown and the Holy Ghost makes it clear that ideal marriage is based on an altogether wider and more inclusive relationship than that attained by Tom and Lydia:

'There must be marriage of body in body, and of spirit in spirit, and Two-in-One. And the marriage in the body must not deny the marriage in the spirit, for that is blasphemy against the Holy Ghost; and the marriage in the spirit shall not deny the marriage in the body, for that is blasphemy against the Holy Ghost. But the two must be for ever reconciled, even if they must exist on occasions apart one from he other.'[2]

Tom and Lydia can hardly be said to be married 'in the spirit'.

What their marriage amounts to is a marriage on 'female' terms—as the following passage implies:

'They were a curious family, a law to themselves, separate from the world, isolated, a small republic set in invisible bounds. The mother was quite indifferent to Ilkeston and Cossethay, to any claims made on her from outside . . .

'To this she had reduced her husband. He existed with her entirely indifferent to the general values of the world. Her very ways, the very mark of her eyebrows were symbols and indication to him. There, on the farm with her, he lived through a mystery of life and death and creation, strange, profound ecstasies and incommunicable satisfactions, of which the rest of the world knew nothing; which made the pair of them apart and respected in the English village, for they were also well-to-do' (pp. 103-4).

Lydia, it is seen, becomes the first pronouncedly 'female' Brangwen woman at the Marsh, indifferent to the outside world and separate from it, living predominantly through her senses. But the effect she has on her husband is reductive—the word, in the light of Tom's original aspirations, is significant. The sexual fulfilment Tom finds

[1] *Son of Woman*, p. 101.   [2] 'Study of Thomas Hardy', *Phoenix*, p. 475.

with Lydia is the sustaining validation of his life; it even (as the passage quoted below confirms) affords him intimations of immortality; but he is reduced in his 'man-being'. In the end he slips back into a submersion in the physical immediacies and mysteries of farm life that characterized the lives of his father and grandfather before him–and against which he initially revolted. Tom's life, therefore, is both a success and a failure; and the sense of failure, the consciousness of a narrow-dimensioned limitation of life, gnaws at and undermines the rooted solidity of his success:

'What was missing in his life, that, in his ravening soul, he was not satisfied? He had had that friend at school, his mother, his wife, and Anna? What had he done? He had failed with his friend, he had been a poor son; but he had known satisfaction with his wife, let it be enough; he loathed himself for the state he was in over Anna [i.e., over Anna's marriage]. Yet he was *not* satisfied. It was agony to know it.

'Was his life nothing? Had he nothing to show, no work? He did not count his work, anybody could have done it. What had he known, but the long, marital embrace with his wife! Curious, that this was what his life amounted to! At any rate, it was something, it was eternal. He would say so to anybody, and be proud of it. He lay with his wife in his arms, and she was still his fulfilment, just the same as ever. And that was the be-all and the end-all. Yes, and he was proud of it.

'But the bitterness, underneath, that there still remained an unsatisfied Tom Brangwen, who suffered agony because a girl cared nothing for him. He loved his sons–he had them also. But it was the further, the creative life with the girl, he wanted as well. Oh, and he was ashamed. He trampled himself to extinguish himself' (p. 129).

III

In the second generation man and woman come together through a reversal of the extra-sexual impulse which moves Tom to woo Lydia. It is the man, Will Brangwen, who appears as a 'stranger' in Anna's world when he comes to Ilkeston to work in a lace factory. It is Anna who turns to him in the hope of enlarging her experience: 'In him the bounds of her experience were transgressed: he was the hole in the wall, beyond which the sunshine blazed on an outside world' (p. 114). Will, moreover, seems to have the capacity, which Tom does not possess, for a creative self-fulfilment. Though his 'curious head' reminds Anna of 'some animal, some mysterious animal that lived in the darkness under the leaves and never came out, but which lived vividly, swift and intense' (p. 107), and though he is 'only half articulate' (p. 113), he comes to utterance in his wood-carving: it is 'a passion for him to have the chisel under his grip' (p. 120). When he meets Anna he is carving the Creation of Eve, and under the impetus of his newly awakened love he is 'at last able to create the new, sharp body of his Eve' (p. 121). It is not only the creation of Eve which is at issue, however; in the developing drama of the relationship between Will and Anna we are implicitly invited to observe whether marriage will prove to be a creative release for him.

In fact, the physical revelations of marriage overwhelm him. The honeymoon frees his sensual self, but it is the beginning of a process which leads to the incarceration of his social being:

'One day, he was a bachelor, living with the world. The next day, he was with her, as remote from the world as if the two of them were buried like a seed in darkness. Suddenly, like a chestnut falling out of a burr, he was shed naked and glistening on to a soft, fecund earth, leaving behind him the hard rind of worldly knowledge and experience . . .' (p. 145).

The images in this passage are interesting. It is from the darkness of the womb that Will and Anna emerge, reborn in the flesh, like Tom and Lydia before them. But if the chestnut simile reinforces this idea, it also points to the fact that, for Will, falling from the burr is–for many years–a final consummation, a ripening which detaches him from the outside world and leaves him on the fecund earth where he is content to stay. Though he at first feels that there is 'something unmanly' about his exclusive preoccupation with Anna, it is he who resents her eventual readiness 'to enjoy again a return to the outside world. . . . He wanted to go on, to go on as they were. He wanted to have done with the outside world, to declare it finished for ever' (p. 150).

Their first violent quarrel is an expression of the fundamental difference between them in regard to the limits of an absorption in each other:

' "Can't you do anything?" she said, as if to a child, impatiently. "Can't you do your wood-work?"

' "Where shall I do it?" he asked, harsh with pain.

' "Anywhere."

'How furious that made him.

' "Or go for a walk," she continued. "Go down to the Marsh. Don't hang about as if you were only half there."

'He winced and hated it. He went away to read. Never had his soul felt so flayed and uncreated.

'And soon he must come down again to her. His hovering near her, wanting her to be with him, the futility of him, the way his hands hung, irritated her beyond bearing. She turned on him blindly and destructively, he became a mad creature, black and electric with fury. The dark storms rose in him, his eyes glowed black and evil, he was fiendish in his thwarted soul.

'There followed two black and ghastly days, when she was set in anguish against him, and he felt as if he were in a black, violent underworld, and his wrists quivered murderously. And she resisted him. He seemed a dark, almost evil thing, pursuing her, hanging on to her, burdening her. She would give anything to have him removed.

' "You need some work to do," she said. "You ought to be at work. Can't you *do* something?" ' (p. 152).

The fact that Anna talks to Will 'as if to a child' effectively indicates the cause of her anger: what she resents is the smothering totality of his unmanly dependence on her, and she fights for the right to be left alone when she wishes, to have an existence apart from him. But Will is immoderately and insatiably compelled to her, and when he is not with her he is annulled – he feels 'flayed and uncreated'. As I shall try to show, the conflict between them – the necessary battle between male and female – has various manifestations, but it is this initial dispute which is at its centre.

Will, for instance, begins to realize that she does not respect him as a man: 'She only respected him as far as he was related to herself. For what he was, beyond her, she had no care. She did not care for what he represented in himself' (p. 171). It is, of course, precisely because Will has ceased to represent anything beyond her that Anna fails to respect him, but this leads him only the more arrogantly to claim consideration as her husband. He asserts his position as 'master of the house' and as 'the captain of the ship' (pp. 173–4), but Anna is not submissive:

'It began well, but it ended always in war between them, till they were both driven almost to madness. He said, she did not respect him. She laughed in hollow scorn of this. For her it was enough that she loved him.

' "Respect what?" she asked.

'But he always answered the wrong thing. And though she cud-gelled her brains, she could not come at it.

' "Why don't you go on with your wood-carving?" she said. "Why don't you finish your Adam and Eve?"

'But she did not care for the Adam and Eve, and he never put another stroke to it. She jeered at the Eve, saying, "She is like a little marionette. Why is she so small? You've made Adam as big as God, and Eve like a doll."

' "It is impudence to say that Woman was made out of Man's body," she continued, "when every man is born of woman. What impudence men have, what arrogance!"

'In a rage one day, after trying to work on the board, and failing, so that his belly was a flame of nausea, he chopped up the whole panel and put it on the fire. She did not know. He went about for some days very quiet and subdued after it' (p. 174).

Anna cannot formulate her idea of what it is in Will that she might respect if it were developed, but her reference to his wood-carving reveals the direction of her thoughts. His chopping-up of the panel is therefore of some consequence, though the immediate cause of the destruction is no doubt his angry realization of technical failure. It is a symbolic act: many years pass before Will again turns to creative work, and the burning of the panel is in a way a self-destruction; it signifies the extinction, under the stress of a sensual obsession, of the man who appeared capable of utterance. Thereafter, like the phoenix he carved as a butter-stamper for Anna when he was courting her, he has to rise painfully from his own ashes. But his abandonment of the panel also seems to represent his resentful acceptance of the validity of Anna's criticism of the work, his recognition that there is a blatant disproportion in size between the Adam and Eve figures, and it marks the tacit modification of his demands that Anna do him obeisance.

Will's dropping of the overt claim to be master is no more than a modification of his attitude, however, for as has been suggested the claim itself is only one of the manifestations of his refusal to recognize Anna's independence of being. Anna realizes that he seems 'to expect her to be part of himself, the extension of his will' (p. 170), and she rouses to fight him off. This aspect of their conflict reflects the col-lision of elemental forces that stir into motion when they first come together–as the following description of an incident during their courting suggests:

'Corn harvest came on. One evening they walked out through the farm buildings at nightfall. A large gold moon hung heavily to the grey horizon, trees hovered tall, standing back in the dusk, waiting. Anna and the young man went on noiselessly by the hedge, along where the farm-carts had made dark ruts in the grass. They came through a gate into a wide open field where still much light seemed to spread against their faces . . .

'They did not want to turn back, yet whither were they to go, towards the moon? For they were separate, single.

' "We will put up some sheaves," said Anna. So they could remain there in the broad, open place. . . .

' "You take this row," she said to the youth, and passing on, she stooped in the next row of lying sheaves, grasping her hands in the tresses of the oats, lifting the heavy corn in either hand, carrying it, as it hung heavily against her, to the cleared space, where she set the two sheaves sharply down, bringing them together with a faint, keen clash. Her two bulks stood leaning together. He was coming, walking shadowily with the gossamer dusk, carrying his two sheaves. She waited near by. He set his sheaves with a keen, faint clash, next to her sheaves. They rode unsteadily. He tangled the tresses of corn. It hissed like a fountain. He looked up and laughed.

'Then she turned away towards the moon, which seemed glowingly to uncover her bosom every time she faced it. He went to the vague emptiness of the field opposite, dutifully.

...

'And always, she was gone before he came. As he came, she drew away, as he drew away, she came. Were they never to meet? Gradually a low, deep-sounding will in him vibrated to her, tried to set her in accord, tried to bring her gradually to him, to a meeting, till they should be together, till they should meet as the sheaves that swished together.

...

'Till at last, they met at the shock, facing each other, sheaves in hand. And he was silvery with moonlight, with a moonlit, shadowy face that frightened her. She waited for him.

' "Put yours down," she said.

' "No, it's your turn." His voice was twanging and insistent.

'She set her sheaves against the shock. He saw her hands glisten among the spray of grain. And he dropped his sheaves and he trembled as he took her in his arms. He had overtaken her, and it was his privilege, to kiss her. She was sweet and fresh with the night air, and sweet with the scent of grain. And the whole rhythm of him beat into his kisses, and still he pursued her, in his kisses, and still she was not quite overcome. He wondered over the moonlight on her nose! All the moonlight upon her, all the darkness within her! All the night in his arms, darkness and shine, he possessed of it all! All the night for him now, to unfold, to venture within, all the mystery to be entered, all the discovery to be made' (pp. 121–4).

The sexual symbolism of this sophisticated pursuit of the bride is obvious enough, but the obscure second paragraph in the quoted passage leads to a somewhat different interpretation of the significance of the incident. What *is* the connection between the moon and separateness or singleness? If the subsequent description does not make the connection at once apparent, Lawrence's pronouncements elsewhere leave us in little doubt as to what it actually is:

'The moon, the planet of women, sways us back from our day-self, sways us back from our real social unison, sways us back, like a retreating tide, in a friction of criticism and separation and social disintegration. That is woman's inevitable mode, let her words be what they will. Her goal is the deep, sensual individualism of secrecy and night-exclusiveness, hostile, with guarded doors. . . .'[1]

What Anna clings to, then, in response to the moon which seems glowingly to uncover her bosom, is her own individual separateness of being. And though her night goal is sensual, it is her deepest 'woman-being' which resists the movement towards Will and which prevents her from being overcome when he finally takes her in his arms. Will, on the other hand, is impervious to the moon. With the full force of his 'man-being' he is intent on bringing about a meeting. The difference between them even shows itself in the way they handle the sheaves: her 'two bulks' stand 'leaning together', but, it would seem, remain distinguishable; he 'tangles' the corn when he puts his sheaves down, and–in a section of the description not quoted–he

[1] *Fantasia*, pp. 173–4. Cf. too: 'The moon is the centre of our terrestrial individuality in the cosmos. She is the declaration of our existence in separateness. Save for the intense white recoil of the moon, the earth would stagger towards the sun. The moon holds us to our own cosmic individuality, as a world individual in space. She is the fierce centre of retraction, of frictional withdrawal into separateness. She it is who sullenly stands with her back to us, and refuses to meet and mingle. She it is who burns white with the intense friction of her withdrawal into separation, that cold, proud white fire of furious, almost malignant apartness, the struggle into fierce, frictional separation. . . .' *Ibid.*, pp. 146–7.

works steadily at 'threading his sheaves with hers' (p. 123). The 'tangling' and the 'threading' are indicative of Will's desire to mingle and merge with Anna in a union which obliterates all singleness and separateness; he wants a union in which, in a word, he is 'possessed of' her. And the conflict between them that is foreshadowed in the cornfield is carried over into their marriage with a ferocious intensity.

The sort of relationship that Anna wants is symbolized by the way in which she walks home with Will from the Marsh on the evening that she tells him she is pregnant: 'She put her hand lightly on his arm, out of her far distance. And out of the distance, he felt her touch him. They walked on, hand in hand, along opposite horizons, touching across the dusk. . . . They continued without saying any more, walking . . . hand in hand across the intervening space, two separate people' (pp. 178–9). But Will is 'afraid' to be alone in his separateness; he wants always to 'be one with her', wants her to come to him 'to complete him', for he is 'ridden by the awful sense of his own limitation' (p. 179). Consequently, he persistently tries to force his will upon her, and she is uncomfortably aware of 'the darkness and otherworld . . . in his soft, sheathed hands' (p. 180). When she comes to him 'with her hands full of love', she receives the 'bitter-corrosive shock of his passion upon her, destroying her in blossom' (p. 182). It is her self-sufficiency that Will tries to 'destroy', and Anna, in a blind effort to save herself, is moved to an exaggerated assertion of defiance:

'In these days she was oblivious of him. Who was he, to come against her? No, he was not even the Philistine, the Giant. He was like Saul proclaiming his own kingship. She laughed in her heart. Who was he, proclaiming his kingship? She laughed in her heart with pride.

'And she had to dance in exultation beyond him. Because he was in the house, she had to dance before her Creator in exemption from the man. On a Saturday afternoon, when she had a fire in the bedroom, again she took off her things and danced, lifting her knees and her hands in a slow, rhythmic exulting. He was in the house, so her pride was fiercer. She would dance his nullification, she would dance to her unseen Lord. She was exalted over him, before the Lord.

'She heard him coming up the stairs, and she flinched. She stood with the firelight on her ankles and feet, naked in the shadowy, late afternoon, fastening up her hair. He was startled. He stood in the doorway, his brows black and lowering.

' "What are you doing?" he said, gratingly. "You'll catch a cold."

'And she lifted her hands and danced again, to annul him, the light glanced on her knees as she made her slow, fine movements down the far side of the room, across the firelight. He stood away near the door in blackness of shadow, watching, transfixed. And with slow, heavy movements she swayed backwards and forwards, like a full ear of corn, pale in the dusky afternoon, threading before the firelight, dancing his non-existence, dancing herself to the Lord, to exultation.

'He watched, and his soul burned in him. He turned aside, he could not look, it hurt his eyes. Her fine limbs lifted and lifted, her hair was sticking out all fierce, and her belly, big, strange, terrifying, uplifted to the Lord. Her face was rapt and beautiful, she danced exulting before her Lord, and knew no man.

'It hurt him as he watched as if he were at the stake. He felt he was being burned alive. The strangeness, the power of her in her dancing consumed him, he was burned, he could not grasp, he could not understand. He waited obliterated. Then his eyes became blind to her, he saw her no more . . .' (pp. 183–4).

F. R. Leavis, in commenting on the conflict between Will and Anna, says: '. . . the nature of the conflict should not, after all, be found defeatingly obscure. Anna, on the face of it, might seem to be the aggressor. The relevant aspect of her has its clear dramatization in the scene that led to the banning of the book; the scene in which she is surprised by Will dancing the defiant triumph of her pregnancy, naked in her bedroom. She is the Magna Mater, the type-figure adverted to so much in *Women in Love* of a feminine dominance that must defeat the growth of any prosperous long-term relation between a man and a woman.'[1] This, it seems to me, is fundamentally to mistake the import of Anna's dancing. It is true that Leavis also states that 'this dominance in Anna has for its complement a dependence in Will. There are passages that convey to us with the most disturbing force the paradoxical insufferableness to Anna of such a dependence, and its self-frustrating disastrousness';[2] but this qualification hardly offsets the impression he gives that Anna is, in general, the 'aggressor' in the relationship and, in particular, a target of attack in the description of her dancing. I have already tried to show the extent to which the conflict between Will and Anna derives, ultimately, from *his* imperfections; the quoted passage, I should say, hardly supports the contention that Anna is to be reprehended for her behaviour. To begin with, the description itself is not hostile: her movements are 'fine', her limbs are 'fine', her face is 'rapt and beautiful', she sways 'like a full

[1] *D. H. Lawrence: Novelist*, p. 123.   [2] *Ibid.*

ear of corn'–even if her belly is 'big, strange, terrifying'. But these are only secondary confirmations of a sympathy for her which is implied within the wider context of her relationship with Will. Anna is not the Magna Mater dancing the triumph of her pregnancy; she is a woman asserting her right to singleness, to separateness of being. It is not in her feminine dominance that she exults but in her independence. Such an interpretation accounts, I think, for a number of insistent references in the passage: Anna laughs with pride because she feels she is successfully defying Will's 'kingship', not because she is seeking to establish a dictatorship of her own; she dances in exultation 'beyond' him, not 'over' him; she dances his 'nullification' in order to win 'exemption' from him. And though Will cannot rationally 'understand' what she is doing, intuitively he registers the meaning of the dance. That is why he reacts so strongly. Anna's 'separateness' is to him a constant deprivation; he feels defrauded of his own life if he cannot be one with her–hence his sensation of being 'burned alive', 'consumed', 'obliterated'. If Anna is criticized at all in this passage it is for the excessiveness of her demonstration, though it is a road of excess which perhaps leads to the palace of wisdom.

The vision of Anna dancing as 'a strange, exalted thing having no relation to himself' (p. 185) continually torments Will, but he depends on her too much for her dramatic protest to be instantaneously effective: 'If she were taken away, he would collapse as a house from which the central pillar is removed' (p. 186). Will, in other words, is–like Tom before him–the weak, if not quite the broken, end of the arch; and he fights doggedly to prevent everything coming down in ruin about him. It takes a great strength of resistance on Anna's part before he eventually learns what it is 'to be able to be alone':

'It was right and peaceful. She had given him a new, deeper freedom. The world might be a welter of uncertainty, but he was himself now. He had come into his own existence. He was born for a second time, born at last unto himself, out of the vast body of humanity. Now at last he had a separate identity, he existed alone, even if he were not quite alone. Before he had only existed in so far as he had relations with another being. Now he had an absolute self–as well as a relative self' (p. 190).

Will, therefore, is reborn twice: first, into the wondering apprehension of his sensual self, and then into the certainty of his 'absolute self'. Yet his attainment of a separate identity still does not qualify the stultification of his 'man-being': he still feels that 'the whole of the man's world [is] exterior and extraneous to his own real life with Anna' (p. 193).

At this stage of the marriage Anna is 'Anna Victrix', but she is 'still . . . not quite fulfilled':

'She had a slight expectant feeling, as of a door half opened. Here she was, safe and still in Cossethay. But she felt as if she were not in Cossethay at all. She was straining her eyes to something beyond. And from her Pisgah mount, which she had attained, what could she see? A faint, gleaming horizon, a long way off, and a rainbow like an archway, a shadow-door with faintly coloured coping above it. Must she be moving thither?

'Something she had not, something she did not grasp, could not arrive at. There was something beyond her. But why must she start on the journey? She stood so safely on the Pisgah mountain.

. . .

'There was another child coming, and Anna lapsed into vague content. If she were not the wayfarer to the unknown, if she were arrived now, settled in her builded house, a rich woman, still her doors opened under the arch of the rainbow, her threshold reflected the passing of the sun and the moon, the great travellers, her house was full of the echo of journeying.

'She was a door and a threshold, she herself. Through her another soul was coming, to stand upon her as upon the threshold, looking out, shading its eyes for the direction to take' (pp. 195–6).

The phrase 'as of a door half opened' provides a clue to the nature of Anna's discontent. It was to Will, we remember, that she originally turned in the hope of enlarging her experience; he was to be 'the hole in the wall, beyond which the sunshine blazed on an outside world'.[1] After years of marriage she has to admit that the door is only half-open; she has found sexual fulfilment with him but he stands for nothing beyond her. Consequently, like the Brangwen women of old, she has to strain her eyes to see that which she had hoped to live. And because the denial of this hope functions as so important an element in the marriage, Anna herself does not gain entry to the Promised Land though she has so arduously climbed 'her Pisgah mount'. All that she is granted is a vision of the rainbow, for if her doors can be said to open 'under the arch of the rainbow', the archway is 'a long way off . . . a shadow-door'. Anna herself is in part to blame for what must be considered an ultimate failure. From the outset she has

[1] See p. 90 above.

resisted the unknown, has even resisted contact with it in the sexual mystery: 'It was always the unknown, always the unknown, and she clung fiercely to her known self. But the rising flood carried her away' (p. 167). It is partly as a result of her own limitations, therefore, that Anna remains 'safe and still in Cossethay', content to relinquish 'the adventure to the unknown'. No wayfarer herself, she looks to her children to do her journeying for her, and 'lapses' – the word is symptomatic of her condition as she placidly proceeds to bear nine children – into a vague physical content.

But first she has one more battle to fight with Will. Previous to this she has attacked his religious beliefs and practices, but this skirmishing is merely the preliminary to the decisive engagement at Lincoln Cathedral:

'[Will] turned his glowing, ecstatic face to [Anna], his mouth opened with a strange, ecstatic grin.

' "There she is," he said.

'The "she" irritated her. Why "she"? It was "it". What was the cathedral, a big building, a thing of the past, obsolete, to excite him to such a pitch? She began to stir herself to readiness. . . .

'In a little ecstasy he found himself in the porch, on the brink of the unrevealed. He looked up to the lovely unfolding of the stone. He was to pass within to the perfect womb.

'Then he pushed open the door, and the great, pillared gloom was before him, in which his soul shuddered and rose from her nest. His soul leapt, soared up into the great church. His body stood still, absorbed by the height. His soul leapt up into the gloom, into possession, it reeled, it swooned with a great escape, it quivered in the womb, in the hush and the gloom of fecundity, like seed of procreation in ecstasy' (pp. 200–1).

Anna stirs herself to readiness in intuitive awareness that it is really the old battle between them that is about to be joined – though it takes the guise of a religious quarrel. Tuned to Will as she is, the sight of his 'ecstatic' face and his use of the feminine pronoun for the cathedral alert her to the covert significance of his entry into the church. Nathan A. Scott writes: 'The Cathedral-arch is obviously a sexual symbol, but it also has more extensive symbolic ramifications which suggest a transcendent world of Mystery, in the attainment of which the idiom of the sex act is merely instrumental and evocative.'[1]

---

[1] *Rehearsals of Discomposure*, p. 147.

It seems to me that to regard the sexual imagery as 'merely instrumental and evocative' is to miss the point of the ensuing altercation between Will and Anna. His entry into the cathedral is described in terms of the sex act because he approaches the religious mystery with the same craving that he brings to the sexual mystery. The suggestion, indeed, is of a spiritual orgasm in which he 'swoons with a great escape' from himself, from the fearsome burden of his lonely singleness, both losing himself in the gloom of the church and taking 'possession' of it.

Until Anna intervenes, Will enjoys, in the cathedral, the same sort of 'consummation' that he has relentlessly been seeking to find in her. It is as if his rebirth into 'separate identity' is annulled, and as if his old desires, secure in the camouflage of religious emotion, triumphantly seize at satisfaction:

'She too was overcome with wonder and awe. She followed him in his progress. Here, the twilight was the very essence of life, the coloured darkness was the embryo of all light, and the day. Here, the very first dawn was breaking, the very last sunset sinking, and the immemorial darkness, whereof life's day would blossom and fall away again, re-echoed peace and profound immemorial silence.

'Away from time, always outside of time! Between east and west, between dawn and sunset, the church lay like a seed in silence, dark before germination, silenced after death. Containing birth and death, potential with all the noise and transition of life, the cathedral remained hushed, a great, involved seed, whereof the flower would be radiant life inconceivable, but whose beginning and whose end were the circle of silence. Spanned round with the rainbow, the jewelled gloom folded music upon silence, light upon darkness, fecundity upon death as a seed folds leaf upon leaf and silence upon the root and the flower, hushing up the secret of all between its parts, the death out of which it fell, the life into which it has dropped, the immortality it involves, and the death it will embrace again.

'Here in the church, "before" and "after" were folded together, all was contained in oneness. Brangwen came to his consummation. . . .

'Here the stone leapt up from the plain of earth, leapt up in a manifold, clustered desire each time, up, away from the horizontal earth, through twilight and dusk and the whole range of desire, through the swerving, the declination, ah, to the ecstasy, the touch, to the meeting and the consummation, the meeting, the clasp, the close embrace, the neutrality, the perfect, swooning consummation, the timeless ecstasy. There his soul remained, at the apex of the arch, clinched in the timeless ecstasy, consummated' (pp. 201–2).

This passage presents Will's experience so sympathetically that only a close scrutiny reveals that Lawrence is not identifying himself with it; and the appearance, at this juncture, of the rainbow symbol makes the greater the temptation to believe that he is. This rainbow, however, is artificial, a compound projection of the cathedral arch and of the 'jewelled gloom'; and what it symbolizes is not unity in diversity, the union of a separate heaven and earth, but the attainment of a 'oneness' that obliterates all distinction. The decisive image in this respect is the twilight, that which is neither light nor darkness but is 'the very essence of life' in the cathedral, and the conclusive concept is the 'neutrality' of the final close embrace of the stone. The passage posits the 'timeless ecstasy' of an absolute which is insidiously compelling, to which Will surrenders in a surging attempt to merge himself with it–but to Lawrence it is anathema. The only absolute that Lawrence is prepared to acknowledge is the 'Holy Ghost', that which relates conflicting forces but does not neutralize them.[1]

Anna's reaction to the cathedral is distinguished from that of Will:

'Her soul too was carried forward to the altar, to the threshold of Eternity, in reverence and fear and joy. But ever she hung back in the transit, mistrusting the culmination of the altar. She was not to be flung forward on the lift and lift of passionate flights, to be cast at last upon the altar steps as upon the shore of the unknown. There was a great joy and a verity in it. But even in the dazed swoon of the cathedral, she claimed another right. The altar was barren, its lights gone out. God burned no more in that bush. It was dead matter lying there. She claimed the right to freedom above her, higher than the roof. She had always a sense of being roofed in.

'So that she caught at little things, which saved her from being swept forward headlong in the tide of passion that leaps on into the Infinite in a great mass, triumphant and flinging its own course. She wanted to get out of this fixed, leaping, forward-travelling movement, to rise from it as a bird rises with wet, limp feet from the sea, to lift herself as a bird lifts its breast and thrusts its body from the pulse and heave of a sea that bears it forward to an unwilling conclusion, tear herself away like a bird on wings, and in the open space where there is clarity, rise up above the fixed, surcharged motion, a separate

[1] See Chap. 1, p. 22 above.

speck that hangs suspended, moves this way and that, seeing and answering before it sinks again, having chosen or found the direction in which it shall be carried forward.

'And it was as if she must grasp at something, as if her wings were too weak to lift her straight off the heaving motion. So she caught sight of the wicked, odd little faces carved in stone, and she stood before them arrested.

'These sly little faces peeped out of the grand tide of the cathedral like something that knew better. They knew quite well, these little imps that retorted on man's own illusion, that the cathedral was not absolute. They winked and leered, giving suggestion of the many things that had been left out of the great concept of the church. "However much there is inside here, there's a good deal they haven't got in," the little faces mocked.

'Apart from the lift and spring of the great impulse towards the altar, these little faces had separate wills, separate motions, separate knowledge, which rippled back in defiance of the tide, and laughed in triumph of their own very littleness.

' "Oh look!" cried Anna. "Oh look, how adorable, the faces! Look at her."

'Brangwen looked unwillingly. This was the voice of the serpent in his Eden . . .' (pp. 203–4).

The characterization of Anna's interjection as 'the voice of the serpent' lends a certain plausibility to John Middleton Murry's interpretation of the scene: 'The meaning of all this symbolism is patent. Through the woman, through sex, the spiritual ideal is destroyed; and it is good that it should be destroyed. For the spiritual ideal is partial and false. It is based on the negation of sex, of the mighty principle of life itself.'[1] This is not only a distortion of Lawrencean doctrine but of scant relevance to the scene in question. Anna, despite her natural scepticism, despite her belief that the lights of the altar have gone out, is not fighting Will's 'spirituality', nor is he a man who places the spirit above the flesh–rather the reverse. What she resents and resists is Will's submission to the overwhelming 'oneness' of the cathedral. Characteristically, she asserts the right of the individual to detach himself from the mass, to rise like a bird above the engulfing sea, separate and distinct. And she clings to the gargoyles not because they symbolize female carnality, as Murry suggests, but because–as for Ruskin–they symbolize individual freedom and point to the existence

[1] *Son of Woman*, p. 81.

of '*separate* wills, *separate* motions, *separate* knowledge'.[1] They also point to the 'many things' that have been 'left out' of the 'grand tide', and reaffirm for Anna the importance of a world beyond the ecstasy–the 'open sky' that the cathedral disdains, the 'man's world' that Will denies in his exclusive absorption both in her and in the church.

In the dispute over the gargoyles that follows her intervention, Anna emerges victorious (though it should be noted that, in the passage quoted, she too is tacitly criticized for a typical limitation of being, for her heavy reluctance to adventure, her instinctive resistance to being 'cast . . . upon the shore of the unknown'). Not only does she herself '[get] free' from the cathedral, she even destroys his passion: 'Strive as he would, he could not keep the cathedral wonderful to him' (p. 205). Thereafter Will continues to devote himself to the church next to his house, labouring at works of restoration, but he is 'like a lover who knows he is betrayed, but who still loves, whose love is only the more tense'. As far as his work at the office is concerned, he '[does] not exist'; he '[keeps] himself suspended', and is content to live by Anna's 'physical love for him' (pp. 208–9). Like Tom, however, he is painfully aware of 'some limit to himself', of 'a darkness in him which he *could* not unfold, which would never unfold in him' (p. 210). Anna, on the other hand, 'lapses', as previously indicated, into her child-bearing; 'every moment' is 'full and busy with productiveness' and she feels 'like the earth, the mother of everything' (pp. 207–8).

Will's ultimate dissatisfaction with his life is presented in a way that quietly emphasizes the rhythmic movement of the book. As Tom turned to Anna when she was a child, so Will turns to Ursula 'for love and for fulfilment', but the repetition is subtly varied. Will encounters in Ursula a determination to 'relapse' into 'her own separate

---

[1] A relevant comment on the significance of the gargoyles is to be found in the Hardy essay: '. . . the art produced [all through the medieval period] was the collective, stupendous, emotional gesture of the Cathedrals, where a blind, collective impulse rose into concrete form. It was the profound, sensuous desire and gratitude which produced an art of architecture, whose essence is in utter stability, of movement resolved and centralized, of absolute movement, that has no relationship with any other form, that admits the existence of no other form, but is conclusive, propounding in its sum the One Being of All.

'There was, however, in the Cathedrals, already the denial of the Monism which the Whole uttered. All the little figures, the gargoyles, the imps, the human faces, whilst subordinated within the Great Conclusion of the Whole, still, from their obscurity, jeered their mockery of the Absolute, and declared for multiplicity, polygeny . . .' *Phoenix*, p. 454.

world of herself', and he frantically fights to dominate her – jumping with her on his back, for instance, from a high canal bridge into the water beneath, or swinging dangerously high with her in a swingboat at the fair (pp. 225–6). He also tries to turn from Anna to another woman, making an unsuccessful attempt to seduce a young girl whom he sits next to at a music-hall, but it is clear that it is not a sexual hunger that he is seeking to appease: 'She would be small, almost like a child, and pretty. Her childishness whetted him keenly. She would be helpless between his hands' (pp. 227–8).

Anna senses the challenge to her old supremacy, and for the first time she willingly goes to meet the unknown. She waits 'for his touch as if he were a marauder who had come in, infinitely unknown and desirable to her' (p. 235), and they begin to live in a renewed 'passion of sensual discovery' (p. 236):

'This was what their love had become, a sensuality violent and extreme as death. They had no conscious intimacy, no tenderness of love. It was all the lust and the infinite, maddening intoxication of the senses, a passion of death.
...
'But still the thing terrified him. Awful and threatening it was, dangerous to a degree, even whilst he gave himself to it. It was pure darkness, also. All the shameful things of the body revealed them-selves to him now with a sort of sinister, tropical beauty. All the shameful natural and unnatural acts of sensual voluptuousness which he and the woman partook of together, created together, they had their heavy beauty and their delight. Shame, what was it? It was part of extreme delight. It was that part of delight of which man is usually afraid. Why afraid? The secret, shameful things are most terribly beautiful.

'They accepted shame, and were one with it in their most un-licensed pleasures. It was incorporated. It was a bud that blossomed into beauty and heavy, fundamental gratification' (pp. 237–8).

When we consider this passage in isolation, we can do no more than guess at the nature of the 'shameful acts' that Will and Anna '[partake] of together'. In the light of Lawrence's later work, however, the phras-ing of the description is suggestive: their love has become 'a sensuality violent and extreme as death' and it debars 'tenderness'; the 'secret, shameful things' are not only accepted but are found to be 'most terribly beautiful'; their 'pleasures' are 'unlicensed' as well as 'un-natural'; and their 'gratification' is 'heavy' and 'fundamental'. The terms used are similar to those employed in *Women in Love*[1] and then again, with a more specific connotation in view of their context, in *Lady Chatterley's Lover*, and I think we can be reasonably confident that one of the practices Will and Anna indulge in is the same as that in which Mellors and Connie engage on their 'night of sensual passion'.[2] Since I shall argue that Mellors engages in this practice as a means of asserting his manhood and, furthermore, that Lawrence does violence to the character of Connie in making her submit to him, it is worth pointing to some important differences between the two couples. First, we note that Will and Anna 'create' their voluptuous sensuality 'together', that they are equal partners in the enterprise, and that there is no suggestion here of a slave-like submission on the part of the woman. Anna '[adheres] as little as he to the moral world' (p. 235), even though, for her, this period of their love is merely an interlude in the 'sleep of motherhood' from which she does not really wake until she has borne her last child and it is growing up (p. 418). Second, and this is a crucial difference between Will and Mellors, though Will's passion may seem to be generated by a lust for dominance– 'the little creature in Nottingham', we are told, 'had but been leading up to this' (p. 235)–he does not attempt in fact to assert his manhood in this way. He seeks, rather, 'gratification pure and simple' (p. 235), and *his* 'sensuality' sets 'another man in him free'. The 'passion of death', in his case, is a prelude to yet a further rebirth. The 'new man' turns to 'public life', to a 'new activity' for which he is 'now created and released': he has 'at length, from his profound sensual activity, developed a real purposive self' (p. 238).

Will tries to take a part in 'public life' by running a woodwork class in Cossethay. The woodwork class is no doubt a meagre achievement of 'man-being', but after the period of his submersion in Anna it is a step forward. As a result of his work, 'the house by the yew trees' is placed 'in connexion with the great human endeavour at last', and it gains 'a new vigour thereby' (p. 239). Later, after twenty years of marriage, Will even returns to his own wood-carving, coming back 'almost to the point where he had left off his Adam and Eve panel, when he was courting', wanting once again 'to carve things that [are] utterances of himself' (p. 355). But his creative force is spent, and his excited experiments in other mediums are nothing more than moderately successful dabblings. To the end both Anna and Will are not 'quite personal, quite defined as individuals' (p. 354).

[1] See pp. 178–9 below.   [2] See Chap. 5, pp. 303–4 below.

IV

The flood at the Marsh, which follows shortly after the final establishment of a settled relationship between Will and Anna and in which Tom is drowned, washes away an epoch. Ursula grows up in a world which, in terms of the novel, is the modern world, and problems of personal adjustment to it are more complex than those which faced the earlier Brangwens. They are more complex because, for one thing, the possibilities of an escape from it are more limited: the industrial machine which clink-clinked near the Marsh when Tom was a boy roars an asseveration of its presence by the time Ursula is a young woman.

Ursula starts life in revolt against her mother. From an early age she finds Anna's placid fecundity a 'nightmare', and she craves for 'some spirituality and stateliness' (pp. 264–5). She is aware that she is 'a separate entity in the midst of an unseparated obscurity', and she determines to 'become something', accepting the 'responsibility of living an undiscovered life' (p. 283). Of all the Brangwens it is in Ursula, indeed, that the desire for an individual fullness of being is shown at its most intense.[1]

In the same way that Anna turned to Will in the hope of enlarging her experience, Ursula is attracted to the young Skrebensky by the sense he gives her of 'the vast world, a sense of distances and large masses of humanity. It drew her as a scent draws a bee from afar. But also it hurt her' (p. 293). It hurts her, we are to understand, because though drawn by the bustle and the noise, her natural feminine inclination (the Anna in her) is to shy away from the vast world, and Ursula has a developed awareness of her 'woman-being': she has a passion 'to know her own maximum self, limited and so defined against [Skrebensky]. She could limit and define herself against him, the male, she could be her maximum self, female, oh female, triumphant for one moment in exquisite assertion against the male, in supreme contradistinction to the male' (p. 303). If Tom sought to conquer the unknown in the sexual connection, and Will to lose himself in a tremendous possession of the infinite, Ursula wants to

[1] Cf. 'In the *Sisters* was the germ of this novel: woman becoming individual, self-responsible, taking her own initiative.' Letter to Edward Garnett (April 1914), *Letters*, p. 190.

stretch her female self to the maximum – and it is this wish which is
the key to her relationship with Skrebensky. Her attitude to him, to
use Lawrencean terminology, might thus be called 'monistic': she is
preoccupied, as a final objective, with defining *herself* against him and
does not attempt to transcend herself, to seek – *with* him – the 'Holy
Ghost'. But Skrebensky, it is soon intimated, would anyway not be a
suitable partner in such a search. The scent of the vast world proves
to be repellent when it is sniffed:

'He was looking, Ursula thought, very beautiful, because of a flush
of sunburn on his hands and face. He was telling her how he had
learned to shoe horses and select cattle fit for killing.

' "Do you like to be a soldier?" she asked.

' "I am not exactly a soldier," he replied.

' "But you only do things for wars," she said.

' "Yes."

' "Would you like to go to war?"

' "I? Well, it would be exciting. If there were a war I would want
to go."

'A strange distracted feeling came over her, a sense of potent unrealities.

' "Why would you want to go?"

' "I should be doing something, it would be genuine. It's a sort of
toy-life as it is."

' "But what would you be doing if you went to war?"

' "I would be making railways or bridges, working like a nigger."

' "But you'd only make them to be pulled down again when the
armies had done with them. It seems just as much a game."

' "If you call war a game."

' "What is it?"

' "It's about the most serious business there is, fighting."

'A sense of hard separateness came over her . . .' (p. 310).

This passage establishes not only that Skrebensky is 'not exactly' a
soldier, but that he is not exactly anything. If, unlike Will, he does not
deny the outside world, he accepts his place in it with a mechanical
and unadventurous complacency. Under the pressure of her question-
ing, the vacuity of the 'serious business' to which he is dedicated is felt
disturbingly by Ursula. War, as he understands it, is simply a 'doing
something', an escape not from the 'toy-life' of peace, but from the
duty of making something of his life as a man, whether in or out of
uniform. Skrebensky is even less defined as a man than either Tom or

Will; lacking the rooted stability of the one and the passionate aspiration of the other, he has no real identity. He is content to belong, amorphously, 'to the nation', and when he is not called on to serve it, to do 'nothing'. By the end of the discussion he himself seems 'like nothing' to Ursula (p. 311).

F. R. Leavis has drawn attention to the connection between what he calls Skrebensky's 'good-citizen acceptance of the social function as the ultimate meaning of life' and his 'inadequacy as a lover'.[1] The inadequacy manifests itself early on in his relationship with Ursula – while she is still a schoolgirl, in fact. Shortly after the quoted discussion between them, Fred Brangwen's wedding is celebrated. After supper the guests go out into the open for coffee and dance on the grass:

' "Come," said Ursula to Skrebensky, laying her hand on his arm.

'At the touch of her hand on his arm, his consciousness melted away from him. He took her into his arms, as if into the sure, subtle power of his will, and they became one movement, one dual movement, dancing on the slippery grass. It would be endless, this movement, it would continue for ever. It was his will and her will locked in a trance of motion, two wills locked in one motion, yet never fusing, never yielding one to the other. It was a glaucous, intertwining, delicious flux and contest in flux.

...

'As the dance surged heavily on, Ursula was aware of some influence looking in upon her. Something was looking at her. Some powerful, glowing sight was looking right into her, not upon her, but right at her. Out of the great distance, and yet imminent, the powerful, overwhelming watch was kept upon her. And she danced on and on with Skrebensky, while the great, white watching continued, balancing all in its revelation.

' "The moon has risen," said Anton, as the music ceased, and they found themselves suddenly stranded, like bits of jetsam on a shore. She turned, and saw a great white moon looking at her over the hill. And her breast opened to it, she was cleaved like a transparent jewel to its light. She stood filled with the full moon, offering herself. Her two breasts opened to make way for it, her body opened wide like a quivering anemone, a soft, dilated invitation touched by the moon. She wanted the moon to fill in to her, she wanted more, more communion with the moon, consummation. But Skrebensky put his arm

[1] *D. H. Lawrence: Novelist*, p. 140.

round her and led her away. He put a big, dark cloak round her, and sat holding her hand, whilst the moonlight streamed above the glowing fires.

'She was not there. Patiently she sat, under the cloak, with Skrebensky holding her hand. But her naked self was away there beating upon the moonlight, dashing the moonlight with her breasts and her knees, in meeting, in communion. She half started, to go in actuality, to fling away her clothing and flee away, away from this dark confusion and chaos of people to the hill and the moon. But the people stood round her like stones, like magnetic stones, and she could not go, in actuality . . .' (pp. 318–19).

The juxtaposition of the descriptions of the dancing and the moon rising is a good example of the way symbolism functions in the novel as a means of concentrated contrast. The dancing of Ursula and Skrebensky is a representation in physical terms of the ideal relation between a man and a woman; the 'two in one'. It is 'one dual movement', and though they are 'locked' in one motion, they do not fuse and neither yields to the other. It is a relationship which Ursula and Skrebensky are incapable of maintaining outside the dance, and it is not only the cessation of the music that is a disintegrating influence. If the account previously offered[1] of Anna's behaviour in the cornfield is accepted, it will at once be apparent what effect the moon has on Ursula. Her offering of herself to the moon is suggestive of auto-erotism because what she wants is a consummation of self: hence the 'but' when Skrebensky puts his arm round her. He puts a cloak round her too, as if to stave off the moon, but her 'naked self' is in flight from the 'dark confusion and chaos of people' to the sharp definition of singleness. Responsive only to the moon, to the imperative of separateness, she replies to Skrebensky's pathetic 'Don't you like me to-night?' by asking him to leave her alone, and when he 'appropriates' her in another dance, she waits coldly for the conjunction to end so that she can assume her 'pure being' (pp. 319–20). But Ursula is aroused by the moon to a fiendish extent unknown to Anna, as the following quotation indicates:

'At last, when the dance was over, she would not sit down, she walked away. . . .

'They went towards the stackyard. There he saw, with something like terror, the great new stacks of corn glistening and gleaming transfigured, silvery and present under the night-blue sky, throwing

[1] See p. 95 above.

dark, substantial shadows, but themselves majestic and dimly present. She, like glimmering gossamer, seemed to burn among them, as they rose like cold fires to the silvery-bluish air. All was intangible, a burning of cold, glimmering, whitish-steely fires. He was afraid of the great moon-conflagration of the cornstacks rising above him. His heart grew smaller, it began to fuse like a bead. He knew he would die.

'She stood for some moments out in the overwhelming luminosity of the moon. She seemed a beam of gleaming power. She was afraid of what she was. Looking at him, at his shadowy, unreal, wavering presence a sudden lust seized her, to lay hold of him and tear him and make him into nothing. Her hands and wrists felt immeasurably hard and strong, like blades. He waited there beside her like a shadow which she wanted to dissipate, destroy as the moonlight destroys a darkness, annihilate, have done with. She looked at him and her face gleamed bright and inspired. She tempted him. . . .

'And temerously, his hands went over her, over the salt, compact brilliance of her body. If he could but have her, how he would enjoy her! If he could but net her brilliant, cold, salt-burning body in the soft iron of his own hands, net her, capture her, hold her down, how madly he would enjoy her. He strove subtly, but with all his energy, to enclose her, to have her. And always she was burning and brilliant and hard as salt, and deadly. Yet obstinately, all his flesh burning and corroding, as if he were invaded by some consuming, scathing poison, still he persisted, thinking at last he might overcome her. Even, in his frenzy, he sought for her mouth with his mouth, though it was like putting his face into some awful death. She yielded to him, and he pressed himself upon her in extremity, his soul groaning over and over:

' "Let me come–let me come."

'She took him in the kiss, hard her kiss seized upon him, hard and fierce and burning corrosive as the moonlight. She seemed to be destroying him. He was reeling, summoning all his strength to keep his kiss upon her, to keep himself in the kiss.

'But hard and fierce she had fastened upon him, cold as the moon and burning as a fierce salt. Till gradually his warm, soft iron yielded, yielded, and she was there fierce, corrosive, seething with his destruction, seething like some cruel, corrosive salt around the last substance of his being, destroying him, destroying him in the kiss. And her soul crystallized with triumph, and his soul was dissolved with agony and annihilation. So she held him there, the victim, consumed, annihilated. She had triumphed: he was not any more' (pp. 320–2).

The passage is a brilliant example of the 'carbon' of character in action. The level of being at which the drama is enacted is evoked by the stacks of corn which throw 'dark, substantial shadows' but are 'themselves majestic and dimly present': it is with the dim presence that Lawrence is concerned, not with the outward shadow that gives a distorted impression of it. We have, therefore, to try to accept the distension of language which, as has been pointed out previously, is almost inevitable in any attempt to render the state of being that Lawrence is interested in. We have, in other words, to reconcile words like 'terror', 'die', 'tear', 'annihilate', and 'destroy' with new contexts. It is at once significant, then, that Skrebensky is terrified by the stacks of corn. In the moon-inflamed scene, where everything burns with 'cold, glimmering, whitish-steely fires', he is called on to produce a 'man-being' to match the 'woman-being' of Ursula, a sun to rival her moon. For Ursula, since Skrebensky will not leave her alone, turns on him, and sets out in the full pride of her female self in search of a maximum intensity which can only be achieved by challenging him to a corresponding assertion of his male being. On both sides the compulsion is to a destructive dominance. He tries with all his might to 'net' her, 'to enclose her, to have her', to 'overcome' her; she resists to 'the death'. In the end she 'annihilates' him because, as we have already been led to expect, he has no genuine male self to oppose to her; he is no sun but a 'shadow', a 'darkness' which the moonlight destroys. He cannot 'keep himself in the kiss'.[1]

The meaning of the experience is neatly summed up, symbolically, by the present Skrebensky chooses for Ursula when shortly afterwards he goes off to fight in the Boer War. He sends her a box of sweets, offering himself, so to speak, to be eaten, and leaving Ursula wondering—after she has guiltily devoured all the sweets herself—why it is that the empty box is 'a crux for her. What was she to think of it?' (p. 327). She sends him some wild snowdrops.

Ursula might well feel guilty. If, in the scene under the moon, she strips Skrebensky to his essential nothingness, her relinquishing of herself to the frictionally disintegrating 'night goal' of 'deep, sensual individualism' is self-lacerating. She succeeds in being her maximum

---

[1] The physical basis of Skrebensky's 'annihilation' both in this scene and in his second encounter with Ursula under the moon (see pp. 118–21 below) is discussed in Chap. 5, pp. 291–2 below.

female self, but it is with a sense of horror that she realizes the consequences. She is filled with an 'overpowering fear of herself' (p. 322), and determining that Skrebensky should never become 'aware of what had been', she tries to caress him 'back from the dead without leaving him one trace of fact to remember his annihilation by' (pp. 322–3). But she does not forgive him that he was not 'strong enough to acknowledge her' (p. 411). As for Skrebensky, the 'form and figure of him' is restored, and he goes about his army duties, 'giving himself up to them', but he ceases to consider personal connections important: 'What did a man matter personally? He was just a brick in the whole great social fabric, the nation, the modern humanity' (p. 328)–the image of the brick fittingly suggests the inert deadness of which he is guilty in the face of life.

When Skrebensky goes off to South Africa, Ursula forms a Lesbian attachment with her schoolmistress, Winifred Inger. It is perhaps not too fanciful to view her subjection to Winifred as an unconscious retreat to a 'minimum' self after her frightening expansion with Skrebensky. The masculine teacher can exact a submission denied to a man, can be a sun without challenging Ursula's moon: 'Then, with the beloved, subtly-intimate teacher present, the girl sat as within the rays of some enriching sun, whose intoxicating heat poured straight into her veins. . . . But what Ursula adored so much was [Winifred's] fine, upright, athletic bearing, and her indomitably proud nature. She was proud and free as a man, yet exquisite as a woman' (pp. 336–7). But Ursula soon suffers a revulsion from the relationship, recoiling from the 'perverted life of the elder woman' (p. 344), and escapes from her by contriving to marry her off to her uncle, Tom Brangwen, to whom, in his 'own dark corruption', Winifred is akin (p. 347).

Ursula's revolt against her mother manifests itself in a determination not to limit everything, as Anna does, to 'the ring of physical considerations' (p. 353), but to adventure upon the 'mysterious man's world . . . the world of daily work and duty, and existence as a working member of the community' (p. 334). She receives a brutally direct impression of that world when she takes Winifred to visit her Uncle Tom, the manager of a new colliery in Yorkshire:

'He lived in a large new house of red brick, standing outside a mass of homogeneous red-brick dwellings, called Wiggiston. Wiggiston was only seven years old. It had been a hamlet of eleven houses on the edge of healthy, half-agricultural country. Then the great seam of coal had been opened. In a year Wiggiston appeared, a great mass of pinkish rows of thin, unreal dwellings of five rooms each. The streets were like visions of pure ugliness; a grey-black macadamized road, asphalt causeways, held in between a flat succession of wall, window, and door, a new-brick channel that began nowhere, and ended nowhere. Everything was amorphous, yet everything repeated itself endlessly. Only now and then, in one of the house-windows vegetables or small groceries were displayed for sale' (p. 345).

The point to register here is that Lawrence is not simply bringing the record up to date, not simply filling in details of the social and economic transformation of England that was first alluded to when the elder Tom Brangwen was a boy. There is a new insistence in the tone of the above description. The advent of Wiggiston has not merely meant the end of the 'healthy' countryside; the pervading ugliness, the 'thin, unreal' houses, are symptomatic of an insidious human malady: the new town lies, spreading rapidly, 'like a skin-disease' (p. 345). If Wiggiston is a product of the industrialization of England, it signifies the dehumanization of man, the subordination of life to an economic function:

' "But that's how they are," [said Tom Brangwen]. "She'll [i.e., his woman servant] be getting married again directly. One man or another–it does not matter very much. They're all colliers."

' "What do you mean?" asked Ursula. "They're all colliers?"

' "It is with the women as with us," he replied. "Her husband was John Smith, loader. We reckoned him as a loader, he reckoned himself as a loader, and so she knew he represented his job. Marriage and home is a little side-show. The women know it right enough, and take it for what it's worth. One man or another, it doesn't matter all the world. The pit matters. Round the pit there will always be the side-shows, plenty of 'em' (pp. 348–9).

Lawrence's bitter awareness of the dehumanizing effect of industrialism is something new in his work. There is not the same kind of awareness in *Sons and Lovers*, for instance; Paul's father, whatever else he may be, is not simply Walter Morel, butty. And in *The Rainbow*, though Will does not consider his work in the lace factory of any importance, he is not negated by it; it is only in the world in which Ursula takes her place that the reductive influence of the machine is not to be evaded. Moreover–and it is here that Lawrence's criticism of the modern world is felt at its most damaging–quite apart from what the machine does to man, it is a man's own attitude to the machine that is seen to determine the sort of part he plays in the 'side-show' of marriage and home. It is a criticism which Lawrence presents even more pungently in *Women in Love* and, finally, in *Lady Chatterley's Lover*; in *The Rainbow* it is substantiated by the kinship in corruption of Ursula's uncle and Winifred (and, as remains to be discussed, by the nature of Ursula's renewed relationship with Skrebensky).

Ursula's response to Wiggiston is to decide that 'her soul's action should be the smashing of the great machine' (p. 350). She is given an opportunity to try her strength against it when she begins to teach at the Brinsley Street school in a poor quarter of Ilkeston. Nothing, it might be thought, could be more remote from the actualities of Wiggiston than teaching, but it soon becomes apparent that the dialectic of the classroom is as harsh as that of the colliery. School has its ordained function in shaping the life that is swept along by the great conveyor belt. Ursula discovers that her class does not consist of individual children but is a 'collective, inhuman thing' (p. 377). She tries, in defiance of the prevailing system, to initiate personal relationships with the children, but soon finds herself in a 'very deep mess' (p. 383). The alternatives, as they present themselves to her, are to accept her own pure instrumentality and so to deny her personal self, or to be dragged down to destruction by the class. After a crisis, she fights for mastery, becoming a chill disciplinarian, at times brutal, always impersonal. She finally establishes herself as a teacher in command of her class, but like John Smith, loader, in the colliery, 'in school, she [is] nothing but Standard Five teacher' (p. 393).

Ursula, then, manages to hold her place in the man's world only by accepting its terms, and the machine, which it was to be her soul's action to smash, proves to be irrefrangible. What distinguishes her from her Uncle Tom and from Winifred, however, is her spiritual invulnerability. Forced to serve the machine, she refuses to capitulate to it, remaining committed to an individual search for fullness of being. She even rejects the university (which she attends after completing her period of elementary-school teaching) as 'only a little side-show to the factories of the town' (p. 434). She is intent at all costs on growing into herself: 'Self was a oneness with the infinite. To be oneself was a supreme, gleaming triumph of infinity' (p. 441).

It is against this background that her renewed relationship with Skrebensky should be viewed, for–*pace* Graham Hough–'the schoolteaching episode' is decidedly along 'the main thematic line'.[1]

[1] Cf.: 'Much of Ursula's subsequent experience is Lawrence's own, imaginatively

Skrebensky has been away from England for about six years, but she does not forget him:

'Often her thoughts returned to him. He seemed like the gleaming dawn, yellow, radiant, of a long, grey, ashy day. The memory of him was like the thought of the first radiant hours of morning. And here was the blank grey ashiness of later daytime. Ah, if he had only remained true to her, she might have known the sunshine, without all this toil and hurt and degradation of a spoiled day. He would have been her angel. He held the keys of the sunshine. Still he held them. He could open to her the gates of succeeding freedom and delight. Nay, if he had remained true to her, he would have been the doorway to her, into the boundless sky of happiness and plunging, inexhaustible freedom which was the paradise of her soul. Ah, the great range he would have opened to her, the illimitable endless space for self-realization and delight for ever' (pp. 438–9).

The imagery of this passage makes it clear why Ursula turns again to Skrebensky, despite their earlier failure together. In her determination 'to learn, to know and to do' (p. 411), she has been seeking to balance her 'night goal' with a 'day goal', has been trying, that is to say, to attain a self which is harmoniously reconciled between its male and female elements. But her experiences in the man's world have not been liberating; she can think of the day only as a 'blank grey ashiness'. Bitterly she reflects that if Skrebensky had been man enough, 'if he had only remained true to her', she could have 'known the sunshine' through him and with him, without the 'toil and hurt and degradation of a spoiled day'. The hurt has been so deep, however, the degradation of being 'Ursula Brangwen, Standard Five teacher' so great, the disappointment in the university so profound, that in her despair she forces herself to believe he still holds 'the keys of the sunshine'. Her hunger for 'self-realization' is so urgent that she becomes a blind mouth: 'her will [fixes] itself to him' (p. 439). When she meets him again and they try to resume an intimacy, she is at once aware that he is 'always side-tracking his own soul', but nevertheless her 'will never [relaxes], though her heart and soul must be imprisoned and silenced' (pp. 443–4).

transferred to a young woman – the school-teaching episode, for example. It is brilliantly done, and helps to keep this increasingly difficult part of the book firmly rooted in actuality. But we must pass it by, as we have passed by earlier episodes, to follow the main thematic line. This continues in Ursula's love for Skrebensky . . .' *The Dark Sun*, p. 68.

Ursula, therefore, demands from Skrebensky a kind of maleness he is incapable of giving. At first he satisfies her sexually, but 'after each contact, her anguished desire for him or for that which she never [has] from him [is] stronger, her love [is] more hopeless' (p. 463), and she realizes sadly that he arouses 'no fruitful fecundity' in her: 'He seemed added up, finished. She knew him all round, not on any side did he lead into the unknown' (pp. 473–4). Her sense of his ultimate 'nothingness' is the more acute because the abnegation of self which the man's world has forced on her leads her, in her relationship with him, to seek to be not smaller than herself, not just Standard Five teacher or university student, but larger: 'She was no mere Ursula Brangwen. She was Woman, she was the whole of Woman in the human order. All-containing, universal, how should she be limited to individuality?' (p. 444). Though it is 'concluded' that she will marry him, the outcome of their relationship is predetermined.

One of the incidental problems for Ursula in considering whether or not to marry Skrebensky is the question of settling in India. He is due to go out to India at the end of his six months' leave in England. Ursula says that she will be 'glad to leave England' where 'everything is so meagre and paltry' (p. 461), but it is apparent that she distrusts the sort of life she will be called on to lead in India with Skrebensky:

‘ "You with . . . your going to India because you will be one of the somebodies there! It's a mere dodge, your going to India."

‘ "In what way a dodge?" he cried, white with anger and fear.

‘ "You think the Indians are simpler than us, and so you'll enjoy being near them and being a lord over them," she said. "And you'll feel so righteous, governing them for their own good. Who are you, to feel righteous? What are you righteous about, in your governing? Your governing stinks. What do you govern for, but to make things there as dead and mean as they are here!"

‘ "I don't feel righteous in the least," he said.

‘ "Then what *do* you feel? It's all such a nothingness, what you feel and what you don't feel."

‘ "What do you feel yourself?" he asked. "Aren't you righteous in your own mind?"

‘ "Yes, I am, because I'm against you, and all your old, dead things," she cried.

‘She seemed, with the last words, uttered in hard knowledge, to strike down the flag that he kept flying. He felt cut off at the knees, a figure made worthless. A horrible sickness gripped him, as if his legs were really cut away, and he could not move, but remained a crippled trunk, dependent, worthless. The ghastly sense of helplessness, as if he were a mere figure that did not exist vitally, made him mad, beside himself.

'Now, even whilst he was with her, this death of himself came over him, when he walked about like a body from which all individual life is gone. In this state he neither heard nor saw nor felt, only the mechanism of his life continued' (pp. 461–2).

Ursula's hostility to Skrebensky's easy acquiescence in all the 'old, dead things' she is passionately committed to resisting is so intense that, in discussions like this, she transfers her enmity against the machine to him as a man. That is why she delivers her opinions with such malevolent, destructive force, and being unable to gainsay her, he is struck where he is most vulnerable, in the soft, pulpy core of his spiritual helplessness; and that is why he walks about 'like a body from which all individual life is gone'. He is reduced to a sense of his own non-existence, and all that remains to complete the rupture between them is for her to translate her piercing penetration of him into physical terms.

This she eventually does – with a shocking and tenacious ferocity:

'Suddenly, cresting the heavy, sandy pass, Ursula lifted her head, and shrank back, momentarily frightened. There was a great whiteness confronting her, the moon was incandescent as a round furnace door, out of which came the high blast of moonlight, over the seaward half of the world, a dazzling, terrifying glare of white light. They shrank back for a moment into shadow, uttering a cry. He felt his chest laid bare, where the secret was heavily hidden. He felt himself fusing down to nothingness, like a bead that rapidly disappears in an incandescent flame.

' "How wonderful!" cried Ursula, in low, calling tones. "How wonderful!"

'And she went forward, plunging into it. He followed behind. She too seemed to melt into the glare, towards the moon.

'The sands were as ground silver, the sea moved in solid brightness, coming towards them, and she went to meet the advance of the flashing, buoyant water. She gave her breast to the moon, her belly to the flashing, heaving water. He stood behind, encompassed, a shadow ever dissolving.

...

'Then there in the great flare of light, she clinched hold of him, hard, as if suddenly she had the strength of destruction, she fastened her arms round him and tightened him in her grip, whilst her mouth sought his in a hard, rending, ever-increasing kiss, till his body was powerless in her grip, his heart melted in fear from the fierce, beaked, harpy's kiss. The water washed again over their feet, but she took no notice. She seemed unaware, she seemed to be pressing in her beaked mouth till she had the heart of him. Then, at last, she drew away and looked at him–looked at him. He knew what she wanted. He took her by the hand and led her across the foreshore back to the sand hills. She went silently. He felt as if the ordeal of proof was upon him, for life or death. He led her to a dark hollow.

' "No, here," she said, going out to the slope full under the moonshine. She lay motionless, with wide-open eyes looking at the moon. He came direct to her, without preliminaries. She held him pinned down at the chest, awful. The fight, the struggle for consummation was terrible. It lasted till it was agony to his soul, till he succumbed, till he gave way as if dead, and lay with his face buried, partly in her hair, partly in the sand, motionless, as if he would be motionless now for ever, hidden away in the dark, buried, only buried, he only wanted to be buried in the goodly darkness, only that, and no more.

'He seemed to swoon. It was a long time before he came to himself. He was aware of an unusual motion of her breast. He looked up. Her face lay like an image in the moonlight, the eyes wide open, rigid. But out of the eyes, slowly, there rolled a tear, that glittered in the moonlight as it ran down her cheek.

'He felt as if the knife were being pushed into his already dead body. With head strained back he watched, drawn tense, for some minutes, watched the unaltering, rigid face like metal in the moonlight, the fixed, unseeing eyes, in which slowly the water gathered, shook with glittering moonlight, then surcharged, brimmed over and ran trickling, a tear with its burden of moonlight, into the darkness, to fall in the sand' (pp. 479–80).

This scene is a complex fusion of the various motives portrayed in the relationship of Ursula and Skrebensky. To begin with, she here gives physical expression to the overpowering, destructive contempt which she feels for him as a man in the 'man's world'. This, I take it, is the implicit significance of the kiss, in so far as that can be distinguished from the intercourse that follows. With a sudden access of the 'strength of destruction' she presses her 'rending', her 'fierce, beaked, harpy's kiss' upon him till it seems that she has 'the heart of him'. But, of course, this is only one aspect of the scene as a whole, and, indeed, of the kiss itself. Their sexual conflict is in large measure a repetition of their earlier encounter under the moon, only exacerbated by Ursula's intervening frustrations of self. The moon functions here, as the sea has served previously, to tantalize her with 'vast suggestions of fulfilment', though in her walks along the foreshore she has recognized Skrebensky's inadequacy as a 'personification' of such fulfilment, has registered that his 'soul [can] not contain her in its waves of strength, nor his breast compel her in burning, salty passion' (p. 478). Her momentary fear when she first sees the moon does not only reflect her shock at its sudden white incandescence; it is a fear of the irresistible urge which she feels taking possession of her, a fear of what surrender to the urge will mean both for herself and for Skrebensky. Her 'low, *calling* tones' mark her submission to the moon, and, like the way in which she looks at him after the kiss, are an invitation to him to pit his maximum male self against her maximum female self. The invitation is to something far removed from ordinary sexual experience; it is not even an invitation to the sort of heightened experience which Lawrence describes as the 'destructive fire' of 'profane love . . . the only fire that will purify us into singleness, fuse us from the chaos into our own unique gem-like separateness of being'.[1] It is an invitation to a battle in which the aim is to conquer and kill, to remain destructively *apart* in the act of intercourse in an insane assertion of self; for Ursula, who has given 'her breast to the moon, her belly to the flashing, heaving water', has passed beyond relationship with him. Skrebensky, though compelled, willed by Ursula, to accept the challenge, is in retreat before he begins the fight. The moon lays bare his chest where his secret is hidden, the shame of her previous exposure of his nothingness, the consciousness of his present inability to meet and match her on these terms. The imagery stresses his nullity: he is 'like a bead that rapidly disappears in an incandescent flame'; he is 'a shadow ever dissolving'. He makes an ineffectual attempt to face his 'ordeal of proof' out of the moonlight but nothing avails: once again he is 'annihilated', and he is left wanting to be 'buried, only buried'. The tear which rolls down Ursula's cheek with its 'burden of moonlight' and which falls 'into the darkness . . . in the sand' is a tacit admission of the vanity of her victory. Its ultimate import is a recognition on her part that she cannot, without disastrous consequences, try to recoup at night the losses

[1] See Chap. 1, p. 39 above.

of the day, cannot be Woman, be more than Ursula Brangwen.

That the tear has this sort of significance is, I think, substantiated by the symbolism of Ursula's nightmarish encounter with the stampeding horses. She is out walking on the common, shortly after the last scene with Skrebensky, when she feels that her way is cut off by the horses:

'But the horses had burst before her. In a sort of lightning of knowledge their movement travelled through her, the quiver and strain and thrust of their powerful flanks, as they burst before her and drew on, beyond.

'She knew they had not gone, she knew they awaited her still. But she went on over the log bridge that their hoofs had churned and drummed, she went on, knowing things about them. She was aware of their breasts gripped, clenched narrow in a hold that never relaxed, she was aware of their red nostrils flaming with long endurance, and of their haunches, so rounded, so massive, pressing, pressing, pressing to burst the grip upon their breasts, pressing forever till they went mad, running against the walls of time, and never bursting free. Their great haunches were smoothed and darkened with rain. But the darkness and wetness of rain could not put out the hard, urgent, massive fire that was locked within these flanks, never, never.
...
'They were behind her. The way was open before her, to the gate in the high hedge in the near distance, so she could pass into the smaller, cultivated field, and so out to the high-road and the ordered world of man. Her way was clear. She lulled her heart. Yet her heart was couched with fear, couched with fear all along.

'Suddenly she hesitated as if seized by lightning. She seemed to fall, yet found herself faltering forward with small steps. The thunder of horses galloping down the path behind her shook her, the weight came down upon her, down, to the moment of extinction. She could not look round, so the horses thundered upon her.
...
'Her heart was gone, she had no more heart. She knew she dare not draw near. That concentrated, knitted flank of the horse-group had conquered. It stirred uneasily, awaiting her, knowing its triumph. . . .

'Her feet faltered, she came to a standstill. It was the crisis. The horses stirred their flanks uneasily. She looked away, failing. On her left, two hundred yards down the slope, the thick hedge ran parallel. At one point there was an oak-tree. She might climb into the boughs of that oak-tree, and so round and drop on the other side of the hedge.

'Shuddering, with limbs like water, dreading every moment to fall, she began to work her way as if making a wide detour round the horse-mass. The horses stirred their flanks in a knot against her. She trembled forward as if in a trance.

'Then suddenly, in a flame of agony, she darted, seized the rugged knots of the oak-tree and began to climb. Her body was weak but her hands were as hard as steel. . . . She was working her way round to the other side of the tree. As they started to canter towards her, she fell in a heap on the other side of the hedge.

'For some moments she could not move. Then she saw through the rabbit-cleared bottom of the hedge the great, working hoofs of the horses as they cantered near. She could not bear it. She rose and walked swiftly, diagonally across the field. The horses galloped along the other side of the hedge to the corner, where they were held up. She could feel them there in their huddled group all the while she hastened across the bare field. They were almost pathetic, now. Her will alone carried her, till, trembling, she climbed the fence under a leaning thorn-tree that overhung the grass by the high-road. The use went from her, she sat on the fence leaning back against the trunk of the thorn-tree, motionless' (pp. 488–90).

Critics are roughly agreed on the symbolic meaning of the horses; the formulation which approximates to my own view is that of E. L. Nicholes: the horses, she says, symbolize 'the anarchy of elemental passion'.[1] What is in question is the significance of the incident as a whole. Graham Hough writes: '. . . I have neglected the part that this episode plays in the book's economy as a whole (it is [as?] a matter of fact, an inadequately prepared conclusion, imperfectly integrated

[1] 'The "Simile of the Sparrow" in *The Rainbow* by D. H. Lawrence', *Modern Language Notes*, 64 (March 1949), 173. Ursula's earlier reflections on the nature of love would seem to substantiate this interpretation: 'She did not see how lambs could love. Lambs could only be loved. They could only be afraid, and tremblingly submit to fear, and become sacrificial; or they could submit to love, and become beloveds. In both they were passive. Raging, destructive lovers, seeking the moment when fear is greatest, and triumph is greatest, the fear not greater than the triumph, the triumph not greater than the fear, these were no lambs nor doves. She stretched her own limbs like a lion or a wild horse, her heart was relentless in its desires. It would suffer a thousand deaths, but it would still be a lion's heart when it rose from death, a fiercer lion she would be, a surer, knowing herself different from and separate from the great, conflicting universe that was not herself' (pp. 342–3).

with the rest). The only point I wish to make is that it is...by submission to the contact of the wild horses, the agents, as it seems, of
passion and ferocity; by the temporary obliteration of personal integrity and awareness, that Ursula's mystic reintegrating vision is
achieved. . . .'[1] I find myself in marked disagreement with Hough,
both in regard to the artistic imperfection that, in this connection, he
attributes to the book and in regard to his reading of the scene itself.
My interpretation is derived from Nicholes' analysis of a simile which
Lawrence uses to describe Ursula's feelings as she makes her way
through a wood towards the common where she meets the horses.
The simile is as follows:

'She felt like a bird that has flown in through the window of a hall
where vast warriors sit at the board. Between their grave, booming
ranks she was hastening, assuming she was unnoticed, till she emerged
with beating heart, through the far window and out into the open,
upon the vivid green, marshy meadow' (p. 487).

In her brief but fascinating article, Nicholes suggests that this 'simile
of the sparrow' can be traced, through Wordsworth (Ecclesiastical
Sonnets, No. XVI) back to Bede's *Ecclesiastical History*, and that the
sparrow's flight symbolizes the journey of the soul, coming from the
unknown and passing to the unknown.[2] That Lawrence had some
such significance in mind seems, on the face of it, to be undeniable. I
suggest, therefore, that in presenting Ursula's encounter with the
horses he gives us a concentrated, symbolic retrospect of crucial
stages along her soul's journey.

The opening paragraphs of the quoted passage, it seems to me, look
back to Ursula's sudden, overwhelming, adolescent experience of
sexual passion, to the time of her frantic consummation under the
moon at the age of sixteen. The 'lightning of knowledge' that travels
through her then is forked. On the one hand, she recognizes, with an
awareness that is never to leave her, the value of her physical being;
and she accepts the presence of the 'hard, urgent, massive fire' that can
never be put out. On the other hand, however, she realizes that the
sort of assertion to which she resorts with Skrebensky, the 'pressing,
pressing, pressing to burst the grip' upon her, is a dead end, a 'running against the walls of time', and that she will not, in that way,
'burst free' to the fullness of being she is seeking.

[1] *Two Exiles: Lord Byron and D. H. Lawrence* (University of Nottingham pamphlet,
1956), p. 9.
[2] 'The "Simile of the Sparrow" . . .', *loc. cit.*, p. 173.

The third paragraph refers to her hope that she has safely put the temptation to an unmitigated assertion 'behind her'. She starts on her teaching and the way seems to be 'open before her', the way to 'the high-road and the ordered world of man'.

The next two paragraphs, I take it, evoke the second of the scenes under the moon. She is 'seized by lightning' for a second time, and the weight comes 'down upon her, down, to the moment of extinction'. Once more she is conquered by the 'concentrated, knitted flank of the horse-group', and is left feeling that her heart is 'gone'.

The remainder of the description is, in terms of the novel as a whole, the most important part of the episode, for it records a vital decision that is not presented dramatically elsewhere. Her last experience with Skrebensky is for Ursula, as it is for him, 'the crisis'. Weakly, 'shuddering, with limbs like water, dreading every moment to fall', she surmounts it. She determines to put the hedge between herself and the horses, and climbing the tree with hands 'as hard as steel', she rises above them, and drops to the other side of the hedge. This time she does not merely hope that she has left the horses 'behind her'; they are 'held up' by the hedge. She still 'feels' them as she hurries across the field, but they are a limited force, 'almost pathetic, now', and she safely reaches 'the high-road'.

If this interpretation is acceptable, then it seems that the point of the episode is not that Ursula submits to the horses, but that, following her bitter experience with Skrebensky (and we remember the tear that rolls down her cheek), she brings them into a new relation with herself. And the 'mystic reintegrating vision' to which Hough refers, Ursula's vision of the rainbow which concludes the book, is not achieved by an obliteration of personal integrity and awareness, no matter how temporary. It is a vision of wholeness which springs from the realignment in a unified self of hitherto violently contending forces, forces which Lawrence symbolizes by the tiger and the lamb or the lion and the unicorn in the expository writings, and which are represented in the scene on the common by the horses and the high-road. With the horses behind her, experienced in all their wonderful terror but now brought into line against the hedge as a result of her determination to make for the road, and with the road lying arduously ahead, running along, as it seems to her, 'between the hedges' (p. 491), in relation, that is to say, to what is bounded by the hedges, Ursula has come to the 'deep, unalterable knowledge' which persists 'under all [the] illness' into which she falls after the

experience (p. 491). The illness is a prelude to her spiritual rebirth:
'And again, to her feverish brain, came the vivid reality of acorns in
February lying on the floor of a wood with their shells burst and discarded and the kernel issued naked to put itself forth. She was the
naked, clear kernel thrusting forth the clear, powerful shoot, and the
world was a bygone winter, discarded, her mother and father and
Anton, and college and all her friends, all cast off like a year that has
gone by, whilst the kernel was free and naked and striving to take
new root, to create a new knowledge of Eternity in the flux of Time.
And the kernel was the only reality; the rest was cast off into oblivion'
(p. 493).

The creation of a knowledge of eternity in the flux of time is the
creation of a consummated self: 'My idea of Eternity', Dorothy Brett
reports Lawrence as saying, 'I can best illustrate by the rainbow: it is
the meeting half-way of two elements. The meeting of the sun and of
the water produce, at exactly the right place and moment, the rainbow. So it is in everything, and that is eternal . . . the Nirvana . . . just
that moment of the meeting of two elements. No one person could
reach it alone without that meeting.'[1] Ursula's painful approach to a
consummated self is convincingly established, and the rainbow, we
see, is a fitting emblem of her personal achievement. What must be
adjudged a weakness in the book, however, is the form given to her
vision of the rainbow; being made new herself, it is her facile assumption that she will find the world changed to measure: 'She saw in the
rainbow the earth's new architecture, the old, brittle corruption of
houses and factories swept away, the world built up in a living
fabric of Truth, fitting to the over-arching heaven' (p. 496). As
F. R. Leavis has remarked, this 'confident note of prophetic hope' is
'wholly unprepared [for] and unsupported, defying the preceding
pages'.[2]

Ursula's miscarriage is the final evidence of her rejection of Skrebensky, and thereafter she is ready 'to recognize a man created by
God', to hail a man who will come 'from the infinite' (p. 494), a man,
that is, who has achieved an individual self. 'The final page of the
manuscript of *The Rainbow*', Lawrence Clark Powell tells us, 'bears the
note "End of Volume I" ';[3] Birkin is the man Ursula hails in *Women
in Love*.

[1] *Lawrence and Brett* (London, 1933), p. 267.

[2] *D. H. Lawrence: Novelist*, p. 142.

[3] *The Manuscripts of D. H. Lawrence: A Descriptive Catalogue* (Los Angeles, 1937), p. 5.

(B) *Women in Love*

'Do not listen to Bertie [i.e., Bertrand Russell] about going to London. You cannot *really* do anything now: no one can do anything. You might as well try to prevent the spring from coming on. This world of ours has got to collapse now, in violence and injustice and destruction, nothing will stop it. Bertie deludes himself about his lectures. There will come a bitter disillusion.

'The only thing now to be done is either to go down with the ship, sink with the ship, or, as much as one can, *leave* the ship, and like a castaway live a life apart. As for me, I do not belong to the ship; I will not, if I can help it, sink with it. I will not live any more in this time. I know what it is. I reject it. As far as I possibly can, I will stand outside this time, I will live my life, and, if possible, be happy, though the whole world slides in horror down into the bottomless pit. There is a greater truth than the truth of the present, there is a God beyond these gods of to-day. Let them fight and fall round their idols, my fellow men: it is their affair. As for me, as far as I can, I will save myself, for I believe that the highest virtue is to be happy, living in the greatest truth, not submitting to the falsehood of these personal times.'[1]

Lawrence's letter to Ottoline Morrell helps to explain why *Women in Love*, though in intention a sequel to *The Rainbow*,[2] is so different from the earlier novel. It is not merely that there is a notable difference in technique between the two books, that, in *Women in Love*, Lawrence seems more easily able to express his apprehension of the 'carbon' of character in scenes which combine a complex symbolic depth with a surface of dramatic naturalism so that this novel is airier and more spacious than its predecessor; *Women in Love*, though conceived as part of a single project which made *The Rainbow* a necessary prior undertaking, was in fact written out of a radically different mood. The passage quoted above (and it is a representative instance of the way in which Lawrence viewed the world in 1916) provides a background to his feeling as he wrote *Women in Love*.[3] His mood, despite his hope of

[1] Letter to Lady Ottoline Morrell (February 1916), *Letters*, p. 317.
[2] Cf.: 'I am half way through a novel, which is a sequel to the *Rainbow*, though quite unlike it.' Letter to J. B. Pinker (May 1916), *Letters*, p. 350.
[3] Lawrence worked at *The Sisters*, which incorporated material that was included in *Women in Love*, in 1913. He then put *The Sisters* aside to work on various versions of *The Rainbow*, and *Women in Love*, as we now know it, was begun in the spring of 1916 and completed the following year.

some sort of personal exemption from the general fate, is clearly one of profound despair, a despair made all the more bitter by a realization of his own powerlessness to prevent the world from sliding down into the bottomless pit. *Women in Love* is, in effect, a sustained dramatization of his belief in a personal immunity amid the public disaster. Though it is set in the same pre-war England as that in which Ursula of *The Rainbow* reaches maturity, the optimism which, in that book, informs her concluding vision of social regeneration, is transmuted into an abiding sense of the imminent collapse into calamity of a whole way of life. The War, as the viciousness of the fighting bit home by 1916, represented for Lawrence the disintegration of English civilization; and though the novel is apparently remote from the international concerns which agitated men at the time of its composition, it is, from one point of view, a novel of war, in that it explores the nature of the deep-seated disease in the body politic of which war is the ultimate death-agony. It is almost as if Lawrence carries out an autopsy on the still-breathing form of pre-war society.[1]

I emphasize this connection between the War and *Women in Love* not only because Lawrence's insistence in the book on the irrevocable doom of England is implicitly related to the catastrophe of 1914, but because it helps to explain the structure of the novel. It accounts, for instance, for what appears to be the dual motion of the book. On the one hand, as I shall try to show, there is a continuation of the search, begun in *The Rainbow*, for a lasting relation between the sexes, a search for the 'two in one'. The marriage of Birkin and Ursula, though markedly different in character from the marriages described in *The Rainbow*, is presented as an achieved relation of this kind, and its significance is heightened by the contrasted destructive passion of Gerald and Gudrun. But at the same time, to use the terms of Lawrence's letter to Ottoline Morrell, both couples are shown to be on board a ship which is rapidly heading for destruction, and their personal relations are not only qualified by their response to the danger but are the measure of a psychic drive towards life or death which such a

[1] Cf. Lawrence's description of the novel: 'There is another novel, sequel to *The Rainbow*, called *Women in Love*. I don't know if Huebsch has got the MS. yet. I don't think anybody will publish this, either. This actually does contain the results in one's soul of the war: it is purely destructive, not like *The Rainbow*, destructive – consummating. It is very wonderful and terrifying, even to me who have written it. I have hardly read it again. I suppose, however, it will be a long time without being printed–if ever it is printed.' Letter to Waldo Frank (July 1917), *Collected Letters*, I, 519.

predicament intensifies. Birkin and Ursula, clinging to the life preserver of their own 'unison in separateness', abandon ship; Gerald
and Gudrun, by trying to destroy each other, symbolically prefigure
in themselves the desire for death of those who do not attempt to
leave the ship–a desire, it is implied, which is to achieve its shattering
consummation in the general wreck that lies ahead. There is, therefore, no internal division in the book between the social and the
personal, for all the 'social scenes' are designed to evoke that background of impending ruin against which the personal drama is
enacted, and in relation to which it derives its ultimate meaning.

The structural principle of *Women in Love* is locative; that is to say,
there is a calculated movement from one place to another, each place
being a representative unit in the social organism and serving as the
focus of a local significance. The places are related to one another not
merely through a juxtaposition which yields a comprehensive view
of the social scene as a whole, but–so to speak–through their common
location on volcanic soil. There are five such foci in the book: Beldover, where Ursula and Gudrun live; Shortlands, the Crich home;
Breadalby, Hermione's country house; the Café Pompadour, the
haunt of London Bohemians; and the Tyrolese hostel, where Birkin,
Ursula, Gudrun and Gerald stay during their Alpine holiday. We are
required, in each place, to register the tell-tale tremors which herald
an inevitable cataclysm.

To view the novel in this way is to do no less than justice to the
compact tightness of its organization. The chapters which describe
the world of London bohemianism, for instance, might appear–at a
glance–to have no real function in the whole; and since, as the biographers have shown, they incorporate incidents in Lawrence's own
life, it becomes easily plausible to suppose that they were included
either in careless animus[1] or for their own sake. Even F. R. Leavis,
who rates *Women in Love* very highly indeed,[2] cites these chapters as

[1] Cf. Cecil Gray's resentment of the 'spiteful way' in which Lawrence caricatured
his 'best friends'. Gray objects particularly to the portrayal of Philip Heseltine as
Halliday, and maintains that Lawrence ascribed his own 'ludicrous or revolting
peculiarities' to his friends. See *Peter Warlock: A Memoir of Philip Heseltine* (London,
1934), pp. 223–4.

[2] He calls it 'one of the most striking works of creative originality that fiction has
to show'–D. H. *Lawrence: Novelist*, p. 146. He has also said that it is 'as astonishing a
work of genius as can be found among novels, and one that would, by itself,
make Lawrence a major value for the critic interested in the possibilities of prose
fiction.' 'D. H. Lawrence–the Novelist', *The Listener*, 42 (September 29, 1949), 543.

representative of one of the two faults he finds in the book: '[The fault] is represented pre-eminently by chapters VI and VII ("Crème de Menthe" and "Totem") and chapter XXVIII ("Gudrun in the Pompadour"). Lawrence here does some astonishingly vivid history: he re-creates, giving us the identifiable individuals, the metropolitan Bohemia he had known after the success of *Sons and Lovers*. A great deal of what he renders with such force is clearly there because it was once actual; he recalls the scene, the detail and the face. The episode that made so deep an impression on him goes in, for that reason–even when it was one he only heard about, as for instance that of the impounding of the letter by Katherine Mansfield at the Café Royal. But all that doesn't owe its presence to the needs of thematic definition and development would have been better excluded; a point to be made with the more emphasis since *Women in Love* has so complex and subtle an organization, and we have to assume in general, as we read, that everything is fully significant.'[1]

But the first paragraph of Chapter VI suggests that the account of Bohemia is in fact relevant to the development of the specific theme of the novel:

'They met again in the café several hours later. Gerald went through the push doors into the large, lofty room where the faces and heads of the drinkers showed dimly through the haze of smoke, reflected more dimly, and repeated *ad infinitum* in the great mirrors on the walls, so that one seemed to enter a vague, dim world of shadowy drinkers humming within an atmosphere of blue tobacco smoke. There was, however, the red plush of the seats to give substance within the bubble of pleasure' (p. 68).

At first sight this passage seems to give no more than a casual impression of the smoke-filled café, but it unobtrusively suggests the unreality of the assembled drinkers and links them with the inhabitants of one of the other 'worlds' of the novel in a way that convincingly places the scene within the determined limits of the book. The 'vague, dim world of shadowy drinkers' which typifies Bohemia on its chosen ground is not so far removed as might be thought from Beldover, 'the world of powerful, underworld men who [spend] most of their time in the darkness' (p. 128): what the two worlds have in common is a failure of meaningful life, the failure to live in bright, vivid distinction of being. I shall refer later to the miners in this connection. The description of London Bohemians is in keeping, too,

[1] *D. H. Lawrence: Novelist*, p. 181.

with Birkin's earlier characterization of them: 'the most pettifogging calculating Bohemia that ever reckoned its pennies. . . . Painters, musicians, writers–hangers-on, models, advanced young people, anybody who is openly at outs with the conventions, and belongs to nowhere particularly' (pp. 65–6). They are the small practitioners of art, and a room in which all individuality is obliterated in an amorphous haze of smoke is a fitting setting for their mediocrity. The café, moreover, is a refuge for those who are 'at outs' with the world of everyday life, but the self-centred narrowness of the world to which they adhere is implied by the unending reflection in the 'great mirrors on the walls'. If we respond to the suggestiveness of the opening description of the Café Pompadour, we are not altogether unprepared, towards the end of the novel, to find it styled 'this small, slow, central whirlpool of disintegration and dissolution' (p. 429), a phrase which unambiguously places the headquarters of London Bohemia along the main line of 'thematic definition and development'. The 'bubble of pleasure' which the drinkers have blown round themselves has nothing more substantial than red-plush seats at its centre, and it is dangerously poised to burst. The reference to the 'bubble of pleasure', moreover, lends added significance to the name of the café. The Café Pompadour is not merely a casual substitution for the Café Royal but neatly evokes the world of the Marquise de Pompadour ('Après nous le déluge!') which was swept away by the French Revolution.

The three chapters which F. R. Leavis implies could be dispensed with without much loss are designed to give body to the impressionism of the initial presentation of the bohemian *milieu*. In Chapter VI, for instance, there is the striking incident in which Minette suddenly slashes a knife across the hand of a young man in the café:

' "I'm not afwaid of anything except black-beetles," said Minette, looking up suddenly and staring with her round eyes, on which there seemed an unseeing film of flame, fully upon Gerald. He laughed dangerously, from the blood. Her childish speech caressed his nerves, and her burning, filmed eyes, turned now full upon him, oblivious of all her antecedents, gave him a sort of licence.

' "I'm not," she protested. "I'm not afraid of other things. But black-beetles–ugh!" She shuddered convulsively, as if the very thought were too much to bear.

...

' "And are you afraid of nothing else, Minette?" asked the young Russian, in his quick, hushed, elegant manner.

' "Not weally," she said. "I am afwaid of some things, but not weally the same. I'm not afwaid of *blood*."

' "Not afwaid of blood!" exclaimed a young man with a thick, pale, jeering face, who had just come to the table and was drinking whisky. 'Minette turned on him a sulky look of dislike, low and ugly.

' "Aren't you really afraid of blud?" the other persisted, a sneer all over his face.

' "No, I'm not," she retorted.

' "Why, have you ever seen blood, except in a dentist's spittoon?" jeered the young man.

' "I wasn't speaking to you," she replied rather superbly.

' "You can answer me, can't you?" he said.

'For reply, she suddenly jabbed a knife across his thick, pale hand. He started up with a vulgar curse.

' "Shows what you are," said Minette in contempt.

' "Curse you," said the young man, standing by the table and looking down at her with acrid malevolence.

' "Stop that," said Gerald, in quick, instinctive command.

'The young man stood looking down at her with sardonic contempt, a cowed, self-conscious look on his thick, pale face. The blood began to flow from his hand' (pp. 76–8).

Some idea of the way in which seemingly disparate scenes in *Women in Love* are interlocked can be gained from a consideration of Minette's apparently illogical, incidental fear of black-beetles. I suggest that her fear of beetles is connected with her memory of one of the West African carvings which she has seen at Halliday's–the carving that has so crucial a significance for Birkin:

'He remembered the African fetishes he had seen at Halliday's so often. There came back to him one, a statuette about two feet high, a tall, slim, elegant figure from West Africa, in dark wood, glossy and suave. It was a woman, with hair dressed high, like a melon-shaped dome. He remembered her vividly: she was one of his soul's intimates. Her body was long and elegant, her face was crushed tiny like a beetle's, she had rows of round heavy collars, like a column of quoits, on her neck. He remembered her: her astonishing cultured elegance, her diminished, beetle face, the astounding long elegant body, on short, ugly legs, with such protuberant buttocks, so weighty and unexpected below her slim long loins. She knew what he himself did not know. She had thousands of years of purely sensual, purely unspiritual knowledge behind her. It must have been thousands of years since her race had died, mystically: that is, since the relation between the senses and the outspoken mind had broken, leaving the experience all in one sort, mystically sensual. Thousands of years ago, that which was imminent in himself must have taken place in these Africans: the goodness, the holiness, the desire for creation and productive happiness must have lapsed, leaving the single impulse for knowledge in one sort, mindless progressive knowledge through the senses, knowledge arrested and ending in the senses, mystic knowledge in disintegration and dissolution, knowledge such as the beetles have, which live purely within the world of corruption and cold dissolution. This was why her face looked like a beetle's: this was why the Egyptians worshipped the ball-rolling scarab: because of the principle of knowledge in dissolution and corruption' (pp. 285–6).

The recurrence of the phrase 'disintegration and dissolution' – it is the key motive of the book, indicative of a general process against which Birkin and Ursula pit themselves – takes us back to the whirlpool of the Pompadour. Minette has so strong a fear of beetles because what she fears is her own inherent tendency to lapse, her own desire to break the complex unity of sense and mind in a disintegration into 'mystic' sensualism. But at the same time she secretly hankers after the beetle world of corruption;[1] and that is why, when she stares at Gerald as she speaks of her fear, there is 'an unseeing film of flame' on her burning eyes. She is 'oblivious of all her antecedents' as she turns her eyes 'full upon him' not only because she is disregarding her liaison with Halliday but, on the psychic level on which so much of the action of the novel is staged, because her look is an invitation to ignore – in the manner of the African fetish – the arduous European search for integrated being. That Gerald responds by laughing 'dangerously, from the blood' is, on this level – that is, at a level deeper than that of an incited sexual arousedness – illustrative of his own suppressed desire for a similar sort of dissolution. In this respect, his reaction to the African statues is revealing. When he first sees them he is 'disapproving' and finds them 'rather obscene' (p. 82), but he is clearly fascinated by them and, the next morning, forces Birkin to tell

[1] There is an interesting anticipation of the beetle image in a 1915 letter: 'We have had another influx of visitors: David Garnett and Francis Birrell turned up the other day – Saturday. I like David, but Birrell I have come to detest. These horrible little frowsty people, men lovers of men, they give me such a sense of corruption, almost putrescence, that I dream of beetles. It is abominable. . . .' Letter to S. S. Koteliansky (April 1915), *Collected Letters*, I, 333.

him what he thinks of a figure carved in the posture of childbirth.
Birkin says, 'It is art':

'Strangely elated, Gerald . . . lifted his eyes to the face of the wooden
figure. And his heart contracted.

'He saw vividly with his spirit the grey, forward-stretching face of
the savage woman, dark and tense, abstracted in utter physical stress.
It was a terrible face, void, peaked, abstracted almost into meaningless-
ness by the weight of sensation beneath. He saw Minette in it. As in a
dream, he knew her.

' "Why is it art?" Gerald asked, shocked, resentful.

' "It conveys a complete truth," said Birkin. "It contains the whole
truth of that state, whatever you feel about it."

' "But you can't call it *high* art," said Gerald.

' "High! There are centuries and hundreds of centuries of development in a straight line, behind that carving; it is an awful pitch of
culture, of a definite sort."

' "What culture?" Gerald asked, in opposition. He hated the sheer
barbaric thing.

' "Pure culture in sensation, culture in the physical consciousness,
really ultimate *physical* consciousness, mindless, utterly sensual. It is
so sensual as to be final, supreme."

'But Gerald resented it. He wanted to keep certain illusions, certain
ideas like clothing' (p. 87).

The relation of this passage to the scene in the Pompadour and to
Gerald's sexual encounter with Minette the night before is at once
apparent. Moreover, the defensive hostility Gerald feels towards the
statue, which expresses itself in a desire 'to keep certain illusions, certain ideas like clothing', is paralleled by his 'slight revulsion' when he
looks at Libidnikov in the nude (the Russian's name is suggestive) and
sees 'the human animal, golden skinned and bare, somehow humiliating' (p. 85). The depiction of the deliberate nudity of Halliday and
Libidnikov which precedes the quoted passage is not, we realize, a
gratuitous *exposé* of bohemian idiosyncrasies. The futility of Halliday's
passionate aspiration 'to live from day to day without *ever* putting on
any sort of clothing whatever' in order to 'feel [he has] lived' (p. 86),
is an implicit criticism of the nullity of the life he actually leads in
the 'vague, dim world' of Bohemia.[1] It might be noticed, too, how

[1] That Lawrence wished to emphasize this point is indicated by an interesting
divergence in the texts of the American and English editions of the novel. In the
American, the earlier text, Birkin also goes naked: 'Birkin suddenly appeared in

Halliday's nudity is indicative of a kind of 'disintegration' at the opposite pole to that represented by the carvings: 'Halliday was different. He had a rather heavy, slack, broken beauty, dark and firm. He was like a Christ in a Pietá. The animal was not there at all, only the heavy, broken beauty' (p. 85).

The cross-references to which a single paragraph of *Women in Love* may give rise are so numerous that it is perhaps necessary for me to state that I am, in effect, following a single line of thought if I now return to the episode in which Minette slashes the hand of the unnamed young man, for the foregoing discussion was occasioned by her fear of beetles. Her urge towards 'disintegration and dissolution' not unexpectedly expresses itself in a violent destructiveness as well as in sexual abandon, and when provoked, as she is, her blood lust issues in the attack on the young man. If Bohemia, as we have been told, does not set much store by the conventions, the scene is an indication of the sort of force that is released when people who are not fitted for the responsibility of freedom do as they like. The incident, in this respect, links up with Hermione's attack on Birkin – manifestations of violence are not restricted to the Pompadour but are a characteristic feature of the various 'worlds' of the novel – and with the conversation at the Crich wedding about the desirability of acting 'spontaneously on one's impulses' (pp. 35–7). Birkin's insistence, in that conversation, on the proposition that 'no man cuts another man's throat unless he wants to cut it, and unless the other man wants it cutting. . . . It takes two people to make a murder: a murderer and a murderee' (p. 36), is an interesting comment on the part played

the doorway, also in a state of nudity, towel and sleeping suit over his arm. He was very narrow and white, and somehow apart' (Avon, published by arrangement with The Viking Press, n.d., p. 71). The corresponding passage in the English text is as follows: 'Birkin suddenly appeared in the doorway, in white pyjamas and wet hair, and a towel over his arm. He was aloof and white, and somehow evanescent' (p. 86).

This change, as far as Birkin is concerned, necessitates a further alteration of the text a little later, one that strengthens the case against Gerald:

'When Gerald went back to his room from the bath, he also carried his clothes. It seemed bad form in this house, not to go about naked. And after all, it was rather nice, there *was* a real simplicity. Still, it was rather funny, everybody being so deliberately nude' (Avon, p. 72).

'When Gerald went back to his room from the bath, he also carried his clothes. He was so conventional at home, that when he was really away, and on the loose, as now, he enjoyed nothing so much as full outrageousness. So he strode with his blue silk wrap over his arm and felt defiant' (p. 88).

by the young man, who, despite his curses, is left with a 'cowed' look on his face. The rage to destroy and to be destroyed, which–in small compass–is present in the café, is of course the sort of rage which, intensified by public sanction, is given free rein in war; war is the ultimate consummation which the state of being of most of the characters in *Women in Love* would seem to require.

Gudrun's triumph over Halliday in respect of the Birkin letter, which forms the subject-matter of the last of the three chapters devoted to London Bohemia, is an instance of how Lawrence turns an experience from life to his own thematic purposes in the novel. No doubt it gave him personal satisfaction to ridicule the original of Halliday for his mockery of *Amores* at the Café Royal,[1] but I do not think the episode 'goes in' simply because it made 'so deep an impression on him'. It is neatly related, to begin with, to what has been previously presented as one of the distinctive characteristics of bohemianism: the jeers of the reader of the letter and his chorus are an expression of a mean, vindictive destructiveness, of the easy, pettifogging violence of words; for the outburst is occasioned by Gerald's slighting of them and by Gudrun's supreme contempt. The object of their fury is Birkin because, as they well know, he stands for a way of life which negates their own impotent existence. It is in the substitution of the letter for the book of poems of the original incident that Lawrence shows the resources of an impersonal art. Some sort of substitution was anyway made necessary since Birkin is not a poet, but the device of a personal letter enables Lawrence to achieve certain effects quite apart from the exposure of Halliday and his friends:

' "Do let me go on! Oh, this is a perfectly wonderful piece! But do listen to this. 'And in the great retrogression, the reducing back of the created body of life, we get knowledge, and beyond knowledge, the phosphorescent ecstasy of acute sensation.' Oh, I do think these phrases are too absurdly wonderful. Oh, but don't you think they *are* –they're nearly as good as Jesus. 'And if, Julius, you want this ecstasy of reduction with Minette, you must go on till it is fulfilled. But surely there is in you also, somewhere, the living desire for positive

---

[1] There is some dispute as to whether it was Heseltine who engaged in the jeering reading. Richard Aldington says that Middleton Murry assured him it was, and that Murry kept the copy of *Amores* impounded by Katherine Mansfield. He also quotes a corroboratory letter by Michael Arlen, who was present at the scene; see *Portrait of a Genius, But . . .* (London, 1950), p. 186. Cecil Gray, on the other hand, maintains, on the authority of S. S. Koteliansky, another eye-witness, that Heseltine was not even in the café at the time of the reading; see *Peter Warlock*, pp. 224–5.

creation, relationships in ultimate faith, when all this process of active
corruption, with all its flowers of mud, is transcended, and more or
less finished–' I do wonder what the flowers of mud are. Minette,
you are a flower of mud."
  ' "Thank you–and what are you?"
  ' "Oh, I'm another, surely, according to this letter! We're all flowers
of mud–*Fleurs–hic! du mal!* It's perfectly wonderful, Birkin harrowing
Hell–harrowing the Pompadour–*Hic!*" . . .
  ' " 'Surely,' " Halliday intoned, " 'surely goodness and mercy hath
followed me all the days of my life–' " he broke off and giggled.
Then he began again, intoning like a clergyman. " 'Surely there will
come an end in us to this desire–for the constant going apart–this
passion for putting asunder–everything–ourselves, reducing ourselves part from part–reacting in intimacy only for destruction–using
sex as a great reducing agent, reducing the two great elements of male
and female from their highly complex unity—reducing the old ideas,
going back to the savages for our sensations–always seeking to *lose*
ourselves in some ultimate black sensation, mindless and infinite–
burning only with destructive fires, raging on with the hope of being
burnt out utterly–' "
  ' "I want to go," said Gudrun to Gerald, as she signalled the waiter.
Her eyes were flashing, her cheeks were flushed. The strange effect of
Birkin's letter read aloud in a perfect clerical sing-song, clear and
resonant, phrase by phrase, made the blood mount into her head as
if she were mad . . .' (pp. 433–4).
  Birkin's letter is a deliberate exaggeration of Lawrencean doctrine,
but the remarkable success of the self-parody should not blind us to
what, in terms of the created world of *Women in Love*, is its core of truth.
The letter serves the additional purposes, therefore, of confirming our
impression of Minette as a reductive force, and–at the same time–of
diagnosing the diseased relationship of Gerald and Gudrun. Gudrun
emerges with credit from the scene for her quietly brave defence of
Birkin, but one wonders whether her intervention comes when it does
because the letter has touched home.
  I have dwelt at some length on the relatively unimportant chapters
which deal with Bohemia both because they have come in for unjustified criticism and because, in this novel, the circumferential leads in a
straight line to the centre. The rottenness of Bohemia, which these
chapters reveal with effortless economy, is an instance of the general
rottenness in the state of England. To move from the Pompadour to

Breadalby, for example, is to move to a different world, but the smell of putrefaction is the same.

At first sight Breadalby might appear to be the seat of no more vicious a vice than escapism: 'There seemed a magic circle drawn about the place, shutting out the present, enclosing the delightful, precious past, trees and deer and silence, like a dream.' The scene is focused more sharply, however, when we are told that 'the attitude' of those who are to be found there is 'mental and very wearying', and that their talk, a characteristic activity, goes on 'like a rattle of small artillery' (p. 93). Breadalby is the home of ideas, and though there are the inevitable hangers-on, it is a meeting-place for the advanced in thought. Under the tutelage of the daughter of the house, Hermione Roddice, there foregather on its lawns men of the calibre of Sir Joshua Mattheson, the learned sociologist; and the house-parties are connected with public affairs through Hermione's brother, a Liberal member of Parliament. The quintessential figure of the group, however, and the one in whom its weaknesses are most rigorously analysed, is Hermione herself.

Hermione is an equivocator. She lives for and through the mind and, characteristically, she vaunts the delights of knowledge: 'To me', she says, 'the pleasure of knowing is *so* great, so *wonderful* – nothing has meant so much to me in all life, as certain knowledge – no, I am sure – nothing' (p. 95); but she also asserts that 'the mind . . . is death', maintaining with demonic innocence that 'it [destroys] all our spontaneity, all our instincts' (p. 44). What lies behind the equivocation is a perverted lust, as Birkin violently tells her: 'You want to clutch things and have them in your power. . . . And why? Because you haven't got any real body, any dark sensual body of life. You have no sensuality. You have only your will and your conceit of consciousness, and your lust for power, to *know*' (p. 46). In other words Hermione typifies an indulgence in what Lawrence elsewhere calls a 'sensational gratification within the mind',[1] and we realize how exactly she is 'placed' by the opening description of her:

'The chief bridesmaids had arrived. Ursula watched them come up the steps. One of them she knew, a tall, slow, reluctant woman with a weight of fair hair and a pale, long face. This was Hermione Roddice, a friend of the Criches. Now she came along, with her head held up, balancing an enormous flat hat of pale yellow velvet, on which were streaks of ostrich feathers, natural and grey. She drifted forward as if

[1] 'The Crown', *Reflections*, p. 56.

scarcely conscious, her long blanched face lifted up, not to see the world. She was rich. She wore a dress of silky, frail velvet, of pale yellow colour, and she carried a lot of small rose-coloured cyclamens. Her shoes and stockings were of brownish grey, like the feathers on her hat, her hair was heavy, she drifted along with a peculiar fixity of the hips, a strange unwilling motion. She was impressive, in her lovely pale-yellow and brownish-rose, yet macabre, something repulsive. People were silent when she passed, impressed, roused, wanting to jeer, yet for some reason silenced. Her long, pale face, that she carried lifted up, somewhat in the Rossetti fashion, seemed almost drugged, as if a strange mass of thoughts coiled in the darkness within her, and she was never allowed to escape' (pp. 16–17).

There is something 'macabre' about her appearance, and people are repelled by her even though they are impressed, because she moves as though she tacitly disowns her body: hence her slow reluctance and her strange unwilling motion as she drifts forward with a peculiar fixity of the hips. Great emphasis, like the distortion in a modern painting, is given to the size of her head: her face, it is repeatedly insisted, is long, and it is balanced by the heavy weight of her hair and by the enormous hat she wears. The distortion, clearly, has a significance which is counter to that of the African carving which has a face 'crushed tiny like a beetle's' and which is so 'weighty' below the loins. Hermione, we are invited to recognize, is a prey to a process of 'disintegration and dissolution' which is the reverse of that epitomized by the fetish but which is as deadly in its effects. Some suggestion of the deadliness is implied, with Lawrencean esotericism, by the 'mass of thoughts' which 'coil' (the word has a serpent-like ominousness) in the 'darkness' within her; it is directly illustrated by the nature of her relationship with Birkin.

Hermione's 'deficiency of being' is attested by the 'terrible void' within her—we are reminded of the bubbles which hover round the Bohemians and round Gerald[1]–and it is to Birkin that she turns to fill the void, 'to close up this deficiency' (p. 18). Believing that she herself is 'the central touchstone of truth', she is convinced that she needs only Birkin and his 'high' knowledge in conjunction with her to be

---

[1] Gerald, too, has a 'great dark void . . . at the centre of his soul' (p. 363), and as his father slowly dies before him, he comes to feel 'more and more like a bubble filled with darkness, round which whirled the iridescence of his consciousness, and upon which the pressure of the outer world, the outer life, roared vastly' (p. 364).

complete (p. 19). But he, who is trying to leave her after having been her lover for some years–his breaking away from her is the first movement in a withdrawal from the world which she represents–in fact relentlessly forces her to an agonized awareness of the 'bottomless pit' of her insufficiency. The way in which she eventually succumbs to her own inadequacy has been brilliantly analysed by F. R. Leavis[1] with a comprehensiveness that leaves little to be added; I should merely like to emphasize some of the thematic implications of her collapse.

Hermione has 'an obsession . . . to know all [Birkin knows]' (p. 99), and when she compels him to explain what knowledge he gets from copying a Chinese drawing of geese, he forces her, as Leavis points out, 'to admit to herself an awareness of "unknown modes of being" ', and to recognize that 'the reality of life is something she can have no command over and cannot take into her possession'. As a result, 'she feels herself for the moment nothing but the play of chaotic forces that the "mental consciousness" had excluded',[2] but her collapse is described in terms which suggest something larger than a personal failure:

' "Yes," she said, as if she did not know what she were saying. "Yes," and she swallowed, and tried to regain her mind. But she could not, she was witless, decentralized. Use all her will as she might, she could not recover. She suffered the ghastliness of dissolution, broken and gone in a horrible corruption. And he stood and looked at her unmoved. She strayed out, pallid and preyed-upon like a ghost, like one attacked by the tomb-influences which dog us. And she was gone like a corpse, that has no presence, no connexion. He remained hard and vindictive' (p. 99).

The simile of the 'tomb-influences' reinforces Leavis's analysis by suggesting how Hermione is suddenly overwhelmed by the buried life within her, and she is simultaneously 'like a ghost' and 'like a corpse' because, confronted by the inefficacy of that which she habitually lives by, her mind and her will, she has no living centre from which to act; she is 'decentralized'. It is the fifth sentence, however, the sentence which seems at first to strain at a rather wilful heightening, that lends the experience a wider significance. The words 'dissolution' and 'corruption' in this sentence have the same force as they have in the more readily understandable context of Birkin's reflections on the African statue: in that passage, it will be remembered, the beetles are

[1] *D. H. Lawrence: Novelist*, pp. 183–91.   [2] *Ibid.*, pp. 188–9.

said to 'live purely within the world of corruption and cold dissolution'. Hermione, as I have previously remarked, typifies a different but related sort of 'dissolution', and–forced by Birkin–she experiences a mystical sense of her own 'disintegration', seeming to apprehend the extent to which a potentially vital union of mind and body has in her been 'reduced' to the deathly sterility of a will-driven intellectuality. And just as the African carvings represent the highest pitch of a mindless civilization, the culture of an 'ultimate *physical* consciousness'[1] which sharply defines its own limitation, Hermione's breakdown is anticipatory of the end of a culture of ultimate *mental* consciousness which is represented by Breadalby. Lawrence's view of her, I imagine, is similar to his estimate of certain Dostoievsky characters, of whom he wrote to Middleton Murry and Katherine Mansfield in 1916: 'The men who represent the will, the pure mental, social, rational, absolved will, Ivan Karamazov, and Pyotr Stepanovitch, and Gavril, they represent the last stages of our social development, the human being become mechanical, absolved from all relation.'[2] That Hermione is intended to have this sort of representative significance, and that the stage of development she exemplifies is putrescence is explicitly borne out by a passage in which the intimation of her cynicism operates as a final irony, for her predicament is an unsolicited confirmation of her own dictum, that 'the mind is death':

'She did not believe in the inner life–it was a trick, not a reality. She did not believe in the spiritual world–it was an affectation. In the last resort, she believed in Mammon, the flesh, and the devil–these at least were not sham. She was a priestess without belief, without conviction, suckled in a creed outworn, and condemned to the reiteration of mysteries that were not divine to her. Yet there was no escape. She was a leaf upon a dying tree. What help was there then, but to fight still for the old, withered truths, to die for the old, outworn belief, to be a sacred and inviolate priestess of desecrated mysteries? The old great truths *had* been true. And she was a leaf of the old great tree of knowledge that was withering now . . .' (p. 329).

One of the questions that *Women in Love* implicitly poses is whether the tree referred to in this passage is not as likely to be violently uprooted as to die by natural process. A conversation at the Crich wedding suggests the answer:

'Hermione was having a discussion with the bridegroom about nationality.

[1] See p. 133 above.   [2] *Letters*, p. 327.

' "No," she said. "I think that the appeal to patriotism is a mistake. . . ."

...

' "But," Gerald insisted, "you don't allow one man to take away his neighbour's living, so why should you allow one nation to take away the living from another nation?" . . .

' "It is not always a question of possessions, is it? It is not all a question of goods?"

'Gerald was nettled by this implication of vulgar materialism.

' "Yes, more or less," he retorted. "If I go and take a man's hat from off his head, that hat becomes a symbol of that man's liberty. When he fights me for his hat, he is fighting me for his liberty."

'Hermione was nonplussed.

' "Yes," she said, irritated. "But that way of arguing by imaginary instances is not supposed to be genuine, is it? A man does *not* come and take my hat from off my head, does he?"

' "Only because the law prevents him," said Gerald.

' "Not only," said Birkin. "Ninety-nine men out of a hundred don't want my hat. . . . And if he does want my hat, such as it is . . . why, surely it is open to me to decide, which is a greater loss to me, my hat, or my liberty as a free and indifferent man. If I am compelled to offer fight, I lose the latter. It is a question which is worth more to me, my pleasant liberty of conduct, or my hat."

' "Yes," said Hermione, watching Birkin strangely. "Yes."

' "But would you let somebody come and snatch your hat off your head?" the bride asked of Hermione.

'The face of the tall straight woman turned slowly and as if drugged to this new speaker.

' "No," she replied, in a low, inhuman tone, that seemed to contain a chuckle. "No, I shouldn't let anybody take my hat off my head."

' "How would you prevent it?" asked Gerald.

' "I don't know," replied Hermione slowly. "Probably I should kill him."

'There was a strange chuckle in her tone, a dangerous and convincing humour in her bearing . . .' (pp. 30–2).

The conversation forcefully suggests Hermione's complacent inconsistency; her intellectual assent to Birkin's defence of the individual right to liberty of action is at once nullified by her reply to the hypothetical question which is put to her. Given the context, moreover, the 'humour' of her reply does not disguise the equanimity with which she, if she were able, would proceed to recover the nation's hat. The inconsistency manifests the dark side of her enlightened idealism, and it clearly has a representative value. When it comes to the test, there is no essential difference between Hermione's free-thinking repudiation of patriotism and Gerald's unabashed advocacy of it. The intellectual and the industrialist, though they might do so under different banners, would be ready, we see, to commit themselves to the same war. In the conversation at the wedding both Hermione and Gerald turn what might be called the implacable other cheek of the benevolent Christian idealism on which their civilization is nominally based.[1]

The strangeness of Hermione's behaviour when the decisive question is put, the way in which she slowly turns to the bride 'as if drugged', is an interesting precedent to her reaction when she absorbs what Birkin has said about the Chinese drawing: 'Hermione looked at him along her narrow, pallid cheeks. Her eyes were strange and drugged, heavy under their heavy, drooping lids' (p. 99)–and indeed her theoretical readiness to kill for a hat is paralleled by her actual attempt to murder Birkin. Birkin, so to speak, is continually snatching her hat off her head. After F. R. Leavis's analysis of what lies behind the attack on Birkin, it should no longer be possible for a critic to say that the scene is 'so emotionally melodramatic as to be almost comic'.[2] That Hermione's rage should issue in the murderous attack on Birkin is a logical extension not only of her deep desire to

[1] That Lawrence intended the conversation to have the sort of significance I have attributed to it is, I think, borne out by portions of a letter he wrote to Catherine Carswell in July 1916: 'This is what Christ's weeping over Jerusalem has brought us to, a whole Jerusalem offering itself to the Cross. To me, this is infinitely more terrifying than Pharisees and Publicans and Sinners taking *their* way to death. This is what the love of our neighbour has brought us to, that, because one man dies, we all die. . . .

'There needs something else besides the love of the neighbour. If all my neighbours chose to go down the slope to Hell, that is no reason why I should go with them. I know in my own soul a truth, a right, and no amount of neighbours can weight it out of the balance. I know that, for me, the war is wrong. I know that if the Germans wanted my little house, I would rather give it them than fight for it: because my little house is not important enough to me. If another man must fight for his house, the more's the pity. But it is his affair. To fight for possessions, goods, is what my soul *will not* do. Therefore it will not fight for the neighbour who fights for his own goods.' *Letters*, pp. 355–6.
[2] 'William Tiverton' [Martin Jarrett-Kerr], *D. H. Lawrence and Human Existence* (London, 1951), p. 35.

kill, of which the conversation at the wedding first gives intimation, but of the inherent destructiveness of the world in which she lives: the attack is a physical expression of the urge which animates the talk at Breadalby, the talk that is 'like a rattle of small artillery'. It is also, as her 'voluptuous ecstasy' (p. 117) indicates, the satisfaction of a perverse lust, which is the counterpart of her lust 'to know'. The blow is tangible evidence of her ultimate disbelief in the 'trick' of the 'inner life' and in the 'affectation' of the 'spiritual world', and indeed it is through a curious combination of the flesh and the devil, if not also of Mammon, that Hermione finally makes contact with reality.

Beldover is reality for the colliers who live there, but it is as far removed from a real meaningfulness as Hermione's customary intellectuality. Though we do not see as much of Beldover as we do of the Café Pompadour or Breadalby, it is at once apparent that it has a representative place in the national scene:

'The two girls were soon walking swiftly down the main road of Beldover, a wide street, part shops, part dwelling-houses, utterly formless and sordid, without poverty. Gudrun, new from her life in Chelsea and Sussex, shrank cruelly from this amorphous ugliness of a small colliery town in the Midlands. Yet forward she went, through the whole sordid gamut of pettiness, the long amorphous, gritty street. . . . She felt like a beetle toiling in the dust. She was filled with repulsion.

'They turned off the main road, past a black patch of common-garden, where sooty cabbage stumps stood shameless. No one thought to be ashamed. No one was ashamed of it all.

' "It is like a country in an underworld," said Gudrun. "The colliers bring it above-ground with them, shovel it up. Ursula, it's marvellous, it's really marvellous–it's really wonderful, another world. The people are all ghouls, and everything is ghostly. Everything is a ghoulish replica of the real world, a replica, a ghoul, all soiled, everything sordid. It's like being mad, Ursula."

'The sisters were crossing a black path through a dark, soiled field. On the left was a large landscape, a valley with collieries, and opposite hills with cornfields and woods, all blackened with distance, as if seen through a veil of crape . . .' (pp. 11–12).

Beldover, like Wiggiston, which Ursula visits in *The Rainbow*,[1] is a gruesome imitation of a town. There is the same 'amorphous ugliness',

[1] See pp. 113–14 above.

and the 'sooty' cabbages and 'soiled' fields point in a sadly similar way to the defacement of the once healthy countryside. But where Wiggiston was 'like a skin-disease', it is indicative of Lawrence's sharper bitterness in *Women in Love* that Beldover, which is separated by a 'veil of crape' from the cornfields and woods, is like a town of the dead. Moreover, it is clearly not accidental–for the beetle is as portentous an insect in this book as the wasp in *A Passage to India*–that Gudrun should respond to the underworld existence which Beldover suggests to her by feeling 'like a beetle toiling in the dust'. The full significance of this opening description is revealed later, in the chapter ('The Industrial Magnate') which analyses what Gerald does to the colliers in the mines. As Gudrun remarks, Beldover is what the colliers shovel up from underground.

Shortlands, where the Criches live, is screened by a wooded hill from the collieries which support its opulence, but the 'industrial sea . . . [surges] in coal-blackened tides against the grounds of the house' (p. 249). It is, so to speak, the home of industry, and it is at once suggestive that 'there [is] a strange freedom, that almost [amounts] to anarchy, in the house' (p. 30). The existence of a state of near-anarchy in the house is immediately attributable to the invalidism of the head of the family and to the fact that Gerald, at Shortlands, does not yet exercise the authority he has assumed in the mines; it is also an intimation of the anarchic principle which both men, in their very different ways, represent in the world of industry.

Thomas Crich tries to smooth the harshness of the economic machine he controls by oiling it with a Christian humanitarianism. Believing that 'in Christ' he is 'one with his workmen', and that 'through poverty and labour' they are 'nearer to God than he' (p. 242), he translates *caritas* into charity, and attempts to mitigate the practices of large-scale industry by encouraging appeals to his heart. But his charity is, of course, corrupting in its effects, and it stimulates a mutual parasitism between donor and recipient. It draws the 'worst sort' among the colliers and their women, who come 'crawling', ready to feed 'on the living body of the public like lice' (p. 242); for Thomas Crich himself it becomes a means of easy self-gratification, and he seems to his wife like 'some subtle funeral bird, feeding on the miseries of the people' (p. 244). She revolts passionately against his philanthropy but, being unable to prevent him from its pursuit, she is driven 'almost mad' and '[wanders] about the house and about the surrounding country, staring keenly and seeing nothing' (p. 244). Just

as Hermione's intellectualism leads, in the end, to the attack on
Birkin, so Crich's 'spirituality' has for an obverse the destructiveness
of his relationship with his wife: theirs is 'a relation of utter inter-
destruction'(p. 244). That, in defiance of the truth of their relationship,
he should always say to himself 'how happy he [has] been, how he
[has] loved her with a pure and consuming love ever since he [knew]
her' (p. 245) stresses the capacity for self-deception which also characterizes his attitude to the facts of the mining industry.

It is by promulgating a belief in spiritual equality–in Christ he is one
with his workmen–that Thomas Crich becomes an anarchic force in
the mines. An apt comment on this doctrine is provided by Birkin,
who (in regard to a similar belief of Hermione's) maintains that 'one
man isn't any better than another, not because they are equal, but
because they are intrinsically *other*, that there is no term of comparison', and insists that 'spiritually there is pure difference' (pp.
115–16). Crich's colliers confuse the issue still further by driving his
ethics to an economic conclusion: manifesting a 'will for chaos'
(p. 255), they press for a complementary functional equality. But their
'passion for equality' is not easily distinguished from 'the passion of
cupidity' when they refuse to accept a reduction in their wages and
the Masters' Federation imposes a lock-out: 'Seething mobs of men
[march] about, their faces lighted up as for holy war, with a smoke of
cupidity' (p. 253). Their simmering destructiveness finally issues in
violence, a pit-head being set on fire and a man shot dead before
soldiers manage to disperse the rioting mob.

In Gerald the 'will for chaos' is subtly rationalized into a will to
power, but the changes he institutes in the mines are a product of
the same anarchic tendency. When he takes over the running of the
mines from his father, he has a 'vision of power': seeing himself as 'the
God of the machine', and believing that 'Man's will' is the 'only
absolute', he seeks the 'pure fulfilment of his own will' in a struggle
to subjugate both man and matter to his own ends (pp. 250–1). His
immediate objective is the profitable extraction of coal from the
earth, and in order to make this as efficient a process as possible, he
ruthlessly abandons his father's humanitarianism and substitutes for
the miners' dream of functional equality the rigid fact of their graded
instrumentality. In place of the 'silliness' of the 'whole democratic-
equality problem' he seeks to construct a mechanism which will contain 'perfect instruments in perfect organization', and the 'inhuman
principle in the mechanism' inspires him with an 'almost religious

exaltation' (pp. 255–6)–a demonic transformation, this, of his father's Christianity.

The way in which Gerald implements his reforms and the nature of the miners' response to them is described in one of the most powerful passages in the novel, a passage remarkable for its penetrative insight:

'Gradually Gerald got hold of everything. And then began the great reform. Expert engineers were introduced in every department. An enormous electric plant was installed, both for lighting and for haulage underground, and for power. The electricity was carried into every mine. New machinery was brought from America, such as the miners had never seen before, great iron men, as the cutting machines were called, and unusual appliances. The working of the pits was thoroughly changed, all the control was taken out of the hands of the miners, the butty system was abolished. Everything was run on the most accurate and delicate scientific method, educated and expert men were in control everywhere, the miners were reduced to mere mechanical instruments. They had to work hard, much harder than before, the work was terrible and heart-breaking in its mechanicalness.

'But they submitted to it all. The joy went out of their lives, the hope seemed to perish as they became more and more mechanized. And yet they accepted the new conditions. They even got a further satisfaction out of them. At first they hated Gerald Crich, they swore to do something to him, to murder him. But as time went on, they accepted everything with some fatal satisfaction. Gerald was their high priest, he represented the religion they really felt. His father was forgotten already. There was a new world, a new order, strict, terrible, inhuman, but satisfying in its very destructiveness. The men were satisfied to belong to the great and wonderful machine, even whilst it destroyed them. It was what they wanted. It was the highest that man had produced, the most wonderful and superhuman. They were exalted by belonging to this great and superhuman system which was beyond feeling or reason, something really godlike. Their hearts died within them, but their souls were satisfied. It was what they wanted. Otherwise Gerald could never have done what he did. He was just ahead of them in giving them what they wanted, this participation in a great and perfect system that subjected life to pure mathematical principles. This was a sort of freedom, the sort they really wanted. It was the first great step in undoing, the first great phase of chaos, the substitution of the mechanical principle for the organic, the destruction of the organic purpose, the organic unity, and the subordination of every organic unit to the great mechanical purpose. It was pure organic disintegration and pure mechanical organization. This is the first and finest state of chaos' (pp. 259–60).

Lawrence's criticism of pre-war England is centred in this devastating analysis of Gerald's efficiency. It is one of the points on which the whole novel converges, for if Shortlands meets Beldover in the mines, the mines in turn are clearly a symbol of the industrial complex which is modern civilization and supports alike Breadalby and the Café Pompadour. It is not surprising, therefore, that the word 'disintegration' recurs in this passage, though it points to a kind of collapse which, in the nature of the renunciation it epitomizes, is more shocking than any yet referred to. This disintegration goes further than the dissolution into separate parts of a whole; the 'reduction' of the miners to 'mere mechanical instruments' is a metamorphosis, the perversity of which is suggested by the name given to the new machines–'great iron men'. The iron men mediate between Gerald and the miners as the vehicles of a mutual destructiveness. That the miners finally accept the machines betokens not only their nihilistic submissiveness but the deflection of their desire for violence into a quiet passion of self-destruction: Beldover, we remember, is like a town of the dead. As far as Gerald is concerned, the anarchic perfection of his system is both the logical culmination of his will to subjugate man and matter and a subtle satisfaction of *his* 'destructive demon': 'As soon as Gerald entered the firm, the convulsion of death ran through the old system. He had all his life been tortured by a furious and destructive demon, which possessed him sometimes like an insanity. This temper now entered like a virus into the firm . . .' (p. 257). His activity in the mines, that is to say, is fundamentally a sublimation of the sort of urges which lead him as a boy to kill his brother 'accidentally' (Birkin points the moral for us here by reflecting that there is no such thing as accident: 'It all hung together, in the deepest sense' (p. 28)) and to long to go with the soldiers to shoot the rioting miners (p. 254). But at the same time his demon proves to be ultimately self-destructive. The system Gerald devises is so perfect that he becomes not so much the God of the machine as a superior instrument, and he eventually realizes that he himself is 'hardly necessary any more' (p. 261). He is consequently thrown back on his resources as a man–only to discover that he has exhausted them in service of the machine. He finds that, outside the mines, he has no identity: he does 'not [know] what he [is]', and he fears that his eyes are 'blue false bubbles' that may 'burst in a moment and leave clear annihilation' (p. 261). The bubbles take us by way of the Pompadour to Halliday's African carvings–those central symbols of disintegration–and to Birkin's further reflections on the beetle-faced woman:

'There remained this way, this awful African process, to be fulfilled. It would be done differently by the white races. The white races, having the Arctic north behind them, the vast abstraction of ice and snow, would fulfil a mystery of ice-destructive knowledge, snow-abstract annihilation. Whereas the West Africans, controlled by the burning death-abstraction of the Sahara, had been fulfilled in sun-destruction, the putrescent mystery of sun-rays. . . .

'Birkin thought of Gerald. He was one of these strange white wonderful demons from the north, fulfilled in the destructive frost mystery. And was he fated to pass away in this knowledge, this one process of frost-knowledge, death by perfect cold? Was he a messenger, an omen of the universal dissolution into whiteness and snow?' (pp. 286–7).

The references to Gerald are unnecessarily explicit. It seems clear without them that by taking 'the first great step in undoing', by substituting 'the mechanical principle for the organic' in his organization of the mines, he initiates the northern miners in 'a mystery of ice-destructive knowledge, snow-abstract annihilation', and that his own actual dissolution in the snow is the physical counterpart of a 'mystical' disintegration. But if Gerald's death by perfect cold has an ominous social significance, it is convincingly precipitated by a personal breakdown. As always in Lawrence, what a man stands for in the 'man's world' is revealed and tested in his personal relations, and Gerald's death is the outcome of his relationship with Gudrun.

The struggle between Gerald and Gudrun is concluded high up in the Alps when they go with Birkin and Ursula to a Tyrolese mountain resort. The description of the view from the hostel at once establishes the significance of this, the fifth, 'world' of the novel:

'[Gudrun] went and crouched down in front of the window, curious.

' "Oh, but this– !" she cried involuntarily, almost in pain.

'In front was a valley shut in under the sky, the last huge slopes of snow and black rock, and at the end, like the navel of the earth, a white-folded wall, and two peaks glimmering in the late light. Straight in front ran the cradle of silent snow, between the great slopes that were fringed with a little roughness of pine trees, like hair, round the base. But the cradle of snow ran on to the eternal closing-in, where the walls of snow and rock rose impenetrable, and the mountain peaks above were in heaven immediate. This was the centre, the knot, the navel of the world, where the earth belonged to the skies, pure, unapproachable, impassable.

'It filled Gudrun with a strange rapture. She crouched in front of the window, clenching her face in her hands, in a sort of trance. At last she had arrived, she had reached her place. Here at last she folded her venture and settled down like a crystal in the navel of snow and was gone.

'Gerald bent above her and was looking out over her shoulder. Already he felt he was alone. She was gone. She was completely gone, and there was icy vapour round his heart. He saw the blind valley, the great cul-de-sac of snow and mountain peaks under the heaven. And there was no way out. The terrible silence and cold and the glamorous whiteness of the dusk wrapped him round, and she remained crouching before the window, as at a shrine, a shadow.
...

'He lifted her close and folded her against him. Her softness, her inert, relaxed weight lay against his own surcharged, bronze-like limbs in a heaviness of desirability that would destroy him, if he were not fulfilled. She moved convulsively, recoiling away from him. His heart went up like a flame of ice, he closed over her like steel. He would destroy her rather than be denied' (pp. 450–2).

I have suggested that Beldover, Shortlands, Breadalby, and the Café Pompadour can be said to converge on the mines; they also cast long shadows out to the snowy mountain heights. The heights, that is to say, serve as a vantage point from which these 'worlds' may be retrospectively surveyed and simultaneously evoke the likelihood of their ultimate metamorphosis into a single frozen world of snow. It is a poetic evocation, the connection being effected by means of two images used in the description of the view. The first image, the repeated references to the end of the valley as 'the navel' of the earth, amplifies the suggestion of deathliness which attaches to the scene; for the navel, it would seem, is not to be regarded here as a symbol of life. It implies, rather, the point at which the life-cord is cut, at which the sustaining link with that which nourishes life is broken; and if this seems to posit the possibility of new, independent life, it is life of an order which on earth means death, for it is the point where the

mountain peaks are 'in heaven immediate' and where the earth
belongs to the skies, 'pure, unapproachable, impassable'.[1] The deathliness which is to be detected beneath the surface of life in the other
worlds of the novel and the death which is to be the end result of that
process of 'disintegration and dissolution' in which they are variously
caught are here exposed as a pervasive presence; the second image of
the valley as a 'great cul-de-sac' makes clear why the road from the
England of Shortlands and Breadalby runs to the Tyrolese mountain
heights. The Lawrencean implications of this image are suggested by
its use in another context:

'True, we must all develop into mental consciousness. But mental
consciousness is not a goal; it is a cul-de-sac. It provides us only with
endless *appliances* which we can use for the all-too-difficult business of
coming to our spontaneous-creative fulness of being. It provides us
with means to adjust ourselves to the external universe. It gives us
further means for subduing the external, materio-mechanical universe to our great end of creative life. And it gives us plain indications
of how to avoid falling into automatism, hints for the *applying* of the
will, the loosening of false, automatic fixations, the brave adherence
to a profound soul-impulse. This is the use of the mind – a great indi-
cator and instrument. The mind as author and director of life is
anathema.'[2]

F. R. Leavis has quoted this passage as 'immediately relevant to
Gerald's case',[3] and has pointed out the connection between the use
of the word 'appliances' and Ursula's comment on Gerald's 'go': 'It
goes in applying the latest appliances.' The passage also helps to
explain the symbolism of the mountain scene. When we relate the
cul-de-sac and navel images, it is not merely in terms of an execrable
pun that we register the direction taken by the 'mental consciousness', which we have seen at work at Breadalby and Shortlands, as a

[1] Some passages in *Twilight in Italy* lend support to such a reading: 'And the ice
and the upper radiance of snow [on the Alps] are brilliant with timeless immunity
from the flux and warmth of life. Overhead they transcend all life, all the soft,
moist fire of the blood. So that a man must needs live under the radiance of his
own negation' (p. 8).

'The valley beds were like deep graves, the sides of the mountains like the collapsing walls of a grave. The very mountain-tops above bright with transcendent
snow, seemed like death, eternal death. . . .

'The very pure source of breaking-down, decomposition, the very quick of
cold death, is the snowy mountain-peak above. . . .' (p. 280).
[2] *Psychoanalysis and the Unconscious*, pp. 126–7.   [3] *D. H. Lawrence: Novelist*, p. 157.

dead end. The 'blind valley' is a symbolic equivalent of the 'vast abstraction of ice and snow' of the Arctic north that Birkin conceives the white races to have behind them, destining them to 'fulfil a mystery of ice-destructive knowledge, snow-abstract annihilation'.

The cul-de-sac, therefore, is another focal point of the novel, and it is an integral part of the total design that a further line should lead from it to Loerke. The German artist is the most impressive–and the most sinister–person whom the English party encounter at the hostel. He is a reptilian figure, who gives the impression of being more closely related to the mud than to the snow of the Alpine setting, but it is through his concept of art as an end in itself that his place in the pattern becomes clear. He maintains that a work of art 'has nothing to do with anything but itself', and that 'the relative work of action' must not be confused with 'the absolute world of art' (p. 484). Gudrun enthusiastically supports Loerke's claim, but Ursula insists–and we are called on to endorse her statement–that 'the world of art is only the truth about the real world' (p. 485), thus indicating to us that the path followed by Loerke and Gudrun in their art leads to yet another impasse. An art which is cut off from life can be said to be 'disintegrative'; it is not by chance that Loerke likes 'the West African wooden figures, the Aztec art, Mexican and Central American', and that he takes refuge with Gudrun in 'the suggestion of primitive art', worshipping 'the inner mysteries of sensation' (p. 504).

Loerke, however, is disdainfully inconsistent, and though he agrees with Gudrun's contention that art 'stands in another world' while the artist is in 'this world' (p. 484), his art is rooted firmly enough in the sort of world represented by Beldover and Shortlands. He finds 'machinery and the acts of labour . . . extremely, maddeningly beautiful', and he believes that 'art should *interpret* industry as art once interpreted religion' (p. 477). He is, indeed, a better interpreter of industry than he realizes. He is doing a frieze for a granite factory in Cologne, and he describes it as a 'representation of a fair, with peasants and artisans in an orgy of enjoyment . . . whirling ridiculously in roundabouts' (p. 476). When Gudrun challenges him to explain how his fair interprets industry, he maintains that a man at a fair fulfils 'the counterpart of labour–the machine works him instead of he the machine' (p. 477); aware of Gerald's anarchic activity in the mines, we realize that the real significance of the frieze is that it is 'a frenzy of chaotic motion'.

By introducing Loerke so late in the novel, Lawrence does more, we see, than merely provide Gudrun with an alternative to Gerald.

II

'Between me and a woman,' Gerald says, 'the social question does not enter. It is my own affair' (p. 114); but the novel makes it clear that his relations with women are, in fact, conditioned by his mechanistic solution of that question. It is not only that women function as safety valves against the perfection of the machine he has created, providing him with his 'most satisfactory relief' from the frightening sense of his own nullity; his desire 'to lose [himself] in some ultimate black sensation' (to use the terms of Birkin's *fleurs du mal* letter to Halliday), the unacknowledged desire, that is to say, to engage in the reductive process epitomized by the West African carving, is the disintegrative counterpart of that 'mystery of ice-destructive knowledge' which Gerald consummates in the mines. It is no accident, as Angelo P. Bertocci acutely points out,[1] that when Gudrun is sketching some water-plants that rise 'succulent' from the 'festering chill' of 'soft, oozy, watery mud' and Gerald rows towards her in a boat, she should see him as '[starting] out of the mud' (pp. 132–3). Gerald, moreover, seeks to satisfy in women that passion for destruction which underlies his reorganization of the mines, seizing on a woman like Minette, for instance, as a victim, and, with 'the electricity . . . turgid and voluptuously rich in his limbs', exulting in the sense that he will be able 'to destroy her utterly in the strength of his discharge' (p. 71).

The connection between Gerald's attitudes as a man in the 'man's world' and as a lover is by no means a matter of explicit comment at different stages of the action; it is conveyed with dramatic immediacy, for instance, in the description of his handling of the red Arab mare as he forces it to stand at a railway crossing while a colliery train slowly passes:

'Gudrun was looking at him with black-dilated, spellbound eyes. But he sat glistening and obstinate, forcing the wheeling mare, which spun and swerved like a wind, and yet could not get out of the grasp of his will, nor escape from the mad clamour of terror that resounded through her, as the trucks thumped slowly, heavily, horrifying, one

[1] 'Symbolism in *Women in Love*', *A D. H. Lawrence Miscellany*, ed. Harry T. Moore (Carbondale, 1959), p. 95.

after the other, one pursuing the other, over the rails of the crossing....

'A sharpened look came on Gerald's face. He bit himself down on the mare like a keen edge biting home, and *forced* her round. She roared as she breathed, her nostrils were two wide, hot holes, her mouth was apart, her eyes frenzied. It was a repulsive sight. But he held on her unrelaxed, with an almost mechanical relentlessness, keen as a sword pressing into her. Both man and horse were sweating with violence. Yet he seemed calm as a ray of cold sunshine.

'Meanwhile the eternal trucks were rumbling on, very slowly, treading one after the other, one after the other, like a disgusting dream that has no end. The connecting chains were grinding and squeaking as the tension varied, the mare pawed and struck away mechanically now, her terror fulfilled in her, for now the man encompassed her; her paws were blind and pathetic as she beat the air, the man closed round her, and brought her down, almost as if she were part of his own physique.

' "And she's bleeding! She's bleeding!" cried Ursula, frantic with opposition and hatred of Gerald. She alone understood him perfectly, in pure opposition.

'Gudrun looked and saw the trickles of blood on the sides of the mare, and she turned white. And then on the very wound the bright spurs came down, pressing relentlessly. The world reeled and passed into nothingness for Gudrun, she could not know any more' (pp. 123-4).

F. R. Leavis aptly suggests that this scene from the chapter 'Coal-Dust' should be 'set over against' the later chapter 'The Industrial Magnate', and he points out that the scene makes us realize 'the energy of will in Gerald as something more cruelly and dangerously ruthless than, for instance, it appears as Ursula and Gudrun discuss it in chapter IV, "The Diver" ',[1] but it seems to me that the relation between the two chapters is more complex than he intimates. Gerald's violation of the mare is a symbolic representation of the outrage he commits against the lives of the miners. It is a *colliery* train that passes, and Gerald's forcing of the mare to stand at the crossing is analogous to the way in which he subdues the instinctively rebellious miners to the machine. Nor is Gerald's behaviour representative of a gratuitous, if ravenous, intensity of will; as in the mines, his will is bent to an overriding purpose, and it is concentrated here on compelling even the mare to recognize its own mere instrumentality: 'She must learn to stand-

[1] *D. H. Lawrence: Novelist*, pp. 155-6.

what use is she to me in this country if she shies and goes off every time an engine whistles', he later justifies himself. When he goes on to deny Ursula's assertion that the mare 'has as much right to her own being' as he has to his, and says, 'I consider that mare is there for my use . . . because that is the natural order' (p. 154), we register the diabolical logic of the industrial magnate, who with 'an almost mechanical relentlessness' has reduced the spontaneous struggle of the mare to a 'mechanical' pawing of the air.

The scene, moreover, as I have already remarked, is also an indication of Gerald's attitudes as a lover. The description has insistent sexual overtones, and there is an obvious sexual symbolism in some of the images employed: 'But he held on her unrelaxed . . . keen as a sword pressing into her.' Read in this way, the scene is an intimation of the imperious need for dominance, the desire to bend the other to his will, that characterizes Gerald's relations with Gudrun. And the strange coldness of his passion–amid all the violence he seems calm 'as a ray of cold sunshine'–is suggestive not only of the 'frost mystery' but also of the 'festering chill' from which rise the flowers of mud. It is yet another instance of the imaginative coherence of the novel that the passion should inevitably be destructive, and that Gerald's deliberate pressing of the spurs on to the mare's bleeding wounds should come as the natural climax of the scene.

Gudrun's reaction to Gerald's treatment of the mare illuminates the development of her relationship with him. She watches him with 'black-dilated, spellbound eyes', and from this moment she both comes under his spell and seeks to cast her own subtle spell over him–when he nearly plunges on to her with the horse, she is not afraid but cries out in a 'strange, high voice, like a gull, or like a witch': 'I should think you're proud' (p. 125). The world reels and passes into nothingness for her as Gerald digs his spurs into the mare, but his savagery is clearly appealing, and the horror he arouses in her is acutely desirable:

'Gudrun was as if numbed in her mind by the sense of indomitable soft weight of the man, bearing down into the living body of the horse: the strong, indomitable thighs of the blond man clenching the palpitating body of the mare into pure control; a sort of soft white magnetic domination from the loins and thighs and calves, enclosing and encompassing the mare heavily into unutterable subordination, soft-blood-subordination, terrible' (p. 126).

It is not only as a victim, however, that Gudrun offers herself to Gerald. With Birkin pointing the moral for us, we register that her involuntary identification with the mare reflects two radically opposed impulses: 'And woman is the same as horses: two wills act in opposition inside her. With one will, she wants to subject herself utterly. With the other she wants to bolt, and pitch her rider to perdition' (p. 157).

The violence that is coiled within Gudrun is strikingly revealed in her encounter with the Highland cattle and in its aftermath. She is dancing 'in the eurhythmic manner' to Ursula's singing when the bullocks appear on the scene, standing 'with their knees planted' and watching 'with their dark, wicked eyes'. Gudrun cries out, 'in a high, strident voice, something like the scream of a sea-gull', and then dances towards the cattle:

'Gudrun, with her arms outspread and her face uplifted, went in a strange palpitating dance towards the cattle, lifting her body towards them as if in a spell, her feet pulsing as if in some little frenzy of unconscious sensation, her arms, her wrists, her hands stretching and heaving and falling and reaching and reaching and falling, her breasts lifted and shaken towards the cattle, her throat exposed as in some voluptuous ecstasy towards them, whilst she drifted imperceptibly nearer, an uncanny white figure, towards them, carried away in its own rapt trance, ebbing in strange fluctuations upon the cattle, that waited, and ducked their heads a little in sudden contraction from her, watching all the time as if hypnotized, their bare horns branching in the clear light, as the white figure of the woman ebbed upon them, in the slow, hypnotizing convulsion of the dance. She could feel them just in front of her, it was as if she had the electric pulse from their breasts running into her hands. Soon she would touch them, actually touch them. A terrible shiver of fear and pleasure went through her. And all the while Ursula, spell-bound, kept up her high-pitched thin, irrelevant song, which pierced the fading evening like an incantation.

'Gudrun could hear the cattle breathing heavily with helpless fear and fascination. Oh, they were brave little beasts, these wild Scotch bullocks, wild and fleecy. Suddenly one of them snorted, ducked its head, and backed' (pp. 187-8).

Gudrun's cry, in a voice 'something like the scream of a sea-gull', recalls the way in which she shouts to Gerald on the mare and suggests that the scene with the cattle should be viewed in relation to the earlier incident. If she is spellbound when she watches Gerald, she succumbs to a self-induced trance here, as the rhythm of the long, rocking, opening sentence which describes the dance emphasizes.

Sexual overtones are insistent in this passage, too, and Gudrun's 'voluptuous ecstasy' is set against Gerald's cold passion. Flaunting herself before the bullocks, her breasts lifting and shaking towards them, the thrill she experiences is compounded of a dangerous courting of violent attack and a triumphant conquest of her own fear. It also stems from a fierce self-assertion in the face of a menacing maleness, and in this respect it is of interest to compare her dance with that of Anna in *The Rainbow*. I have earlier suggested that Anna dances her right to singleness and independence;[1] Gudrun dances her desire for dominance, matching her will against that of the bullocks and testing her power. When Gerald and Birkin appear and Gerald scatters the cattle with a loud shout, it comes as no surprise that, with Gerald trailing after her, the observer this time, Gudrun defiantly follows the cattle to where they have regrouped and then '[rushes] sheer upon the long-horned bullocks, in shuddering irregular runs, pausing for a second and looking at them, then lifting her hands and running forward with a flash', till they give way before her, 'snorting with terror', and gallop off (pp. 189–90). Her victory over Gerald's cattle almost at once releases her desire for violence against him, and she suddenly strikes him on the face with the back of her hand.[2] The extent to which Gerald and Gudrun declare themselves to each other in the scenes with the mare and with the bullocks is suggested by his reply when, after the blow, she softly asks him not to be angry with her: 'I'm not angry with you', he says. 'I'm in love with you' (p. 192).

The two scenes should be compared with that in which Gerald and Gudrun collaborate against Winifred's 'great, lusty rabbit' in a passion of sadistic cruelty which is at the same time masochistic. The recurrent image of Gudrun crying out 'in a high voice, like the crying of a seagull, strange and vindictive' (p. 270), reveals how deeply the scenes were linked in Lawrence's imagination; and, indeed, the import of the incident is so clearly an elaboration of the earlier significances that it hardly requires detailed analysis. It is perhaps worth pointing out, however, that whereas Gerald subdues the mare to the 'machine',

[1] See p. 98 above.
[2] At this point there is another interesting divergence between the English and American texts of the novel. In the (later) English text Lawrence softens the violence and avoids an explicit sexual reference to it by substituting 'a light blow on the face' (p. 190) for 'a blow on the face' (Avon, p. 156), and 'she felt in her soul an unconquerable desire for deep violence against him' (p. 190) for 'she felt in her soul an unconquerable lust for deep brutality against him' (Avon, p. 156).

the rabbit is removed from its hutch to be drawn–for purposes of 'art', so to speak; and that, despite Loerke's insistence, a connection between 'the relative work of action' and 'the absolute world of art' is here implicitly established. For the rest, it is in keeping with the subtleties of their relationship that, after the rabbit has been forced to submit, Gudrun should look at Gerald with 'strange, darkened eyes, strained with underworld knowledge, almost supplicating, like those of a creature which is at his mercy, yet which is his ultimate victor', and that they should feel a 'mutual hellish recognition'. Finally, they show each other the 'red gashes' they have received from the rabbit and they are 'implicated with each other in abhorrent mysteries' (p. 272). 'This is their bond or pledge', Mark Spilka remarks, 'to that future violent ripping at each other's souls which ends in Gerald's death'.[1] These three powerful and original scenes suggest the nature of Gerald and Gudrun's relationship and testify to the rich effectiveness of symbolic action as a technique.

In his direct treatment of their relationship, however, Lawrence does not merely take up the significances conveyed by the 'animal scenes' but adds to them and qualifies them. The description of their sexual relations, for instance, considerably expands the meaning of their implication with each other:

'He had come for vindication. She let him hold her in his arms, clasp her close against him. He found in her an infinite relief. Into her he poured all his pent-up darkness and corrosive death, and he was whole again. It was wonderful, marvellous, it was a miracle. This was the ever-recurrent miracle of his life, at the knowledge of which he was lost in an ecstasy of relief and wonder. And she, subject, received him as a vessel filled with his bitter potion of death. She had no power at this crisis to resist. The terrible frictional violence of death filled her, and she received it in an ecstasy of subjection, in throes of acute, violent sensation....

'And she, she was the great bath of life, he worshipped her. Mother and substance of all life she was. And he, child and man, received of her and was made whole. His pure body was almost killed. But the miraculous, soft effluence of her breast suffused over him, over his seared, damaged brain, like a healing lymph, like a soft, soothing flow of life itself, perfect as if he were bathed in the womb again....

'He buried his small, hard head between her breasts and pressed her breasts against him with his hands. And she with quivering hands

[1] *The Love Ethic*, p. 136.

pressed his head against her, as he lay suffused out, and she lay fully conscious. The lovely creative warmth flooded through him like a sleep of fecundity within the womb. Ah, if only she would grant him the flow of this living effluence, he would be restored, he would be complete again. He was afraid she would deny him before it was finished. Like a child at the breast, he cleaved intensely to her, and she could not put him away. And his seared, ruined membrane relaxed, softened, that which was seared and stiff and blasted yielded again, became soft and flexible, palpitating with new life. He was infinitely grateful, as to God, or as an infant is at its mother's breast. He was glad and grateful like a delirium, as he felt his own wholeness come over him again, as he felt the full, unutterable sleep coming over him, the sleep of complete exhaustion and restoration.

'But Gudrun lay wide awake, destroyed into perfect consciousness. She lay motionless, with wide eyes staring motionless into the darkness, whilst he was sunk away in sleep, his arms round her' (pp. 388–90).

This passage exposes the irresolvable conflicts of desire which confound the relationship of Gerald and Gudrun. I have previously suggested that Gudrun oscillates between a desire for victimization and for dominance; and if she capitulates here in 'an ecstasy of subjection' to his need of her – he has stolen into her house in the middle of the night, seeming fixed in 'an odd supernatural steadfastness' (p. 388) which she feels powerless to oppose – she soon enough resents the 'burden' of his beauty which can 'compel her and subjugate her' (p. 393). It is only a matter of time before she forms 'the deep resolve ... to combat him', steeling her soul with strength in the knowledge that 'one of them must triumph over the other' (p. 465). The first of the new factors in their relationship which emerges in this passage is the indication that Gerald's will to dominate has as a disturbing counterpart a child-like tendency to be utterly dependent on Gudrun, as his cleaving intensely to her, 'like a child at the breast', makes clear.[1] Worshipping her as the 'mother and substance of all life', he does obeisance to her as a *magna mater* figure; and it is in relation to his conduct that Birkin's stoning of the moon's reflection (which I shall discuss later) has a pointed significance. It is true that he is under considerable strain when he goes to her on this occasion – his father's death makes him realize that unless he can 'find reinforcements' he

[1] Gerald's childlike dependence on Gudrun prefigures that of Clifford Chatterley, another effective industrialist, on Mrs Bolton – see Chap. 5, p. 301 below.

will 'collapse inwards upon the great dark void which [circles] at the centre of his soul' (p. 363)–but his dependence on her becomes a continued, harassingly gnawing, and humiliating need. It is only by taking her life or by giving up his own that he can ultimately free himself.

Gerald's dependence is obviously the result of his inability to achieve a self of his own, and in this respect Lawrence again takes up the question that pervades *The Rainbow*, Gerald's predicament, indeed, being analogous in many ways to that of Will. It is because he does not 'believe in his own single self' (p. 381) that he is forced to seek reinforcement against a collapse into the void; it is characteristic that, when he first turns physically to Gudrun as his father slowly dies, his love should be selfish: he is 'blind to her' and '[thinks] only of himself' (p. 371). But 'ego reacts upon ego', Lawrence says in 'The Crown', 'only in friction. . . . And then, when a man seeks a woman, he seeks not a consummation in union, but a frictional reduction.'[1] It is the frictional 'reduction' from the union of single selves which the sex act should yield that enables Gerald to believe there is a self where there is none and that accounts, in the passage quoted, for his spurious sense of being 'made whole' again.[2] Gerald's 'selfishness', however, also has its paradoxical counterpart: a deep desire for a surrender of self. It is this desire which gives a sinister connotation to his wish for abandonment–'I believe in love, in a real *abandon*, if you're capable of it', he says, and Gudrun echoes her agreement (p. 327)–and which, in the description of their intercourse, manifests itself in images of containment: she is 'the great bath of life' and he feels 'as if he were bathed in the womb again'; he buries his head between her breasts. Gudrun, too, though she is more naturally self-sufficient than Gerald, succumbs on occasion to the desire for containment; and though in the passage quoted she is the 'vessel' that receives, when she kisses Gerald under the bridge, she is the one who seems 'to melt, to flow into him', and he is the 'firm, strong cup that receives the wine of her life' (p. 373). It is against the failure of self which vitiates this kind of love and which the love-making itself perpetuates that Birkin, of course, pits himself.

The third pair of conflicting desires is one which torments Gudrun

---

[1] *Reflections*, p. 58.

[2] The sort of 'self-realisation' that is involved in this kind of love is described by Lawrence in a letter written while he was at work on *Women in Love*: '. . . that act of love, which is a pure thrill, is a kind of friction between opposites, inter-destructive, an act of death. There is an extreme *self-realisation*, *self-sensation*, in this friction against the really hostile, opposite.' Letter to Catherine Carswell (July 1916), *Letters*, p. 363.

alone. In her relationship with Gerald she is torn between the temptation to mindless submission to him and the compulsive necessity for knowledge. Consequently, though she responds to his treatment of the mare with a 'numbed' mind, she reaches up, when she kisses him under the bridge, 'like Eve reaching to the apples on the tree of knowledge', and she wants to touch him till she has 'strained him into her knowledge. Ah, if she could have the precious *knowledge* of him, she would be filled, and nothing could deprive her of this' (p. 374). That it is forbidden fruit she reaches for is subsequently intimated by her being 'destroyed into perfect consciousness' while Gerald lies asleep beside her. She is also 'destroyed', of course, because it is into her that he pours 'all his pent-up darkness and corrosive death' as he seizes at life in her, but she too is roused to destructiveness: she is 'driven up against his perfect sleeping motion like a knife white-hot on a grindstone' (p. 391). The ultimate paradox of their relationship, the catastrophe towards which their mutually hostile purposes inevitably carry them, is that life for the one means death for the other. Death is the only resolvent.

That Gerald and Gudrun are poised for death by the time they reach the Tyrolese hostel is indicated in the passage, already quoted,[1] which describes their reactions to the view from their window. Gudrun's 'strange rapture' and her crouching before the window 'in a sort of trance' recall the ecstatic trance in which she dances dangerously towards the bullocks, but her fascinated desire for death is registered even more clearly here by her readiness to settle down 'like a crystal in the navel of snow' and to be gone. Gerald, on the other hand, feels that there is 'icy vapour round his heart' when he senses that she has passed beyond him; and it is with a sinister coldness of passion reminiscent of his attitude as he struggles with the mare – his heart now goes up 'like a flame of ice'–that he determines to destroy her rather than be denied.

When Gudrun eventually 'denies' Gerald, when she tells him that their relationship has been a failure and mockingly adds: 'But we can try again elsewhere' (p. 519), he can think only of the 'perfect voluptuous finality' of killing her. The attack, when it comes, is the culminating act of violence in the novel, in which destructiveness surges beneath the surface of life as it is lived by most of the characters. The destructiveness which issues in the attack on Gudrun is a concomitant of that which underlies Gerald's work in the mines. If Gerald seeks

[1] See pp. 148–9 above.

refuge in 'sensual ecstasy' from the redundancy of a life in which ultimately there is no need even for the God of the machine, the sensual
ecstasy is, in the end, indistinguishable from the ecstasy of murder–
Gudrun's struggling, as he tightens his grip on her throat, is for him
'her reciprocal lustful passion in this embrace' (p. 531)–and the murderous passions, the desire to kill and to be killed, are equivalent to the
passions which are gratified in war.[1] The War of 1914–18, as I have
earlier suggested, is the objective correlative of the violence in *Women
in Love*. But Gerald's destructive demon, of course, is inherently self-
destructive. In 'a revulsion of contempt and disgust' (p. 351) he releases Gudrun before he has strangled her, and wanders off to die in
the cul-de-sac of snow.

III

Of the characters in *Women in Love* it is Birkin and Ursula who are most
aware of the disintegration of life that the novel variously discloses.
When he tells her that he is 'tired of the life that belongs to death–our
kind of life' (p. 208), he gives expression to her own intuitive sense of
life as 'a rotary motion, mechanized, cut off from reality. There was
nothing to look for from life–it was the same in all countries and all
peoples. The only window was death' (p. 216); and it is their mutual
recoil from a society *in extremis* that, in part, brings them together.
Their relationship is the more momentous in that it is all they have
to set against the general disaster, Birkin going so far as to say, in an
early conversation with Gerald, that 'there remains only this perfect
union with a woman–sort of ultimate marriage–and there isn't anything else' (p. 64). It is not surprising that, rejecting the society he lives
in, Birkin feels forced to seek a new kind of relation with Ursula, for
it is clearly shown in the novel that the personal relations to which
that society gives rise are themselves an alarming symptom of disease
in the body politic.

The problem, as it presents itself in both its personal and social
aspects, is primarily concerned with the difficulty of achieving a self,
and this difficulty is seen to be at the centre of a particularly vicious

---

[1] A further extract from Lawrence's letter on Dostoievsky (February 1916) to
Katherine Mansfield and Middleton Murry seems to be relevant to his intentions
here: 'The Christian ecstasy leads to imbecility (*The Idiot*). The sensual ecstasy
leads to universal murder: for mind, the acme of sensual ecstasy, lies in *devouring*,
like a tiger drinking blood. . . .' *Letters*, p. 327.

circle. In the case of Gerald, for instance, it is because he loses all sense of an organic wholeness of being in his work in the mines that he has no independent self on which to lean in his fatal relationship with Gudrun; but it is only because he has no real self to start with, and no respect for the claims of individuality, that he lends himself to the monstrous perversity which degrades the miners to mere instruments. It is the failure to consummate a self that undermines life, and in considering the sort of relationship he wishes to establish with Ursula, Birkin fastens on this deficiency in 'the old way of love' as that which it is essential to avoid. Birkin meditates on this subject at length and with some obscurity, but in so far as his views are identifiable with those of Lawrence himself, as would seem likely, they are of central importance for an understanding of the development of Lawrence's thought:

'On the whole, he hated sex, it was such a limitation. It was sex that turned a man into a broken half of a couple, the woman into the other broken half. And he wanted to be single in himself, the woman single in herself. He wanted sex to revert to the level of the other appetites, to be regarded as a functional process, not as a fulfilment. He believed in sex marriage. But beyond this, he wanted a further conjunction, where man had being and woman had being, two pure beings, each constituting the freedom of the other, balancing each other like two poles of one force, like two angels, or two demons.

'He wanted so much to be free, not under the compulsion of any need for unification, or tortured by unsatisfied desire. Desire and aspiration should find their object without all this torture, as now, in a world of plenty of water, simple thirst is inconsiderable, satisfied almost unconsciously. And he wanted to be with Ursula as free as with himself, single and clear and cool, yet balanced, polarized with her. The merging, the clutching, the mingling of love was become madly abhorrent to him.

'But it seemed to him, woman was always so horrible and clutching, she had such a lust for possession, a greed of self-importance in love. She wanted to have, to own, to control, to be dominant. Everything must be referred back to her, to Woman, the Great Mother of everything, out of whom proceeded everything and to whom everything must finally be rendered up.

'It filled him with almost insane fury, this calm assumption of the Magna Mater, that all was hers, because she had borne it. Man was hers because she had borne him. A Mater Dolorosa, she had borne him, a Magna Mater, she now claimed him again, soul and body, sex, meaning, and all. He had a horror of the Magna Mater, she was detestable.

...

'It was intolerable, this possession at the hands of woman. Always a man must be considered as the broken-off fragment of a woman, and the sex was the still aching scar of the laceration. Man must be added on to a woman, before he had any real place or wholeness.

'And why? Why should we consider ourselves, men and women, as broken fragments of one whole? It is not true. We are not broken fragments of one whole. Rather we are the singling away into purity and clear being, of things that were mixed. Rather the sex is that which remains in us of the mixed, the unresolved. And passion is the further separating of this mixture, that which is manly being taken into the being of the man, that which is womanly passing to the woman, till the two are clear and whole as angels, the admixture of sex in the highest sense surpassed, leaving two single beings constellated together like two stars.

'In the old age, before sex was, we were mixed, each one a mixture. The process of singling into individuality resulted into the great polarization of sex. The womanly drew to one side, the manly to the other. But the separation was imperfect even then. And so our world-cycle passes. There is now to come the new day, when we are beings each of us, fulfilled in difference. The man is pure man, the woman pure woman, they are perfectly polarized. But there is no longer any of the horrible merging, mingling self-abnegation of love. There is only the pure duality of polarization, each one free from any contamination of the other. In each, the individual is primal, sex is subordinate, but perfectly polarized. Each has a single, separate being, with its own laws. The man has his pure freedom, the woman hers. Each acknowledges the perfection of the polarized sex-circuit. Each admits the different nature in the other' (pp. 223–5).

The repeated phrases in which man is described as 'a broken half of a couple', 'the broken-off fragment of a woman', and the 'broken fragment of one whole' recall passages in *The Rainbow* in which Tom is said to be 'the broken end of the arch' and in which Will realizes that 'if [Anna] were taken away, he would collapse as a house from which the central pillar is removed'.[1] The phrases indicate, then, that Birkin is pursuing a line of thought which leads straight from the earlier novel;

[1] See pp. 87, 98 above.

the quoted passage as a whole suggests that the line here curves in a new direction. The ideal relationship that Lawrence posits for the men and women of *The Rainbow* can be said to be the 'two in one' that is symbolized by the rainbow arch; the relationship to which Birkin aspires with Usrula can best be described (in the terms in which Ursula thinks of it) as a 'mutual unison in separateness' (p. 299), a phrase which registers a significant shift in emphasis. Though both phrases suggest a coming together in a union which does not obliterate singleness, it seems to me that in the earlier phrase the emphasis is on union, whereas in the later it is on separateness. Birkin, certainly, is markedly preoccupied with the idea of 'single, separate being'. What, one wonders, is responsible for the change?

I suggest, in the first place, that the change reflects Lawrence's growing awareness of the extent to which individuality is threatened in the 'man's world'. In *The Rainbow*, Ursula declares that her life's task is to be the smashing of the machine; but the machine is so massively established in *Women in Love* that both she and Birkin abjure the fight and–as remains to be discussed–ultimately solve the difficulty by withdrawing from the world of work. The increasing menace of the machine is further indicated by the progression in the novels from Walter Morel, man and butty, to John Smith, loader, to Gerald's anonymous miner, instrument. It is as if man is now so squashed by the inexorable pressure of the outer world that the maintenance of individuality in his personal relations becomes of overriding importance. For Birkin it is clearly of prime concern that what he refuses to yield to the machine should not be yielded to a woman, the more especially since he maintains that a 'perfect union with a woman' is all that there is left to believe in. To yield to a woman, moreover, would likewise mean to submit to being exploited, to being reduced to an instrument.

Second, the change in emphasis is a measure of Lawrence's changed valuation of the significance of sexual intercourse. Hitherto the sex act has had a transcendent value in the sense that it has been regarded not merely as the means by which man and woman consummate their coming together but as the means by which they transcend their separateness in a union which is greater than either. In Lawrence's own terminology, indeed, the act may be said to have been viewed hitherto as a tangible manifestation of the Holy Ghost, the unifying Third Person of the Trinity. Birkin is the first character in Lawrence to think of sex 'as a functional process, not as a fulfilment', and to regard the satisfaction of sexual desire as analogous to the satisfaction of thirst in a world of plenty of water. His 'hatred' of 'sex' is founded on the perception that it is destructive of the independence of man and woman, that, if it is once allowed a transcendent value, man and woman must of necessity be incomplete in themselves. In his insistent desire to be 'single in himself' despite his conjunction with a woman, Birkin apparently wishes to fashion the house of marriage not round an arch but behind separate columns.

Birkin's demand that the individual be primal gains in force from our knowledge of Gerald's predicament, for Gerald's relationship with Gudrun, in one of its aspects, affords an instance of the 'merging, mingling self-abnegation of love' which Birkin characterizes as 'horrible'. I suggest, however, that Birkin's demand should also be considered against the background of *The Rainbow*. It is not merely that Will's relations with Anna furnish us with an even better example of the attitudes Birkin castigates; in *The Rainbow* we can clearly see the limitations which attend the pursuit of 'fulfilment' in a 'sex marriage'. Both Tom and Will do eventually find fulfilment in their marriages but only after an arduous struggle–and without succeeding in finding themselves. Neither, in the end, is 'quite defined' as an individual. In *The Rainbow*, moreover, and it is this concept which seems to be especially pertinent to Birkin's meditations, the achievement of true individuality is regarded as being dependent on the reconciliation of male and female elements within the individual and on their maximum expression in a coherent personality; both Tom and Will, consequently, fail to attain to fullness of being because they manifestly exhaust their 'man-being' in the sexual relation. It is a typical Lawrencean paradox that, as Birkin points out, and as Lawrence consistently asserts in his own person,[1] the sex act is the means by which 'the admixture of sex' is 'surpassed', is the means, that is to say, by which the complex union of male and female components in the individual man and woman is reduced to elemental singleness, the man becoming 'pure' man, the woman 'pure' woman. The dilemma is formidable: 'man-being' is exhausted in a consuming sexual relation; only the sex act is productive of an unadulterated 'man-being'. Birkin's reflections take a disconcerting turn when, in order to resolve the dilemma, he first minimizes the importance of the sex act and then predicates a 'pure man' and 'pure woman' who are 'fulfilled in

[1] Cf. the passages from the essay on Hardy and from 'Love' cited in Chap. 1, pp. 29, 39 above.

difference' not during sexual intercourse but, on the contrary, quite independently of such conjunction. Manhood and womanhood outside of the sexual relation are no longer, in other words, to be regarded as achievements, as the consummation of selves which have male and female components, but as singular blessings.

Birkin's conclusions are anticipatory of Lawrence's assertion in *Fantasia of the Unconscious* that 'a child is either male or female, in the whole of its psyche and physique is either male or female'.[1] Whereas Lawrence takes his stand in the *Fantasia* statement, however, with unabashed dogmatism, it seems to me that in Birkin's meditations he resorts to obfuscation: we are first asked to accept the possibility of an 'old age, before sex was' when we were 'mixed'; then, while we are still bewildered by the curious phrase which qualifies the 'old age', we are told of 'the process of singling into individuality' which, even then, results in an imperfect separation between the manly and the womanly; finally, we are hastened on to the passing of 'our world-cycle' and to the coming of 'the new day' when man is 'pure man' and woman 'pure woman'. In his depiction of the relations of Birkin and Ursula, I think we must assume, Lawrence tries to inaugurate the new day, and it is because he thereby drives himself into an untenable position that his treatment of their relationship, as I shall try to show, tends to be unsatisfactory. That it is an untenable position for him is sufficiently indicated in the quoted passage by the fact that, though a key concept governing the envisaged relation between man and woman is 'the pure duality of polarization', when it comes to the individual, an arbitrary limit is set to the characteristic Lawrencean dualism. It is set, too, with such a violence of distaste–the 'pure' man and woman are said to be 'free from any contamination of the other'–as to be at once suspect. It is perhaps worth pointing out, in addition, that the images used to amplify the desiderated state of polarity are suggestive of a 'non-human' relationship: the 'two pure beings' balance each other 'like two angels, or two demons' or they are 'constellated together like two stars'.

I have devoted so much attention to an analysis of Birkin's thoughts not only because they define the nature of the relationship he wishes to establish with Ursula, but also because they provide us with a key to an understanding of the symbolic action by which their relations are, in part, developed. There is a direct connection, for instance, between the passage I have quoted and the strange scene in which

[1] For the full quotation see Chap. 1, p. 33 above.

Birkin, unknowingly watched by Ursula, throws stone after stone at the reflection of the moon in the millpond. The scene itself is a central one, and it has links not only with other incidents in *Women in Love* but with *The Rainbow*. The effectiveness of the scene is increased if we realize that the moon has a symbolic value for Ursula as well as for Birkin, and that she in some measure intuitively comprehends the meaning of the stoning. The moon that is reflected in the pond is the moon that shone devastatingly on Skrebensky, the moon that is the planet of the self-assertive, sensual, devouring woman; and the chastening effect of Ursula's experiences with Skrebensky is suggested by her reaction when, on her way to the mill, she suddenly becomes aware of the moon: she '[suffers] from being exposed to it' and is glad 'to pass into the shade', wishing for 'something else out of the night . . . not this moon-brilliant hardness' (pp. 276–7). She is 'dazed' by Birkin's obsessive behaviour, feeling as if she has fallen and is 'spilled out, like water on the earth' (p. 279), but in so far as she can understand what is occurring, she responds to his mood: after she has revealed herself they discuss their relationship, and she at once charges him with thinking that she only wants 'physical things' (p. 281). The climax of the scene comes–and it is perhaps the best direct comment on one aspect of its complex symbolism–when Birkin's soft and gentle kisses none the less kindle 'the old destructive fires' in Ursula: the fires, like the shattered moon which re-forms in the pond, are not easily extinguished, and though she at first submits to his plaintive request that they 'be still', she cannot help cleaving close to him as he continues to kiss her. It is only by imposing 'his idea and his will' that Birkin gets his way; rebuffed, Ursula puts on her hat and goes home (pp. 284–5).

I have said that the scene is also connected with Birkin's reflections on the 'pure man' and 'pure woman'. His comments, in the quoted passage, on the possessive 'Great Mother of everything' provide an obvious link with his stoning of the moon's reflection, for, putting a name to what Ursula vaguely but instinctively apprehends, he invokes Cybele, the 'accursed *Syria Dea*', just before he begins to throw the stones (p. 278).[1] In a section (which I did not cite) from the same

---

[1] Oskar Seyffert describes 'the Asiatic Cybele or Cybebe' as ' "the Great Mother", a goddess of the powers of nature and the arts of cultivation, who was worshipped upon mountains in Mysia, Lydia, and Phrygia', and he states that Syria Dea, 'a deity of generation and fecundity worshipped in Syrian Hierapolis under the name Atargatis, whom the later Greeks and Romans simply called the Syrian goddess',

passage, Birkin indeed explicitly identifies both Ursula and Hermione with qualities of the Great Mother, 'out of whom proceeded everything and to whom everything must finally be rendered up', thinking of Hermione as 'the Mater Dolorosa, in her subservience, claiming with horrible, insidious arrogance and female tyranny, her own again', and of Ursula as 'the same–or the inverse . . . the awful, arrogant queen of life' with 'the unthinkable overweening assumption of primacy in her' (pp. 224–5). We may add the name of Gudrun to the list, for, as we have seen, it is to a *magna mater* figure that Gerald does obeisance. While he is cursing Cybele, Birkin also throws the dead husks of flowers on to the water, apparently intimating, in a more restrained fashion than the frenzied stoning which follows, his determination to discard the forms of relationships that have gone dead.

Critical opinion evinces agreement, in general terms, on the immediate motivation of Birkin's unusual behaviour. It is only Eliseo Vivas who suggests a greater complexity of motivation. He finds the stoning revelatory of 'the threat and the frustration that are tearing' Birkin:

'He curses Cybele, the Syria Dea, identified–or was it, confused?–in Greece with Aphrodite. She was a terrible goddess, for she destroyed the sacred king who mated with her on a mountain top by tearing out his sexual organs. She was served by sodomitic priests who dressed as women, castrated themselves, and sought ecstasy in union with her. I take it therefore that Birkin is expressing the ancient and deep-rooted fear some men have felt towards women.

came in the course of time to share the attributes of Cybele, among other goddesses. *A Dictionary of Classical Antiquities* (New York, 1959), pp. 542, 609.

In *The Golden Bough*, which we know Lawrence read (see *D. H. Lawrence's Letters to Bertrand Russell*, ed. Harry T. Moore (New York, 1948), p. 63), James Frazer describes certain rites associated with Cybele. His description, I imagine, is the source of Lawrence-Birkin's view of the goddess as fiendishly destructive of the male: 'The great spring festival of Cybele and Attis is best known to us in the form in which it was celebrated at Rome; but as we are informed that the Roman ceremonies were also Phrygian, we may assume that they differed hardly, if at all, from their Asiatic original. . . . Further, we may conjecture, though we are not expressly told, that it was on the same Dy of Blood [i.e., the third day of the festival] . . . that the novices sacrificed their virility. Wrought up to the highest pitch of religious excitement they dashed the severed portions of themselves against the image of the cruel goddess. These broken instruments of fertility were afterwards reverently wrapt up and buried in the earth or in subterranean chambers sacred to Cybele, where, like the offering of blood, they may have been deemed instrumental in recalling Attis to life and hastening the general resurrection of nature . . .' (London, 1950), pp. 348–9.

'. . . Wanting Ursula, Birkin is also afraid that she will accept him, on any terms whatever. But it is not Ursula alone whom he has feared. He has feared Hermione and has broken with her for what he made to appear to be genuinely good reasons. Are we to gather that Birkin fears women and that at the root of his fear there is a component that he faces in the moon scene but does not dare face in its own literal terms, a component that taken together with his fear of woman leads us to the deep and sickly roots of the conflict between his need for love and his inability to accept or to give love?'[1]

This is an interesting interpretation, but I do not think it is supported by the facts of *Women in Love* as we have them. There is no indication I know of, other than the bare naming of Cybele, which by itself is hardly conclusive, that Birkin's relations with Ursula are undermined by the sort of fear Vivas suggests. The attribution of such a fear to Skrebensky, for instance, might be plausible, but the sexual relations of Birkin and Ursula, as described, are singularly free of the strain which attaches to Ursula's relations with Skrebensky in *The Rainbow*. Vivas stresses that the scene at the pond 'takes place before the relationship between Birkin and Ursula becomes intimate' (p. 259), but this is simply not the case: the following passage from the earlier chapter, 'Water-Party', is, I should say, quite unambiguous in that respect:

'And soon he was a perfect hard flame of passionate desire for her. Yet in the small core of the flame was an unyielding anguish of another thing. But this also was lost; he only wanted her, with an extreme desire that seemed inevitable as death, beyond question.

'Then, satisfied and shattered, fulfilled and destroyed, he went home away from her, drifting vaguely through the darkness, lapsed into the old fire of burning passion. Far away, far away, there seemed to be a small lament in the darkness. But what did it matter? What did it matter, what did anything matter save this ultimate and triumphant experience of physical passion, that had blazed up anew like a new spell of life. "I was becoming quite dead-alive, nothing but a word-bag," he said in triumph, scorning his other self. Yet somewhere far off and small, the other hovered' (p. 210).

This does not read like an experience which gives ground for the fear Vivas believes underlies the stone-throwing–Birkin feels 'shattered' and 'destroyed' only because he has been unable to resist what he conceives of as the destructive fire of passion, destructive in a way which I

[1] *D. H. Lawrence*, pp. 259–60.

hope I have sufficiently discussed–nor is his supposed fear fed in any way by what follows. As for Hermione, it certainly seems a random speculation to suggest that Birkin's relations with her are vitiated by the same fear. Of that there is not the remotest indication, and Birkin does not have to make his reasons for breaking with her 'appear to be genuinely good'; they are objectively established as such, and on quite other grounds. Birkin's cursing of Cybele, as I have tried to show, has a more general reference than that which Vivas attributes to it, though (as I intimated in relation to the passage cited from Frazer) the castration rites associated with the goddess make her an appropriate symbol of all that Birkin fears is destructive of the male. When Vivas further contends–since Cybele's priests were not only 'holy eunuchs' but also 'sodomitic' (p. 260)–that 'another one of the frustrations' the scene at the pond expresses is related to the *Blutbrüderschaft* Birkin proposes to Gerald and to their naked wrestling (pp. 263–4), and hence to the possibility that Birkin is 'projecting into [Ursula], or trying to find in her, what she [is] not and [cannot] be' (p. 266),[1] I feel that, in regard to Birkin and Ursula, his attention should be drawn to his own stricture, in another connection, on 'critics who inquire how many children Lady Macbeth had' (p. 267). As far as Birkin and Gerald are concerned, I shall try to show later that the significance of their wrestling is not that it points to a 'theme of homosexuality', even if 'we [use] the term ["homosexual"] in the broad sense we have learned from psychoanalysts' (p. 264), but that it helps to explain more clearly than 'the myth of the *Vulva Dentata*' Birkin's 'conflict between his need for love and his inability to accept or to give love'.[2]

[1] Vivas refers specifically here to 'statements such as those found in Chapter XXIII, in which we are told that Birkin found Ursula beautiful, beyond womanhood, but in which we read: "Yet something was tight and unfree in him." . . . it may be that the relationship left him tight and unfree, because he found her beautiful beyond *womanhood*, because he was projecting into her, or trying to find in her, what she was not and could not be' (pp. 265–6). That Vivas is forcing an interpretation on a text which cannot support it is perhaps suggested by the fact that the context of the 'statements', which he does not quote, furnishes an adequate explanation of why Birkin felt 'tight and unfree': 'She was beautiful as a new marvellous flower opened at his knees, a paradisal flower she was, beyond womanhood, such a flower of luminousness. Yet something was tight and unfree in him. He did not like this crouching, this radiance–not altogether' (p. 353). For a discussion of the whole passage from which this is an excerpt, see pp. 174–80 below.

[2] Vivas refers to this myth in an article, 'The Substance of *Women in Love*', *The Sewa-*

There is, however, more to the stone-throwing than is at once apparent. A curious remark Birkin makes in reply to Ursula, when they are discussing his behaviour, alerts us to a further complexity of motivation on his part:

' "You won't throw any more stones, will you?"

' "I wanted to see if I could make it be quite gone off the pond," he said.

' "Yes, it was horrible, really. Why should you hate the moon? It hasn't done you any harm, has it?"

' "Was it hate?" he said.

'And they were silent for a few minutes' (p. 280).

When Birkin thinks of the *magna mater* in the passage which precedes the scene at the pond, he is so unambiguous and pronounced in his hatred of her–he has a 'horror' of her, she is 'detestable'–that we begin to wonder what else it is he sees in the reflected moon that gives rise to his ambivalent feeling. A clue to the additional meaning of the scene, I suggest, is to be found in the terms in which it is described: the smashing of the moon's reflection is persistently viewed in terms of a clash of opposites. The scene is set for us, so to speak, by Ursula, for we watch it through her eyes, and from the outset we are aware of the contrast between the brightness of the reflected moon and the darkness of the water: a fish leaps, 'revealing the light in the pond', and 'this fire of the chill night breaking constantly on to the pure darkness' repels her; she wishes it were 'perfectly dark, perfectly, and noiseless and without motion' (p. 277). The image of the moon, we begin to understand, violates the purity of the dark waters, and it is the contaminating reflection that Birkin attempts to obliterate. The ambivalence of Birkin's feeling towards the moon, after he has compulsively continued, 'like a madness', to try to expunge it from the pond, may be attributed to the fact that the moon–quite apart from an esoteric mythology–is susceptible of a generalized identification with the feminine.[1] The final 'triumphant reassumption' of the reflected moon, which the dark waters cannot but contain, is in ironic opposition to Birkin's concept of the 'pure man'.

nee Review, 66 (Autumn 1958), 620. The reference is deleted from the equivalent passage in his book, but it helps to define the nature of the fear he attributes to Birkin. For a discussion of the wrestling bout, see pp. 183–6 below.

[1] Cf. Maud Bodkin's comment in *Archetypal Patterns in Poetry* (London, 1951): '. . . we find . . . in the background of the mind, some sense of the moon-image as related in man's imagination to the lives of women, and burdened with the obscure mingled feelings they excite' (p. 291).

It strikes me as significant that the symbolic action which is used to develop the relationship of Birkin and Ursula should either, as in the case of the convincingly dramatic scene at the pond, be subversive of Birkin's pretensions both to eliminate the sensual *magna mater* in Ursula and to regard himself as a 'pure' man, or, as in the case of the episode of the cats, to which I shall now refer, that it should be so palely ineffective, artistically. This incident, which is apparently intended to serve as an endorsement of the positive values which Birkin woos Ursula to acclaim in their relationship, can only be unfavourably compared with the brilliance of the scenes with the mare, the bullocks, or the rabbit, where the negative implications of Gerald and Gudrun's involvement with each other are subtly presented:

' "What I want is a strange conjunction with you–" [Birkin] said quietly; "–not meeting and mingling–you are quite right:–but an equilibrium, a pure balance of two single beings:–as the stars balance each other." . . .

' "Isn't this rather sudden?" [Ursula] mocked.

'He began to laugh.

' "Best to read the terms of the contract, before we sign," he said.

'A young grey cat that had been sleeping on the sofa jumped down and stretched . . . Then it sat considering for a moment, erect and kingly. And then, like a dart, it had shot out of the room, through the open window-doors, and into the garden.

' "What's he after?" said Birkin, rising.

'The young cat trotted lordly down the path, waving his tail. He was an ordinary tabby with white paws, a slender young gentleman. A crouching, fluffy, brownish-grey cat was stealing up the side of the fence. The Mino walked statelily up to her, with manly nonchalance. She crouched before him and pressed herself on the ground in humility . . . He looked casually down on her. So she crept a few inches further, proceeding on her way to the back door, crouching in a wonderful, soft, self-obliterating manner, and moving like a shadow.

'He, going statelily on his slim legs, walked after her, then suddenly, for pure excess, he gave her a light cuff with his paw on the side of her face. She ran off a few steps, like a blown leaf along the ground, then crouched unobtrusively, in submissive, wild patience. . . .

' "She is a wild cat," said Birkin. "She has come in from the woods" '
(pp. 164–5).

...

' "The wild cat," said Birkin, "doesn't mind. She perceives that it is justified."

' "Does she!" cried Ursula. "And tell it to the Horse Marines."

' "To them also."

' "It is just like Gerald Crich with his horse–a lust for bullying–a real *Wille zur Macht*–so base, so petty."

' "I agree that the *Wille zur Macht* is a base and petty thing. But with the Mino, it is the desire to bring this female cat into a pure stable equilibrium, a transcendent and abiding *rapport* with the single male. Whereas without him, as you see, she is a mere stray, a fluffy sporadic bit of chaos . . ." ' (p. 167).

Ursula's reference to Gerald at once invites comparison between this scene and the episode at the railway crossing. It is obvious that, though the encounter of the cats is a pleasant enough interlude, and though it is an instance of Lawrence's gift for communicating his sense of the special quality, the 'inwardness', of animal life, it is presented with nothing like the sustained power that characterizes the earlier description. It might be objected that power is hardly a fair criterion of comparison and that the account of the cats is deliberately modulated, but the power of Lawrence's writing is always a sure measure of the depth of his conviction; and if a lack of power is viewed here as a limitation, it is by way of suggesting that Lawrence has been unable to find an adequate symbolic equivalent for the idea of 'a strange conjunction' to which Birkin alludes. Birkin's opening remarks, indeed, are a rather ostentatious prelude to what follows, and the crudity of the symbolic action in this case further sets it off from the incident at the crossing. The crudity betrays the employment of a clearly inferior technique: whereas Gerald and Gudrun are themselves participants in a self-contained and revelatory action which requires no overt comment as to its 'meaning' on the part of the author, Birkin and Ursula are merely onlookers at the random meeting of the cats, which is introduced into the narrative in much the same way as the *exemplum* in a medieval sermon, with suitable embellishments both before and after and for similar purposes of edification. Finally, we ought not to be blind to the fact that the incident, as described, is itself inconsistent with Birkin's interpretation of its symbolism. An analysis of the encounter between the cats would seem to confirm Ursula's conclusion that what Birkin really wants is 'a satellite' (p. 167), for Mino's behaviour is hardly illustrative, as he maintains, of a desire to bring the female cat into 'a pure stable equilibrium, a transcendent and abiding *rapport* with the single male'. The Mino's proudly single maleness is no doubt heavily asseverated–though 'an ordinary tabby', he is 'erect and kingly', he is 'lordly', and he walks 'statelily', with 'manly nonchalance'–but whereas the supposed state of pure and stable equilibrium would seem to demand that he have a queenly consort, the sad truth is that the 'wild cat' is very easily tamed. She starts off by 'crouching' and by 'stealing' up the fence; at the Mino's approach she presses herself on the ground 'in humility' and creeps 'a few inches' at a time; after the cuff she is duly 'submissive'. Perhaps the most revealing phrase, however, is that which refers to her 'wonderful, soft, self-obliterating manner': the Mino remains unchallenged in his manly singleness, we see, because he has had the good fortune to encounter a self-less female, so utterly lacking in an independent being of her own, indeed, that she even moves 'like a shadow'. It begins regrettably but unavoidably to seem that Lawrence has demolished Cybele only to set up a new graven image in her stead–that of the triumphant male.

Pace Leavis, who says it seems to him that 'the position for which Birkin contends in his wooing of Ursula does emerge from the "tale" vindicated, in the sense that the norm he proposes for the relations of man and woman in marriage has been made, by the varied resources of Lawrence's art, sufficiently clear, and, in its intelligibility, sufficiently cogent, to compel us to a serious pondering',[1] I must confess that I find the norm Birkin proposes, in so far as it is defined by the values he advocates rather than by those he rejects, neither clear nor cogent. I think that Lawrence's attempt to portray Birkin and Ursula's achievement of 'the pure duality of polarization' (with all that the phrase, in its context, implies) is as unsatisfactory and unconvincing as the 'doctrinal' passages in which he makes a frontal attack on our credence, and as the 'symbolic' scenes in which he presents external support for his position. The means by which they achieve 'polarity' are detailed in a crucial chapter called 'Excurse'; the title, it seems, serves as an announcement, among other things, of a fresh sortie.

Some ten pages of 'Excurse' are devoted to a description of the special kind of experience Birkin and Ursula have together and of its effect on them; I quote a representative passage, of manageable length:

'She looked at him. He seemed still so separate. New eyes were opened in her soul. She saw a strange creature from another world in

[1] *D. H. Lawrence: Novelist*, p. 176.

him. It was as if she were enchanted, and everything were meta-morphosed. She recalled again the old magic of the Book of Genesis, where the sons of God saw the daughters of men, that they were fair. And he was one of these, one of these strange creatures from the beyond, looking down at her, and seeing she was fair.

'He stood on the hearth-rug looking at her, at her face that was upturned exactly like a flower, a fresh, luminous flower, glinting faintly golden with the dew of the first light. And he was smiling faintly as if there were no speech in the world, save the silent delight of flowers in each other. Smilingly they delighted in each other's presence, pure presence, not to be thought of, even known. But his eyes had a faintly ironical contraction.

'And she was drawn to him strangely, as in a spell. Kneeling on the hearth-rug before him, she put her arms round his loins, and put her face against his thighs. Riches! Riches! She was overwhelmed with a sense of a heavenful of riches.

' "We love each other," she said in delight.

' "More than that," he answered, looking down at her with his glimmering, easy face.

'Unconsciously, with her sensitive finger-tips, she was tracing the back of his thighs, following some mysterious life-flow there. She had discovered something, something more than wonderful, more won-derful than life itself. It was the strange mystery of his life-motion, there, at the back of the thighs, down the flanks. It was a strange reality of his being, the very stuff of being, there in the straight down-flow of the thighs. It was here she discovered him one of the sons of God such as were in the beginning of the world, not a man, something other, something more.

'This was release at last. She had had lovers, she had known passion. But this was neither love nor passion. It was the daughters of men coming back to the sons of God, the strange inhuman sons of God, who are in the beginning.

'Her face was now one dazzle of released, golden light, as she looked up at him and laid her hands full on his thighs, behind, as he stood before her. He looked down at her with a rich bright brow like a diadem above his eyes. She was beautiful as a new marvellous flower opened at his knees, a paradisal flower she was, beyond womanhood, such a flower of luminousness. Yet something was tight and unfree in him. He did not like this crouching, this radiance—not altogether.

'It was all achieved for her. She had found one of the sons of God from the Beginning, and he had found one of the first most luminous daughters of men' (pp. 352–3).

The ostensible meaning of this experience in the parlour of the inn is, I think, sufficiently clear – it is the means by which Birkin and Ursula establish their 'unison in separateness' – but the experience, as described, is one in which, to say the least, it is difficult to participate imaginatively, and which leaves us both dissatisfied and puzzled. There is, for instance, the confusing issue of individual singleness. The delight they take in each other's presence, 'pure presence', suggests that what we have here is the realization of the hopes that are set out in Birkin's reflections on the relations of men and women; but it is not clear whether the achieved 'purity' is a product of the experience, or whether it is antecedent to it and merely ratified by what happens. On the one hand, even before Ursula touches Birkin, she sees him as one of 'the sons of God': the reference to the mysterious passage in the Book of Genesis, it seems, does not only serve to assert Birkin's established independence of being[1] but obscurely implies that his pure presence is also a matter of pure maleness, for the man who is 'no son of Adam' can be assumed to be free from any contamination of the other sex. This, I take it, is what underlies the related assertions that he is 'a strange creature from another world', and that he is 'not a man' but 'something other, something more'. Similarly, Ursula is 'beyond womanhood'. If, then, the achievement of 'pure individuality' is antecedent to the experience, we would like to know, for we are not told, just how it is that they are 'metamorphosed'.

On the other hand, it is later stated that their 'accession into being' is directly due to the experience itself: 'She seemed to faint beneath, and he seemed to faint, stooping over her. It was a perfect passing away for both of them, and at the same time the most intolerable accession into being . . .' (p. 354). If the experience described were a phallic one, an accession into pure male and female being would be acceptably in line with typical Lawrencean thought,[2] but the fact that

---

[1] A passage in *The Rainbow* provides a gloss on the overt meaning of Birkin's identity with the biblical giants: '[Ursula] laid hold of [Skrebensky] at once for her dreams. Here was one such as those Sons of God who saw the daughters of men, that they were fair. He was no son of Adam. Adam was servile. Had not Adam been driven cringing out of his native place, had not the human race been a beggar ever since, seeking its own being? But Anton Skrebensky could not beg. He was in possession of himself, of that, and no more. Other people could not really give him anything nor take anything from him. His soul stood alone' (p. 292).   [2] See p. 165 above.

it is not raises further difficulties. In the first place, though the non-phallic nature of the experience is stressed, it seems that we are intended to attribute to it the sort of transcendent value that is usually associated in Lawrence with the sex act: Ursula discovers 'something more than wonderful, more wonderful than life itself', but what she discovers is 'neither love nor passion'. The 'floods of ineffable darkness and ineffable riches', we are later told, that spring from 'the smitten rock of the man's body, from the strange marvellous flanks and thighs', come from 'deeper, further in mystery than the phallic source' (p. 354). I do not wish to suggest, of course, that the experience is represented as a substitute for sexual intercourse; on the contrary, once supreme value is attached to it and not to intercourse, sex, so to speak, is put safely in its place and ceases to be a menace. It is as if the experience is a means of controlling the 'old destructive fires' which, as was earlier intimated in relation to Birkin's stoning of the moon's reflection, can never be entirely extinguished. Birkin and Ursula, indeed, after they have had tea at the inn, drive off into Sherwood Forest and, on a moonless night–'It was a night all darkness, with low cloud' (p. 360)–consummate their union in a more usual fashion. If what transpires in the forest, as the following quotation suggests, cannot be said to be analogous to the satisfaction of thirst in a world of plenty of water, its 'perfection', I think, is intended to be viewed as a consequence of the revelation at the inn and its significance as subordinate to it:

'She had her desire of him, she touched, she received the maximum of unspeakable communication in touch, dark, subtle, positively silent, a magnificent gift and give again, a perfect acceptance and yielding, a mystery, the reality of that which can never be known, vital, sensual reality that can never be transmuted into mind content, but remains outside, living body of darkness and silence and subtlety, the mystic body of reality. She had her desire fulfilled. He had his desire fulfilled. For she was to him what he was to her, the immemorial magnificence of mystic, palpable, real otherness' (p. 361).

If this analysis is acceptable, then it must further be urged that the experience at the inn is presented, rather too obviously, as an expedient by which the paradoxes inherent in Birkin's position are resolved; it is presented from one point of view, that is to say, as the means by which 'pure' male and female being are attainable outside of sexual intercourse, and at the same time, in regard to the careful avoidance of any suggestion of 'mingling and merging', or of any sense of containment, it is offered as a kind of sexual contact which, by its nature, cannot be either destructive or subversive of singleness. That it is an expedient is, in part, suggested by the poor quality of the writing. There is no call, I should say, for a detailed analysis of this weakness, for it is plainly evident in the passages I have cited, and there is general critical agreement, moreover, that the combined vagueness and stridency of the style hardly does Lawrence credit.[1] The special pleading is also betrayed by the ridiculous lengths to which Lawrence is driven in attributing significance to the experience: after it, Ursula, who is said to be 'usually nervous and uncertain at performing . . . public duties, such as giving tea', is 'at her ease, entirely forgetting to have misgivings', and 'the tea-pot [pours] beautifully from a proud slender spout' (p. 354); similarly, when they are driving to Sherwood Forest, Birkin is described as sitting still 'like an Egyptian Pharaoh, driving the car. He felt as if he were seated in immemorial potency, like the great carven statues of real Egypt, as real and as fulfilled with subtle strength, as these are, with a vague inscrutable smile on the lips' (p. 358), but lest there should be any doubt as to his ability to steer the vehicle, it is hastily asserted that the Egyptian in him is duly tempered by a touch of the Greek:

'But with a sort of second consciousness he steered the car towards a destination. For he had the free intelligence to direct his own ends. His arms and his breast and his head were rounded and living like those of the Greek, he had not the unawakened straight arms of the Egyptian, nor the sealed, slumbering head. A lambent intelligence played secondarily above his pure Egyptian concentration in darkness' (p. 359).

Even if we consider the description of the ultra-phallic revelation not so much as an expedient on Lawrence's part as a failure to communicate a genuine mystical experience, it seems open to serious objection. The failure in communication means that, at best, the experience remains the author's own, personal and not transmuted into the imaginative terms which alone could secure it a rightful place in a work of art; we are left, consequently, with little, if any, idea of what it is that actually happens to Birkin and Ursula at the inn. G. Wilson Knight attempts to relate the incident to the later account of anal intercourse in *Lady Chatterley's Lover*. He writes – I omit his parenthetical page references:

[1] See, for instance, F. R. Leavis, *D. H. Lawrence: Novelist*, p. 148, and Graham Hough, *The Dark Sun*, p. 82.

'Frontal, phallic, sexuality is surpassed, and an otherness touched "more wonderful than life itself"–a deathly otherness–"the very stuff of being" at "the darkest poles of the body" by the "rounded" loins, "the darkest, deepest, strangest life-source of the human body at the back and base of the loins". . . . In *Women in Love* the implements are fingers; but, as again in *Lady Chatterley*, it is a matter less of love than of deliberate and "impersonal" "sensual reality", and is to this extent "inhuman". . . .'[1]

Though I think we cannot be sure of the meaning of certain references in *Women in Love* if we attempt to explain them as they stand, there are passages which appear to be related to the description of "the shameful natural and unnatural acts of sensual voluptuousness' of Will and Anna in *The Rainbow*,[2] and which, when read in the light of *Lady Chatterley's Lover*, would seem to confirm Wilson Knight's argument. Before Birkin and Ursula go to the inn, for instance, he thinks of how 'he [has] taken her at the roots of her darkness and shame–like a demon' (p. 343); and later, Ursula is glad to realize 'they might do as they liked . . . How could anything that gave one satisfaction be excluded? What was degrading?' (p. 464). Nevertheless, I do not believe that the incident at the inn should be interpreted in this way. It is not merely that it is difficult to reconcile Wilson Knight's interpretation with the description, as we have it, of what transpires in the public parlour of the inn; after Birkin and Ursula leave the inn, we are told that he is still waiting 'for her to take this knowledge of him as he [has] taken it of her' (p. 360). Nor, as I have already pointed out, does it seem to me that the description of the intercourse which follows (p. 361) suggests anything unconventional.[3]

The failure in communication, then, would seem to preclude the relationship which Birkin ostensibly succeeds in establishing with Ursula from being regarded as in any sense normative, the norm which he proposes being, in the crucial instance of their sexual relations, if in no other, neither exoteric nor intelligible. Moreover, even if we assume, for the moment, that the description of the experience at the inn succeeds in suggesting the means by which a 'pure stable equilibrium' between the lovers is to be assured, we cannot help noticing that the state of balance supposedly attained is precarious, if

[1] 'Lawrence, Joyce and Powys', *Essays in Criticism*, 11 (October 1961), 406–7.
[2] See pp. 105–6 above.
[3] See Chap. 5, pp. 303–9 below, for a discussion of the more certainly established unorthodoxy in *Lady Chatterley's Lover*.

not equivocal. The scene, as Ursula kneels before Birkin, is a little too reminiscent of the wild cat and the Mino to be quite comfortable, and though it is said that Birkin does 'not like this crouching, this radiance –not altogether', the disavowal, in its half-heartedness, is a disquieting intimation of what we are to expect in the next phase of Lawrence's writing, the phase which culminates in the blatant one-sidedness of the main relationships in *The Plumed Serpent*.

Ostensibly secure in their singleness, Birkin and Ursula are now ready for marriage, ready, that is, to be 'transcended into a new oneness', to consummate their separate being in 'a new, paradisal unit regained from the duality' (p. 417). The kind of marriage they wish to make, however, is more expressive of revolt against the established order, against 'the horrible privacy of domestic and connubial satisfaction' and 'the hot narrow intimacy between man and wife' (p. 223), than is the liaison of Gerald and Gudrun, and it implies no surrender to the society they despise. Indeed, it is over tea at the inn, immediately after the climactic revelation, that Birkin declares they must 'drop [their] jobs', that 'there's nothing for it but to get out, quick'; and it is 'when they [wake] again from the pure swoon' which ensues on Ursula's '[pressing] her hands . . . down upon the source of darkness in him', that they decide 'to write their resignations from the world of work there and then' (pp. 355–6). Even fighting the old, as Ursula later tells Gudrun (p. 492), means belonging to it, and their rejection of the world they know is absolute. It extends to a renunciation of all possessions, for Birkin maintains that 'houses and furniture and clothes' are 'all terms of an old base world, a detestable society of man' (p. 402), and in their determination to avoid having things of their own, they refuse to be bound even by a chair they have bought at a jumble market and give it away. Just what they will do and where they will go is not precisely defined. Birkin, who is fortunately possessed of a private income, suggests that they should 'wander away from the world's somewheres into [their] own nowhere', contending that it is possible 'to be free, in a free place, with a few other people', though he admits that it is not so much 'a locality' he is seeking as 'a perfected relation between [them], and others' (pp. 355–6).[1] In the

[1] Here, plainly, is the first expression in the novels of the project which Lawrence cherished in his own life; and his 'wandering' from country to country after the war is, of course, reflected in the novels which follow *Women in Love*, all of which, until *Lady Chatterley's Lover*, are set, either in whole or in part, outside of England. Lawrence remarked on the project in a letter early in 1915: 'We will also talk of my

event, they embark, together with Gerald and Gudrun, on the Alpine holiday. Though their decision to leave the mountain resort should be viewed, in contrast to the enthusiasm which Gerald and Gudrun evince for the cold whiteness, as indicative of the bid they are making for life, Gerald's death nevertheless forces them to return. It is with his death, so ominous in its implications for the 'world' from which they are fleeing, that ultimately they are faced.

I have stressed Birkin and Ursula's desire to withdraw from the world because, in so far as Lawrence's feelings in this respect can be identified with theirs, their attitude represents a significant reversal of the attempt, begun in *The Rainbow*, to come to terms with it. In the earlier novel, it will be remembered, the realization of 'man-being' was seen to be dependent on effective 'utterance' in the 'man's world', and Tom and Will and Skrebensky were, in different measure, condemned for a failure in manhood; it was only Ursula who could be said to have achieved full individuality. At the opening of *Women in Love* the prior struggles for integrated being of *The Rainbow* are, so to speak, taken for granted, in the sense that none of the four leading characters is subject to the limitations of 'blood-intimacy': they are articulate, self-conscious, and intellectual; and all are active in the 'world of work'. The problem Lawrence apparently set himself was that of exploring the development of individuality with ever more and more complex characters, of proceeding, as it were, to a Birkin and an Ursula and a Gerald and a Gudrun through a Tom and a Lydia and a Will and an Anna. In *Women in Love* it becomes evident, however, that true being is more than a matter of having a day, as well as a night, goal. In the end, as I have previously pointed out, Gerald's work in the mines and Gudrun's art are revealed as 'disintegrative', as an abuse of organic life; and the black sensuality of their relationship is productive of the violence which, in the novel, is seen as an inevitable concomitant of any process of 'dissolution'. What, then, of Birkin and Ursula? What are we to make of the fact that their 'accession into being' is followed at once by their resignations from the 'world of work'? Whether or not we are inclined to accept their ostensible achievement of genuine

pet scheme. I want to gather together about twenty souls and sail away from this world of war and squalor and found a little colony where there shall be no money but a sort of communism as far as necessaries of life go, and some real decency. It is to be a colony built up on the real decency which is in each member of the community. A community which is established upon the assumption of goodness in the members, instead of the assumption of badness.' Letter to W. E. Hopkin (January 1915), *Letters*, p. 215.

individuality, their withdrawal from the world–though it may perhaps be justified by the hopeless state of the society in which they
would have to live if they did not withdraw from it–must be deemed,
in the context of the two books, a serious qualification of their fullness
of being. Accordingly, it should come as no surprise that, in the next
phase of his writing, Lawrence should assiduously seek to determine
the conditions under which a return to the world is possible, and that,
given the collapse of the pre-war world of *The Rainbow* and of *Women
in Love*, such a return should ultimately necessitate the emergence of
a leader who will try to refashion it.

With the crucial Hardy essay in mind, we may also view the arduous
movement to the world and away from it and then back again as
having a different, though of course related, motive force. Unlike the
main male protagonists in *The Rainbow*, who strive to reconcile their
male and female elements but who fail to do so, and who are on the
whole dominated by tendencies which, in the essay, are said to exem-
plify the female principle, Birkin, a most Lawrence-like figure, is
presented as believing in an unadulterated masculinity. The dis-
tinguishing quality of his manhood, however, his insistence on the
primacy of being, turns out (again in terms of the essay) to be disconcertingly feminine in character. This insistence manifests itself as the
most pronounced feature of his relationship with Ursula: separateness
of being is a prime condition of their unison, and it is because the
maintenance of individual being is paramount that he urges her to
withdraw with him from the world.[1] 'Doing', 'Public Good', and
'Community' are typical attributes of the male principle as opposed to
female 'Being' and 'Self-Establishment'.[2] It is therefore on essentially
female terms, though in the name of a clear and determined manhood, that Birkin is set to live his life with Ursula. Again, it should not
be found surprising that, in the next phase, there ultimately evolves
the stern and relentless male who, in his personal relations with a
woman, is an assertive and dominating figure, and who plays his part
in the world as a leader of men.

Male elements in Birkin, which I think we must now view as existing

---

[1] Cf. Lawrence's own view: 'One must forget, only forget, turn one's eyes from
the world: that is all. One must live quite apart, forgetting, having another
world, a world as yet uncreated. Everything lies in *being*, although the whole
world is one colossal madness, falsity, a stupendous assertion of not-being.' Letter
to Lady Ottoline Morrell (April 1916), *Letters*, p. 344.

[2] See Chap. 1, p. 30 above.

in a state of insidious war with female elements rather than in a condition of triumphant and uncontaminated assumption, are manifested in his relationship with Gerald. He tells Gerald that he believes
in 'the *additional* perfect relationship between man and man–additional
to marriage', and that this relationship should be 'equally important,
equally creative, equally sacred, if you like' (pp. 397–8). His desire for
such a relationship may be regarded as expressive of his revolt against
the conventional relations of men and women, of defiance of the
'whole community of mistrustful couples insulated in private houses
or private rooms, always in couples, and no further life, no further
immediate, no disinterested relationship admitted' (p. 223); but it also
suggests, as I shall now try to show, that he is urged to satisfy longings
which, in relation to a woman, he feels compelled to resist. This is
indicated when he proposes to Gerald that they should swear a *Blutbrüderschaft*. He makes the proposal when he realizes that he must face
'the problem of love and eternal conjunction between two men', and
when he first admits to himself that 'to love a man purely and fully'
has been 'a necessity inside himself all his life':

' "You know how the old German knights used to swear a *Blutbrüderschaft*," he said to Gerald, with quite a new happy activity in his
eyes.

' "Make a little wound in their arms, and rub each other's blood into
the cut?" said Gerald.

' "Yes–and swear to be true to each other, of one blood, all their
lives. That is what we ought to do. No wounds, that is obsolete. But
we ought to swear to love each other, you and I, implicitly, and perfectly, finally, without any possibility of going back on it."

'He looked at Gerald with clear, happy eyes of discovery. Gerald
looked down at him, attracted, so deeply bondaged in fascinated
attraction, that he was mistrustful, resenting the bondage, hating the
attraction.

' "We will swear to each other, one day, shall we?" pleaded Birkin.
"We will swear to stand by each other–be true to each other–ultimately–infallibly–given to each other, organically–without possibility of taking back" ' (pp. 231–2).

Birkin later adds, as Gerald shows less and less inclination to accept
the offer, that what he wants is 'an impersonal union that leaves one
free' (p. 232), but it is noticeable that he actually lays more stress on
unison than on separateness: they, like the German knights, should
be 'of one blood'; they should be 'given to each other, organically'.

Moreover, though Birkin strenuously opposes (albeit not always successfully) Ursula's efforts to make him declare his love for her, since the word is tainted in his mind with connotations of 'mingling and merging', he proposes a swearing of love as the oath of brother-hood. In other words, the typically 'male' desire for a 'melting into pure communion', for a 'fusing together into oneness',[1] is allowed expression only in relation to a man; for in such a relation, it seems, there is no defensive compulsion, as there is in regard to a woman, to realize the 'otherness' of the partner.

I suggest that strong confirmation of this interpretation is to be found in the description of the well-known wrestling bout between Gerald and Birkin, which functions as a non-bloody, if not altogether acknowledged, pledge of brotherhood. The two men strip naked and begin 'a real struggle', driving 'deeper and deeper against each other, as if they would break into a oneness':

'So the two men entwined and wrestled with each other, working nearer and nearer. . . . [Birkin] seemed to penetrate into Gerald's more solid, more diffuse bulk, to interfuse his body through the body of the other, as if to bring it subtly into subjection, always seizing with some rapid necromantic foreknowledge every motion of the other flesh, converting and counteracting it, playing upon the limbs and trunk of Gerald like some hard wind. It was as if Birkin's whole physical intelligence interpenetrated into Gerald's body, as if his fine, sublimated energy entered into the flesh of the fuller man, like some potency, casting a fine net, a prison, through the muscles into the very depths of Gerald's physical being.

'So they wrestled swiftly, rapturously, intent and mindless at last, two essential white figures working into a tighter, closer oneness of struggle, with a strange, octopus-like knotting and flashing of limbs in the subdued light of the room; a tense white knot of flesh gripped in silence between the walls of old brown books. Now and again came a sharp gasp of breath, or a sound like a sigh, then the rapid thudding of movement on the thickly-carpeted floor, then the strange sound of flesh escaping under flesh. Often, in the white interlaced knot of violent living being that swayed silently, there was no head to be seen, only the swift, tight limbs, the solid white backs, the physical junction of two bodies clinched into oneness. Then would appear the gleaming, ruffled head of Gerald, as the struggle changed, then for a moment the dun-coloured, shadowlike head of the other man would lift

[1] See Chap. 1, pp. 39–41 above.

up from the conflict, the eyes wide and dreadful and sightless. 'At length Gerald lay back inert on the carpet . . .' (pp. 304–5).

We can be reasonably confident, I think, that Lawrence did not intend this description to be overtly homosexual in character, though there is not much evidence of what he thought about homosexual practices. Cecil Gray, who is for the most part hostile to Lawrence, reports that in 1916 he read the typescript of an unpublished work called *Goats and Compasses*, which he describes as 'a bombastic, pseudo-mystical, psycho-philosophical treatise dealing largely with homosexuality'; but since the only two copies of the 'treatise' were destroyed, one by Lawrence himself and the other by Philip Heseltine, Gray's description of it testifies to nothing more than that Lawrence was interested in the subject–though Gray found his interest 'suspiciously lively'.[1] In *The Rainbow*, however, Lawrence is clearly critical of the 'perverted life' of Winifred;[2] and in his essay on Whitman he unequivocally states: 'For the great mergers, woman at last becomes inadequate. . . . So the next step is the merging of man-for-man love. And this is on the brink of death. It slides over into death.'[3] Moreover, Catherine Carswell, who knew Lawrence well, records his detestation of sexual 'perversion',[4] and Knud Merrild, who lived for some time with him in New Mexico, insists on his undoubted 'normality'.[5] It would seem, therefore, that the distinct homosexual colouring of the description of the wrestling bout–and of other scenes (such as the bathing scene in *The White Peacock*, the sick-room scene in *Aaron's Rod*, the scenes in which there are physical encounters between Somers and Kangaroo in *Kangaroo*, and the initiation scene in *The Plumed Serpent*[6]) in which Lawrence portrays a close physical intimacy between men with one of whom he is more or less identified–is evidence of the pronounced feminine component in his make-up, of a latent or repressed homosexual tendency, rather than of any overt homosexual intention on his part.

The emotional force of the quoted description, however, suggests that the bout is meant to have an extra-physical significance, and indeed we are told that the wrestling has 'some deep meaning to them–

[1] *Peter Warlock*, p. 114. [2] See p. 113 above.
[3] *Studies in Classic American Literature*, p. 251. [4] *The Savage Pilgrimage*, p. 95.
[5] *A Poet and Two Painters* (London, 1938), p. 208.
[6] The scenes from *Aaron's Rod* and *The Plumed Serpent* are discussed in Chap. 4, pp. 202–3, 234–6 below. See the appendix for an analysis of the scene from *The White Peacock*.

an unfinished meaning' (p. 307). It seems to me that we should regard it as parallel in function to the means by which Birkin and Ursula establish contact at the inn, though in the case of the man and the woman, of course, the occasion marks their full acceptance of the bond between them; whereas here the pledge to brotherhood–Birkin's reply to Gerald's question as to whether this is the *Brüder-schaft* he wants being a noncommittal 'Perhaps' (p. 308)–is only tenta-tively affirmed. If there is a parallelism between the scenes, then the differences between them are striking. First, the description of the wrestling is not marred by any of the mystical fogginess which clings to the account of what happens at the inn. Second, whereas the con-tact between man and woman preserves their separateness, that between man and man knots them together. It might be argued that 'knotting' is an inescapable consequence of wrestling, but the refer-ences to their 'oneness', as they wrestle 'rapturously', are too insistent and (in the context of the book as a whole) too charged with meaning to be limited in their application to the merely physical facts of the tussle: they seem to drive deeper against each other, 'as if they would break into a oneness'; as they 'entwine', Birkin seems 'to interfuse his body through the body of the other'; Birkin's 'sublimated energy' casts 'a fine net, a prison, through the muscles into the very depths of Gerald's physical being'; they work into a 'tighter, closer oneness of struggle' as they become a 'white interlaced knot of violent living being'; and, finally, there is to be seen only 'the physical junction of two bodies clinched into oneness'.

It is scarcely surprising that this pledge of brotherhood should come to nothing, for Birkin and Gerald obviously stand for radically differ-ent ways of life–virtually, indeed, for life as opposed to death. Never-theless, at the end of the novel, Birkin is left to regret the fact that Gerald's death has put an effective end to his hopes of union with a man:

' "Did you need Gerald?" [Ursula] asked one evening.

' "Yes," he said.

' "Aren't I enough for you?" she asked.

' "No," he said. "You are enough for me, as far as a woman is con-cerned. You are all women to me. But I wanted a man friend, as eter-nal as you and I are eternal."

' "Why aren't I enough?" she said. "You are enough for me. I don't want anybody else but you. Why isn't it the same with you?"

' "Having you, I can live all my life without anybody else, any other sheer intimacy. But to make it complete, really happy, I wanted eternal union with a man too: another kind of love," he said.

' "I don't believe it," she said. "It's an obstinacy, a theory, a perversity."

' "Well–" he said.

' "You can't have two kinds of love. Why should you!"

' "It seems as if I can't," he said. "Yet I wanted it."

' "You can't have it, because it's false, impossible," she said.

' "I don't believe that," he answered' (p. 541).

The 'two kinds of love' which Birkin says he wanted should not be distinguished simply as love for a woman and love for a man: what is involved, as I have tried to show, is a need on his part both for firm singleness and for melting union. That Lawrence believes it is possible to reconcile these needs is suggested by the closing words of the novel, which, in their inconclusiveness, are anticipatory of the further consideration this problem is given in the next phase of his work. After the rigorous trial of *The Rainbow* and *Women in Love* he has, at last, in his portrayal of the relationship of Birkin and Ursula, ostensibly established the conditions of fruitful marriage; in *Aaron's Rod* we are, so to speak, invited to support Birkin's contention that a married man's desire for 'eternal union with a man too' is not an obstinacy, nor a theory, nor a perversity.

4. One Up, One Down: The Third Period

(A) *Aaron's Rod*

'AND BETWEEN MEN LET THERE BE A NEW, SPONTANEOUS RELA-tionship, a new fidelity. Let men realize that their life lies ahead, in the dangerous wilds of advance and increase. Let them realize that they must go beyond their women, projected into a region of greater abstraction, more inhuman activity.

'There, in these womanless regions of fight, and pure thought and abstracted instrumentality, let men have a new attitude to one another. Let them have a new reverence for their heroes, a new regard for their comrades: deep, deep as life and death.

'Let there be again the old passion of deathless friendship between man and man. Humanity can never advance into the new regions of unexplored futurity otherwise. Men who can only hark back to woman become automatic, static. In the great move ahead, in the wild hope which rides on the brink of death, men go side by side, and faith in each other alone stays them. They go side by side. And the

188

extreme bond of deathless friendship supports them over the edge of the known and into the unknown.

'Friendship should be a rare, choice, immortal thing, sacred and inviolable as marriage. Marriage and deathless friendship, both should be inviolable and sacred: two great creative passions, separate, apart, but complementary: the one pivotal, the other adventurous: the one, marriage, the centre of human life; and the other, the leap ahead.'[1]

This passage, which concludes Lawrence's long essay on education, may serve as a formal statement of characteristic interests in the novels of the third phase. It is also an indication of the transition which *Women in Love* has led us to expect. Written in 1918,[2] it suggests, in the first place, that the black mood occasioned by the War has lightened; and it presages a readiness to grapple once again with a world which had previously been abandoned in despair: the 'wild hope which rides on the brink of death' refers, in its context, to the hope held by men who, 'in the endless trek across life', leave the women and children with the wagons and go on ahead, 'running on the brink of death and at the tip of the life advance', but it may also be read as an expression of expectations roused by peace. Second, the mention of 'reverence for heroes' in conjunction with the hope of a 'great move ahead' implies the emergence of a leadership theme. Third, we note that 'the outriders' are to be concerned with 'advance and increase', that they are to be 'projected into a region of greater abstraction', of 'pure thought and abstracted instrumentality', in their journey 'into the unknown'; in terms of Lawrence's attribution of male and female qualities, that is to say, they are to be engaged in characteristic *male* activity.

In *Aaron's Rod* Lawrence is no more specific about the tasks he believes men should undertake together than he is in 'Education of the People' with which it is contemporaneous.[3] The novel ultimately

---

[1] 'Education of the People', *Phoenix*, p. 665.

[2] A letter, tentatively dated 'early Dec., 1918' by Huxley, in which Lawrence remarks that he has done 'three little essays, "Education of the People"', and asks for the address of *The Times Educational Supplement* (*Letters*, p. 459), makes it possible that the conclusion of the essay was written after the armistice. Moore tentatively dates the letter '21 November 1918' (*Collected Letters*, p. 565).

[3] I think it likely that the novel referred to in two 1918 letters is *Aaron's Rod*: 'I have begun a novel now—done 150 pages, which is as blameless as Cranford. It shall not have one garment disarranged, but shall be buttoned up like a Member of Parliament. Still, I wouldn't vouch that it is like *Sons and Lovers*: it is funny. It amuses me terribly' (Letter to Lady Cynthia Asquith, dated only 'Sunday', but placed by

implies the necessity for action in the 'man's world', but the non-particularized action which is contemplated remains a merely vague aspiration. What the novel is concerned with essentially, and what puts some backbone, if not an articulated skeleton, into the flabby flesh of its structure, is the question of 'deathless friendship between man and man'. Whereas such friendship, however, is viewed both in *Women in Love* and in the 1918 essay as 'complementary' to marriage, it is presented in *Aaron's Rod* as suspiciously like an alternative to it. We become uncomfortably aware that Lawrence so urgently desires to verify the possibility of a close connection between men that he seems to avoid considering 'inviolable and sacred' male friendship in relation to marriage (the 'centre of human life'), to which it is said to be additional but which we may presume to be an obstacle to its establishment: Lilly's wife, Tanny, though vigorously alive as a character, is for the most part kept at a distance and is discreetly absent at crucial moments of contact between him and Aaron; while Aaron's abandonment of his wife and his failure to find satisfaction in other women appear calculated to drive him into the arms of Lilly.

The conflicting desires for 'separateness of being' and for 'communion', which covertly contended for satisfaction in Birkin, are almost at once seen to be operative in Aaron:

'He recognised it as a secret malady he suffered from: this strained, unacknowledged opposition to his surroundings, a hard core of irrational, exhausting withholding of himself. Irritating, because he still *wanted* to give himself. A woman and whiskey, these were usually a remedy–and music. But lately these had begun to fail him. No, there was something in him that would not give in–neither to the whiskey, nor the woman, nor even the music. Even in the midst of

Huxley among the January 1918 letters, *Letters*, p. 427)–and: 'I am doing some philosophic essays, also, very spasmodically, another daft novel. It goes slowly–very slowly and fitfully. But I don't care' (Letter to Mark Gertler (February 1918), *Letters*, p. 432). Though F. R. Leavis tentatively identifies this novel as *The Lost Girl* (*D. H. Lawrence: Novelist*, p. 30), two of Lawrence's biographers, Richard Aldington (*Portrait of a Genius, But . . .*, p. 201) and Harry T. Moore (*The Intelligent Heart*, p. 237) suggest it was *Aaron's Rod*. It appears that Lawrence put *Aaron's Rod* aside in 1918 after he had written some eleven chapters or about half the novel as we now have it. Chapter XI would seem a likely place for him to have broken off since Aaron's relations both with his wife and with Lilly reach a deadlock at this point, and Aaron's sudden departure for Novara in Chapter XII would seem to be connected as much with Lawrence's own post-war stay in Italy and with his resumption of the novel outside England as with Aaron's desire to join Lilly. *Aaron's Rod* was completed in June 1921 (see *Letters*, p. 518).

his best music, it sat deep established in him, this obstinate black dog, and growled and was never cajoled. He knew of its presence–and was a little uneasy. For, of course, he *wanted* to let himself go; to feel rosy and loving and all that. But at the very thought, the black dog showed its teeth' (p. 31).

Despite the jocularly defensive irony of the comments which pertain, in the Lawrencean view of things, to the pernicious desire to 'give oneself', the passage is a remarkably explicit formulation of a dilemma which I take to be central to Lawrence himself. The free explicitness in regard to Aaron is perhaps due to his curious standing in the novel as a sort of second self to Lilly, the character with whom Lawrence is immediately identified. In his presentment of Aaron, that is to say, Lawrence manages both to project and to withhold himself, and though he is close enough to Aaron for personal revelation, he is sufficiently removed to be unambiguous about the uncomfortable. As far as Aaron is concerned, at all events, the cleavage of feeling alluded to early in the book manifests itself disruptively in the relationships in which he is involved. It is even projected on to Michelangelo's David in one of those passages in which Aaron sees through Lawrence's eyes: the David has nothing like the binding force of the African carvings in *Women in Love*, but it stands as an oblique affirmation, an externalization, of Aaron's own ambivalence:

'He may be ugly, too naturalistic, too big, and anything else you like. But the David in the Piazza della Signoria, there under the dark great Palace, in the position Michelangelo chose for him, there, standing forward stripped and exposed and eternally half-shrinking, half-wishing to expose himself, he is the genius of Florence . . .' (p. 253).

It is Aaron's desire to keep himself tight and compact that is responsible, at least in part, for his desertion of his wife. It is only more than half-way through the book (in a passage to which I shall refer presently) that his motives for leaving Lottie are clarified; to begin with, we take it on trust that her continual and resentful carping has stiffened him to breaking-point. We realize, however, that what he is stolidly resisting is her possessiveness, that her ranting at him is a kindred manifestation of the 'curious, irritating possession' with which their daughter Millicent 'cleaves' to the ornaments for the Christmas tree (p. 15). When Millicent wilfully smashes a ball of 'hardened glass, of a magnificent full dark blue colour' and stands biting her lip, with a look 'half of pure misery and dismay, half of

satisfaction, on her pretty, sharp face', the comments of the parents seem dangerously to expose their own conflict:
' "She wanted to break it," said the father.
' "No she didn't! What do you say that for!" said the mother. And Millicent burst into a flood of tears' (pp. 17–18).

Chapter I is entitled 'The Blue Ball', and for Aaron the smashing of the ornament sets up reverberations which are not easily stilled: 'So-this was what it was. And this was the end of it', he reflects, as he looks at the pieces, still feeling 'the curious soft explosion of its breaking in his ears' (p. 18). It is on this night that he abandons his family, leaving his wife to decry *his* limitations: 'We were all right at first', she later says. 'I was fond of *him*. But he'd kill anything. He kept himself back, always kept himself back, couldn't give himself–' (p. 56). It has been a destructive relationship, we see, in which possessiveness and self-possession clash and recoil. Aaron and Lottie are too fixed in their attitudes, moreover, for the conflict between them to be resolved. Aaron's faltering return home, some nine months after he has left it, results in a bitter scene and makes him determine on 'life single, not life double':

'As for future unions, too soon to think about it. Let there be clean and pure division first, perfected singleness. That is the only way to final, living unison: through sheer, finished singleness' (p. 156).

The way to unison through singleness is straight and narrow, and it is strewn with obstacles which impede the progress of many more than Aaron and his wife. When he finally meditates, at somewhat repetitive length, on the causes of the division between them, we see, indeed, that the obstacles are those encountered time and again in *The Rainbow* and *Women in Love*. With these books in mind we can understand well enough what he means, but it must be said that, in *Aaron's Rod*, Lawrence seems to take a lot for granted. Aaron's relationship with his wife is flimsily, almost cursorily, presented, and we have little more than the hints conveyed in 'The Blue Ball' chapter and the wrangling scene which ensues on his return to set against his partisan view of its history:

'During the early months of the marriage he had, of course, continued the spoiling of the young wife. But this never altered the fact that, by his very nature, he considered himself as first and almost as single in any relationship. First and single he felt, and as such he bore himself. It had taken him years to realise that Lottie also felt herself first and single: under all her whimsicalness and fretfulness was a conviction as firm as steel: that she, as woman, was the centre of creation, the man was but an adjunct. She, as woman, and particularly as mother, was the first great source of life and being, and also of culture. The man was but the instrument and the finisher. She was the source and the substance.

'Sure enough, Lottie had never formulated this belief inside herself. But it was formulated for her in the whole world. It is the substantial and professed belief of the whole white world. She did but inevitably represent what the whole world around her asserted: the life-centrality of woman. Woman, the life-bearer, the life-source' (p. 192).
...

'. . . all her instinct, all her impulse, all her desire, and above all, all her *will*, was to possess her man in very fulness once: just once: and once and for all. Once, just once: and it would be once and for all' (p. 195).

The discord adumbrated here is familiar. The will to dominate and the wish to remain single in marriage are hardly likely to be productive of harmony, but it appears tendentious on Lawrence's part–for I doubt whether Aaron is being exposed to criticism in this respect–to ratify the man's desire to be 'first and single' as 'natural' and to castigate the woman for hers. In analysing the breakdown of the marriage it is not sufficient to adduce Lottie as a possessive *magna mater* figure, secure in her sense of herself as 'the first great source of life and being' and representative of the deluded formulations of 'the whole white world', when Aaron's refusal to be an 'adjunct' (that is, 'the broken-off fragment of a woman', in Birkin's phrase) has, from Lottie's point of view, manifested itself in a destructive withholding of himself. Lawrence's consideration of this aspect of the relationship is equivocal. He notes that the spirit which refuses to worship a woman expresses itself as the 'arrogance' of a 'self-unyielding male', and Aaron, presumably, is condemned for withholding himself even in the sex act:

'He never gave himself. He never came to her, *really*. He withheld himself. Yes, in those supreme and sacred times which for her were the whole culmination of life and being, the ecstasy of unspeakable passional conjunction, he was not really hers. He was withheld. He withheld the central core of himself, like the devil and hell-fiend he was . . .' (p. 194).

But, by implication, he is simultaneously exonerated:

'He realised that he had never intended to yield himself fully to her or to anything: that he did not intend ever to yield himself up entirely to her or to anything: that his very being pivoted on the fact of his isolate self-responsibility, aloneness. His intrinsic and central aloneness was the very centre of his being. Break it, and he broke his being . . .' (p. 197).

Aaron's determination not to break his 'central aloneness' for fear of breaking his being is based not only on his experience with Lottie but also on what he conceives to be the result of an abortive affair he has with Josephine, whom he meets after he has left his wife. 'I felt, the minute I was loving her, I'd done myself', he tells Lilly, who nurses him when he falls ill after the affair. 'If I'd kept myself back, my liver wouldn't have broken inside me, and I shouldn't have been sick' (p. 110). This apparent justification of Aaron's *idée fixe* makes Lawrence's attitude to the part it plays in undermining his marriage the more equivocal. What lies behind the equivocation, it seems, is a failure to distinguish between extremes of conduct in sexual relations. Such relations, we are moved to urge, must surely not necessarily involve either the humiliating prostration of a Gerald before a Gudrun or the destructive withdrawal of an Ursula from a Skrebensky. Safety and sanity would seem to lie neither in a surrender nor in a withholding but in a maintenance of self. Towards the end of Aaron's reflections, however, there is a change of emphasis, and the fear of giving himself is modified into the idea of never giving himself away: 'The more generous and the more passionate a soul, the more it *gives* itself. But the more absolute remains the law, that it shall never give itself away' (p. 200). Aaron's final conclusion about love is in keeping with this important modification, but when we read it in the context of what he has revealed of his attitude to Lottie, we are not altogether convinced that it is an authentic expression of his desires:

'Love too. But there also, taking one's way alone, happily alone in all the wonders of communion, swept up on the winds, but never swept away from one's very self. Two eagles in mid-air, maybe, like Whitman's Dalliance of Eagles. Two eagles in mid-air, grappling, whirling, coming to their intensification of love-oneness there in mid-air. In mid-air the love consummation. But all the time each lifted on its own wings: each bearing itself on its own wings at every moment of the mid-air love consummation. That is the splendid love-way' (pp. 201–2).

This, we see, is another formulation of Birkin's 'unison in separateness', though Whitman's eagles are a more apposite simile for the kind

of relation envisaged than Birkin's stars.[1] The simile, indeed, is of
some significance. Not only does it suggest a relationship which is
alive; it also frankly acknowledges the moment of 'love-oneness',
even though this is balanced by the eagles bearing themselves on their
own wings 'at every moment of the mid-air love consummation'. In
effect, the simile marks the tacit abandonment of the previously felt
need of an 'ultra-phallic' safeguard for sexual contact. Though
Aaron's experiences with women tend to duplicate situations described in *The Rainbow* and *Women in Love*, Lawrence makes no attempt,
either in *Aaron's Rod* or in the subsequent novels, to follow up the
method which supposedly leads to an 'accession into being' for Birkin
and Ursula and which, in its ostensible success as a means of preserving singleness while establishing union, seems to call for emula-
tion. 'Unison in separateness', as it is now defined, has some claim to
being regarded as 'the splendid love-way', though it is evidently still
difficult to achieve. Lilly, for instance, gives a more prosaic account of
the desired relationship (the simile he uses by way of an introductory
negation being effectively expressive of the end of 'two in one'), but a
struggle for domination clearly besets his own marriage:

' "I hate married people who are two in one–stuck together like
two jujube lozenges," said Lilly.

' "Me an' all. I hate 'em myself," said Aaron.

' "Everybody ought to stand by themselves, in the first place–men
and women as well. They can come together, in the second place, if
they like. But nothing is any good unless each one stands alone,
intrinsically"' (pp. 111–12).

...

' "Tanny's the same," [thought Lilly]. "She does nothing really but
resist me: my authority, or my influence, or just *me*. At the bottom of

---

[1] Lawrence had completed a first draft of his *Studies in Classic American Literature* by
1918. Despite the reservations expressed in the critical essay, he clearly had a
strong sense of kinship with Whitman, 'the great poet' who 'meant so much' to
him. Lawrence, of course, went his own individual way, but he must have found
confirmation of many of his beliefs in Whitman, the poem referred to above being
an obvious instance of a congenial similarity of view. His ideas of male friendship,
too, are akin to Whitman's. In the final version of the essay he caustically dis-
sociates himself from Whitman's 'man-for-man love' which he maintains becomes a deathly 'merging', but in 1919 he came close, despite characteristic insistences, to an acceptance of it–see the letter to Godwin Baynes in which he suggests that Whitman's concept of male friendship may provide a solution to the
difficulties of marriage; Edward Nehls, I, 500–1.

her heart she just blindly and persistently opposes me. God knows what it is she opposes: just me myself. She thinks I want her to submit to me. So I do, in a measure natural to our two selves. Somewhere, she ought to submit to me. But they all prefer to kick against the pricks . . ."' (p. 119).

As far as Aaron himself is concerned, his deep-rooted ambivalence towards personal relations inclines him, like Balaam's ass (to use a favourite Lawrencean comparison), to turn from the 'love-way' he has espied:

'He could not persuade himself that he was seeking for love, for any kind of unison or communion. . . . No–he was not moving *towards* anything: he was moving almost violently away from everything. . . . Only let him *not* run into any sort of embrace with anything or any-body–this was what he asked. Let no new connection be made be-tween himself and anything on earth. Let all old connections break. This was his craving' (pp. 214–15).

At this juncture it appears that Aaron's black dog is triumphant, but the extreme terms in which the craving for withdrawal is expressed are suggestive of the strength of the temptation to cling to connection rather than of a determination to remain alone. And indeed, not very long afterwards, in a conversation with Lilly, Argyle, and the Marchese del Torre (which incidentally serves to ratify Aaron's criticism of his wife, for all the men unite in condemning what they take to be the firmly established *magna mater* characteristics of modern woman), Aaron is forced to confess that to break all connections is easier said than done: 'I can't stand by myself in the middle of the world and in the middle of people', he says, 'and know I am quite by myself, and nowhere to go, and nothing to hold on to. I can for a day or two–But then, it becomes unbearable as well. You get frightened . . .' (p. 289). Sexual desire, for one thing, is the spectre which haunts the isolated; and Aaron is soon drawn by the attractiveness of the Marchese's wife, despite the fact that her husband has adduced her as the epitome of detestable womanhood in the conversation to which I have just alluded. Though Aaron is aware of what he is doing, we can only expect that the cake which he wishes both to have and to eat will prove to be indigestible: 'Cost what may, he must come to her. And yet he knew at the same time that, cost what may, he must keep the power to recover himself from her. He must have his cake and eat it' (p. 294).

Aaron woos the Marchesa with his flute. She has 'a beautiful, strong, sweet voice', but when she sings for him she falters to an end, 'bitterly chagrined', after three verses of the song (p. 298). Aaron asks if he may accompany her:

'His flute was at his mouth, he was watching her. He sounded the note, but she did not begin. She was twisting her handkerchief. So he played the melody alone. At the end of the verse, he looked up at her again, and a half mocking smile played in his eyes. Again he sounded the note, a challenge. And this time, as at his bidding, she began to sing. The flute instantly swung with a lovely soft firmness into the song, and she wavered only for a minute or two. Then her soul and her voice got free, and she sang–she sang as she wanted to sing, as she had always wanted to sing, without that awful scotch, that impediment inside her own soul, which prevented her.

'She sang free, with the flute gliding along with her. And oh, how beautiful it was for her! How beautiful it was to sing the little song in the sweetness of her own spirit. How sweet it was to move pure and unhampered at last in the music! The lovely ease and lilt of her own soul in its motion through the music! She wasn't aware of the flute. She didn't know there was anything except her own pure lovely song-drift. Her soul seemed to breathe as a butterfly breathes, as it rests on a leaf and slowly breathes its wings. For the first time! For the first time her soul drew its own deep breath. All her life, the breath had caught half-way. And now she breathed full, deep, to the deepest extent of her being' (p. 299).

This description is not as innocent as it might appear. Innuendoes link it with the conversation of Lilly, Aaron, Argyle, and the Marchese in a way which suggests that woman perhaps assumes the role of a *magna mater* because man lacks the sexual prowess to keep her in her place. In that conversation the Marchese complains bitterly that his wife always puts him off if he comes to her of his own desire: 'I do not think', he says, 'in all my life, my wife has loved me from *my* initiative, you know' (p. 285). When Aaron, therefore, sounds his 'challenge', I think we are to infer not only that the wooing has begun in earnest but that he announces to the Marchesa that he is a man of a different calibre from her husband. She begins to sing, we note, 'as at his bidding', and afterwards the Marchese, whose face looks 'strange and withered and gnome-like', realizes that Aaron has done 'what he himself never could do, for this woman', realizes, in a word, that he is 'displaced' (p. 300). The implication that Aaron is here vaunting his superiority as a male as well as assuming the initiative is the more disturbing in that the passage is otherwise suggestive of a harmonious equality, of the equality of status that is to be attained in a true 'unison in separateness': singing 'in the sweetness of her own spirit', she sings 'free, with the flute gliding along with her', and later, in phrases which recall the dalliance of the eagles, she feels 'what a joy it was to float and move like a swan in the high air, flying upon the wings of her own spirit' (p. 300). Aaron is more directly associated with the eagles:

'So he left, and went to his own place, and there to his own remote room. As he laid his flute on the table he looked at it and smiled. He remembered that Lilly had called it Aaron's Rod.

' "So you blossom, do you?–and thorn as well," said he. . . .

'And now came his desire back. But strong, fierce as iron. Like the strength of an eagle with the lightning in its talons. Something to glory in, something overweening, the powerful male passion, arrogant, royal, Jove's thunderbolt. Aaron's black rod of power, blossoming again with red Florentine lilies and fierce thorns. He moved about in the splendour of the male passion-power. He had got it back, the male godliness, the male godhead' (p. 301).

Aaron's flute, clearly, has not only won the Marchesa; it has become an emblem of phallic potency, and if the eagles are to meet in mid-air, each borne aloft on its own wings, there is to be no doubt, in the drive of the overweening, arrogant, royal, godly male passion, as to who is master. Birkin, as Mino the cat, has suffered a sea change into Aaron the eagle, or, to put it differently, Aaron's flute sounds the note of male domination which is to resound in the novels of this period. It is a note which is not unexpected, for it is needed to assert the 'maleness' of a stance on the 'female' ground of 'the flesh' and of 'being'.

When Aaron finally has his desire (and when, for the first time in the novels since *Sons and Lovers*, a man is shown, through a suggestive reversal of a tell-tale comparison, to be dominant in the sex act), he is surprised to find that the Marchesa is 'not powerful, as he had imagined her', but seems 'almost like a clinging child in his arms'. He is bewildered, too, when he senses that she is nevertheless opposed to him–'In some strange and incomprehensible way, as a girl-child blindly obstinate in her deepest nature, she was against him'–and he feels that she is 'not his woman' (p. 305). In other words, if he has proved that he is superior to the maligning husband, he has only succeeded in bearing witness to the sagacity of Argyle, who, when asked (in the discussion previously referred to) whether there cannot be a 'balancing of wills' between man and woman, replies: 'My dear boy, the balance lies in that, that when one goes up, the other goes down. One acts, the other takes. It is the only way in love' (p. 287). 'Two in one', we see, has given way to 'unison in separateness', which to judge from the experience of Lilly and Aaron who advocate it, means, in effect, 'one up, one down'. It seems to be the intention behind the novels of the third period that the man should not be down.

It is perhaps a measure of Lawrence's uncertainty in the position in which he now finds himself that he should be equivocal about Aaron's reasons for breaking with the Marchesa. Aaron at first tells himself that it is 'fate, and not her fault' that he feels 'blasted', but then he is made to realize that it is his marriage which is inviolable: 'he would tell her that he was a married man, and that though he had left his wife, and though he had no dogma of fidelity, still, the years of marriage had made a married man of him, and any other woman than his wife was a strange woman to him, a violation' (p. 310). This sounds plausible, but it is not altogether convincing when weighed against his violent dissatisfaction with Lottie. It is still less convincing when we reflect that his discomfort is probably due to the cake sticking in his throat: when he returns home after intercourse with the Marchesa, he is glad that he can 'go to bed, alone, in his own cold bed, alone, thank God' (p. 308). Despite 'the magic feeling of phallic immortality', what repels him is the way she seems 'to love clinging to him and curling strangely on his breast'. Like Lottie's assumption of primacy, the Marchesa's very submissiveness is felt as a threat to his 'own central life. It simply blighted him' (p. 317). From there it is a short step to conclude that she is afraid of his 'actual male physique' as of 'a fetish, fetish-afraid and fetish-fascinated', and that she is using him as 'a mere magic implement', ignoring 'himself, the individual man which he was'. He recognizes that he too has attempted 'to strike a magic fire out of her, for his own ecstasy', but whereas 'she was absolutely gone in her own incantations', in him there was 'all the time something hard and reckless and defiant, which stood apart'. Finally, and by now the way out has been satisfactorily found, he reflects that 'she would drink the one drop of his innermost heart's blood, and he would be carrion' (p. 318). It begins very much to look as though Aaron's experiences with women must, at all costs, result in disillusion so that he will be left free for Lilly.

This, at any rate, is what I take to be the meaning of the symbolism which follows Aaron's break with the Marchesa. First, there is the smashing of his flute when a bomb is thrown into the café where he is drinking with Lilly and some others:

' "Is that your flute?" asked Lilly.

' "Bit of it. Smashed."

' "Let me look."

'He looked, and gave it back.

' "No good," he said.

' "Oh no," said Aaron.

' "Throw it in the river, Aaron," said Lilly.

'Aaron turned and looked at him.

' "Throw it in the river," repeated Lilly. "It's an end."

'Aaron nervelessly dropped the flute into the stream. The two men stood leaning on the bridge-parapet, as if unable to move.

' "We shall have to go home," said Lilly. "Tanny may hear of it and be anxious."

'Aaron was quite dumbfounded by the night's event: the loss of his flute. Here was a blow he had not expected. And the loss was for him symbolistic. It chimed with something in his soul: the bomb, the smashed flute, the end.

' "There goes Aaron's Rod, then," he said to Lilly.

' "It'll grow again. It's a reed, a water-plant. You can't kill it," said Lilly, unheeding.

' "And me?"

' "You'll have to live without a rod, meanwhile."

'To which pleasant remark Aaron made no reply' (p. 331).

If we accept that the flute is a phallic symbol, we begin to understand why Lilly is so briskly unsympathetic, so 'unheeding'. The 'end' which he imperturbably pronounces and which chimes 'with something in Aaron's soul' is, of course, to be the end of Aaron's sexual misadventures. The meaning of Lilly's reassurance that the rod will grow again is, I think, illuminated by relating it to a comment in *Women in Love*: we are told there that if Gerald 'pledged himself with the man he would later be able to pledge himself with the woman' (p. 398). That, presumably, is the sort of hope that is held out to Aaron. Aaron, in other words, has come to the parting of the ways; he must live without a rod, meanwhile, and all that is left him is the connection with Lilly – Lawrence makes us realize that:

'His flute was broken, and broken finally. The bomb had settled it.

The bomb had settled it and everything. It was an end, no matter how he tried to patch things up. The only thing he felt was a thread of destiny attaching him to Lilly. The rest had all gone as bare and bald as the dead orb of the moon. So he made up his mind, if he could, to make some plan that would bring his life together with that of his evanescent friend' (p. 335).

In the narrative the thoughts I have just quoted follow a 'strange dream' Aaron has after the smashing of his flute, and they seem to be also applicable to the dream. The dream symbolism reinforces that of the flute. At one stage of the dream Aaron finds that he is in a boat, and that he is 'two people': an 'invisible, *conscious* self' and a 'palpable' self:

'The palpable or visible Aaron sat at the side of the boat, on the end of the middle seat, with his naked right elbow leaning out over the side. And now the boat entered upon shallows. The impalpable Aaron in the bows saw the whitish clay of the bottom swirl up in clouds at each thrust of the oars, whitish clayey clouds which would envelop the strange fishes in a sudden mist. And on the right hand of the course stakes stood up in the water, at intervals, to mark the course.

'The boat must pass very near these stakes, almost touching. And Aaron's naked elbow was leaning right over the side. As they approached the first stake, the boatmen all uttered a strange cry of warning, in a foreign language. The flesh-and-blood Aaron seemed not even to hear. The invisible Aaron heard, but did not comprehend the words of the cry. So the naked elbow struck smartly against the stake as the boat passed . . .' (pp. 333–4).

It hardly seems necessary to quote the rest of the dream in full. The palpable Aaron still does not heed the warning cries, and his elbow strikes against a second, and then a third, stake. Thereupon he draws in his arm, and the boat swings steadily on, 'into the deep, unfathomable water again'. The last thing Aaron remembers is that they draw near a lake-city and he sees an idol, which he knows as Astarte. . . . It requires no subtlety to understand the symbolism of the 'naked right elbow'. The moon goddess presides over the painful progress of Aaron's relationships with three women – Lottie, Josephine, and the Marchesa – and it is only after he has been hurt for the third time that the palpable Aaron changes his position, though even then he is 'not aware of any need to do so'. The invisible Aaron, nevertheless, '[breathes] with relief in the bows' as they leave the shallows and head for deeper water, for the deep waters, I take it, of an unfathomable relation with Lilly.

Aaron's relationship with Lilly is the crux of *Aaron's Rod* though, in a curious way, its portrayal does not bulk large in the narrative. Aaron's experiences, however, which might otherwise appear merely random, seem designed to lead him towards Lilly, and that is why I remarked earlier that it is the friendship theme alone which gives the novel direction.

Lilly, the lively, sophisticated writer, and Aaron, the stolid ex-checkweighman, do not, when they are together, seem at first to have much in common, though when they are apart, as has been pointed out, Aaron disconcertingly tends to be Lilly's *alter ego*. They are attracted to each other, initially, in somewhat negative fashion: when Josephine declares passionately that she hates 'the house' they 'live in', hates, that is to say, England and America, Lilly tells her that he 'can't get much fire' in his hatred, that 'they pall' on him; and it is Aaron's phlegmatically uttered 'Ay!' that causes them to glance at each other 'with a look of recognition' (p. 77). They are drawn further together when Lilly nurses Aaron during his illness after the affair with Josephine. Their friendship is tentatively affirmed then by the closeness of their physical contact, for Lilly rubs Aaron with oil, rubbing 'every speck of the man's lower body' as if 'in a sort of incantation', until 'the spark [comes] back into the sick eyes' and Aaron 'regains' himself (p. 118). This is yet another instance of a naked intimacy between men, but if, as Mark Spilka claims, we are to regard the episode as a 'spontaneous rite' of brotherhood, as a 'sudden radical pledge to some more than casual relationship between two men',[1] we should at least be aware of what the 'pledge' implies about the nature of the relationship. This is how the scene begins:

'Suddenly Lilly rose and went to the dressing-table.

' "I'm going to rub you with oil," he said. "I'm going to rub you as mothers do their babies whose bowels don't work."

'Aaron frowned slightly as he glanced at the dark, self-possessed face of the little man.

' "What's the good of that?" he said irritably. "I'd rather be left alone."

' "Then you won't be."

'Quickly he uncovered the blond lower body of his patient, and began to rub the abdomen with oil . . .' (p. 118).

[1] *The Love Ethic*, pp. 157, 159.

The surface innocence of this description conceals weighty thematic matter in much the same way as the account of Aaron's accompaniment of the Marchesa on the flute. Lilly, we see, remains 'self-possessed', but Aaron's characteristic desire to withhold himself, to be 'left alone', which is allowed a decisive importance in his relations with women, is here simply overruled. It is overruled, too, in a manner which considerably modifies the idea of brotherhood as first advanced in *Women in Love*. When Lawrence uses a comparison involving babies or children in connection with adult relationships, it is usually significant; Lilly's announced intention to rub Aaron 'as mothers do their babies', though it is of course directly motivated by concern for Aaron's health, is an indirect assertion of the dominance he is claiming in their relationship. Rubbing Aaron, he has him in his hands, as it were. That this is the symbolic meaning of the scene is borne out, I think, by Lilly's reflections as he watches 'his patient fall into a proper sleep':

'And he sat and watched him sleep. And he thought to himself, "I wonder why I do it. . . . As soon as this man's really better he'll punch me in the wind, metaphorically if not actually, for having interfered with him. And Tanny would say he was quite right to do it. She says I want power over them. What if I do? They don't care how much power the mob has over them, the nation. . . . Why can't they submit to a bit of healthy individual authority? The fool would die, without me . . ."' (pp. 118–19).

Male friendship, it begins to appear, has also become a matter of 'one up, one down', and it is at this juncture, indeed, that Lilly, as he continues to sit and brood, concludes that Tanny 'ought to submit' to him.[1] That Tanny is said to do 'nothing really but resist' him makes it look, moreover, as if male friendship is to be an alternative means of satisfying an authoritarian impulse.

Neither the friendship nor Lilly's authority is, in fact, easily established. Lilly, differing markedly in this respect from Birkin, insists that the kind of friendship he has in mind precludes disagreement on important issues: 'I *don't* have friends who don't fundamentally agree with me', he tells Aaron. 'A friend means one who is at one with me in matters of life and death' (p. 146). Aaron knows that 'a certain call' has been made 'upon his soul', but he does 'not intend to obey' (p. 147). He is not ready, at this stage, to submit to Lilly, feeling, if anything, that he is 'superior' to him; and the two men part coldly.

[1] I have quoted the passage in full on pp. 195–6 above.

204 One Up, One Down: The Third Period

Aaron, however, remains drawn to Lilly. Determining 'to clear out' of London, which is '[getting] on his nerves' (p. 158), he writes to Lilly, asking if he should join him in Italy. Despite the apparent indifference with which Lilly responds to the proposal–'Come if you want to', he says (p. 159)–Aaron leaves England and finally meets Lilly in Florence. After the crucial incident which results in the smashing of Aaron's flute, they walk into the country together and engage in a portentous discussion that brings the book to a close. The discussion, which raises issues that go beyond the immediate question of their relationship, calls for detailed consideration.

Lilly accuses Aaron of wanting 'to whoosh off in a nice little love-whoosh and lose [himself]', but he insists that Aaron will be 'had' if he tries to 'get excited and carried away loving a woman, or humanity, or God' since it is impossible for him really to lose himself (pp. 341–2). 'You *are* yourself,' he tells him, 'and so *be* yourself. Stick to it and abide by it. . . . Your own single oneness is your destiny' (p. 343):

' "I told you there were two urges–two great life-urges, didn't I? There may be more. But it comes on me so strongly, now, that there are two: love, and power. And we've been trying to work ourselves, at least as individuals, from the love urge exclusively, hating the power-urge, and repressing it. And now I find we've got to accept the very thing we've hated.

' ". . . It is a vast dark source of life and strength in us now, waiting either to issue into true action, or to burst into cataclysm. Power–the power-urge. The will-to-power–but not in Nietzsche's sense. Not intellectual power. Not mental power. Not conscious will-power. Not even wisdom. But dark, living, fructifying power. Do you know what I mean?

...

' "And, of course, there must be one who urges, and one who is impelled. Just as in love there is a beloved and a lover: the man is supposed to be the lover, the woman the beloved. Now, in the urge of power, it is the reverse. The woman must submit, but deeply, deeply submit. Not to any foolish fixed authority, not to any foolish and arbitrary will. But to something deep, deeper. To the soul in its dark motion of power and pride. We must reverse the poles. The woman must now submit–but deeply, deeply, and richly! No subservience. None of that. No slavery. A deep, unfathomable free submission."

...

' "Woman yield–?" Aaron [said].

' "Woman–and man too. Yield to the deep power-soul in the individual man, and obey implicitly. I don't go back on what I said before. I do believe that every man must fulfil his own soul, every woman must be herself, herself only, not some man's instrument, or some embodied theory. But the mode of our being is such that we can only live and have our being whilst we are implicit in one of the great dynamic modes. We *must* either love, or rule. And once the love-mode changes, as change it must, for we are worn out and becoming evil in its persistence, then the other mode will take place in us. And there will be profound, profound obedience in place of this love-crying, obedience to the incalculable power-urge. And men must submit to the greater soul in a man, for their guidance: and women must submit to the positive power-soul in man, for their being."

' "You'll never get it," said Aaron.

' "You will, when all men want it. All men say, they want a leader. Then let them in their souls *submit* to some greater soul than theirs. At present, when they say they want a leader, they mean they want an instrument, like Lloyd George. A mere instrument for their use. But it's more than that. It's the reverse. It's the deep, fathomless submission to the heroic soul in a greater man. You, Aaron, you too have the need to submit. You, too, have the need livingly to yield to a more heroic soul, to give yourself. You know you have. And you know it isn't love. It is life-submission. And you know it. But you kick against the pricks. And perhaps you'd rather die than yield. And so, die you must. It is your affair."

'There was a long pause. Then Aaron looked up into Lilly's face. It was dark and remote-seeming. It was like a Byzantine eikon at the moment.

' "And whom shall I submit to?" he said.

' "Your soul will tell you," replied the other' (pp. 345–7).

This, as far as both man and woman are concerned, is 'one up, one down' with a vengeance, but though Lilly expounds the new doctrine of 'life-submission' so confidently in these closing pages, it is a doctrine, we cannot help realizing, that the book itself has done little to support. Lilly's own relations with Tanny, like those of Aaron with his wife, do not suggest that 'the woman' is prepared to submit at all, and certainly neither 'freely' nor 'deeply, deeply, and richly'; while even the Marchesa, we remember, who does submit physically to Aaron's 'male super-power', continues to resist him 'in some strange and incomprehensible way'. Clearly, the theme of female submission has not yet been conclusively explored. It has become significantly linked, however, to the theme of male friendship, and not only, as I intimated earlier, because it seems at times that such friendship is valued, at least in part, for the opportunity it provides of exercising an authority which is opposed by the woman; Lilly's reference to the replacement of 'the love-mode' by 'the power-mode', which will bring 'profound, profound obedience in place of this love-crying', obscurely implies that a man's willing submission to the 'greater soul' in another man may perhaps be a means of inducing the woman to submit as well.[1] The interaction of these two themes is investigated further in *Kangaroo* and *The Plumed Serpent*.

What, then, of Lilly and Aaron? Are we to believe that Aaron, though '[kicking] against the pricks', has finally been brought to a 'deep fathomless submission' to Lilly? Lawrence is curiously ambiguous on this point. It is not merely that the novel ends inconclusively, for if Lilly, with a face 'like a Byzantine eikon', seems to command veneration, Aaron's last question is delicately poised between acceptance and rejection; it is that Lawrence throughout speaks disconcertingly with two voices in regard to their relationship. Both the smashing of Aaron's flute and his dream (Lilly's talk of 'deep unfathomable' and 'deep fathomless' submission representing, I think, more than a verbal link with 'the deep unfathomable water' into which the dream-boat ultimately swings) point to the strong likelihood of his giving in to Lilly; and indeed Lawrence does not rely on symbolism alone to suggest this:

'But no! If he had to give in to something; if he really had to give in, and it seemed he had: then he would rather give in to the devilish little Lilly than to the beastly people of the world. If he had to give in, then it should be to no woman, and to no social ideal, and to no social institution. No!–if he had to yield his wilful independence, and give himself, then he would rather give himself to the little, individual *man* than to any of the rest. For to tell the truth, in the man was something incomprehensible, which had dominion over him, if he chose to allow it.

[1] Cf., in this respect, some of Lilly's earlier remarks: ' "Men have got to stand up to the fact that manhood is more than childhood–and then force women to admit it," said Lilly. "But the rotten whiners, they're all grovelling before a baby's napkin and a woman's petticoat. . . . The man's spirit has gone out of the world. Men can't move an inch unless they can grovel humbly at the end of the journey. . . . That's why marriage wants readjusting–or extending–to get men on to their own legs once more, and to give them the adventure again . . ." ' (pp. 123–4).

'As he lay pondering this over, escaping from the *cul de sac* in which he had been running for so long, by yielding to one of his pursuers ... as Aaron lay so relaxing, finding a peculiar delight in giving his soul to his mind's hero, the self-same hero tapped and entered' (pp. 336–7).

Since the discussion, which I have quoted in part above, follows almost immediately after this passage, and since Aaron's thoughts lead us to expect an unqualified surrender to the little man, it is remarkable that Lawrence is, in the end, so indecisive. His indecisiveness, however, is a redeeming feature of the book, for it suggests that his artistic integrity will not allow him blatantly to force Aaron into a yielding which would negate a great deal of what has gone before. It is symptomatic of the strain that Aaron's private mental surrender should be so unconvincing. Why, we wonder, does he 'have to give in to something'? To make the smashing of his flute of such inordinate consequence, to make it, indeed, 'the end',[1] is surely to put symbolism to illegitimate use. His steadfast refusal to give in either to woman or to society is hardly a preparation for yielding to Lilly; and, in any event, it is not clear why yielding in the name of 'life-submission' should not be as much a 'cul de sac' as less pretentious forms of surrender. Aaron, moreover, as we have seen, is scarcely the kind of man to 'give himself' to anyone, let alone to yield pride of place, for 'wherever he [is] he [likes] to be given, tacitly, the first place – or a place among the first' (p. 158); and nothing, bar the destruction of the flute, has served to alter this preference. But there is a still more obtrusive contradiction of this sort to be faced: even if we accept Lilly's contention that the submission he is demanding will not prevent Aaron from 'fulfilling his own soul', though the distinction between 'giving oneself' and giving oneself away' is drawn fine here, it is difficult to reconcile the choice he offers him with what he has previously said about the difficulty of 'learning to possess' his own soul 'in isolation': 'It's what you get to after a lot of fighting and a lot of sensual fulfilment', he tells Aaron. 'And it never does away with the fighting and with the sensual passion. It flowers on top of them, and it would never flower save on top of them' (p. 128). The friendship may be additional to marriage for Lilly, but for Aaron it is presented, virtually, as an alternative; given Lilly's necessary conditions for 'self-possession', therefore, we can only conclude that Aaron will be made to follow a will-o'-the-wisp if his soul should tell him to submit to Lilly.

[1] See the passage quoted on p. 200 above.

A new development in the last pages of the book is the linking of the personal to the political, for the qualities of soul that will enable a man to exact submission from both wife and friend are the very qualities, it is intimated, that make him a leader. An interest in power and in leadership is, of course, not new in Lawrence,[1] though this is the first time it is explicitly formulated in the novels. The 'power motive' that Lawrence is interested in, however, is not at this stage given a precise political application. Lilly's definition of it by negation does not do much to clarify the meaning of the 'dark, living, fructifying power' of which he talks. The power which the leader possesses is to be used for the 'guidance' of men, but the nature of the 'true action' into which it is 'waiting to issue' is indefinite; action, indeed, is left to the future,[2] and it is only in *Kangaroo* and *The Plumed Serpent* that the actual exercise of power in the world is explored.

From the point of view of this study, a development of some importance in *Aaron's Rod* is the postulation of 'power' as an alternative to 'love', for in the Hardy essay, it might be remembered, the 'Epoch of Love' was set against the 'Epoch of the Law'.[3] Lawrence's new insistence on 'power', however, does not represent a movement to a mode that is opposed to 'love' (for, as I think I can show, 'power' is simply 'love' in another guise), but is evidence, rather, of a reaction against the 'feminine' implications of a life which posits individual 'being' as the supreme object. I suggested, in the discussion of *Women in Love*, that Birkin's emphasis on 'being' constituted a rejection of the 'merging' and the 'oneness' which he found to be inherent in 'love', and that this rejection, in turn, implied a need for assurance that, in

[1] I quote a representative earlier instance in his correspondence: 'You must drop all your democracy. You must not believe in "the people". One class is no better than another. It must be a case of Wisdom, or Truth. Let the working classes *be* working classes. That is the truth. There must be an aristocracy of people who have wisdom, & there must be a Ruler: a Kaiser: no Presidents & democracies. . . .' Letter to Bertrand Russell (conjecturally dated 6.7.1915), *D. H. Lawrence's Letters to Bertrand Russell*, p. 50. See, too, letter to Dollie Radford (December 1916), published in Edward Nehls, I, 409.

[2] The conclusion of Lawrence's history textbook, which was completed in 1919, also proclaims the necessity for a leader, but does not indicate how he is to function: 'It all depends on the will of the people. But the will of the people must concentrate in one figure, who is also supreme over the will of the people. He must be chosen, but at the same time responsible to God alone. Here is a problem of which a stormy future will have to evolve the solution.' *Movements in European History*, p. 306.

[3] See Chap. 1, pp. 26–7 above.

relation to a woman, he was 'other'. I also pointed out that his determination to maintain his 'separateness of being' and his corresponding
decision to withdraw from the world meant, in effect, that he was set
to live his life on 'female' terms, and I intimated that, in so far as
Lawrence was identified with Birkin, a 'swing to the other extreme'
was to be expected. The Lawrencean Lilly's advocacy of 'power' as a
concomitant of 'being' marks the first stage in such a movement[1]–
marks, that is to say, the establishment of a new 'male' interest
which will not only enable the man to return to the world but to do
so on terms apparently remote from the rejected conception of 'love'
as 'communion'. But 'love' is disposed of only by sleight of hand, for
Lilly's wish for a male friend is, in part, an expression of a desire to be
'at one' with a man;[2] and his pretensions to being a leader betoken a
tendency, however much disguised, to 'spread himself over humanity'.[3] It is evident that he is fighting a weakness he discerns in himself
when he violently denounces Aaron's supposed desire 'to whoosh off
in a nice little love-whoosh'. 'Power' and 'love', indeed, as Lawrence
says elsewhere, are the 'same thing, at the very last':

'It is a radical passion in man, however, the passion to include
everything in himself, grasp it all. There are two ways of gratifying this
passion. The first is Alexander's way, the way of power, power over
the material universe. . . . And power, we know, is a bubble: a platitu-
dinous bubble.

'But Jesus chose the other way: not to *have* all, but to *be* all. Not to
grasp everything into supreme possession: but to *be* everything,
through supreme acceptance. It is the same thing, at the very last. The
king-god and the crucified-God hold the same bubble in their hands:

---

[1] Lawrence had earlier given us reason to anticipate that a belief in 'being' would
lead eventually to a belief in 'power': '. . . according to his idea of fulfilment, man
establishes the whole order of life. If my fulfilment is the fulfilment and establishment of the unknown divine Self which I am, then I shall proceed in the realising
of the greatest idea of the self, the highest conception of the I, my order of life
will be kingly, imperial, aristocratic. The body politic also will culminate in this
divinity of the flesh, this body imbued with glory, invested with divine power and
might, the King, the Emperor. In the body politic also I shall desire a king, an
emperor, a tyrant, glorious, mighty, in whom I see myself consummated and
fulfilled. This is inevitable!' *Twilight in Italy* (1916), pp. 127–8.
[2] See p. 203 above.
[3] Cf. Lilly on Christ and Lincoln: ' "Well, if one will be a Jesus he must expect his
Judas. That's why Abraham Lincoln gets shot. A Jesus makes a Judas inevitable.
A man should remain himself, not try to spread himself over humanity. He
should pivot himself on his own pride" ' (p. 120).

210 One Up, One Down: The Third Period

the bubble of the All, the Infinite. The king-god extends the dominion of his will and consciousness over all things: the crucified identifies his will and consciousness with all things. But the submission of love is at last a process of pure materialism, like the supreme extension of power. . . .'[1]

Lawrence, in other words, in terms of his own division of the world, is divided against himself, for he is engaged in asserting and defending a 'male' doctrine of 'power', which in its kindred manifestation as a creed of 'love' he violently condemns, and which, anyway, runs counter to his deepest 'feminine' inclination to 'be':

'We must go very, very carefully at first. The great serpent to destroy, is the will to Power: the desire for one man to have some dominion over his fellow-men. Let us have no personal influence, if possible– nor personal magnetism, as they used to call it, nor persuasion–no "Follow me"–but only "Behold". And a man shall not come to save his own soul. Let his soul go to hell. He shall come because he knows that his own soul is not the be-all and the end-all, but that all souls of all things do but compose the body of God, and that God indeed shall Be.'[2]

This passage is premonitory of the ultimate rejection of 'power', but it is not until Lawrence, with logical persistence, drives himself, through *Kangaroo*, to a clearly repugnant position in *The Plumed Serpent* that his revulsion swings him round and compels him to retread the road he has come.

Signs of strain are already clearly evident in *Aaron's Rod*. If the treatment of the main themes, the nature of the relationships of man and

---

[1] 'Democracy', *Phoenix*, p. 707. The essay is tentatively assigned to the years 1919–21 by E. W. Tedlock, *The Frieda Lawrence Collection of D. H. Lawrence Manuscripts: A Descriptive Bibliography* (Albuquerque, 1948), p. 133. Edward D. McDonald says it 'may have been written . . . as early as, say, 1923'. Introduction to *Phoenix*, p. xxv.

[2] Letter to Lady Ottoline Morrell (February 1915), *Letters*, p. 221. Eric Bentley maintains that 'in Lawrence the dichotomy [i.e., "the dichotomy of religion and politics, the eternal and the temporal, the metaphysical and the historical" which he states has been "at the back" of his study of Heroic Vitalism] is clarified into that of Love and Power. All his endeavours, personal and literary, are attempts to know more fully the meaning of these two words. . . .' 'D. H. Lawrence, John Thomas and Dionysos', *The Cult of the Superman* (London, 1947), p. 212. I disagree with Bentley, for I think the major dichotomy in Lawrence is that between Love and/or Power and 'Separateness of Being'; Love and Power are, if anything, a dichotomy within a dichotomy. A preoccupation with Love and Power, moreover, is characteristic only of Lawrence's third phase of writing and is certainly not the mark of 'all his endeavours'.

man and of man and woman and their interaction, is marred, as I believe I have shown, by serious contradictions, the plot and the structure of the novel are equally uncertain. Important events in the plot, such as Aaron's astonishingly quick success in London or his abrupt departure from England, to specify but two obvious instances, are presented with no great concern for verisimilitude. As far as the structure is concerned, the opening of the book, with its sharp differentiation between the Christmas festivities in the houses of a miner and the mine-owner, leads us to expect that, in the manner of *Women in Love*, different 'worlds' are to be juxtaposed in relation to a unifying theme; in fact, however, there is not a juxtaposition but a succession of 'worlds', on which the central drama barely impinges, and Aaron's progress from the mines and the 'Royal Oak' pub to the orchestra and the 'half Bohemians' of London, and then to Italy and the tourist and expatriate English, is detailed in a manner which becomes negligently diffuse–picaresque by default, as it were. By the end of the book it is apparent that Lawrence has simply made prodigal use both of situations he experienced and of people he encountered in his own life;[1] and we are scarcely surprised when Richard Aldington tells us that Lawrence's literary agent at first reported that *Aaron's Rod* 'could "not be accepted", it was full of libellous matter'.[2] Nor does the verve with which the extraneous scenes are described–the delightful appearances of Francis and Angus come particularly to mind–minimize the artistic recklessness with which they are included in the book.

When we consider the technical brilliance and originality of *The Rainbow* and of *Women in Love*, we can only conclude that Lawrence is now no longer concerned with form in the novel. But he still has a conscience, and his discomfort reveals itself again and again: 'Our

---

[1] The extent to which Lawrence drew on his own life is suggested by Edward Nehls' listing of the originals of some of the characters: Norman Douglas–James Argyle; Sir Walter Becker and his wife–Sir William and Lady Franks; Reggie Turner–Algy Constable; Capt. James Robert White–Jim Bricknell; Alfred Brentnall–Alfred Bricknell; Dorothy Yorke–Josephine Ford; Richard Aldington–Robert Cunningham; Hilda Aldington, 'H.D.'–Julia Cunningham; Cecil Gray–Cyril Scott; Augustus John–Struthers; Dr Feroze–Sherardy; Brigit Patmore–Clariss Browning. See *D. H. Lawrence*, II, 452.

[2] *Portrait of a Genius, But . . .*, p. 242. The chagrin aroused by the book was certainly considerable; see, for instance, Norman Douglas, *D. H. Lawrence and Maurice Magnus: A Plea for Better Manners* (privately printed, 1925), pp. 40–1, and *Looking Back* (London, 1933), II, 348; and Cecil Gray, *Musical Chairs*, p. 136.

story will not yet see daylight' is the opening sentence of Chapter IV; the uncertainty with which Chapter V begins–'A friend had given Josephine Ford a box at the opera for one evening: our story continues by night'–is made even more noticeable by Lawrence's failure to remember, as Middleton Murry has pointed out, that Josephine Ford, when she is first introduced some twenty pages back, is called Josephine Hay; and Aaron's weakly motivated departure from England is side-stepped with too overt a jauntiness: 'Therefore behold our hero alighting at Novara, two hours late, on a wet dark evening' (p. 159). Lawrence is no genial Thackeray, and his intrusions in the first person are a sign of weakness, not of strength–as the following passage, which refers to Aaron's centrally important attempt to understand his relations with Lottie, perhaps sufficiently indicates:

'In his own powerful but subconscious fashion Aaron realised this. He was a musician. And hence even his deepest *ideas* were not word-ideas, his very thoughts were not composed of words and ideal concepts. They too, his thoughts and his ideas, were dark and invisible, as electric vibrations are invisible no matter how many words they may purport. If I, as a word-user, must translate his deep conscious vibrations into finite words, that is my own business. I do but make a translation of the man. He would speak in music. I speak with words.

'The inaudible music of his conscious soul conveyed his meaning in him quite as clearly as I convey it in words: probably much more clearly. But in his own mode only: and it was in his own mode only he realised what I must put into words. These words are my own affair. His mind was music.

'Don't grumble at me then, gentle reader, and swear at me that this damned fellow wasn't half clever enough to think all these smart things, and realise all these fine-drawn-out subtleties. You are quite right, he wasn't, yet it all resolved itself in him as I say, and it is for you to prove that it didn't' (p. 199).

Finally, Lawrence almost explicitly admits that the novel, as he now views it, has become something radically different from the art form which he has previously handled with such rigorous assurance, for this is how he comments on a letter Aaron writes to Sir William Franks:

'Well, here was a letter for a poor old man to receive. But, in the dryness of his withered mind, Aaron got it out of himself. When a man writes a letter to himself, it is a pity to post it to somebody else. Perhaps the same is true of a book' (pp. 307–8).

Lawrence's defensive reservation betrays an inner uncertainty as to where he is heading. The trail was to lead, by way of the novel as a private 'thought-adventure' (to use the term he employs in *Kangaroo*), to the cul-de-sac of *The Plumed Serpent*.

(B) *The Plumed Serpent*

'It all seemed so far from the dark God [Somers] wished to serve, the God from whom the dark, sensual passion of love emanates, not only the spiritual love of Christ. He wanted men once more to refer the sensual passion of love sacredly to the great dark God, the ithyphallic, of the first dark religions. . . .'[1]

In *Aaron's Rod*, it will be remembered, the world was to be saved, prospectively, by a leader who would know how to exercise power. In *Kangaroo* power is considered in relation to politics and to possible alternatives to an outmoded system of democracy, but in the end political programmes are found to be wholly inefficacious. Somers, the Lawrence-like protagonist of the novel, finally realizes that 'the only thing is the God who is the source of all passion. Once go down before the God-passion and human passions take their right rhythm' (p. 221). As the passage quoted above indicates, it is to 'the great dark God, the ithyphallic, of the first dark religions' that he turns–and it is this God who is resurrected in *The Plumed Serpent*.[2] The myth, however, leaves us with the uncomfortable suspicion that the God is reborn as much to vindicate a mode of personal relations that Lawrence seems determined to establish as to point the way to salvation.

The opening chapters of the novel forcefully suggest that Mexico is much in need of saving. As Kate, Owen, and Villiers enter the stadium where the bull-fight is to take place, a characteristic image adverts to the nature of life in Mexico City:

'They emerged out of a tunnel in the hollow of the concrete-and-iron amphitheatre. A real gutter-lout came to look at their counter-slips, to see which seats they had booked. He jerked his head downwards, and slouched off. Now Kate knew she was in a trap–a big concrete beetle trap' (p. 12).

[1] *Kangaroo*, p. 224. *Kangaroo* was written in two months in 1922 and published in 1923.
[2] *The Plumed Serpent*, published in 1926, was begun in May 1923 (see *Letters*, p. 567) and completed in February 1925 (see *Letters*, p. 629).

Though its purport is somewhat different here, the last phrase in this passage has behind it the weight of the numerous and crucial references to the beetle, and to 'the principle of knowledge in dissolution and corruption' which it represents, in *Women in Love*.[1] The beetlemen of Mexico City figure a principle of evil–they have 'faces of pure brutish evil, cold and insect-like' (p. 83)–the evil manifesting itself, in part, in their odious degeneration. The allusions to men prowling round the stadium 'like lost mongrels' (p. 16) and to 'the mongrel men of a mongrel city', two of whom stand 'making water against the wall, in the interval of their excitement' (p. 25), do more than evoke Kate's angry response to a half-breed people; taken in conjunction with the beetle imagery (it is a 'beetle-like intruder' (p. 18) who insinuates himself into the place reserved for Villiers' feet), they point to a reversion to a lower form of life. This is man as insect or dog.

Violence is as revealing an index of the Mexican degeneracy as it was of the 'disintegration' of life in the various worlds of *Women in Love*. Long after the bull-fight, when Kate is a witness to the way in which two four-year-old urchins persecute a water-fowl on the Lake of Sayula, she reflects that Mexico seems to demand a victim and that the whole American continent will always be 'divided between Victims and Victimizers' (p. 232). Her thoughts are an apt comment on the afternoon's sport in Mexico City. While they await the bulls and the toreadors, the crowd seek a release for the tension of violence within them by victimizing selected members of the audience whose straw hats are snatched off their heads and sent skimming away or whose heads are made the targets for hurled oranges. The bull itself, we begin to realize, is venerated because it plays a satisfyingly dual role: doomed, more likely than not, to be a victim, it is first taunted into being a victimizer. A 'bold picador', mounted on an 'ancient steed', points his lance into a bull's shoulder and the bull '[dives] its horns upwards into [the horse's] belly, rolling him over with his rider as one might push over a hat-stand'. The bull is drawn off and the horse is led away, but the bull returns:

'Kate knew what was coming. Before she could look away, the bull had charged on the limping horse from behind, the attendants had fled, the horse was up-ended absurdly, one of the bull's horns between his hind legs and deep in his inside. Down went the horse, collapsing in front, but his rear was still heaved up, with the bull's horn working

[1] See, for instance, Chap. 3, pp. 131–2 above.

vigorously up and down inside him, while he lay on his neck all twisted. And a huge heap of bowels coming out. And a nauseous stench. And the cries of pleased amusement among the crowd' (p. 23).

There is something so obscene in the way the crowd feed on this spectacle of violence that we are not surprised to find that Mexican degeneracy is associated with a sense of sexual perversion. The contest between the bull and the toreadors is described in terms which suggest a grotesque sexual encounter: the bull has 'long flourishing horns' (p. 19) and is an epitome of 'massive maleness' (p. 21); the 'precious toreadors' look 'like eunuchs, or women in tight pants' (p. 19), they skip 'like fat-hipped girls showing off', and it is 'from his erectness' that one of them '[rears] himself on tiptoe, his plump posterior much in evidence', and pushes 'two razor-sharp darts with frills at the top into the bull's shoulder' (p. 22). It is no wonder that 'fat mammas' in the crowd have 'a pleased, excited look in their eyes, almost sexual, and very distasteful in contrast to their soft passive bodies' (p. 25). Kate flees from the stadium before a bull is killed (the afternoon's toll is seven, Villiers later informs her), feeling that Mexico lies 'in her destiny almost as a doom. Something so heavy, so oppressive, like the folds of some huge serpent that seemed as if it could hardly raise itself' (p. 29).

The snake or serpent image is used in the first part of the book to characterize the failure of life in the aboriginal Indians of Mexico as distinguished from that in the half-breed beetle-men. The Indian failure is of the spirit. Kate is later able to attribute her sense of Mexico pulling her down, 'with a slow, reptilian insistence' (p. 79), to 'the curious, radical opposition of the Indians to the thing we call the spirit' (p. 125). In the Indians there is a cramping limitation of life to the physical, a heavy one-sidedness in which the country itself is involved:

'No lovely fusion, no communion. No beautiful mingling of sun and mist, no softness in the air, never. Either hard heat or hard chill. Hard, straight lines and zigzags, wounding the breast. No soft, sweet smell of earth. The smell of Mexico, however subtle, suggested violence and things in chemical conflict' (p. 228).

Unlike the loutish half-breeds, the Indians do possess a beauty, 'a certain sensitive tenderness of the heavy blood' such as emanates from the men who ply their wares in the *plaza* of Mexico City (p. 57), but they also have 'black, centreless eyes' which bespeak the fact that they 'aren't really there', as Kate puts it; 'they have no centre, no real *I*'

(p. 46). The Indian failure to develop, 'the fear of not being able to find full creation', like the degeneration of the half-breeds, is productive of evil: in 'the uncreated centre' of their eyes there lurk 'evil and . . . insolence', the insolence 'against a higher creation, the same thing that is in the striking of a snake' (p. 84). Kate can 'well understand the potency of the snake upon the Aztec and Maya imagination'; even in Cipriano, the Indian general (whom she eventually marries), she detects 'something smooth, undeveloped, yet vital' which suggests 'the heavy-ebbing blood of reptiles in his veins' (p. 74). The inability of the ordinary Indian to consummate a self makes him 'a half-being', 'a part-thing', and if he has 'smooth thighs and supple loins like a snake', he has too 'a will to disintegration and death' (p. 115). The failure of being inevitably generates violence, 'a demonish hatred of life itself'; 'caught in the toils of old lusts and old activities as in the folds of a black serpent that strangles the heart', the Indian is subject to a lust to kill which 'no lust of women can equal' (p. 145).

Beetle, mongrel, snake–the fall of man in Mexico is vividly and forcefully evoked. The collapse naturally takes a different form from that portrayed in the highly industrialized society of *Women in Love*, but it is as complete and manifests itself in a similar craving for consummation in violence and in death. Nor, until the Quetzalcoatl movement is launched, does there seem to be much prospect of the Mexicans being raised to life. It is soon intimated that the church, for instance, is unlikely to effect a change:

'[Kate] sat on a parapet of the old roof. The street beyond was like a black abyss, but around her was the rough glare of uneven flat roofs, with loose telephone wires trailing across, and the sudden, deep, dark wells of the *patios*, showing flowers blooming in shade.

'Just behind was a huge old church, its barrel roof humping up like some crouching animal, and its domes, like bubbles inflated, glittering with yellow tiles, and blue and white tiles, against the intense blue heaven. Quiet native women in long skirts were moving on the roofs, hanging out washing or spreading it on the stones. Chickens perched here and there. An occasional bird soared huge overhead, trailing a shadow. And not far away stood the brownish tower-stumps of the Cathedral, the profound old bell trembling huge and deep, so soft as to be almost inaudible, upon the air' (p. 56).

Neither the church nor the cathedral, we see, is able to lift itself above the 'black abyss' of the streets of Mexico City: the 'tower-stumps' of the cathedral suggest that it is cut off in its lifelessness from the 'intense blue heaven' overhead; while the church, with its roof 'humping up like some crouching animal', is bound to the earth, it seems, in the way that mongrels and snakes are. The fact that the cathedral bell is 'almost inaudible' neatly implies the essential failure of the church in Mexico, a failure to make itself heard, to appeal to the Mexican consciousness in terms that it can understand; and the soft inaudibility of the bell is in striking contrast to the insistent drum-beats which are eventually substituted for it under the new dispensation. The empty bubbles of the church domes – we are reminded of the bubble imagery in *Women in Love* – are indeed premonitory of that substitution.

All that the church can do in Mexico is to exert itself in works of charity. There is, for instance, the *Cuna*, the foundlings' home, of which Ramón's wife, Carlota, is the director: 'waste, unwanted babies could be delivered in at the door of the *Cuna*, like parcels', and the Carmelite sisters 'equip them for life' (a concentrated venom of irony is directed at Carlota, who uses the expression) by farming out most of the children to 'decent' Indian women, who are paid a small monthly sum to take them into their homes (p. 167). When it comes to religious observance, the effect of the church is shown to be pernicious. The Mexicans indulge themselves in the spectacle of yet another victim, 'the Crucified streaked with blood', and kneel with 'a sensual, almost victimized self-abandon to the god of death' (p. 288). Christianity, it is clear, does not help the Indians to find a 'centre', and, in Lilly's phrase, the 'love-whoosh' it stimulates, the self-abandon, is as vicious as the death-worship:

'The day of Corpus Christi came, with high mass and the church full to the doors with kneeling peons, from dawn till noon. Then a feeble little procession of children within the church, because the law forbids religious processions outside. But all, somehow, for nothing. Just so that the people could call it a *fiesta*, and so have an excuse to be more slack, more sloshy and uncontrolled than ever. The one Mexican desire; to let themselves go in sloppy inertia.

'And this was the all-in-all of the religion. Instead of doing as it should, collecting the soul into its own strength and integrity, the religious day left it all the more decomposed and degenerate' (pp. 290–1).

If the church is ineffectual, the state is simply inconsequential. It is soon borne in on Kate that Mexico cannot be revitalized through political action. Revolution, the Mexican panacea, is the support of prestige not principle, and we are to view the violence it begets as only another aspect of the deathly struggle between victim and victimizer in which Mexicans are enthralled. At the bull-fight, for instance, 'the degenerate mob of Mexico City' yell for music from some military bands 'with the voice of mob authority', for they are 'the People, and the revolutions had been their revolutions, and they had won them all'. The shouting of the mob becomes 'brutal and violent' (Kate can never forget it), but the bands remain nonchalantly indifferent, for it is the army which has won all the revolutions: 'So the revolutions were *their* revolutions, and they were present for their own glory alone' (p. 15). The socialist reformers get no nearer the quick of the problem. The impulse behind their activity is hate: the young intellectual who accompanies Kate and her party on a tour of the University insists on the need to 'kill all the capitalists' as a primary objective, though he later confesses that he is 'sorry [he has] to hate so much' (pp. 60, 62). Even in the famous Ribera frescoes the 'flat Indians' are merely 'symbols in the weary script of socialism and anarchy'; and Kate, who remembers the 'certain richness of physical being' and the 'helplessness, a profound unbelief' of an Indian she has just seen in the *plaza*, cannot help reflecting that 'all the liberty, all the progress, all the socialism in the world would not help him. Nay, it would only help further to destroy him' (p. 58). Early on in her stay in Mexico Kate thus takes up a position which is in line with that of Ramón:

' "Politics and all this *social* religion that Montes [the newly installed president] has got is like washing the outside of the egg, to make it look clean," [he tells Cipriano]. "But I, myself, I want to get inside the egg, right to the middle, to start it growing into a new bird. . . . Montes wants to clean the nest and wash the egg. But meanwhile, the egg will go cold and die. The more you save these people from poverty and ignorance, the quicker they will die: like a dirty egg that you take from under the hen-eagle, to wash it. While you wash the egg, it chills and dies . . ." ' (pp. 203–4).

Put in the scales against the nature of the Mexican collapse, Ramón's analogy carries weight. It also leads, of course, straight to Quetzalcoatl, for the 'new bird' Ramón wishes to hatch is to stand within the ring of a coiled snake. The firmness of movement of the novel is impressive, the more so since we cannot help contrasting it with the slackness of *Aaron's Rod* and *Kangaroo*. The book proceeds with a manifest certainty from the old to the new, from Mexico City, with its bull-fights and its mob, with its cathedral and its peons and its socialists, to the Lake of Sayula, where the gods are reborn; proceeds, that is to say, from a depiction of degeneration to an assertion of regeneration. The regeneration, however, is too much a matter of *assertion*, and it is when we are confronted with the living gods in action that we begin to doubt. As in *Women in Love*, the hand that demolishes does so with a surer strength than the hand that builds.

While Kate is still in Mexico City, the return of the old gods is reported as a 'fantasy' in an item in the newspaper:

'The name Quetzalcoatl, too, fascinated her. She had read bits about the god. Quetzal is the name of a bird that lives high up in the mists of tropical mountains, and has very beautiful tail-feathers, precious to the Aztecs. Coatl is a serpent. Quetzalcoatl is the Plumed Serpent, so hideous in the fanged, feathered, writhing stone of the National Museum.

'But Quetzalcoatl was, she vaguely remembered, a sort of fair-faced bearded god; the wind, the breath of life, the eyes that see and are unseen, like the stars by day. . . . Quetzalcoatl! Who knows what he meant to the dead Aztecs, and to the older Indians, who knew him before the Aztecs raised their deity to heights of horror and vindictiveness?

'All a confusion of contradictory gleams of meaning, Quetzalcoatl. But why not? Her Irish spirit was weary to death of definite meanings, and a God of one fixed purport. Gods should be iridescent, like the rainbow in the storm . . .' (pp. 64–5).

Kate's initial reactions to Quetzalcoatl indicate the significance of Lawrence's attempt to revive the old gods. In the first place, amid the 'confusion of contradictory gleams of meaning', it seems that Lawrence undertakes to redeem the very gods themselves; that is to say, he does not shirk the 'horror and vindictiveness' associated with the Aztec deity–as we shall see, he regrettably incorporates this aspect in his myth–but it is essentially as 'the breath of life' that he presents Quetzalcoatl. Second, we can assume that Lawrence, like Kate, is 'weary to death' of a God 'of one fixed purport', is weary to death, that is, of Christ as the God of the Spirit alone; and in one sense *The Plumed Serpent* is a statement of his break with Christianity, the break being ultimately symbolized in the ritual burning of images of Christ and the Virgin. Concurrently the novel is also an attempt to express a fundamental apprehension of the duality of existence in religious terms, to translate a philosophy, we might say, into a religion. Coatl and Quetzal, serpent and bird, are merely new and alternative symbols for the tiger and the lamb, the lion and the unicorn, the horses and the highway; and Lawrence's 'savage pilgrimage' is, as ever, a search for a means of reconciling the opposites, is still, in a word, a search for the Holy Ghost.[1] It is no accident that the image which conveys Kate's sense of an iridescent God should be 'the rainbow in the storm'. In *The Plumed Serpent* the symbol that is substituted for the Holy Ghost of the expository writings and for the rainbow of the earlier novel is the Morning Star, 'that watches between the night and the day, the gleaming clue to the two opposites' (p. 102), 'the poignant intermediate flashing its quiet between the energies of the cosmos' (p. 105).[2] The energies of the cosmos are further symbolized by the serpent and the bird, and it is Ramón's effort as the living manifestation of the God Quetzalcoatl, as the 'lord of two ways' (p. 241), to rouse the snake of Mexico from its torpor, to fire it into a living relation with the eagle. This is how he addresses a group of peons:

' "How shall we men become Men of the Morning Star? And the women the Dawn-Star Women?

' "Lower your fingers to the caress of the Snake of the earth.

' "Lift your wrist for a perch to the far-lying [*sic*] Bird.

' "Have the courage of both, the courage of lightning and the earthquake.

' "And wisdom of both, the wisdom of the snake and the eagle.

' "And the peace of both, the peace of the serpent and the sun.

[1] Though a serpent and a bird figure in Will Brangwen's carving of the Creation of Eve–'there was a bird on a bough overhead, lifting its wings for flight, and a serpent wreathing up to it' (*The Rainbow*, p. 121)–this is the first time Lawrence makes extensive use of these symbols. Eric Bentley refers to their use by Nietzsche: 'Fused with [the myth of Zarathustra] is a myth of sun-worship. At the very beginning, Zarathustra prays to the sun before undertaking his mission among men. The consummation of his task is called "the great noontide". It is not reached in the book itself. . . .

'Under the sun the proudest creature is the eagle and the wisest is the serpent. The union of these two, an emblem which D. H. Lawrence later discovered to his great joy in Mexico, is the emblem of Zarathustra. Lawrence, too, connected them with sun-worship. The symbolism is admirably expressive of Heroic Vitalism.' *The Cult of the Superman*, p. 94.

[2] Cf. Lawrence's account of the god of the morning star in *Apocalypse*: 'The morning-star was always a god, from the time when gods began. But when the cult of dying and re-born gods started all over the world, about 600 B.C., he became symbolic of the new god because he rules in the twilight, between day and night, and for the same reason he is supposed to be lord of both, and to stand gleaming with one foot on the flood of night and one foot on the world of day, one foot on sea and one on shore. . .' (p. 184).

' "And the power of both, the power of the innermost earth and the outermost heaven.

' "But on your brow, Men! the undimmed Morning Star, that neither day nor night, nor earth nor sky can swallow and put out.

' "And between your breasts, Women! the Dawn-Star, that cannot be dimmed . . ." ' (p. 212).

The Morning Star that can neither be swallowed nor put out nor dimmed is the consummated self, the self that is born of an acceptance of man's dual nature, of a struggle to reconcile both flesh and spirit in a union which denies neither – as Kate comes to realize:

'And when the spirit and the blood in man begin to go asunder, bringing the great death, most stars die out.

'Only the man of a great star, a great divinity, can bring the opposites together again, in a new unison.

'And this was Ramón, and this was his great effort: to bring the great opposites into contact and into unison again. And this is the god-power in man. By this power you shall know the god in man. By none other.

'Ramón was a man as the least of his peons was a man, with the beating heart and the secret loins and the lips closed on the same secret of manhood. And he was human as Kate was human, with the same yearning of the spirit, for pure knowledge and communion, the soul in the greatness of its comprehending.

'But only he had that starry power for bringing together the two great human impulses to a point of fusion, for being the bird between the vast wings of the dual-created power to which man has access and in which man has his being. The Morning Star, between the breath of dawn and the deeps of the dark. . . .

'The star between the two wings of power: that alone was divinity in a man, and final manhood' (p. 435).

The terminology used in this passage recalls that of the Hardy essay and reminds us that the duality of 'the two great human impulses' is a duality of the male and female principles. It is a duality of 'the spirit and the blood'; of 'knowledge' and the 'soul' (for soul, in Lawrence, is 'of the blood' (p. 125), is the consciousness of the body); of 'communion' and 'the secret loins'. It is a duality of 'the word' and 'the roots': 'All that matters to me', Ramón tells Kate, 'are the roots that reach down beyond all destruction. The roots and the life are there. What else it needs is the word, for the forest to begin to rise again. And some man among men must speak the word' (p. 88). It is a duality of the Bird which '[sits] in the middle of the sun' (p. 210) and of the Snake of earth, 'of the heart of the world' (p. 209). It is not only reminiscences of the Hardy essay which help us to interpret the Quetzalcoatl symbolism; a revealing simile recalls Lawrence's father (who, it will be remembered, embodied 'female' qualities) in a way which would link him with the serpent heaviness of the Mexican:

'[The Mexicans] are caught in the toils of old lusts and old activities as in the folds of a black serpent that strangles the heart. The heavy, evil-smelling weight of an unconquered past. . . .

'For Jesus is no Saviour to the Mexicans. He is a dead god in their tomb. As a miner who is entombed underground by the collapsing of the earth in the gangways, so do whole nations become entombed under the slow subsidence of their past. Unless there comes some Saviour, some Redeemer to drive a new way out, to the sun' (p. 145).

I have drawn attention to this male-female duality because I believe the elaboration of the Quetzalcoatl religion marks yet another attempt by Lawrence to bring the two opposing principles into harmonious relation, marks, indeed, his most concerted effort in this respect since *The Rainbow*, though (as I shall try to show) it results in failure.

One of the ways in which Ramón tries to rouse the peons is to induce them to join in the singing of hymns and in the old Indian dances. Trained Quetzalcoatl men lead the way in the *plaza* at Sayula:

'The one singer had finished, and only the drum kept on, touching the sensitive membrane of the night subtly and knowingly. Then a voice in the circle rose again on the song, and like birds flying from a tree, one after the other, the individual voices arose, till there was a strong, intense, curiously weighty soaring and sweeping of male voices, like a dark flock of birds flying and dipping in unison. And all the dark birds seemed to have launched out of the heart, in the inner forest of the masculine chest.

'And one by one, voices in the crowd broke free, like birds launching and coming in from a distance, caught by the spell. The words did not matter. Any verse, any words, no words, the song remained the same: a strong, deep wind rushing from the caverns of the breast, from the everlasting soul! Kate herself was too shy and wincing to sing: too blenched with disillusion. But she heard the answer away back in her soul, like a far-off mocking-bird at night. And Juana was

singing in spite of herself, in a crooning feminine voice, making up the words unconsciously.
...

'Then the drum started again, with a new, strong pulse. One of the seated men, in his white *poncho* with the dark blackish-and-blue border, got up, taking off his sandals as he did so, and began softly to dance the dance step. Mindless, dancing heavily and with a curious bird-like sensitiveness of the feet, he began to tread the earth with his bare soles, as if treading himself deep into the earth. Alone, with a curious pendulum rhythm, leaning a little forward from a powerful backbone, he trod to the drum beat, his white knees lifting and lifting alternately against the dark fringe of his blanket, with a queer dark splash. And another man put his *huaraches* into the centre of the ring, near the fire, and stood up to dance. The man at the drum lifted up his voice in a wild, blind song. The men were taking off their *ponchos*. And soon, with the firelight on their breasts and on their darkly abstracted faces, they were all afoot, with bare torsos and bare feet, dancing the savage bird-tread.
...

'Till the young peons could stand it no more. They put off their sandals and their hats and their blankets, and shyly, with inexpert feet that yet knew the old echo of the tread, they stood behind the wheeling dancers, and danced without changing place. Till soon the revolving circle had a fixed yet throbbing circle of men outside' (pp. 136–8).

I imagine it is an exultation in the tone of this description of 'the savage bird-tread', and of analogous descriptions both in the novel and in *Mornings in Mexico*, that has led certain critics to charge Lawrence with advocating a deliberate primitivism, with wanting us to 'allow our "consciousness" to be overpowered by the alien "consciousness" of the Indian'.[1] The charge is absurd enough, as a minimally careful reading of the novel–not to mention the repeated insistences in the expository writings[2]–clearly shows. Lawrence believes that primitive intuitions may well serve as a point of fresh departure in the onward

[1] Wyndham Lewis, *Paleface* (London, 1929), p. 175. Cf. Frederick J. Hoffman, 'From Surrealism to "The Apocalypse": A Development in Twentieth Century Irrationalism', *A Journal of English Literary History*, 15 (June 1948), 157; and William York Tindall, *D. H. Lawrence and Susan His Cow* (New York, 1939), p. 113.
[2] See, for instance, 'Indians and an Englishman', *Phoenix*, pp. 98–9, and *Studies in Classic American Literature*, pp. 75, 201, 204.

movement of our civilization; the direction to be taken, however, is forward, not backward, and if this means going back in order to go forward, it is by way of adding something to our lives, not reducing them. In the novel the revival of old customs, and particularly of the old dances, serves a specific function: it is intended not only to stir the sluggish peon into life but to re-establish contact between him and the circumambient universe. That Lawrence is not indulging in a perverse primitivism is amply borne out by Kate's reflections soon after she witnesses the dancing in the *plaza*:

'She grew quieter, shut up with the dusky glow of her candle. And her heart, still wrenched with the pain of fear, was thinking: "Joachim [i.e., her deceased second husband] said that evil was the lapsing back to old life-modes that have been surpassed in us. This brings murder and lust. But the drums of Saturday night are the old rhythm, and that dancing round the drum is the old savage form of expression. Consciously reverting to the savage. So perhaps it is evil."

'But then again her instinct to believe came up.

' "No! It's not a helpless, panic reversal. It is conscious, carefully chosen. We must go back to pick up old threads. We must take up the old, broken impulse that will connect us with the mystery of the cosmos again, now we are at the end of our own tether . . ." ' (pp. 147–8).

Lawrence might well say, with E. M. Forster, 'Only connect', though the connection he insists on, the connection between man and 'the mystery of the cosmos', goes beyond that between the prose and the passion, between the spirit and the blood. Ramón believes that only in 'the heart of the cosmos' can man look for strength, that if he can keep his soul 'in touch with the heart of the world, then from the heart of the world new blood will beat in strength and stillness into him, fulfilling his manhood' (p. 207). When Quetzalcoatl supersedes Jesus at Sayula, the church bells are silenced and the clock ceases to strike. Instead, there is a turning 'from the clock to the sun and from metal to membrane' (p. 376), and 'moments of change' are marked by the sounding of drums: there is a heavy drum at dawn, and a man chants 'the Dawn-Verse' from the church tower; at about nine o'clock a light drum '[rattles] quickly' and a voice cries, 'Half-way up the slope of the morning!'; the heavy drum sounds again at noon, and at about three o'clock the light drum is followed by the cry, 'Half-way down the slope of the afternoon'; at sunset the 'great drum [rolls]' and there is an evening verse. And Kate finds that 'the world

[is] different, different. The drums seemed to leave the air soft and vulnerable, as if it were alive' (pp. 373–4).[1]

More pertinent than the allegation of primitivism on Lawrence's part is the failure of the new religious practices to live up to the aims of the Quetzalcoatl movement, to point clearly, that is to say, to the Morning Star. An examination of the passage, quoted above, in which the religious songs and dances are described, is in this respect revealing. 'Who sleeps shall wake!' (p. 137), sing the dancing Quetzalcoatl men; and it must be admitted that the surging prose of the description admirably conveys the irresistible attraction of the dance to the watching peons, felicitously rendering the hypnotic rhythm of the movement which urges them out of their inertia. But to what, we ask, do the peons wake? It is only by a sort of legerdemain that Lawrence tries to suggest that the singing and dancing are a means of establishing contact between the snake and the bird. He attempts to do so by relying on an insistent bird imagery: individual voices arise, one after the other, 'like birds flying from a tree'; there is a soaring and sweeping of male voices, 'like a dark flock of birds flying and dipping in unison'; one by one, voices in the crowd break free, 'like birds launching and coming in from a distance'; a man dances 'heavily' but 'with a curious bird-like sensitiveness of the feet', and the dance itself is 'the savage bird-tread'. Yet it is abundantly clear that this is no blithe bird of the spirit that is evoked: the words of the song '[do] not matter', the man who dances with bird-like sensitiveness is 'mindless', the man at the drum lifts up his voice 'in a wild, blind song'. What the singing and dancing achieve is a release of soul–the song is 'a strong, deep wind rushing from the caverns of the breast, from the everlasting soul!' and Kate hears the answer 'away back in her soul'–but then soul, we remember, is 'of the blood'. It is the lethargic snake alone that is roused here.

What is true of this passage is true, it seems to me, of the overall presentation of the religion. It can be claimed that the Mexicans are galvanized into establishing a new connection with the cosmos, but this leads to an enhanced state of physical being, not to a union of

[1] Lawrence's work at this time, both fictional and non-fictional, shows a marked preoccupation with the necessity for a vital contact between man and the cosmos. See, for instance, 'The Woman Who Rode Away' (written in 1924) and 'Sun' (written in 1925), *The Tales of D. H. Lawrence* (London, 1948); and 'Morality and the Novel' (written in 1925), *Phoenix*, p. 528, and 'Aristocracy', *Reflections* (1925), pp. 228–229. Lawrence maintained this view just as strongly at the end of his life–cf. the moving passage with which *Apocalypse* (1931) ends, pp. 222–4.

blood and spirit. Indeed, if Christianity can be characterized as 'a religion of the spirit', as Ramón says to the Bishop (p. 276), the Quetzalcoatl movement emerges as a religion of being. This seems to be the tenor of one of Ramón's prayers:

' "When the plasm of the body, and the plasm of the soul, and the plasm of the spirit are at one, in the Snake *I Am*.

' "I am Now.

' "Was-not is a dream, and shall-be is a dream, like two separate, heavy feet.

' "But Now, I Am.

...

' "And what falls away is a dream, and what accrues is a dream. There is always and only Now, Now and I Am"' (pp. 188–9).

No doubt a union of body and soul and spirit is asserted in the opening lines of this passage, but it is not by the Morning Star that it is blessed: the reference to 'the Snake' is subversive of the assertion and suggests that the man Who Is is alive in the flesh, but no more. In this respect, Cipriano, at least, is quite explicit:

' "And when you have [the second strength], where will you feel it?

' "Not here!"–and he struck his forehead. "Not where the cunning *gringos* have it, in the head, and in their books. Not we. We are men, we are not spiders.

' "We shall have it here!"–he struck his breast–"and here!"–he struck his belly–"and here!"–he struck his loins' (p. 379).

And even Ramón, the apotheosis of the aspiration that is symbolized by the Morning Star, at times craves simply to be:

'This was how Ramón felt at the moment:–I am attempting the impossible. I had better either go and take my pleasure of life while it lasts, hopeless of the pleasure which is beyond all pleasures. Or else I had better go into the desert and take my way all alone, to the Star where at last I have my wholeness, holiness. The way of the anchorites and the men who went into the wilderness to pray. For surely my soul is craving for her consummation, and I am weary of the thing men call life. Living, I want to depart to where *I am*' (p. 267).

The Morning Star, we note, is invoked, but it is a lone consummation of *soul* that is desired. An enriched state of physical being, a vital connection with the cosmos, that is what Quetzalcoatl in fact brings. But that was where the men of *The Rainbow* started, not ended.

'Being', as opposed to 'Doing' or 'Knowing', is a typical attribute of the female principle. We see that, in terms of the Hardy essay, Quetzalcoatl is essentially a 'female' religion, and we begin to realize that the fierce male assertion which characterizes Lawrence's amplification of the religion is an attempt to camouflage an exposed position. If the bird is dragged down by the serpent, it will nevertheless pretend to a stance of invincible male power, like that of Aaron's overweening eagle. In this respect, the very postures of worship assigned to converts to the new religion are revealing: Cipriano gives the following instructions to those about to enter 'the house of Quetzalcoatl' for the first time:

' "Hear me, people. You may enter the house of Quetzalcoatl. Men must go to the right and left, and remove their shoes, and stand erect. To the new God no man shall kneel.

' "Women must go down the centre, and cover their faces. And they may sit upon the floor.

' "But men must stand erect.

' "Pass now, those who dare" ' (p. 353).

As shrubs set off mighty forest trees, the sitting women are clearly meant to enhance the power of the erect men, are intended, it seems, to be submissive participants in a strongly male affirmation:

'So that around the low dark shrubs of the crouching women stood a forest of erect, upthrusting men, powerful and tense with inexplicable passion. It was a forest of dark wrists and hands up-pressing, with the striped wall vibrating above, and higher, the maze of green going to the little, iron-barred windows that stood open, letting in the light and air of the roof.

' "I am the living Quetzalcoatl," came the solemn, impassive voice of Ramón' (p. 355).

The male affirmation is made even more strenuously in the presentation of Cipriano's Huitzilopochtli. The religion of being, we disconcertingly find, is concomitantly to be a religion of power. When Cipriano engages in the old savage dances with his men, he is 'at once tired and surcharged with extraordinary power', and he feels 'the black mystery of power go out of him over all his soldiers'. The soldiers, indeed, are said to be conscious 'not through themselves but through him. . . . It was in him they were supreme. They got their splendour from his power and their greatest consciousness was his consciousness diffusing them.' And Cipriano triumphantly tells them that he is not of himself: 'I am of the red Huitzilopochtli and the power from behind the sun. And you are not of yourselves. Of yourselves you are nothing. You are of me, my men' (p. 381). Cipriano is crudely forthright in his utterance, but this self-glorification, this direct propagation of a cult of the hero and leader of men, has its counterpart in the obeisance which Ramón exacts:

'Ramón rose to his feet. The men of Quetzalcoatl turned to face him, and shot up their naked right arms in the gesture of the statue, Ramón lifted his arm, so that his blanket fell in towards his shoulder, revealing the naked side and the blue sash.

' "All men salute Quetzalcoatl!" said a clear voice in command' (p. 354).

Lawrence, who was writing in 1925, cannot, of course, be held responsible for our unhappy memories of the Nazi salute and of a German people who accepted that they existed only in and for the Führer; but it is symptomatic of the strain under which he is labouring, of his imperative need to assert a fierce masculinity, that such passages should so darkly cloud the book of the Morning Star–for Lawrence was no fascist. The vast bulk of his work outside *The Plumed Serpent* bears witness to the fact that he was too impatient an individualist, too firmly committed to a rigorous and nonconformist self-responsibility, too sensitive a venerator of life itself, to be thought of as a fascist. This is not the view of a considerable body of critics who regard him as a proto-fascist and who resort to quite unwarranted generalizations to lend verisimilitude to the charge. It is easy to condemn Lawrence with allegations of 'unreason' and 'mindlessness' and 'sexuality', but such allegations merely betray an obstinate incomprehension of his work–as the following quotation reveals (and it is a representative instance):

'[Lawrence] turned away from the mental and moral sanities that make life wholesome and willed himself into the blind life of instinct and unreason. He cultivated mindlessness and made a religion of sexuality–going back, as he was for ever saying, to the phallic source; he took refuge from thought in the sub-human awareness of the "solar plexus"–whatever he meant by that–and the "blood". And in all this he was anticipating the anarchism which before long would intoxicate the German soul, talking the language of Rosenberg and Ludendorff, yielding to the power-madness that already possessed Hitler and was driving him on to destroy the world....'[1]

[1] W. S. Handley Jones, 'D. H. Lawrence and the Revolt against Reason', *The London Quarterly and Holborn Review*, 173 (January 1948), 27–8. Cf. Stebelton H. Nulle, 'D. H. Lawrence and the Fascist Movement', *The New Mexico Quarterly*, 10 (February 1940), 4, 6; Cecil Gray, *Musical Chairs*, p. 130; Bertrand Russell, *Portraits from Memory*

The Plumed Serpent (I shall refer in a moment to more damning instances of a fascist tendency in the novel) is best regarded as an aberration, a blind alley into which Lawrence was driven by the psychological forces I have attempted to describe in this study. His own aversion to fascism, moreover, is indisputable. In the middle twenties, while he was at work on *The Plumed Serpent* and before Hitler brought out the full implications of fascism for the uncritical, Lawrence was unequivocal in his denunciation of it:

'What did they want to do, those Manby girls? Undermine, undermine, undermine. They wanted to undermine Rico, just as that fair young man would have liked to undermine her. Believe in nothing, care about nothing: but keep the surface easy, and have a good time. *Let us undermine one another. There is nothing to believe in, so let us undermine everything.* . . .

'The evil! The mysterious potency of evil. She could see it all the time, in individuals, in society, in the press. There it was in socialism and bolshevism: the same evil. But bolshevism made a mess of the outside of life, so turn it down. Try fascism. Fascism would keep the surface of life intact, and carry on the undermining business all the better. All the better sport. Never draw blood. Keep the haemorrhage internal, invisible.

'And as soon as fascism makes a break—which it is bound to, because all evil works up to a break—then turn it down. With gusto, turn it down.

'Mankind, like a horse, ridden by a stranger, smooth-faced, evil rider. Evil himself, smooth-faced and pseudo-handsome, riding mankind past the dead snake, to the last break.'[1]

It must be admitted, however, that a reader unacquainted with the rest of Lawrence's work would find sufficient justification in *The*

---

and *Other Things* (London, 1956), pp. 105, 107, 108; William York Tindall, *D. H. Lawrence and Susan His Cow*, pp. 174–5, and *Forces in Modern British Literature*, p. 84; Eliseo Vivas, *D. H. Lawrence*, p. 103; and Eric Bentley, *The Cult of the Superman*, p. 230.

[1] 'St Mawr' (written in 1924), *Tales*, p. 613. Cf. the following extract from a letter to Rolf Gardiner (March 1928): 'When leadership has died—it is very nearly dead, save for Mussolini and you and White Fox and Annie Besant and Gandhi—then it will be born again, perhaps, new and changed, and based on reciprocity of tenderness. The reciprocity of power is obsolete. When you get down to the basis of life, to the depth of the warm creative stir, there is no power. . . .

'Yes, one can ignore Fascism in Italy for a time. But after a while, the sense of false power forced against life is very depressing. And one can't escape—except by the trick of abstraction, which is no good.' *Letters*, pp. 704–5.

Plumed Serpent for linking the author with Nazism. When the Quetzal-coatl movement goes into action, its ethos is all too clear. Ramón, for instance, when challenged by the Bishop as to the legality of his intention to burn the holy images of the church at Sayula, replies: 'What is illegal in Mexico? What is weak is illegal. I will not be weak, My Lord' (p. 278). And then, most damagingly, there is the description of the executions which mark Cipriano's assumption of godhood:

'The song ceased, and there was silence. Then Cipriano beckoned to the men to bring forward the peon with the black cross painted on his front and back. He limped forward.

'Cipriano: "What man is that, limping?"

'Guards: "It is Guillermo, overseer of Don Ramón, who betrayed Don Ramón, his master." . . .

'Cipriano: "What made him wish to betray his master?"

'Guards: "His heart is a grey dog, and a woman, a grey bitch, enticed him forth."

'Cipriano: "What woman enticed the grey dog forth?"

'The guards came forward with the woman.

'Guards: "This woman, Maruca, my Lord, with the grey bitch heart." . . .

'Cipriano: "The grey dog, and the grey bitch, we kill, for their mouths are yellow with poison. Is it well, men of Huitzilopochtli?"

'Guards: "It is very well, my Lord." . . .

'Cipriano: ". . . Bind them with the grey cords, put ash on their heads."

'The guards quickly obeyed. The prisoners, ash-grey, gazed with black, glittering eyes, making not a sound. A guard stood behind each of them. Cipriano gave a sign, and quick as lightning the guards had got the throats of the two victims in a grey cloth, and with a sharp jerk had broken their necks, lifting them backwards in one movement. The grey cloths they tied hard and tight round the throats, laying the twitching bodies on the floor.

'Cipriano turned to the crowd.

> "The Lords of Life are the Masters of Death.
> Blue is the breath of Quetzalcoatl.
> Red is Huitzilopochtli's blood.
> But the grey dog belongs to the ash of the world. . . ."

'Then he turned once more, to the other, imprisoned peons.

'Cipriano: "Who are these four?"

'Guards: "Four who came to kill Don Ramón." ' . . .

'Cipriano: "When many men come against one, what is the name of the many?"

'Guards: "Cowards, my Lord."

'Cipriano: "Cowards it is. They are less than men. Men that are less than men are not good enough for the light of the sun. If men that are men will live, men that are less than men must be put away, lest they multiply too much. Men that are more than men have the judgment of men that are less than men. Shall they die?"

'Guards: "They shall surely die, my Lord."

...

'The eyes of the three men were blindfolded with black cloths, their blouses and pantaloons were taken away. Cipriano took a bright, thin dagger.

' "The Lords of Life are Masters of Death," he said in a loud, clear voice.

'And swift as lightning he stabbed the blindfolded men to the heart, with three swift, heavy stabs. Then he lifted the red dagger and threw it down.

' "The Lords of Life are Masters of Death," he repeated . . .' (pp. 393–6).

It is painful to realize that Lawrence approves of this travesty of a trial in which Cipriano, as a 'Lord of Life', arrogantly assumes the power of death, in which justice is glibly pronounced in the rehearsed responses of drilled guards, and in which the only refinement is a varying of the manner of death to fit the crime. It hardly needs saying, moreover, that Cipriano's ethics are blatantly fascist: granted hindsight, we can see how easily the category of those who are 'not good enough for the light of the sun' might be extended, how simply Jews and gipsies, for instance, might be classed along with cowards as 'less than men'. Not that we need to invoke the susceptibilities of a post-Nazi generation; it is enough that Lawrence should so wantonly trample on his own feelings, for the executions at Sayula are surely a more repugnant spectacle than the bitterly criticized bull-fight in Mexico City. And the point to register here is that the executions *are* a spectacle, a public show which caters for the same depraved lust as that satisfied at the bull-fight, the death lust of the victimizer for the victim. But whereas Lawrence vividly depicted the reactions of the crowd at the bull-fight, he does not attempt to describe the effect of the executions on the assembled peons. This is the more notable in that the responses of the peons at crucial stages in the development of the Quetzalcoatl movement are otherwise consistently recorded, are a ready means, indeed, of conveying the attractiveness of the new religion. Is it, we wonder, that Lawrence dare not visualize the expression on faces in the crowd, whether of bestial complicity or of aversion, and stops short at faking a pure enthusiasm? As it is, the strain of prostituting the imagination is great enough – as the quality of the writing suggests. The prose is singularly flat and uninspired, lapsing easily into the repetitive cliché of 'quick as lightning' and 'swift as lightning' or into the studied quaintness of 'What woman enticed the grey dog forth?' In addition, where Lawrence apparently aims at a dramatic heightening in his direct rendering of the exchanges between Cipriano and the guards, he succeeds only in being stiff, if not in betraying how his creative impulse has been stifled by a willed automatism. The automatism, of course, is necessary, for Lawrence is deliberately forcing himself to be demonic in the interests of making a grand male assertion. Kate's reflections after the executions both point to the true significance of the scene and convey Lawrence's own ambivalence to his bastard child:

'When Cipriano said: *Man that is man is more than a man*, he seemed to be driving the male significance to its utmost, and beyond, with a sort of demonism. It seemed to her all terrible *will*, the exertion of pure, awful will.

'And deep in her soul came a revulsion against this manifestation of pure will. It was fascinating also. There was something dark and lustrous and fascinating to her in Cipriano, and in Ramón. The black, relentless power, even passion of the will in men! The strange, sombre, lustrous beauty of it! She knew herself under the spell.

'At the same time, as is so often the case with any spell, it did not bind her completely. She was spellbound, but not utterly acquiescent. In one corner of her soul was revulsion and a touch of nausea' (pp. 401-2).

The 'male significance' that is asseverated in the executions is in sad contrast to the creative 'man-being' that is defined in *The Rainbow*, and we can only regret that Lawrence should have felt obliged to descend so low. A Cipriano is provided to make good Ramón's deficiencies as a 'lord of two ways' – there are repeated references to the 'hard drums of Huitzilopochtli' as opposed to the 'soft roll of the drums of Quetzalcoatl' (pp. 396, 397, 399) – and the resurrection of Huitzilopochtli becomes, in effect, a celebration of human sacrifice. Having driven himself to a repugnant conclusion, it is with little conviction and no fire that Lawrence details the subsequent fortunes of the movement. Ramón's name becomes 'a name to conjure with' throughout Mexico, but the living Quetzalcoatl suffers from 'the deep, devilish animosity' which the country sends out against him; and the Mexicans seem 'to steam with invisible, grudging hate, the hate of demons foiled in their own souls, whose only motive is to foil everything, everybody, in the everlasting hell of cramped frustration' (pp. 419, 420). We see, moreover, the crippling limitations of a movement which is dependent on one man: Kate reflects that if Ramón should kill himself with his efforts, 'Cipriano would come apart, and it would be all finished' (p. 423). Finally–and this development is noted with a surprising perfunctoriness–the religion of Quetzalcoatl is by law declared to be 'the national religion of the Republic'; but, though the whole country is said to be 'thrilling with a new thing, with a release of new energy', there is 'a sense of violence and crudity in it all, a touch of horror' (p. 437).

II

In *Aaron's Rod*, it will be remembered, Lilly tells Aaron that 'men must submit to the greater soul in a man, for their guidance', but if it is clear that he has himself in mind as the leader to whom Aaron should submit, it is uncertain whither he proposes to lead. In *The Plumed Serpent* Cipriano follows Ramón into the Quetzalcoatl movement. From the beginning of the book he is quite simply Ramón's 'man', and for the first time in the novels a 'sacred' relationship between men is presented as being successfully established.

It is a relationship, however, which is vastly different from the *Blutbrüderschaft* into which Birkin vainly tries to draw Gerald in *Women in Love*, the book in which this theme first appears. It is not friendship in any ordinary sense. Nor is it a relation which solves 'the problem of love and eternal conjunction between two men'.[1] In accordance with the revulsion from 'love' in *Aaron's Rod*, it is a relationship which is founded on Ramón's power to compel submission:

' "But you don't believe in [Ramón]," [Kate says to Cipriano]. . . .

' "How not believe? I not believe in Ramón?–Well, perhaps not, in that way of kneeling before him and spreading out my arms and shedding tears on his feet. But I–I believe in him, too. Not in your way,

[1] See Chap. 3, p. 183 above.

234 One Up, One Down: The Third Period

but in mine. I tell you why. Because he has the power to compel me. If he hadn't the power to *compel* me, how should I believe?" ' (p. 217).

Gone, we see, are the hesitancies which qualified Aaron's attitude towards Lilly. Ramón's power, moreover, is merely asserted, either flatly, as above, or with tremulous awe, as in the passage below. When Lawrence does try to evoke the heroic presence, we wait in vain for the quiet conviction of a 'Keep up your bright swords, for the dew will rust them':

'Don Ramón stood a moment to look around. This was his own world. His own spirit was spread over it like a soft, nourishing shadow, and the silence of his own power gave it peace.

'The men working were almost instantly aware of his presence. One after the other the dark, hot faces glanced up at him, and glanced away again. They were men, and his presence was wonderful to them; but they were afraid to approach him, even by staring at him. They worked the quicker for having seen him, as if it gave them new life' (p. 182).

What Cipriano's submission to Ramón means is suggested by the symbolism of the scene in which Ramón prevails on his follower 'to assume the living Huitzilopochtli' and initiates him into the mysteries of godhood:

'They were sitting on the mats in Ramón's room . . .

' "Stand up!" said Ramón.

'Cipriano stood up at once, with that soft, startling alertness in his movement.

'Ramón came quickly to him, placed one of his hands over Cipriano's eyes, closing them. Ramón stood behind Cipriano, who remained motionless in the warm dark, his consciousness reeling in strange concentric waves, towards a centre where it suddenly plunges into the bottomless deeps, like sleep.

' "Cipriano?"—the voice sounded so far off.

' "Yes."

' "Is it dark?"

' "It is dark."

' "Is it alive? Is the darkness alive?"

' "Surely it is alive." . . .

'Ramón then bound Cipriano's eyes and head with a strip of black fur. Then again, with a warm, soft pressure, he pressed one naked hand over Cipriano's naked breast, and one between his shoulders. Cipriano stood in profound darkness, erect and silent.

' "Cipriano?"

' "Yes."

' "Is it dark in your heart?"

' "It is coming dark."

'Ramón felt the thud of the man's heart slowly slackening. . . .

' "Is it dark?"

' "It is dark."

' "Who lives?"

' "I."

'Ramón bound Cipriano's arms at his sides, with a belt of fur round the breast. Then he put his one hand over the navel, his other hand in the small of the other man's back, pressing with slow, warm, powerful pressure.

' "Cipriano?"

' "Yes."

'The voice and the answer going farther and farther away.

' "Is it dark?"

' "No, my Lord."

...

'Ramón bound him fast round the middle, then, pressing his head against the hip, folded the arms round Cipriano's loins, closing with his hands the secret places.

' "Cipriano?"

' "Yes."

' "Is it all dark?"

'But Cipriano could not answer. . . . Ramón kneeled with pressed head and arms and hands, for some moments still. Then he bound the loins, binding the wrists to the hips. . . .

'Then Ramón bound the ankles, lifted Cipriano suddenly, with a sleep-moving softness, laid him on the skin of a big mountain-lion, which was spread upon the blankets, threw over him the red and black *serape* of Huitzilopochtli, and lay down at his feet, holding Cipriano's feet to his own abdomen.

'And both men passed into perfect unconsciousness, Cipriano within the womb of undisturbed creation, Ramón in the death sleep' (pp. 383–5).

William York Tindall states that this ceremony is 'modeled roughly upon the initiations described by Pryse and Mme Blavatsky',[1] and it is no doubt meant to be regarded as an arcane rite, but I suggest that its

[1] *D. H. Lawrence and Susan His Cow*, p. 155.

covert significance is analogous to that of the scene in which Lilly
rubs Aaron's body with oil.[1] The emphasis on the nakedness and
intimacy, if not on the sexuality, of the physical contact between the
two men is reminiscent of that in the earlier novel and charges the
initiation with a similar emotional undercurrent. And if we saw that
Lilly's having Aaron in his hands was a symbolic assertion of 'the deep,
fathomless submission' he wished to exact, we should not find it
impossible to fathom 'the bottomless deeps' into which Cipriano's
consciousness plunges. Ramón closes Cipriano's eyes with his hand
and then binds them with a strip of black fur because what he is in
effect demanding of the living Huitzilopochtli is a blind allegiance. It
is surely not coincidental that when for an instant it is not 'all dark',
when Cipriano, that is to say, sees the light, he should address Ramón
as 'my Lord', this being the only appellation he uses throughout the
scene and this being the psychological moment at which it is elicited.
After this admission of a due subordination it should come as
no surprise that Cipriano is ultimately bound hand and foot. Nor
should we view Ramón's lying down at Cipriano's feet at the end
of the ceremony as evidence of a sudden and inconsistent humility;
he lies, I take it, at right angles to Cipriano, for he '[holds] Cipriano's
feet to his own abdomen', and we are given graphic confirmation
that their relationship is to conform to the pattern of 'one up, one
down'.

That Cipriano, the ambitious, bloodthirsty general, should so easily
submit to Ramón's pre-eminence hardly carries conviction, but then
verisimilitude is of little relevance as a criterion in judging their
wooden relationship. Lawrence, it seems, is so intent on demon-
strating the delights of submission that he fails utterly to evoke the
sort of living interchange that characterizes the more tentative relationships of Birkin and Gerald, Aaron and Lilly, and Somers and Jack.
Ramón and Cipriano do not grow into a relationship; like rocks, they
are fixed in preordained positions, and all we are given are mutual
declarations of satisfaction at the arrangement. Until he marries
Teresa, it seems that the only relationship Ramón can tolerate is that
with Cipriano, for 'mere *personal* contact, mere human contact' fills
him 'with disgust'.

'He had to meet [people] on another plane, where the contact was
different; intangible, remote, and without *intimacy*. His soul was concerned elsewhere. So that the quick of him need not be bound to

[1] See pp. 202–3 above.

anybody. The quick of a man must turn to God alone: in some way or other.

'With Cipriano he was most sure. Cipriano and he, even when they embraced each other with passion, when they met after an absence, embraced in the recognition of each other's eternal and abiding loneliness; like the Morning Star' (pp. 264–5).

Ramón's confidence in Cipriano is matched by the latter's strenuous protestations of belief in him: 'You may respect [Ramón]', he tells Kate, 'more than any other man in the world' (p. 90). And, for good measure, we have this: Kate asks Cipriano whether it would have meant very much to him if Ramón had been killed:

' "To me!" he said, and he pressed his hand against the buttons of his tunic. "To me Ramón is *more* than life. *More* than life." His eyes seemed to glare and go sightless, as he said it, the ferocity melting in a strange blind, confiding glare, that seemed sightless, either looking inward, or out at the whole vast void of the cosmos, where no vision is left' (p. 323).

The melodramatic stridency of this passage, the bathetic straining after effect, is symptomatic of Lawrence's inner uncertainty as to what he is doing. It is to be regretted that in this novel there is no obvious Lawrence-figure, such as that of Birkin or Lilly or Somers in the previous novels, to act as a check against such extravagances, for I imagine Lawrence would have found it difficult, if not inconceivable, to direct an adulation expressed in such terms to a character with whom he was closely identified. The excesses of the novel can in part be ascribed to the absence of the critical consciousness which a Lawrence-figure would perforce have provided, for Lawrence's insubstantial and equivocal presence as Kate merely prompts him at times to demur, not forcibly to challenge and contest; and *her* hesitations, as we shall see, are all too easily overcome. Lawrence evidently wished to be unfettered in his flight to excess.[1]

[1] Cf. F. R. Leavis, who takes a similar view of this weakness: 'And here we have an answer to a question that naturally occurs to anyone who reads the novels in succession: Why should the main character, the centre of sympathetic interest and the dramatized consciousness through which things are presented, be, in this book, a woman? A man as imaginative centre would inevitably have been a Rawdon Lilly or a Richard Lovat Somers, and inevitably have been involved in Lawrence's relations with Frieda–and so in all the disabling complexities of attitude' (*D. H. Lawrence: Novelist*, p. 67).

I might add that there is perhaps an additional answer to the question Leavis poses. Lawrence's ambiguous presence in the book as a woman gives some ground

Kate's reservations in regard to the relationship of Ramón and
Cipriano merely serve further to undermine our belief in it. When
Cipriano tells her that he is 'Ramón's man', she mistrusts him:
'In the long run he was nobody's man. He was that old, masterless
Pan-male, that could not even conceive of service; particularly the
service of mankind. He saw only glory; the black mystery of glory
consummated. And himself like a wind of glory' (p. 327).

Kate's intuition is matched by Ramón's feeling that 'Cipriano would
betray him' (p. 205); but, though these suspicions are not validated
by any corroborative action, for the relationship, as presented, is static,
they do throw doubt on the reality of Cipriano's submission to
Ramón. We see, indeed, that their relationship is also in other respects
not quite what Lawrence would have us believe it to be:
'[Ramón] pushed back his hair and rose, and very quickly went out,
as he was, with naked torso. . . .

'They had a tea-table out on the terrace, and Cipriano, in uniform,
was there. He got up quickly, and came down the terrace with out-
stretched arms, his black eyes gleaming with an intensity almost like
pain, upon the face of the other man. And Ramón looked back at him
with wide, seeing, yet unchanging eyes.

'The two men embraced, breast to breast, and for a moment
Cipriano laid his little blackish hands on the naked shoulders of
the bigger man, and for a moment was perfectly still on his breast.
Then very softly, he stood back and looked at him, saying not a
word.

'Ramón abstractedly laid his hand on Cipriano's shoulder, looking
down at him with a little smile.

' "*Qué tal?*" he said, from the edge of his lips. "How goes it?"

' "*Bien! Muy bien!*" said Cipriano, still gazing into the other man's
face with black, wondering, childlike, searching eyes, as if he, Cipriano, were searching for *himself*, in Ramón's face. Ramón looked back
into Cipriano's black, Indian eyes with a faint, kind smile of recognition, and Cipriano hung his head as if to hide his face, the black hair,
which he wore rather long and brushed sideways, dropping over his
forehead.

'The women watched in absolute silence. Then, as the two men
began slowly to come along the terrace to the tea-table, Carlota
began to pour tea. But her hand trembled so much, the teapot

for thinking that he was psychologically incapable of placing himself at the centre
of a work in which he makes his most unrestrained 'male' affirmation.

wobbled as she held it, and she had to put it down and clasp her hands in the lap of her white muslin dress.

...

'Doña Carlota had made a great effort over herself, and with eyes fixed on the tea-cups, she poured out the tea. She handed [Ramón] his cup without looking at him. She did not trust herself to look at him. It made her tremble with a strange, hysterical anger: she, who had been married to him for years, and knew him, ah, knew him: and yet, and yet, had not got him at all. None of him' (pp. 193–5).

For a brief moment here the relationship between Ramón and Cipriano pulses into life, taking on an unaccustomed solidity. It is instructive to note that Lawrence keeps his eyes firmly on the scene and so succeeds in evoking the strong feeling that exists between the two men without having recourse to the sort of embarrassing declaration we have noticed earlier. It is also instructive to note that the kind of relationship the scene suggests is different from that which Ramón, in the passage quoted on pp. 236–7 above, desiderates as a norm and professes they maintain. Despite the fact that Ramón is said to be 'abstracted', that he speaks 'from the edge of his lips', and that his smile of recognition is 'faint', the contact between the two men can hardly be described as 'intangible, remote, and without *intimacy*'. Indeed, it is the sense of a very close, personal intimacy which, among other things I shall refer to, is responsible for Carlota's agitation. Nor does it appear that the men '[embrace] in the recognition of each other's eternal and abiding loneliness; like the Morning Star'. The simile points to a meeting of two men of achieved selves; the actual embrace suggests that Cipriano leans heavily on the strength of Ramón: he '[searches] for *himself*, in Ramón's face'. Lawrence, moreover, generally castigates a childlike dependence in adult relationships, whether between man and man or man and woman; but Cipriano's eyes are 'childlike', and *his* dependence is apparently acceptable not only to Ramón. What the relationship of Ramón and Cipriano turns out to be, when its stiff contours are softened into life, as here, or when they are filled out by a covert symbolism, as in the initiation scene, is subversive of what Lawrence would seem to contend it is–an ideal relation between two men, each of whom has consummated a self and one of whom, while maintaining his independence, willingly submits to the greater soul of the other.

The scene on the terrace suggests that the male embrace is also intended to serve as an edifying model for the women who observe it.

The sweetness of homage and submission, exemplified in the way Cipriano mutely looks at Ramón and then hangs his head as if to hide his face, is a lesson that Kate and Carlota yet have to learn. That the women watch the men 'in absolute silence' apparently indicates that they are impressed in spite of themselves, though Carlota's agitation, I take it, is attributable not merely to her fear of the men's association in the Quetzalcoatl movement, nor to her realization that she has not 'got' Ramón, but to her inchoate determination not to yield her husband the sort of blind devotion he receives from his friend. The moral, moreover, is clear. Carlota persists in her wilful independence of Ramón and brings about her own death; Kate is less extreme and comes eventually to pay due obeisance to Cipriano.

III

Jascha Kessler has analysed *The Plumed Serpent* in terms of universal 'ritual myths' associated with the 'rites of passage'. Following Joseph Campbell's outline in *The Hero with the Thousand Faces*, he states that 'the myths are based on a simple formula: *separation–initiation–return*', and maintains that 'Kate's story in *The Plumed Serpent* comprises . . . the first two parts of this formula . . .' though Lawrence 'seems not to have been conscious' of the mythic pattern to which the book conforms. In accordance with this pattern Kessler suggests that Kate's voyage across the Lake of Sayula to Sayula village indicates the crossing of 'the first threshold' which is 'usually denoted by a trip across water', and that 'this crossing marks a dying to the old self and figures the promise of rebirth'.[1] It is an interesting suggestion and one which prompts questions as to the nature of Kate's new mode of being, for she is 'reborn' into a role played by no other woman in the novels.

The things Kate initially rejects are familiar to us from the earlier novels. Like Birkin and Ursula, she makes up her mind 'to cut herself off from all the mechanical widdershin contacts' ('widdershin' being defined as 'unwinding the sensations of disintegration and anti-life'), and 'to turn [her] back on the cog-wheel world' (p. 113). And like Birkin and Lilly, she rejects 'love': she realizes that 'human love has its limits, that there is a beyond', and that 'the yearning for companionship and sympathy and human love [has] left her' (p. 65).

[1] 'Descent in Darkness: The Myth of *The Plumed Serpent*', *A D. H. Lawrence Miscellany*, pp. 243, 239, 244.

In her revulsion from 'the cog-wheel world' Kate turns to 'a soft world of potency' and succeeds in establishing the kind of connection with the cosmos that the Quetzalcoatl movement strives to ritualize:

'She was surprised at herself, suddenly using this language. But her weariness and her sense of devastation had been so complete, that the Other Breath in the air, and the bluish dark power in the earth had become, almost suddenly, more real to her than so-called reality. Concrete, jarring, exasperating reality had melted away, and a soft world of potency stood in its place, the velvety dark flux from the earth, the delicate yet supreme life-breath in the inner air. Behind the fierce sun the dark eyes of a deeper sun were watching, and between the bluish ribs of the mountains a powerful heart was secretly beating, the heart of the earth' (p. 118).

In her aversion from 'love' Kate arrives at a new conception of sex. I propose to examine this conception in some detail, for it gives cause for disquiet, making us suspect that Lawrence uses the Quetzalcoatl theme as an unacknowledged means of forcing a desiderated submissiveness on his main female character.

Kate first senses a 'greater sex' when, like the watching peons, she too is impelled to join in the dancing of the Quetzalcoatl men in the *plaza* at Sayula:

'The outer wheel was all men. She seemed to feel the strange dark glow of them upon her back. Men, dark, collective men, non-individual. And herself woman, wheeling upon the great wheel of womanhood.

'Men and women alike danced with faces lowered and expressionless, abstract, gone in the deep absorption of men into the greater manhood, women into the great womanhood. It was sex, but the greater, not the lesser sex. The waters over the earth wheeling upon the waters under the earth, like an eagle silently wheeling above its own shadow.

'She felt her sex and her womanhood caught up and identified in the slowly revolving ocean of nascent life, the dark sky of the men lowering and wheeling above. She was not herself, she was gone, and her own desires were gone in the ocean of the great desire. As the man whose fingers touched hers was gone in the ocean that is male, stooping over the face of the waters.

'The slow, vast, soft-touching revolution of the ocean above upon ocean below, with no vestige of rustling or foam. Only the pure sliding conjunction. Herself gone into her greater self, her woman-hood consummated in the greater womanhood. And where her fingers touched the fingers of the man, the quiet spark, like the dawn-star, shining between her and the greater manhood of men.

'How strange, to be merged in desire beyond desire, to be gone in the body beyond the individualism of the body, with the spark of contact lingering like a morning star between her and the man, her woman's greater self, and the greater self of man. Even of the two men next to her. What a beautiful slow wheel of dance, two great streams streaming in contact, in opposite directions.

'She did not know the face of the man whose fingers she held. Her personal eyes had gone blind, his face was the face of dark heaven, only the touch of his fingers a star that was both hers and his' (pp. 140–1).

Considered as an evocation of Kate's reactions to the dance, this description is inoffensive, though the vacuity of some of the phraseology is reminiscent of the mystical obfuscation of parts of *Women in Love*. It is the sexual symbolism that is disturbing. At first sight the dance might seem to figure the kind of contact between men and women which Lawrence advocates in *The Rainbow*, 'two great streams streaming in contact, in opposite directions', but the eagle simile gives us pause. If it brings to mind the eagle image in *Aaron's Rod*,[1] it suggests a strikingly different sexual relationship. No longer are there two eagles, meeting in 'the love consummation' in mid-air; the eagle 'silently wheeling above its own shadow' is clearly, in terms of the water imagery, a male eagle, and the simile implies that the woman is merely a projection of the man, a pale reflection of him, and that he is wholeheartedly and self-centredly concerned only with his own needs. It begins to appear that the description of the dance is an insidious preparation for Kate's capitulation to Cipriano:

'Kate watched [Cipriano's] deep, strong Indian chest lift as his arms quickly fought to free his head. How dark he was, and how primitively physical, beautiful, and deep-breasted, with soft, full flesh! But all, as it were, for himself. Nothing that came forth from him to meet with one outside. All oblivious of the outside, all for himself' (pp. 214–15).

This interpretation of the dance is borne out, I think, by other tell-tale images in the passage quoted. While Kate's desires are 'gone in the ocean of the great desire', are submerged, that is to say, in a desire that transcends sex, the man whose fingers touch hers is 'gone in the ocean that is male', in the waters, that is, which '[wheel] upon the waters

[1] See p. 194 above.

under the earth', and the 'male ocean' remains pointedly 'stooping *over* the face of the waters' that are 'female'. Once Kate's desires are gone, she is 'consummated in the greater womanhood', but what this consummation entails is unwittingly revealed by the insistence that there is 'no vestige of rustling or foam': the seemingly innocuous phrase looks ahead, as we shall see, to 'the death in her of the Aphrodite of the foam' (p. 439), to her voluntary foregoing of orgasm.

This, at any rate, is the conclusion to which the book inexorably leads, and where the path to it is not covertly prepared, it is exultantly hacked out. After the dancing there is the description of Kate's drive with Cipriano:

'As they sat side by side in the motor-car, silent, swaying to the broken road, she could feel the curious tingling heat of his blood, and the heavy power of the *will* that lay unemerged in his blood. She could see again the skies go dark, and the phallic mystery rearing itself like a whirling dark cloud, to the zenith, till it pierced the sombre, twilit zenith; the old, supreme phallic mystery. And herself in the everlasting twilight, a sky above where the sun ran smokily, an earth below where the trees and creatures rose up in blackness, and man strode along naked, dark, half-visible, and suddenly whirled in supreme power, towering like a dark whirlwind column, whirling to pierce the very zenith.

'The mystery of the primeval world! She could feel it now in all its shadowy, furious magnificence. She knew now what was the black, glinting look in Cipriano's eyes. She could understand marrying him, now. In the shadowy world where men were visionless, and winds of fury rose up from the earth, Cipriano was still a power. Once you entered his mystery the scale of all things changed, and he became a living male power, undefined, and unconfined. The smallness, the limitations ceased to exist. In his black, glinting eyes the power was limitless, and it was as if, from him, from his body of blood could rise up that pillar of cloud which swayed and swung, like a rearing serpent or a rising tree, till it swept the zenith, and all the earth below was dark and prone, and consummated. . . .

'As he sat in silence, casting the old, twilit Pan-power over her, she felt herself submitting, succumbing. He was once more the old dominant male, shadowy, intangible, looming suddenly tall, and covering the sky, making a darkness that was himself and nothing but himself, the Pan male. And she was swooned prone beneath, perfect in her proneness. . . .

'He would never woo; she saw this. When the power of his blood rose in him, the dark aura streamed from him like a cloud pregnant with power, like thunder, and rose like a whirlwind that rises suddenly in the twilight and raises a great pliant column, swaying and leaning with power, clear between heaven and earth.

'Ah! and what a mystery of prone submission, on her part, this huge erection would imply! Submission absolute, like the earth under the sky. Beneath an over-arching absolute. . . .

'She could conceive now her marriage with Cipriano; the supreme passivity, like the earth below the twilight, consummate in living lifelessness, the sheer solid mystery of passivity. Ah, what an abandon, what an abandon, what an abandon!–of so many things she wanted to abandon.

'Cipriano put his hand, with its strange soft warmth and weight, upon her knee, and her soul melted like fused metal . . .' (pp. 324–5).

The sort of excess noted earlier in regard to Cipriano's protestations of devotion to Ramón pales before the blatancy of this hymn to the power of the phallus, this utterly humourless paean of awe. Indeed, the single-mindedness of what, after Ruskin, we might call the phallic fallacy is obsessive: the phallic mystery rears itself 'like a whirling dark cloud' and '[pierces] the sombre, twilit zenith'; man towers 'like a dark whirlwind column'; 'winds of fury [rise] up from the earth'; it is as if from Cipriano's body of blood there rises up a 'pillar of cloud which [sways and swings], like a rearing serpent or a rising tree'; the dark aura streams from Cipriano and raises 'a great pliant column, swaying and leaning with power, clear between heaven and earth'. The thematic implications of the passage are in accordance with what the description of the dancing has led us to expect. Cipriano, the epitome of an admired maleness, is 'the Pan male', and his masculinity gives threatening promise of a 'huge erection'. The previous aim of a creative male utterance in the 'man's world' is thus supplanted not only by the 'male significance' asserted in Cipriano's conduct of the executions but by the 'supreme power' of the phallic mystery. That this power of 'the old dominant male' is indeed linked in Lawrence's mind with a capacity for violence is indicated by an earlier passage: after Ramón has 'with one stroke' driven a knife into the throat of one of the men who attacks him, his brow seems to Kate to be 'very pure and primitive' and his eyes have 'a certain primitive gleaming look of virginity. As men must have been, in the first awful days, with that strange beauty that goes with pristine rudimentariness' (p. 310).

It is scarcely surprising that Cipriano's 'living male power' should remain 'undefined' as well as 'unconfined', for Lawrence seems singularly unwilling to face its limitations. Before her revelation Kate no doubt thinks of Cipriano as being 'limited as a snake or a lizard is limited' (p. 324), but after it 'the limitations [cease] to exist'; the limited snake, that is to say, is speedily transformed into the 'rearing serpent', and the weakness which the Quetzalcoatl movement is dedicated to eliminate becomes, in Cipriano, the aspirant to godhood, a strength to be celebrated – as does 'the heavy power of the will' which in Carlota, is insistently reprehended.

It is during the drive that Kate can first 'understand marrying [Cipriano]', but she is clearly won by an unsubtle serpent, not a bird, and we might expect (though this does not prove to be the case) that their marriage will hardly qualify for the blessing of Quetzalcoatl. Nor is it to be a marriage in which the man and the woman meet in the rainbow, the only absolute, that which unites heaven and earth; for the 'great pliant column' which sways 'clear between heaven and earth' has itself become 'an over-arching absolute', and for the female partner to such a marriage there is left only submission, 'submission absolute, like the earth under the sky'. Proneness is the distinctive feature of this submission: the earth below the pillar of cloud is 'dark and prone and consummated', and Kate imagines herself 'swooned prone beneath, perfect in her proneness'. The proneness does not merely imply an utter prostration before the male, a meet tribute to the huge erection; the 'mystery of prone submission' betokens a 'supreme passivity', a 'living lifelessness', betokens, in a word, the extinction of the raging Aphrodite. Kate's glorification of proneness, 'the sheer solid mystery of passivity', also implies her acceptance of a relationship which is 'one up, one down', and indeed, when the car stops, she thinks of Cipriano as 'the Master. The everlasting Pan' (p. 326).

Perhaps the most sinister sentence in the passage describing the drive is: 'Ah, what an abandon, what an abandon, what an abandon! – of so many things she wanted to abandon.' What this looks forward to primarily, and hence, no doubt, the insistence of the repetition, is Kate's abandonment of 'orgiastic "satisfaction" ' (p. 439); but it also has other implications, as the reference to the 'many things' indicates. When Ramón sees Kate after the drive, he notices that she has 'the face of one waking from the dead, curiously dipped in death, with a tenderness far more new and vulnerable than a child's' (p. 326). Kate,

in other words, is 'reborn', but not to a new self; it is rather to a re-
linquishment of the self, to what we might call a personal abandon,
that she wakes from the dead. After Cipriano puts his hand on her
knee and her soul '[melts] like fused metal', Kate realizes that 'her self
[has] abandoned her' (p. 326); and when he subsequently makes love
to her, she '[fuses] into a molten unconsciousness, her will, her very
self gone, leaving her lying in molten life, like a lake of still fire,
unconscious of everything save the eternality of the fire in which she
[is] gone' (p. 334). The rape of Kate's character which ensures that she
can accept Cipriano on the terms discussed above doubtless makes it
necessary for Lawrence to emphasize her 'unconsciousness', but this
does not alter the fact that the abandonment of self in the sexual
relation has, since *The Rainbow*, been consistently regarded as a cardinal
sin. Images of melting are associated, it will be remembered, with an
abhorred 'mingling and merging'. Yet now loss of self in a woman, it
seems, is permissible, if not desirable. Lawrence's attitude is the more
suspect in that he simultaneously tries to maintain his old position:
' "With a woman," [Ramón tells Kate], "a man always wants to let
himself go. And it is precisely with a woman that he should never let
himself go. It is precisely with a woman that he should never let himself go, but stick to his innermost belief, and meet her just there.
Because when the innermost belief coincides in them both, if it's
physical, there, and then, and nowhere else, they can meet. And it's
no good unless there is a meeting. It's no good a man ravishing a
woman, and it's absolutely no good a woman ravishing a man. It's a
sin, that is. There is such a thing as sin, and that's the centre of it.
Men and women keep on ravishing one another. . . . Letting oneself
go, is either ravishing or being ravished . . ." ' (pp. 284–5).

Following her rhapsodic reflections in the motor-car, Kate agrees to
marry Cipriano. She is first married to him informally by Ramón, the
'marriage by Quetzalcoatl' (the title of the chapter in which the
mystic ceremony is performed) preceding the civil marriage:

'Ramón took off his blouse and threw it on the stairs. Then with
naked breast he led her into the garden, into the massive rain. Cipriano came forward, barefoot, with naked breast, bareheaded, in the
floppy white pantaloons.

'They stood barefoot on the earth, that still threw back a white
smoke of waters. The rain drenched them in a moment.

' "Barefoot on the living earth, with faces to the living rain," said
Ramón in Spanish, quietly; "at twilight, between the night and the

day; man, and woman, in presence of the unfading star, meet to be perfect in one another. Lift your face, Caterina, and say: *This man is my rain from heaven*."

'Kate lifted her face and shut her eyes in the downpour.

' "This man is my rain from heaven," she said.

' "This woman is the earth to me–say that, Cipriano," said Ramón, kneeling on one knee and laying his hand flat on the earth.

'Cipriano kneeled and laid his hand on the earth.

' "This woman is the earth to me," he said.

' "I, woman, kiss the feet and the heels of this man, for I will be strength to him, throughout the long twilight of the Morning Star."

'Kate kneeled and kissed the feet and heels of Cipriano, and said her say.

' "I, man, kiss the brow and the breast of this woman, for I will be her peace and her increase, through the long twilight of the Morning Star."

'Cipriano kissed her, and said his say.

'Then Ramón put Cipriano's hand over the rain-wet eyes of Kate, and Kate's hand over the rain-wet eyes of Cipriano.

' "I, a woman, beneath the darkness of this covering hand, pray to this man to meet me in the heart of the night, and never deny me," said Kate. "But let it be an abiding place between us, for ever."

' "I, a man, beneath the darkness of this covering hand, pray to this woman to receive me in the heart of the night, in the abiding place that is between us for ever."

' "Man shall betray a woman, and woman shall betray a man," said Ramón, "and it shall be forgiven them, each of them. But if they have met as earth and rain, between day and night, in the hour of the Star; if the man has met the woman with his body and the star of his hope, and the woman has met the man with her body and the star of her yearning, so that a meeting has come to pass, and an abiding place for the two where they are as one star, then shall neither of them betray the abiding place where the meeting lives like an unsetting star. For if either betray the abiding place of the two, it shall not be forgiven, neither by day nor by night nor in the twilight of the star."

'The rain was leaving off, the night was dark . . .' (pp. 344-5).

The ceremony would seem merely to be designed to conform to Quetzalcoatl doctrine: in the 'massive rain' and barefoot, in 'living' connection, that is, with the cosmos, man and woman meet in presence of the Star, the man, like the rain, to be a fertilizing power to the woman, the woman, like the earth, to sustain him. But the foregoing discussion should make it clear, I think, that this is not all that Lawrence is doing. The Quetzalcoatl ritual is used as yet another means of emphasizing the nature of Kate's position in relation to Cipriano. That position is appropriately a kneeling one, and Kate's submission is symbolized by her kissing of Cipriano's feet and heels, while he, on his manly legs, kisses her brow and breast. If Kate is the earth, it appears that she is there to be trampled on.[1]

It is also instructive to note that, though Kate and Cipriano marry in the twilight and under the Star, they pray to meet 'in the heart of the night', and that the ceremony concludes in the dark. This would appear to confirm that their marriage is to be exclusively a meeting in the flesh, for Cipriano's words indicate that it is a serpent night of phallic power that is envisaged, and it emphasizes that the Star is scarcely an apposite emblem of their union. It is not merely that their marriage makes no allowance for the day; it does not, like the Star, signalize a distinction between day and night, between man and woman. Indeed, when we remember Birkin's insistence that in marriage man and woman should remain 'two single beings constellated together like two stars', it becomes significant that Ramón should enjoin Kate and Cipriano to be 'as one star'.[2] The twilight in which the marriage ceremony begins, like the twilight in the cathedral in *The Rainbow*, is deceptive: what it posits (if we think, as we must, of Kate as the day and of Cipriano as the night, though this inverts Lawrence's characteristic sexual symbolism) is not a still point between day and night, a meeting of opposites in which separateness is preserved, but a sliding of the day into the night, a swallowing of the woman by the man. Kate later accuses Cipriano of treating her 'as if [she] had no life of [her] own', and maintains that she 'can't be just

---

[1] While Lawrence is benignly receptive to the idea of a woman's kissing a man's feet, he is quick to resent such adulation on the part of a man. In 'The Ladybird' (completed in 1922), for instance, when Basil kisses his wife's feet 'again and again, without the slightest self-consciousness, or the slightest misgiving', Lawrence ridicules his 'ecstatic, deadly love'. See *Tales*, pp. 390, 414.

[2] See Chap. 3, p. 163 above. Kate, in the end, is led to adopt a position which is diametrically opposed to that of Birkin: 'Now, must she admit that the individual was an illusion and a falsification? There was no such animal. Except in the mechanical world. In the world of machines, the individual machine is effectual. The individual, like the perfect being, does not and cannot exist, in the vivid world. We are all fragments. And at the best, halves. The only whole thing is the Morning Star. Which can only rise between two: or between many' (p. 405).

swallowed up' (p. 386); but her acceptance of the 'death of her individual self' and her belief in the 'deep communion of blood-oneness'
suggest that she is prepared to reconcile herself to that eventuality:

'Now she understood Ramón's assertion: Man is a column of blood:
Woman is a valley of blood. It was the primeval oneness of mankind,
the opposite of the oneness of the spirit.

'But Kate had always looked upon her blood as absolutely her own,
her individual own. Her spirit she shared, in the spirit she communed.
But her blood stayed by her in individuality.

'Now she was confronted by the other great assertion: The blood is
one blood.–It meant a strange, marginless death of her individual
self. . . .

'Now she understood the strange unison she could always feel
between Ramón and his men, and Cipriano and his men. It was the
soft, quaking, deep communion of blood-oneness. Sometimes it made
her feel sick. Sometimes it made her revolt. But it was the power she
could not get beyond . . .' (pp. 433–4).

Mingling and merging, we see, are no longer anathema. At last the
'male' desire for communion, for a 'fusing together into oneness' in
the sexual relation,[1] can be gratified–because the self-less woman, it
seems, constitutes no threat to the individuality of the man. It goes
without saying that the man retains his self intact. Cipriano, it is true,
counters Kate's objections to their relationship by saying: 'I am the
living Huitzilopochtli. And I am swallowed up. I thought, so could
you be, Malintzi' (p. 387); but if he is devoured by his own construct
of grandeur, he is manifestly not swallowed up by her. And it is surely
not without design that, in the same passage in which Kate con-
templates the 'strange, marginless death of her individual self',
reference should be made to Ramón's 'individuality', which is said to
lie in 'the mysterious star which unites the vast universal blood with
the universal breath of the spirit, and shines between them both'
(p. 434).

Cipriano, clearly, can make no claim to a similar star–he is man as 'a
column of blood'–and if his vaunted masculinity is shown to be
grounded in the 'female', it is paid the tribute of a craven submission
by Kate. The totality of her capitulation, indeed, is astonishing. She
consents to a marriage entirely on his terms, and eased of the
last challenge to which a woman can resort, Cipriano is the male
rampant:

[1] See Chap. 1, pp. 39–41 above.

'She realized, almost with wonder, the death in her of the Aphrodite of the foam: the seething, frictional, ecstatic Aphrodite. By a swift dark instinct, Cipriano drew away from this in her. When, in their love, it came back on her, the seething electric female ecstasy, which knows such spasms of delirium, he recoiled from her. It was what she used to call her "satisfaction". She had loved Joachim for this, that again, and again, and again he could give her this orgiastic "satisfaction", in spasms that made her cry aloud.

'But Cipriano would not. By a dark and powerful instinct he drew away from her as soon as this desire rose again in her, for the white ecstasy of frictional satisfaction, the throes of Aphrodite of the foam. She could see that to him, it was repulsive. He just removed himself, dark and unchangeable, away from her.

'And she, as she lay, would realize the worthlessness of this foam-effervescence, its strange externality to her. . . .

'And he, in his dark, hot silence would bring her back to the new, soft, heavy, hot flow, when she was like a fountain gushing noiseless and with urgent softness from the volcanic deeps. . . . What happened was dark and untellable. So different from the beak-like friction of Aphrodite of the foam, the friction which flares out in circles of phosphorescent ecstasy, to the last wild spasm which utters the involuntary cry, like a death-cry, the final love-cry. . . .

'And as it was in the love-act, so it was with him. She could not *know* him. . . .

'Now she found herself accepting him finally and forever as the stranger in whose presence she lived. It was his impersonal presence which enveloped her. She lived in his aura, and he, she knew, lived in hers, with nothing said, and no personal or spiritual intimacy whatever. A mindless communion of the blood' (pp. 439–40).

Sufficient has been said, I hope, to make an analysis of this passage, crucial though it is, superfluous. I should merely like to point out that the sort of marriage which is imposed on the woman by the triumphantly dominant man, the 'mindless communion of the blood', is, ironically enough, thoroughly 'female' in quality. Perhaps the best single comment on the passage is that provided by Lawrence himself. Immediately after it, Kate encounters a snake when she is out walking by the lake-shore. It disappears down a hole in a wall, and she wonders whether it is 'disappointed at not being able to rise higher in creation: to be able to run on four feet, and not keep its belly on the ground'. She decides that perhaps it has 'its own peace', and feels 'a certain reconciliation between herself and it' (p. 442). Her feeling is pathetic evidence of the failure of the Quetzalcoatl aspiration in her own life, of her abashed acceptance of a lower, snake-like form of existence and marriage.

IV

Writing some ten years earlier, while he was at work, that is to say, on the final draft of *The Rainbow*, Lawrence penetratingly said:

'Because a novel is a microcosm, and because man in viewing the universe must view it in the light of a theory, therefore every novel must have the background or the structural skeleton of some theory of being, some metaphysic. But the metaphysic must always subserve the artistic purpose beyond the artist's conscious aim. Otherwise the novel becomes a treatise.

'And the danger is, that a man shall make himself a metaphysic to excuse or cover his own faults or failure. Indeed, a sense of fault or failure is the usual cause of a man's making himself a metaphysic, to justify himself.

'Then, having made himself a metaphysic of self-justification, or a metaphysic of self-denial, the novelist proceeds to apply the world to this, instead of applying this to the world.

'Tolstoi is a flagrant example of this. Probably because of profligacy in his youth, because he had disgusted himself in his own flesh, by excess or by prostitution, therefore Tolstoi, in his metaphysic, renounced the flesh altogether, later on, when he had tried and had failed to achieve complete marriage in the flesh. But above all things, Tolstoi was a child of the Law, he belonged to the Father. He had a marvellous sensuous understanding, and very little clarity of mind.

'So that, in his metaphysic, he had to deny himself, his own being, in order to escape his own disgust of what he had done to himself, and to escape admission of his own failure.'[1]

If Lawrence's criticism of Tolstoy as the author of *War and Peace* and of *Anna Karenina*, if not as a man, is open to question, it might have been designed to describe his own problem as it manifests itself in *The Plumed Serpent*. This novel, indeed, is a sad testimony to what happens when art is 'subdued to a metaphysic';[2] and the metaphysic is so harshly

[1] 'Study of Thomas Hardy', *Phoenix*, p. 479.
[2] Cf. Lawrence in the full flush of *Sons and Lovers*: 'Oh, Lord, and if I don't "subdue my art as a metaphysic", as somebody very beautifully said of Hardy, I do write

clamorous in it just because Lawrence 'had to deny himself, his own being'. He, more obviously than Tolstoy, was 'a child of the Law' and 'belonged to the Father', was a child, that is, of the female principle;[1] and if his lifelong effort to reconcile the female with the male resulted in a body of work which, in its organic development, is unrivalled in English fiction of this century, his attempt, in *The Plumed Serpent*, to assert a 'male' metaphysic in order 'to justify himself' is disastrous. In making the assertion, he not only drove himself to conclusions which I imagine most readers would consider repugnant; more damagingly, he compromised his integrity as an artist, lapsing, according to his own definition of the term, into 'immorality':

'. . . morality is that delicate, for ever trembling and changing *balance* between me and my circumambient universe, which precedes and accompanies a true relatedness. . . .

'Morality in the novel is the trembling instability of the balance. When the novelist puts his thumb in the scale, to pull down the balance to his own predilection, that is immorality.'[2]

Nowhere does Lawrence put his thumb more heavily in the scale than in his presentation of Kate. Kate is not only reduced to an abject acceptance of Cipriano; she is violated. That she should even have been brought to marry him, let alone to bow to his terms of marriage, is a wilful defiance of verisimilitude. In the first place, there are numerous indications that she is actually in love with Ramón–I quote only two of the many instances which suggest this:

'Kate looked at [Ramón] in wonder, with a little fear. Why was he confessing to her? Was he going to love her? She almost suspended her breathing. He looked at her with a sort of sorrow on his brow, and in his dark eyes, anger, vexation, wisdom, and a dull pain' (p. 285).

' "You go ahead so grandly," [Kate says to Ramón], "one would not think you needed help: especially from a mere woman who–who after all is only the wife of your friend." . . .

' "The wife of my friend!" he said. "What could you be better?"

' "Of course," she said, more than equivocal' (p. 444).[3]

We are inclined to conclude that it is disappointment which drives Kate into Cipriano's arms.

---

because I want folk–English folk–to alter, and have more sense.' Letter to A. W. McLeod (April 1913), *Letters*, p. 120.
[1] See Chap. 1, pp. 24–8 above, for a discussion of the way in which Lawrence uses these terms.
[2] 'Morality and the Novel', *Phoenix*, p. 528.   [3] Cf. pp. 200, 217–18, 287, 304, 415, 418.

Second, it is clear that Kate initially finds Cipriano sexually repugnant: after he has asked her to marry him, she tells Ramón, 'with a faint shudder', that she is glad she is white and that she feels there could be 'no contact' with a 'brown-skinned people' (p. 200). The way in which Lawrence surmounts this barrier to the marriage is representative of the equivocation which makes of Kate a dummy, not a person. She is led–perversely, we feel–to 'see the physical possibility of marrying' Cipriano when he maintains that 'the bit of horror' which marriage to him will entail is 'like the sesame seed in the nougat, it gives the sharp wild flavour. It is good to have it there.' And where Kate is concerned, Lawrence is always able to produce a familiar *deus ex machina*: 'But surely, surely it would not be *herself* who could marry him. It would be some curious female within her, whom she did not know and did not own' (p. 249).

Third, it is difficult to believe that Kate, the western woman of delicate sensibility, can stomach the brutality of Cipriano. This, for instance, is how he behaves to Carlota when she is dying:

' "My children!" murmured Carlota.

' "It is well you must leave them," [said Cipriano]. "With your beggar's bowl of charity you have stolen their oil and their wine as well. It is good for you to steal from them no more, you stale virgin, you spinster, you born widow, you weeping mother, you impeccable wife, you just woman. You stole the very sunshine out of the sky and the sap out of the earth. Because back again, what did you pour? Only the water of dead dilution into the mixing-bowl of life, you thief. Oh die!–die!–die! Die and be a thousand times dead! Do nothing but utterly die!"

'Doña Carlota had relapsed into unconsciousness; even her ghost refused to hear. Cipriano flung his sinisterly-flaming *serape* over his shoulders and his face, over his nose, till only his black, glittering eyes were visible as he blew out of the room.

'Kate sat by the window, and laughed a little. The primeval woman inside her laughed to herself, for she had known all the time about the two thieves on the Cross with Jesus; the bullying, marauding thief of the male in his own rights, and the much more subtle, cold, sly, charitable thief of the woman in *her* own rights, forever chanting her beggar's whine about the love of God and the God of pity.

'But Kate, too, was a modern woman and a woman in her own right. So she sat on with Carlota. And when the doctor came, she accepted the obsequiousness of the man as part of her rights. And when the priest came, she accepted the obsequiousness from him, just the same, as part of her woman's rights. These two ministers of love, what were they for, but to be obsequious to her? As for herself, she could hardly be called a thief, and a sneak-thief of the world's virility, when these men came forcing their obsequiousness upon her, whining to her to take it and relieve them of the responsibility of their own manhood. No, if women are thieves, it is only because men want to be thieved from. If women thieve the world's virility it is only because men want to have it thieved, since for men to be responsible for their own manhood seems to be the last thing men want' (pp. 362–3).

This passage reveals what inroads a metaphysic can make on an art. Not only must Kate be made to condone Cipriano's savage insensitivity –when we expect that she will be appalled–she must laugh. But then, of course, it is not really Kate who laughs: it is 'the primeval woman inside her'. And it is only because she is flagrantly not 'a woman in her own rights', as Lawrence wantonly assures us she is, that she can, with equanimity, contemplate Cipriano as 'the bullying, marauding thief of the male in his own rights'. Lawrence, moreover, even fails to be convincing in his presentment of Cipriano. No one, still less the general, talks quite like that, we feel; and that his stream of invective should issue with such passionate vehemence in response to a wrong done to Ramón, not himself, is strikingly out of character. But then Lawrence is oblivious to the demands of character here. He is single-mindedly intent on execrating a 'spiritual' woman and on gloating over her death which he seems to equate with the death-pangs of the Christian idealism she lives by. The burning of the images of Christ and of the Virgin is preceded, as it were, by a human sacrifice. So single-minded is he, indeed, that he seems to be unaware how even Ramón, unobsequious though he may be, is worsted in the assault, for if women are thieves only because men want to be thieved from, the maligned Carlota is not altogether responsible for her sins.

Kate's attitude to Cipriano here is no doubt intended to prepare us for her response to him as Huitzilopochtli, the red god of blood. At the bull-fight, we remember, Kate's horror at the death of a horse is so intense that she fears she will 'go into hysterics' if she sees any more (p. 23); not unexpectedly, therefore, 'the executions [shock] and [depress] her' (p. 401), but it is on the same day, nevertheless, that she consents to become Malintzi, 'the bride of the Living Huitzilopochtli', and to salute his statue in the church (pp. 406–7). In the interval, as

she sits 'rocking in her terrible loneliness and misgiving' (p. 405), Kate
has earnestly pondered the issues raised by the executions, but it is
with a surprising ease that she overcomes her revulsion when Cipriano
appears and invites her to accompany him to the church. He seems
to her to be 'flashing with a flame of virgin youth' and to be 'sensitive
as a boy': 'And calling her only with his boyish flame. The living,
flickering, fiery *Wish*. This was first. The *Will* she had seen was subsidiary and instrumental, the *Wish* in armour' (p. 406). In the end, it
appears, the much-married woman finds the call of the boyish flame
irresistible, and, responding to it, she haplessly indulges in utter
irresponsibility:

'So, when she thought of him and his soldiers, tales of swift cruelty
she had heard of him: when she remembered his stabbing the three
helpless peons, she thought: Why should I judge him? He is of the
gods. And when he comes to me he lays his pure, quick flame to mine,
and every time I am a young girl again, and every time he takes the
flower of my virginity, and I his. It leaves me *insouciante* like a young
girl. What do I care if he kills people? His flame is young and clean. He
is Huitzilopochtli, and I am Malintzi. What do I care, what Cipriano
Viedma does or doesn't do? Or even what Kate Leslie does or doesn't
do!' (pp. 409–10).

Finally, once Kate has been prevailed on to take the brown-skinned
executioner, the friend of the man she secretly loves, as her husband,
we should not be disturbed, I suppose, at her blindness to the nature
of the marriage she has contracted. For blind Lawrence makes her,
with a determination and inconsistency that can only be ascribed to
the confused stirring of his artistic conscience. We might conceivably
believe, for instance, that Kate is innocently unaware of the symbolism of the marriage ceremony performed by Ramón; but when,
towards the end of the book and following her reflections on a perfect
proneness and on the death in her of Aphrodite of the foam, she
detects an adoration of her 'full-breasted, glorious' womanhood in
the eyes of a peon she meets, her thoughts violate all credibility: 'How
wonderful sex can be, when men keep it powerful and sacred, and it
fills the world! Like sunshine through and through one!–But I'm not
going to submit, even there. Why should one give in, to anything!'
(p. 453). And when Kate finally decides to stay on in Mexico as Cipriano's wife rather than face the 'horror' of 'the grimalkin women, her
contemporaries', the nature of her submission is equivocally qualified: 'Ah yes! Rather than become elderly and a bit grisly, I will make

my submission; as far as I need, and no further' (pp. 456–7). Repeatedly, moreover, in the jealous aspersions she spatters on Teresa, Ramón's second wife, Kate is made to be infinitely obtuse. 'Harem', 'self-prostitution', 'the *slave* approach' are what she calls Teresa's power 'to make Ramón great and gorgeous in the flesh, whilst she herself [becomes] inconspicuous, almost *invisible*' (p. 414). She accuses Teresa of sacrificing herself to Ramón, and when Teresa asserts that Ramón is her life, she unabashedly retorts: 'Surely it is better for one to live one's own life!' (pp. 424–5). And in her last discussion with Teresa she remains incorrigibly defiant:

' "Different men must have different wives," [Teresa] said. "Cipriano would never want a wife like me."

' "And different women must have different husbands," said Kate. "Ramón would always be too abstract and overbearing for me."

'Teresa flushed slowly, looking down at the ground.

' "Ramón needs far too much submission from a woman, to please me," Kate added. "He takes too much upon himself" ' (p. 451).

In *The Plumed Serpent*, it is evident, Lawrence had taken cover in a position which he could not defend, either as thinker or as artist. He retreated with dignity, and, discarding the encumbrance of a 'one up, one down' metaphysic of personal relations, proceeded to fight a new battle in *Lady Chatterley's Lover*:

'I sniffed the red herring in your last letter a long time: then at last decide it's a live sprat. I mean about *The Plumed Serpent* and the "hero". On the whole, I think you're right. The hero is obsolete, and the leader of men is a back number. After all, at the back of the hero is the militant ideal: and the militant ideal, or the ideal militant seems to me also a cold egg. We're sort of sick of all forms of militarism and militantism, and *Miles* is a name no more, for a man. On the whole I agree with you, the leader-cum-follower relationship is a bore. And the new relationship will be some sort of tenderness, sensitive, between men and men and men and women, and not the one up one down, lead on I follow, *ich dien* sort of business. So you see I'm becoming a lamb at last, and you'll even find it hard to take umbrage at me. Do you think?

'But still, *in a way*, one has to fight. But not in the O Glory! sort of way. I feel one still has to fight for the phallic reality, as against the non-phallic cerebration unrealities. I suppose the phallic consciousness is part of the whole consciousness which is your aim. To me it's a vital part.

'So I wrote my novel, which I want to call *John Thomas and Lady Jane*. But that I have to submerge into a subtitle, and call it *Lady Chatterley's Lover*. But I am printing here in Florence an unexpurgated edition of this tender and phallic novel, far too good for the public. . . .'[1]

[1] Letter to Witter Bynner (March 1928), *Journey with Genius* (London, 1953), p. 334.

5. The Return: The Fourth Period

Lady Chatterley's Lover

'MAN NEED NOT SACRIFICE THE INTELLECT TO THE PENIS, NOR the penis to the intellect. But there is an eternal hostility between the two, and life is forever torn across by the conflict between them. Yet man has a holy ghost inside him which partakes of the nature of both. And hence man has a new aim in life, to maintain a truce between the two and some sort of fluctuating harmony. Instead of deliberately, as science and Socrates, Christianity and Buddha have all done, deliberately setting out to murder the one in order to exalt the other.'[1]

[1] *The First Lady Chatterley* (New York, 1946), p. 192. Lawrence rewrote his last novel three times. The first version, which he began in October 1926 and completed in March 1927 (see E. W. Tedlock, *The Frieda Lawrence Collection*, pp. 20-1), was published in 1944 as *The First Lady Chatterley*. Tedlock suggests that the second version was written in the spring and summer of 1927 (p. 23). It was first published in Italian in 1954, and appeared in English as *John Thomas and Lady Jane* in 1972. The final version was begun in December 1927 (see *Collected Letters*, p. 1025), completed in January 1928 (see *Letters*, p. 697), and published privately in Florence in June of the same year.

'As I say it's a novel of the phallic Consciousness: or the phallic Consciousness versus the mental-spiritual Consciousness: and of course you know which side I take. The *versus* is not my fault: there should be no *versus*. The two things must be reconciled in us. But now they're daggers drawn.'[1]

We might well be inclined to suppose that it would be difficult to find two more dissimilar novels by the same author than *The Plumed Serpent* and *Lady Chatterley's Lover*, but Connie's reflections in *The First Lady Chatterley*, which bear the distinctive imprint of Lawrence's own thought, indicate that Lawrence initially intended to pursue the same theme, fundamentally, in the English novel as in the Mexican. The terms, of course, are different – the serpent, the bird, and the Morning Star are replaced by the penis, the intellect, and the Holy Ghost – and there is a shift of emphasis consequent on the change of scene. In Mexico Lawrence was struck by the way in which the bird was swallowed by the serpent (as it was in the pre-industrial England which is described at the beginning of *The Rainbow*); when he returned to England, he became acutely aware, once again, of the way in which the spirit was stifling the flesh, of the way in which the flesh was being 'murdered' by 'science and Socrates, Christianity and Buddha'. His concern throughout the years in which he worked at *Lady Chatterley's Lover* was that the 'penis' and the 'intellect' should be reconciled; but faced by what he thought was the 'exaltation' of the one at the expense of the other, he determined in this novel to do justice to the former.[2] He determined, that is to say, to do justice to those qualities

---

[1] 1928 letter to the Brewsters, Earl and Achsah Brewster, *Reminiscences and Correspondence*, p. 166.

[2] I stress this point because Lawrence is so often misrepresented. The sort of misrepresentation to which he is subjected is perhaps nowhere more concisely and more flagrantly exemplified than in this passage from Eric Bentley's *The Cult of the Superman*: 'Klage's vitalism ends like Lawrence's in blasphemy against life itself, and *Lady Chatterley's Lover* is a shocking book, not for what it mentions but for what it advocates. . . . The romantic quest for a life of sensations rather than thoughts reaches its culmination in a religion of sex and power, of his own John Thomas and Nietzsche's Dionysos' (p. 230). Bentley might have pondered the distinction Lawrence draws, in another context, between an insistence and a negation: 'Christ Himself is always going against the Holy Spirit. He must *insist* on the love, because it has been overlooked. But insistence on the one is not to be interpreted as negation of the other. In His purest moments, Christ knew that the Holy Spirit was both love and hate – not one only.' Letter to Eleanor Farjeon (October 1915), *Letters*, p. 261. Bentley might also have considered Lawrence's specific defence of the novel: 'But I stick to my book and my position: Life is only bearable when the

which he felt were undervalued in an industrial civilization, to those qualities, we might add, which were undervalued in his Eastwood home and which he had undervalued in himself in the writing of parts of *The Plumed Serpent*. In view of the phallic paean in that novel this may appear to be a wilful assertion; but we have to distinguish between a glorification of 'the phallus', of male power, that is, and an adherence to the 'phallic consciousness', to what Lawrence elsewhere calls the 'primal consciousness' or 'blood consciousness', an adherence to a sensitive if earthy physical awareness, to the senses (particularly the sense of touch), to a vital spontaneity, to tenderness–in a word, to the female principle. Indeed, Lawrence's invocation of the 'phallic consciousness' betrays the infirmity of a divided self, for it is a subterfuge which enables him to identify himself with 'female' qualities while preserving a 'male' turn of phrase.[1] The identification is obvious enough, as the extract from the letter to the Brewsters shows. It would seem, moreover, that in between the first and final versions of the novel this identification became more and more defiant and strongly altered the emphasis of the finished work. Even in *The First Lady Chatterley* I do not think that the emphasis falls on the 'new aim in mind and the body are in harmony, and there is a natural balance between them, and each has a natural respect for the other.' 'A Propos of *Lady Chatterley's Lover*', *Sex, Literature and Censorship*, ed. Harry T. Moore (London, 1955), p. 231.

[1] It is interesting to trace the changes in the phrasing of an opposition that Lawrence formulated early in his career. In the Hardy essay (1914), that workshop of Lawrence's ideas, there are isolated and tentative references to the 'consciousness of the flesh' which came into being 'through woman' and 'with the Fall', and to 'Knowledge in the blood' (*Phoenix*, pp. 453, 500), but, in defining the differences between the male and female principles, Lawrence is content, for the most part, to distinguish between the 'mind', which he calls 'the consciousness', and the 'senses' (p. 496). The first concise formulation of the opposition that I know of is to be found in a letter of December 1915 to Bertrand Russell, in which Lawrence contrasts 'the blood-consciousness' and 'the mental consciousness' (*Collected Letters*, p. 393). In 'Education of the People' (written in 1918) Lawrence uses the terms 'the primal consciousness', 'the affective consciousness', 'the vital consciousness', 'the spontaneous consciousness', and 'the affective or physical consciousness' in contradistinction to 'mental consciousness' and 'ideal consciousness' (*Phoenix*, pp. 629, 655). In the first version of *Studies in Classic American Literature* he talks of 'the sensual consciousness' or 'the centres of sensual cognition' as opposed to 'the upper centres' ('Fenimore Cooper's Anglo-American Novels', *The English Review*, 28 (February 1919), 90). In *Fantasia of the Unconscious* (1922) 'pure blood-consciousness' is equated with sex, which is said to be 'the basic consciousness of the blood, the nearest thing in us to pure material consciousness' (p. 157). As far as I know, it is only in the late twenties and in connection with *Lady Chatterley's Lover* that Lawrence begins to employ the term 'phallic consciousness'.

life', on the depiction of the 'sort of fluctuating harmony' that should be attained between the 'penis' and the 'intellect'; in *Lady Chatterley's Lover* it seems Lawrence felt 'a truce' could not be established between the two until the 'mental consciousness' had been decisively routed.

Lawrence's defiant identification with the 'phallic consciousness', his 'taking of sides', helps to explain several features of the final version of the book. It accounts, in the first place, for an obtrusive element, the deliberate use of the so-called obscene words. Since the unexpurgated edition of *Lady Chatterley's Lover* has at long last been legally instated in England, there is now no call to discuss whether the use of these words is obscene or not; but what must be considered is the curious critical response to their use, the apparently liberal understanding of Lawrence's intention and the firm disapproval of the practice. I quote what I take to be a representative instance of the prevailing critical attitude:

'... when we come to the obscene words ... I think we encounter an excessive reaction to censorship and prudery. ... Lawrence uses them probably not more than a hundred times in all ... in the course of a longish novel. So in any case they cannot make much difference. They ... are meant to show [Mellors'] frank carnality and its vivifying power. So far they are an integral part of Lawrence's purpose. But still more, one suspects, they are part of the extracurricular activity of bringing "sex out into the open", and like all such secondary purposes in a work of fiction they are so far an irrelevance. Of course, it is quite true, we have no proper vocabulary to discuss sex. ... Lawrence's remedy is to use the obscene words familiarly and seriously, so that the tabooed acts and parts of the body can be talked about in natural and native words. An admirable intention, no doubt, but doing no great credit to his literary sense. Writers are masters of language, but they can only become so by respecting its nature. No writer can alter the connotations of a whole section of the vocabulary by mere fiat; and the fact remains that the connotations of the obscene physical words are either facetious or vulgar. And very useful they are in these contexts. But in any context where dignity, tenderness, respect for one's own person or that of another is concerned, they are impossible. The effect of putting them into Mellors' mouth as they are is either to create the impression that he is, as one of Lawrence's acquaintance described him, a crude sexual moron, or that whole passages of his discourse are disastrously out of character.'[1]

[1] Graham Hough, *The Dark Sun*, pp. 160–1.

It seems to me that, if we respond to the novel as I think Lawrence intended us to, we cannot say that the words do not 'make much difference'; nor, if we understand that Lawrence was not engaging in an 'extracurricular activity' (the book is an organic whole), can we regard them as 'an irrelevance'. Lawrence himself would certainly have been surprised at such an estimate: referring to the first version of the novel, he wrote to his Italian publisher: 'I believe it has hardly any fucks or shits, and no address to the penis, in fact hardly any of the root of the matter at all.'[1] Furthermore, I should say that Lawrence uses the words in an assault on the 'mental consciousness' of the reader, and that the assault, to judge from the letter to the Brewsters, is as much an integral part of his purpose as the effort to show Mellors' 'frank carnality and its vivifying power'. He deliberately tries to shock us out of a false mental position. He violently attempts to dislodge the grip which the 'mental consciousness' exerts on the 'phallic consciousness' in order to bring about an adjustment between the two modes of consciousness; that is to say, he seeks to overcome the superficial aversion of the mind to the words by forcing a response from a deeper consciousness which is not shocked. What he hopes for is a calm, *rational* acceptance both of the words and the physical facts they denote, for a shrinking from the word implies a shrinking from the fact:

'But I want, with *Lady C.*, to make an *adjustment in consciousness* to the basic physical realities. . . . If a man had been able to say to you when you were young and in love: an' if tha shits, an' if tha pisses, I' glad, I shouldna want a woman who couldna shit nor piss—surely it would have been a liberation to you, and it would have helped to keep your heart warm. Think of poor Swift's insane *But* of horror at the end of every verse of that poem to Celia. But Celia shits!—you see the very fact that it should horrify him, and simply devastate his consciousness, is all wrong, and a bitter shame to poor Celia. It's the awful and truly unnecessary *recoil* from these things that I would like to break. It's a question of conscious acceptance and adjustment—only that. . . .'[2]

If Lawrence's use of the words is thus directed at effecting an adjustment in the individual consciousness, his deliberate violation of a literary convention is also intended to shock us out of a social insanity. That adult men and women should have judged the following passage, for instance, to be socially acceptable goes far to justifying the

[1] Letter to G. Orioli (July 1929), *Collected Letters*, p. 1167.
[2] Letter to Lady Ottoline Morrell (December 1928), *Collected Letters*, p. 1111.

thoroughness with which Lawrence rejected the convention; for it is, of course, the dash, and not the missing guts of the word, which is obscene and perniciously perpetuates the attitudes he was attacking:

' "Ay!" he said. "I'm a gamekeeper, at thirty-five bob a week. Ay! I'm all right. I'm Sir Clifford's servant, an' I'm Lady Chatterley's–" he looked her in the face–"What do you call me, in *your* sort of talk?" '

' "My lover!" she stammered.

' "Lover!" he re-echoed. A queer flash went over his face.

' "F–er!" he said, and his eyes darted a flash at her, as if he shot her.'[1]

Lawrence, indeed, saw clearly enough that social sanity is indivisible, and his prophecy of 'a howling manifestation of mob-insanity' has been too horrifyingly borne out for us not to take him seriously:

'The result of taboo is insanity. And insanity, especially mob-insanity, mass-insanity, is the fearful danger that threatens our civilization. . . . If the young do not watch out, they will find themselves, before so very many years are past, engulfed in a howling manifestation of mob-insanity, truly terrifying to think of. . . . In the name of piety and purity, what a mass of disgusting insanity is spoken and written. We shall have to fight the mob, in order to keep sane, and to keep society sane.'[2]

Lawrence, however, did not intend merely to shock. His use of the words should be linked with an overt concern at what might be called the mortification of language: 'All the great words, it seemed to Connie, were cancelled for her generation: love, joy, happiness, home, mother, father, husband, all these great, dynamic words were half dead now, and dying from day to day' (p. 64). Lawrence, that is to say, in attempting to cleanse the grime from the 'obscene' words, sought to revitalize the 'great' words by providing them with a new content. The new content is provided, of course, by the novel as a whole, but the use of the 'obscene' words is an essential part of the undertaking which is the whole. Connie later reflects that one can be ravished without ever being touched, 'ravished by dead words become obscene'

[1] *The First Lady Chatterley*, p. 151. I assume the dash was judiciously inserted by the publisher. Esther Forbes, who contributes 'A Manuscript Report' but who does not indicate to what extent the manuscript was tampered with, merely says: 'This brings up the question of whether the first draft is "printable". Several times Parkin uses simple words suitable to an ex-miner. It is appropriate all right. There are none of the purple patches which made the Italian edition notorious' (p. xviii).

[2] Preface to *Pansies*, *Phoenix*, p. 282.

(p. 97); we might say that Lawrence seeks to show how one can be warmed by obscene words become tender. He seeks, that is, to enhance the value of the words by fashioning new contexts for their use, employing them seriously in contexts which support neither an abusive nor a shameful nor a scornful connotation. His practice, in this respect, is markedly different from that of James Joyce in *Ulysses*, for Joyce's use of the words in the last section of the book, though admirably revelatory of the character of Molly Bloom, in effect perpetuates their debasement.[1] Lawrence, unlike Joyce, was trying to use the words in two different ways at the same time. He wished, on the one hand, to retain their earthy character, for he detested the 'spiritualizing' of sex: '. . . We shall never free the phallic reality from the "uplift" taint till we give it its own phallic language, and use the obscene words. The greatest blasphemy of all against the phallic reality is this "lifting it to a higher plane".'[2] On the other hand, he believed that 'a proper reverence for sex' entailed the use of 'the so-called obscene words, because these are a natural part of the mind's consciousness of the body'.[3]

What, then, is the overall effect of Lawrence's use of the words as distinguished from his intentions? I deliberately quote a passage in which these words preponderate:

' "Why should I say *maun* when you said *mun*," she protested. "You're not playing fair."

' "Arena Ah!" he said, leaning forward and softly stroking her face. ' "Th'art good cunt, though, aren't ter? Best bit o' cunt left on earth. When ter likes! When tha'rt willin'!"

' "What is cunt?" she said.

' "An' doesn't ter know? Cunt! It's thee down theer; an' what I get when I'm i'side thee, and what tha gets when I'm i'side thee; it's a' as it is, all on't."

' "All on't," she teased. "Cunt! It's like fuck then."

' "Nay nay! Fuck's only what you do. Animals fuck. But cunt's a lot more than that. It's thee, dost see: an' tha'rt a lot besides an animal, aren't ter? even ter fuck! Cunt! Eh, that's the beauty o' thee, lass!" ' (p. 185).

First, I think it should be said that the words do shock in exactly the

[1] See, for instance, pp. 739–40 of the John Lane edition (London, 1947). Dorothy Brett reports Lawrence as saying that the last part of *Ulysses* was 'the dirtiest, most indecent, obscene thing ever written'. *Lawrence and Brett*, p. 79.
[2] 'A Propos of *Lady Chatterley's Lover*', loc. cit., p. 267.   [3] *Ibid.*, p. 229.

way Lawrence intended them to; that is, if we are shocked on first encountering them, we soon cease to be so and realize how absurd it was to be shocked at all. Second, I contest Hough's judgement that the words are 'impossible' in a context of dignity, tenderness, and personal respect. Mellors uses them, it seems to me, in a manifestly tender manner, with full respect for Connie's person, and without impairing either his dignity or hers; the soft stroking of her face, indeed, is a physical equivalent of the caressive gentleness of his speech. Nor does it strike me that he speaks out of character or like 'a crude sexual moron'. A more valid objection against Lawrence's use of the words, I should say, is that it is too deliberate, if not self-conscious; and, in this passage at any rate, their use is open to the same sort of criticism that we would level, for instance, at an over-elaborate metaphor. It would be idle to pretend, moreover, that Lawrence is able to employ the words with the effortless simplicity and freshness of a Chaucer; like the special but very different terminology used in *The Rainbow*, the words do undoubtedly carry with them at least a residue of their more usual, contemporary associations. But that does not mean to say, as Hough seems to imply, and as other critics emphatically state, that their use should be restricted to facetious or vulgar contexts.[1] It is, after all, a context which determines the meaning of a word, not a word the context; and a reinstatement of these words would not inhibit their use as invective either in literature or in life.

II

Lawrence's conception of the novel as a dramatization of a conflict between the 'phallic consciousness' and the 'mental consciousness' also throws light on its structure. The structure seems designed to accommodate a juxtaposing of antitheses or oppositions. There are, in the first place, the two opposed 'worlds' of the novel, the two main and contrasted symbols, the house, Wragby, and the wood. Second, there are the two opposed characters, Clifford, the owner of Wragby, and Mellors, the keeper of the wood. Their personal antagonism projects a wider conflict of interest, a conflict between the dilettante writer, the 'mental-lifer', to use Dukes's term (p. 41), and the preserver of wild life from those who would poach on it, between the

[1] Cf. Eliseo Vivas, *D. H. Lawrence*, pp. 146-7, and Katherine Anne Porter, 'A Wreath for the Gamekeeper', *Encounter*, 14 (February 1960), 72.

affluent industrialist and the impecunious worker, between the upper-class gentleman and the lower-class man of the people, between the gregarious conversationalist and the solitary, between crippled impotence and generous potency–to name some of the oppositions that come readily to mind. Caught between the two 'worlds' and between the two men, the link between the two oppositions, is Connie. Suffering at Wragby, turning to the wood as a refuge, Connie, so to speak, tests the values of the two men on her own pulses. The action of the novel traces her slow movement from one 'world' to another, from the one man to the other.

The structure thus has an admirable clarity and sharpness of line, but it seems to me to be deficient in depth, in true solidity. This lack of depth is perhaps most evident in the characterization of both Clifford and Mellors. I should say at once that I believe the characterization of the two men is convincing, that it succeeds, with direct and unstrained immediacy, in evoking them as firm presences, and that it is incorporated, as I shall try to show, with an unbending, even merciless, precision in the thematic design; but I would add that what it gains in ready intelligibility, it loses by its simplicity. I do not, of course, balk at the simplicity as such; I do maintain, however, that complexity and inclusiveness, as *War and Peace* and *The Brothers Kara-mazov* amply demonstrate, are necessary constituents of quality in the novel. Nor do I invoke Tolstoy and Dostoievsky at random, for with Lawrence, perhaps alone among twentieth-century English novelists, the best is the only fitting criterion. I might press the distinction I am making by comparing *Lady Chatterley's Lover* with the best of Lawrence's own work, with *The Rainbow*. In the earlier novel the conflict between the 'penis' and the 'intellect' was located in the individual psyche, and Lawrence was impelled to present his characters in depth, was impelled, indeed, to invent a new and uniquely rich method of characterization in order to do so. In *Lady Chatterley's Lover* this conflict is externalized in the clash between Clifford and Mellors with the result that, while issues are clarified, characters are simplified, and in the novel, as in life, it is, ultimately, people who count. A passage in *The First Lady Chatterley* suggests that Lawrence was aware of this limitation, and though he incomparably strengthened the verisimilitude of the final version, it seems to me that Connie's reflections are an apt comment on it too:

'She sighed wearily. Apparently it was impossible to have a whole man in any man. Her two men were two halves. And she did not want to forfeit either half, to forego either man. Yet neither would she be bullied by either of them in his halfness' (p. 77).

. The same default of complexity is apparent in Lawrence's presentation of the social scene. This deficiency is perhaps most readily comprehended if we compare *Lady Chatterley's Lover*, in this respect, with *Women in Love*, Lawrence's earlier, but more profound, attempt at an anatomy of modern England. What strikes us at once, then, when we recall the spaciousness of *Women in Love*, is the narrowness of the later work, the small-dimensioned compactness of its two 'worlds' in comparison with the sweep, the multifariousness, of the 'worlds' of the earlier novel. The narrowness is a consequence of a deliberate concentration aimed at in the interests of a clear-cut thematic opposition, but the limitation of this technique is perhaps best apprehended if we grasp that Wragby, by itself, is intended to represent something like a combination of Shortlands, Breadalby, and the Café Pompadour. It is meant, that is to say, to be simultaneously the seat of industry, the abode of the 'mental life', and the home of a pettifogging art. As the seat of industry, moreover, it incorporates the dreary blackness of Tevershall, the mining village on which it depends and the equivalent of Beldover in *Women in Love*. These significances are brilliantly communicated, but Wragby, clearly, cannot equal the combined weight of Shortlands, Breadalby, and the Pompadour, just as Clifford, its owner, cannot be made to possess the substantiality of a Gerald *and* a Hermione, to say nothing of a Halliday.

Quarried stone, rooted trees – Wragby and the wood are inherently apt symbols for the sort of contrast Lawrence wishes to emphasize. The contrast, of course, is more profound than that, and it is amplified in a number of ways throughout the novel, but from the outset Wragby and the wood are juxtaposed in meaningful antithesis:

'Wragby was a long low old house in brown stone, begun about the middle of the eighteenth century, and added on to, till it was a warren of a place without much distinction. It stood on an eminence in a rather fine old park of oak trees, but alas, one could see in the near distance the chimney of Tevershall pit, with its clouds of steam and smoke, and on the damp, hazy distance of the hill the raw straggle of Tevershall village, a village which began almost at the park gates, and trailed in utter hopeless ugliness for a long and gruesome mile: houses, rows of wretched, small, begrimed, brick houses, with black slate roofs for lids, sharp angles and wilful, blank dreariness' (pp. 13–14).

Wragby, we learn, is an old house, but it has none of the distinction of age; nor, in its warren-like ramifications, and like its owner, is it an organic whole. The warren image recurs with expanded meaning when Connie later sorts out 'one of the Wragby lumber rooms. There were several: the house was a warren, and the family never sold anything' (p. 152). It is not too fanciful, I believe, to view Clifford's home as the repository of inherited mental attitudes, as well as of family possessions, the attitudes which are associated with 'science and Socrates, Christianity and Buddha', and which, preserved–like lumber–in disregard of their dead weight, have had the effect of disconnecting Clifford from organic life. Wragby, indeed, is disconnected from what human life there is in the neighbourhood, for though Tevershall is virtually part of it, has sprung from it and begins almost at its park gates, there is a 'gulf impassable' between it and the village: 'There was no communication between Wragby Hall and Tevershall village, none' (p. 15). It is not surprising that when Connie is out in the wood and feels, among the trees, that she has '[got] into the current of her own proper destiny', she should hate the prospect of returning to Wragby and its thick walls, even though they afford protection against the wind: 'She would have to go back to Wragby and its walls, and now she hated it, especially its thick walls. Walls! Always walls! Yet one needed them in this wind' (p. 89). Within the walls of Wragby there is a 'mechanical cleanliness' and a 'mechanical order', but Connie believes this masks a 'methodical anarchy', for 'no warmth of feeling [unites] it organically' (p. 18). The continuity of life at Wragby, in its mechanicalness, is both symptomatic of a wider failure, and representative of it:

'This is history. One England blots out another. The mines had made the halls wealthy. Now they were blotting them out, as they had already blotted out the cottages. The industrial England blots out the agricultural England. One meaning blots out another. The new England blots out the old England. And the continuity is not organic, but mechanical' (p. 163).

Lawrence had had personal experience of the way in which the agricultural England was being blotted out by the industrial, and as a youth he had eagerly sought to escape from his home in Eastwood, his Tevershall, to the woods near the farm of Jessie Chambers and her family. The wood in *Lady Chatterley's Lover* is invested, we feel, with a nostalgia not only for the old England but for his own youth. It is a self-contained 'world', the home of the solitary Mellors (who does not exchange a word with Connie during the first eight months of his employment there as gamekeeper), and of that wild life which has not yet been killed off. Like Wragby, it too is 'old', but it is 'rather fine', whereas the house is undistinguished. It is, indeed, 'a remnant of the great forest where Robin Hood hunted', and it still has 'some of the mystery of wild, old England'. Unlike Wragby with its lumber rooms, but like the house Howards End and its wych-elm, it represents, that is to say, an organic connection with the past, a vital rootedness and continuity. But the wood has been violated. Parts of it are denuded of trees, felled by Clifford's father, Sir Geoffrey, for trench timber during the war, and 'big sawn stumps' show their tops and 'their grasping roots, lifeless'. This smashing of roots has a parallel in the enclosure of the wood. The park gates shut out Tevershall, and the miners of Tevershall, among others, are despoiled of their natural heritage, for what is now a riding through a 'private wood' was once 'an old, old thoroughfare coming across country'. It is typical of Clifford's disconnectedness that he should love the wood with a possessive exclusiveness. He wants to keep it 'inviolate, shut off from the world', and ironically, in ignorance of how out of touch he is with the old England he invokes ('This is the old England, the heart of it; and I intend to keep it intact'), he tells Connie: 'I want this wood perfect . . . untouched. I want nobody to trespass in it' (pp. 43–4).

The wood, though, is symbolic of much more than a connection with the past. As opposed to 'the harsh insentience of the outer world', it possesses inwardness and vitality: Connie likes 'the *inwardness* of the remnant of forest, the unspeaking reticence of the old trees. They seemed a very power of silence, and yet a vital presence' (p. 67). Its vitality is generous, prodigal of itself–the oak trees are 'round and vital, throwing off reckless limbs' (p. 97)–expending itself in the profusion of spring, with the 'leaf-buds on the hazels . . . opening like the spatter of green rain' (p. 117), and yet preserving the secret of renewal. It is a vitality which is at once tender and powerful, for in the wood there is the 'tenderness of the growing hyacinths' (p. 124), the 'mystery of eggs and half-open buds, half-unsheathed flowers' (p. 127) and 'the huge heave of the sap in the massive trees' (p. 126). The tenderness and the power are, in turn, associated with another mystery, the phallic: 'Constance sat down with her back to a young pine tree that swayed against her with curious life, elastic, and powerful, rising up. The erect, alive thing, with its top in the sun!' (p. 88). Indeed, when Connie realizes that Mellors is 'beautiful in the phallic mystery' and feels 'his child in all her veins, like a twilight', she is said to be 'like a forest, like the dark interlacing of the oak wood, humming inaudibly with myriad unfolding buds' (p. 143).

III

The significances conveyed through the description of Wragby are forcefully extended by the characterization of Clifford. Any discussion of the presentation of Clifford must start, I think, with a consideration of his paralysis. Julian Moynahan makes the following reservation in regard to Lawrence's treatment of him:

'As a portrait of the modern business man Clifford is surely no better than a monstrous caricature.'. . . He is always an illustration of disconnectedness; never for a moment does he emerge as a man who has suffered a terrible wound and is to be pitied for it. If even briefly the reader could feel with him as a human being, then his whole characterization would seem terribly cruel, and Lawrence's demonstration would be fatally flawed. But the truth is that Clifford in this novel is himself a man entirely defined by his functions. There is nothing left over to pity. Riding about the estate in his motorized chair he is a kind of mechanical centaur who, because he is only half human, is not human at all. Voidness cannot be villainous, nor can it become an object of sympathy.'[1]

The characterization of Clifford may not be complex, but it seems to me, as I have previously remarked and as I shall now try to show, that it is convincingly rendered–and in undoubtedly 'human' terms. The point to register here, then, is that Clifford does start with our sympathy; if he forfeits it quickly, this is due, in much the same way as with Casaubon in *Middlemarch*, for instance, to the fully realized unpleasantness of his actions and attitudes–and not to a failure of imaginative insight on the part of the novelist. Admittedly, no great attention is paid to Clifford's suffering, but then there are two good reasons for this. In the first place, he is presented to us, at the outset, as 'having suffered so much' that he has virtually lost 'the capacity for suffering'; he has been 'so much hurt that something inside him [has] perished, some of his feelings [have] gone. There [is] a blank of insentience' (p. 6). This, it seems to me, is a legitimate starting-point for any novelist. It is surely legitimate, too, for Lawrence to present Clifford to us from the outside; if he does not adhere with a Jamesian closeness to a restricted point of view, the point of view in the novel is

[1] '*Lady Chatterley's Lover*: The Deed of Life', *E.L.H.*, 26 (March 1959), 76–7.

predominantly that of Connie, and we feel for and with Clifford to
the extent that she does. Her feeling for him is not inconsiderable; if
it were, her final decision to leave him (which is at the dramatic centre
of the action) would not be as difficult to arrive at as it is shown to be,
for Connie is nothing if not unconventional. I think that Lawrence's
characterization of Clifford is mercilessly objective, rather than 'cruel',
and that it reflects an uncompromising awareness of one kind of
experience in the 'tragic age' which, we are told in the opening words
of the book, ours essentially is: 'Poor Clifford, he was not to blame.
His was the greater misfortune. It was all part of the general catastrophe.' That Connie should be made to feel that he is 'in a way to
blame' for his 'lack of warmth', for his lack of 'simple, warm, physical
contact' (p. 74), is just, not cruel; and the harshness of the portrait of
Clifford should not be taken to invalidate its truth.

   Clifford's paralysis, of course, is not merely of primary importance
in the plot; through it Lawrence, at one stroke, conveys a great deal
of what he wishes to say in the novel. We are immediately made to
think of Clifford as an impotent cripple, and the impotence of his
way of life (if not of the class of which he is a member) and the crippled
indignity of a body that is wasted by the mind are fundamental to
Lawrence's theme. It is here, however, that further objection is taken
to the paralysis. Clifford's body, it is argued, is not laid waste by his
mind but by the war, and this 'has the effect of removing the target
which Lawrence was most of all aiming at'.[1] A close reading of the
novel should indicate how wide of the mark this is. Even before he is
'shipped home smashed', the 'sex part' of marriage does 'not mean
much' to Clifford, and Connie exults a little that he is not 'just keen
on his "satisfaction" ' and that their intimacy is 'deeper, more personal
than that' (p. 13). After he is wounded, the limitations of their particular kind of intimacy are speedily revealed:

   'He wanted to say something later to Connie about the demi-
vierge business . . . the half-virgin state of her affairs. But he could not
bring himself to do it. He was at once too intimate with her and not
intimate enough. He was so very much at one with her, in his mind
and hers, but bodily they were non-existent to one another, and
neither could bear to drag in the *corpus delicti*. They were so intimate,
and utterly out of touch' (p. 19).

   The paralysis, which makes sexual contact between them impossible,

[1] Harry T. Moore, *'Lady Chatterley's Lover* as Romance', *A D. H. Lawrence Miscellany*,
p. 264.

is representative, we see, of an inherent incapacity, of that loss of the fullness of touch and of a vital connectedness that it, indeed, so vividly figures. Connie's attitude to the 'sex part' is, of course, as inadequate as Clifford's, and she is slowly and painfully taught to recognize its inadequacy, but Clifford never realizes that he is deficient in other ways than in the body:

'"And what about you, Clifford?" [said Dukes]. "Do you think sex is a dynamo to help a man on to success in the world?"

'Clifford rarely talked much at these times. He never held forth; his ideas were really not vital enough for it, he was too confused and emotional. Now he blushed and looked uncomfortable.

' "Well!" he said, "being myself *hors de combat*, I don't see I've anything to say on the matter."

' "Not at all," said Dukes; "the top of you's by no means *hors de combat*. You've got the life of the mind sound and intact. So let us hear your ideas."

' "Well," stammered Clifford, "even then I don't suppose I have much idea . . . I suppose marry-and-have-done-with-it would pretty well stand for what I think. Though of course between a man and a woman who care for one another, it is a great thing."

' "What sort of great thing?" said Tommy.

' "Oh . . . it perfects the intimacy," said Clifford, uneasy as a woman in such talk' (p. 36).

Clifford's incomprehension of the significance of a sexual relation is neatly revealed in this passage of dialogue. It is not merely that his 'marry-and-have-done-with-it' is expressive of his incomprehension; his reticence on the subject of sex, when he is so insatiable a conversationalist on other topics, is revelatory of a blank spot in his mind, of a paralysis of thought, as it were. Under Dukes's remorseless probing, moreover, Clifford's attempt to qualify the initial phrase he has used suggests his mental confusion, if not dishonesty: we know that sex in his own marriage, far from being thought of as 'perfecting an intimacy', has been deemed irrelevant to a truly 'deep' and 'personal' intimacy. It is also worth noting that Clifford, who is generally both precise and robust in his use of language, speaks here in a singularly vague and commonplace manner ('it is a great thing', 'it perfects the intimacy'); the lifelessness of his speech, like his reticence, betrays a deep-seated lack of vitality where sex is concerned, betrays his emotional desiccation. And this lack, it appears, is not due to his being *hors de combat*.

That Clifford's deficiency is not attributable to his physical condition alone is again brought out when he proposes to Connie that she should have a child by another man. The proposal is prompted by a desire to produce an heir to Wragby, not in consideration of any deprivation that Connie might be supposed to feel, and it is expressed in terms that reveal he has no conception of the meaning of the connection he would have her establish. It would be, he tells her, an 'occasional excitement', and he maintains that what matters in a relationship is 'the life-long companionship . . . the living together from day to day, not the sleeping together once or twice' (p. 46). Just what their living together has meant to Connie has earlier been intimated: 'Connie and Clifford had now been nearly two years at Wragby, living their vague life of absorption in Clifford and his work. Their interests had never ceased to flow together over his work' (p. 19). He tries, further, to dispose of her doubts about 'the other man' by saying they ought to be able to arrange 'this sex thing' as they arrange 'going to the dentist' (p. 46). It is, of course, only because he can think in such terms that he can make his self-assured proposal. The shrinking distaste for sex, implicit both in the phrase he uses to talk of it and in the comparison he draws; the blithe and blind falsification of a fundamental issue of life; the denial of the body by the mind – these are the 'targets', among others, that Clifford readily presents for Lawrence to 'aim at'. It is his approach to the question of her having a child and to all the vital concerns of a marriage, quite as much as his actual paralysis, that has a deadening effect on Connie. Though she tells Dukes, who comments on her appearance, that she is not ill, she begins to be afraid of 'the ghastly white tombstones' near the church, the tombstones which she thinks of (in a revelatory comparison) as having the 'peculiar loathsome whiteness of Carrara marble, detestable as false teeth'; the 'bristling of the hideous false teeth of tombstones on the hill' affects her with 'a grisly kind of horror', and she feels 'the time not far off' when she will be buried there (p. 78).

Clifford's paralysis, therefore, is a rich and immediately suggestive symbol of a failure in the functioning of his passional self, of his phallic self, we might say; and it is a scrupulously fair image of his sexual attitudes. Nor is it a symbol that is deliberately and awkwardly imposed on the novel. It is an integral part of Lawrence's conception, as he himself confirms in 'A Propos of *Lady Chatterley's Lover*':

'I have been asked many times if I intentionally made Clifford paralysed, if it is symbolic. And literary friends say, it would have been better to have left him whole and potent, and to have made the woman leave him nevertheless.

'As to whether the "symbolism" is intentional–I don't know. Certainly not in the beginning, when Clifford was created. When I created Clifford and Connie, I had no idea what they were or why they were. They just came, pretty much as they are. But the novel was written, from start to finish, three times. And when I read the first version, I recognised that the lameness of Clifford was symbolic of the paralysis, the deeper emotional or passional paralysis, of most men of his sort and class today. I realised that it was perhaps taking an unfair advantage of Connie, to paralyse him technically. It made it so much more vulgar of her to leave him. Yet the story came as it did, by itself, so I left it alone. Whether we call it symbolism or not, it is, in the sense of its happening, inevitable.'[1]

Though this is a fascinating description of Lawrence's literary procedure, we would not need it to know that Clifford's paralysis is integrally related to the whole. Its symbolic significance is linked, for instance, as I have intimated, to that of Wragby: like the house, Clifford is not an organic whole; the dead weight of his legs, as well as of his ideas, is analogous to that of its lumber rooms; the severing of connection between the two halves of his body should be related to that between Wragby and TeWishall.

Clifford's paralysis, moreover, is also symbolic of the disconnectedness of his relations with other people, as well as with Connie. He is 'just a little bit frightened', for instance, 'of middle and lower class humanity, and of foreigners not of his own class', for, 'in some paralysing way', he is 'conscious of his own defencelessness' though he has 'all the defence of privilege' (p. 10). While his father is alive, he and his brother and sister are 'cut off' even from 'their own class' (p. 12). This disconnectedness manifests itself, too, in his writing: his stories are 'curious, very personal stories' about people he has known, but though the observation is 'extraordinary and peculiar' they are 'in some mysterious way, meaningless', for there is 'no touch, no actual contact' (p. 17). His work, that is to say, does not give the impression of a man writing in his wholeness; it is 'rather like puppies tearing the sofa cushions to bits' (p. 53).

This lack of contact is strikingly apparent in his relations with the

[1] *Sex, Literature and Censorship*, pp. 266–7.

miners, who are, 'in a sense, his own men'. His interest in them is like that of 'a man looking down a microscope, or up a telescope. He [is] not in touch' (p. 16). His inability to feel a warm connection between the miners and himself reveals itself in the chilling insentience of his economic doctrines, on which he expatiates to Connie in the most powerful symbolic scene in the novel.

One day he goes into the wood with her, 'puffing along' in his bath-chair. Seated in the bath-chair, he is clearly meant to be seen as a symbolic figure: 'I ride', he says self-consciously, 'upon the achievements of the mind of man, and that beats a horse'. The thematic opposition on which the book is constructed emerges here with a natural explicitness, the more especially when Connie invokes Plato's steeds and points out that in the modern world there seems to be 'no more black horse to thrash and maltreat' (p. 186). What the elimination of the black steed means in Clifford's case is revealed when he begins to talk of the mining industry. Maintaining that the ownership of property 'has now become a religious question' and that 'the point is *not*: take all thou hast and give to the poor, but use all thou hast to encourage industry and give work to the poor', Clifford betrays the self-centred ruthlessness of his economic paternalism when he declares that, in the miners' own interests, 'strikes will be made as good as impossible', and adds that 'they'll starve if there are no pits. I've got other provision' (pp. 187–8). His paternalism, moreover, gives way to a *laissez-faire* insouciance when Connie taxes him with the hideous ugliness of Tevershall:

' "They built their own Tevershall, that's part of their display of freedom. They built themselves their pretty Tevershall, and they live their own pretty lives. I can't live their lives for them. Every beetle must live its own life." '

' "But you make them work for you. They live the life of your coal-mine." '

' "Not at all. Every beetle finds its own food. Not one man is forced to work for me" ' (p. 189).

Tevershall, as I have pointed out, resembles Beldover in *Women in Love*, and Clifford's use of the beetle image, though scornful and derogatory in intention, suggestively recalls the way in which it is used in the earlier novel. Beldover, indeed, has been insistently brought to mind during Connie's earlier drive through Tevershall. She finds 'the utter negation of natural beauty, the utter negation of the gladness of life, the utter absence of the instinct for shapely beauty which every

bird and beast has, the utter death of the human intuitive faculty . . . appalling' (p. 158):
'Tevershall! That was Tevershall! Merrie England! Shakespeare's England! No, but the England of to-day, as Connie had realized since she had come to live in it. It was producing a new race of mankind, over-conscious in the money and social and political side, on the spontaneous, intuitive side dead, but dead. Half-corpses, all of them: but with a terrible insistent consciousness in the other half. There was something uncanny and underground about it all. It was an underworld . . .' (p. 159).

Gudrun, we remember, says that Beldover is 'like a country in an underworld', and responds to its appalling ugliness by feeling 'like a beetle toiling in the dust'.[1] If we bear in mind that the beetle in *Women in Love* is a central symbol of 'disintegration', then Clifford's refusal of responsibility for the lives of his miners takes on added meaning. The miners of Tevershall, like those of Beldover, have also been subjected to the 'iron men', the 'machines for hewing the coal' (p. 109), and if, as a result, they have become like 'half-corpses', that is at least in part due to the complacency of the cripple in the bath-chair, to the iron logic of the detached 'mental consciousness'.

Clifford, moreover, like Gerald, believes in a rigid functionalism: 'The individual hardly matters', he says. 'It is a question of which function you are brought up to and adapted to' (p. 191). And because he insists that the miners 'are *not* men' in Connie's 'sense of the word', but merely the undistinguished masses, he can invoke the Roman *panem et circenses* and trace modern industrial unrest to the fact that the authorities have made 'a profound hash of the circuses part of the programme, and poisoned [the] masses with a little education'. He goes on to say that 'whips, not swords' should now be taken up: 'The masses have been ruled since time began, and till time ends, ruled they will have to be.' When Connie asks him whether he can rule them, he confidently replies, 'Oh yes! Neither my mind nor my will is crippled, and I don't rule with my legs' (p. 190). As they proceed into the wood, we, if not Clifford, are made forcefully aware of the limitations of both the mind and the will.

Once in the wood Clifford exclaims at its beauty: 'You are quite right about it's being beautiful', he says. 'It is so amazingly. What is *quite* so lovely as an English spring!' Later, he also comments on the colour of the bluebells, which '[wash] blue like flood-water over the

[1] See Chap. 3, p. 143 above.

broad riding': 'It's a very fine colour in itself', he remarks, 'but useless for making a painting'. Ironically, though he has steered his chair along the channel made through the spring flowers by passing feet, he is quite unaware that the wheels have jolted 'over the wood-ruff and the bugle, and [squashed] the little yellow cups of the creeping jenny', and that they have 'made a wake through the forget-me-nots'. Clifford, we see, is insulated both by his mechanical contrivance and by his utilitarian ideas not only from establishing any real contact with the beauty he praises, but even from realizing that he is responsible for destroying it.[1] The smashing of the flowers, moreover, following on his talk of beetles, if not of whips, should be related to the violence done to the lives of the miners by the machines and the mind of a man like Clifford. His immunity to the wood prevents him from understanding a secret which could perhaps help to regenerate the 'half-corpses', for the wood *has* a secret to divulge: the bracken lifts 'its brown curled heads, like legions of young snakes with a new secret to whisper to Eve. . . . Everything came tenderly out of the old hardness.' It is tenderness, not knowledge, Lawrence seems to insist, that alone can save. It is a pity he should spoil the delicacy of this scene by jeering at Clifford; as the chair moves on through the hyacinths, he cannot refrain from saying:

'O last of all ships, through the hyacinthian shallows! O pinnace on the last wild waters, sailing on the last voyage of our civilization! Whither, O weird wheeled ship, your slow course steering! Quiet and complacent, Clifford sat at the wheel of adventure: in his old black hat and tweed jacket, motionless and cautious. O Captain, my Captain, our splendid trip is done! Not yet though! . . .' (pp. 191–2). The scene is not yet done either, and its consummate mastery is marred by no further lapse of this kind.

---

[1] A passage in *Studies in Classic American Literature*, written well before the novel, throws strong light on the scene and helps to illuminate yet another aspect of Clifford's paralysis: 'It is [the] perfect adjusting of ourselves to the elements, the perfect equipoise between them and us, which gives us a great part of our life-joy. The more we intervene machinery between us and the naked forces the more we numb and atrophy our own senses. Every time we turn on a tap to have water, every time we turn a handle to have fire or light, we deny ourselves and annul our being. The great elements, the earth, air, fire, water are there like some great mistress whom we woo and struggle with, whom we heave and wrestle with. And all our appliances do but deny us these fine embraces, take the miracle of life away from us. The machine is the great neuter. It is the eunuch of eunuchs. In the end it emasculates us all . . .' (pp. 185–6).

After Clifford and Connie stop at the well, they start on the return journey and come to the foot of a steep slope; the chair cannot make the ascent and jogs to a halt. Clifford makes repeated efforts to get it moving again, but to no avail, and when Connie offers to push it, he angrily refuses her help. 'What's the good of the damned thing', he says, 'if it has to be pushed!' (p. 194). His remark recalls Gerald's defence of his conduct with the mare at the railway crossing: 'She must learn to stand–what use is she to me in this country if she shies and goes off every time an engine whistles.'[1] The two scenes, indeed, are similar in several respects. Clifford's smashing of the flowers is analogous to the way in which Gerald subdues both his mare and his miners to the machine; both men insist on the absolute instrumentality of all that they command. But there is also a profound difference between the two scenes. Gerald triumphantly exerts his will, the mare is forced to stand, and Gudrun, who is watching, is irresistibly attracted to him. Clifford makes 'shattering efforts' in the exercise of his will, but he cannot get the chair to move, and by the end of the scene Connie has determined to leave him.

At length, in desperate exasperation, Clifford summons Mellors to inspect the motor. Mellors, who calmly disclaims all knowledge of 'these mechanical things', finally reports that 'there's certainly nothing obviously broken' (pp. 195–6). What is conveyed to us in this scene, then, as distinguished from that in which Gerald figures, are both the inherent limitations of the machine and the impotence of the will, its inability to impose a mechanical solution on every problem with which it is confronted. When Clifford nevertheless persists, with a sick fanaticism of the will, in trying to have his way, he endangers his own body: he refuses Mellors' offer to push the chair, succeeds in starting the engine, puts the motor in gear, and jerks off the brake–but the chair charges 'in a sick lurch sideways at the ditch', and it is only because Mellors manages to catch it by the rail that he avoids an accident. He contrives to steer the chair into the riding and, with it 'fighting the hill', he is momentarily triumphant, until he infuriatedly discovers that Mellors is pushing and orders him to stop. The chair comes to a halt once more, and again Mellors is forced into unwilling service of the machine; he lies on his stomach to do 'something or other to the engine', and Connie cannot help reflecting on 'the ruling classes and the serving classes!' Once again Clifford gets

[1] See Chap. 3, pp. 153–4 above.

the chair to move, and the previous chain of incidents is repeated with a mechanical consistency (pp. 196–8).

What is needed to get Clifford up the hill, of course, is a combination of man and machine, and if Clifford stubbornly tries to deny the man, he is ultimately forced to realize this. In 'a cool, superior tone', he asks Mellors to push the chair, but the brake is jammed, and in struggling to heave up the chair 'and the bulky Clifford', Mellors' face goes 'white with the effort, semi-conscious'. We are given yet another indication, that is to say, of the toll that an insensate will, if not the machine itself, takes of the human body. Mellors begins to push, and the chair moves up the hill. Connie fears that Mellors may be hurt, and much to Clifford's indignation, insists on helping him to push:

'She looked at [Mellors'] smallish, short, alive hand, browned by the weather. It was the hand that caressed her. She had never even looked at it before. It seemed so still, like him, with a curious inward stillness that made her want to clutch it, as if she could not reach it. All her soul suddenly swept towards him: he was so silent, and out of reach! And he felt his limbs revive. Shoving with his left hand, he laid his right on her round white wrist, softly enfolding her wrist, with a caress. And the flame of strength went down his back and his loins, reviving him. And she bent suddenly and kissed his hand. Meanwhile the back of Clifford's head was held sleek and motionless, just in front of them' (pp. 198–200).

This further '*tableau vivant*' (p. 198) vividly epitomizes the difference between the 'mental consciousness' and the 'phallic consciousness'. Though Mellors' hand is just behind his head, Clifford is quite unaware of any vital connection between the gamekeeper and himself. Mellors is simply instrumental to his purpose, and he remains sleekly impervious to the other man's condition. When he is safely returned to the Hall, moreover, he not only shows that he is blind to the meaning of the experience, but patronizes Mellors, bestowing on him the only sort of recognition he seems capable of giving, a reward in goods for services rendered: 'Thanks so much, Mellors', he says. 'I must get a different sort of motor, that's all. Won't you go to the kitchen and have a meal? It must be about time' (p. 201). Connie, in contradistinction to Clifford, is sensitively aware of Mellors' hand, of its aliveness, and though she feels she cannot reach it, she is not out of touch with him. When he caresses her wrist and when she kisses his hand, they are united in an instinctive tenderness that is more than an expression of their love. It seems to me inadequate merely to say, as Mark Spilka does, that the tenderness is 'based upon their past communions'; it is also a silent repudiation of Clifford's inhuman coldness and an affirmation of the saving grace of warmth. I think Spilka is again mistaken when he states 'the wider meaning of the passage' is that ' "phallic tenderness" is the force . . . which moves the dead burden of industrial civilization up the hill'.[1] The point of the novel is that an industrial civilization inevitably draws man downhill, as it were, impressing him into service of the machine and destroying his natural wholeness. Tenderness *is* associated with power–that, as I have pointed out, is part of the symbolism of the wood–but it is not a power that seeks to propel an 'industrial civilization' on its way; it is, rather, a human counter to the machine, a restorative, a force that revives. In the quoted passage we note how Mellors feels 'his limbs revive' when Connie's soul suddenly sweeps towards him; and when his caressing of her wrist generates warmth and establishes the tenderness of touch between them, the 'flame of strength' goes down him, 'reviving him'.

The restorative power of tenderness, indeed, is a fundamental theme of Lawrence's fiction at this time, and the exploration of the theme is productive of a number of interesting interconnections among the three major works of the period. In 'The Virgin and the Gipsy', completed by January 1926, the gipsy saves Yvette from drowning in the flood and then takes her in his arms when she feels that she will 'die of shivering', with the result that 'the warmth [revives] between them'.[2] Charles earlier tells Yvette that the gipsy, during the war, 'was the best man we had, with horses. Nearly died of pneumonia. I thought he *was* dead. He's a resurrected man to me' (p. 1078). Mellors is so severely strained by his exertions with Clifford's chair because, as he explains, the pneumonia, which he contracted during his army service, 'took a lot out of [him]' (p. 199); and he has been 'overhead blacksmith at Tevershall, shoeing horses mostly' (p. 209). The gipsy, rather than the fierce Annable of *The White Peacock*, as is often claimed,[3] thus seems to be the prototype of Mellors; for Mellors, of course, is not only the recipient of a healing tenderness but (as remains to be discussed) also the liberal donor. As 'a resurrected man', the gipsy also

---

[1] *The Love Ethic*, p. 190.   [2] *Tales*, p. 1094.
[3] See, for instance, John Middleton Murry, *Son of Woman*, p. 361, and Mark Schorer, 'On *Lady Chatterley's Lover*', *Modern British Fiction*, ed. Mark Schorer (New York, 1961), p. 294.

.

looks forward to 'The Man Who Died', completed in the summer of 1928. The climax of the story is the coming together of the man who had died and the priestess of Isis. The following passage explicitly conveys the significance of their union:

'So he went down to the shore, in great trouble, saying to himself: "Shall I give myself into this touch? Shall I give myself into this touch? Men have tortured me to death with their touch. Yet this girl of Isis is a tender flame of healing. I am a physician, yet I have no healing like the flame of this tender girl. The flame of this tender girl! Like the first pale crocus of the spring. How could I have been blind to the healing and the bliss in the crocus-like body of a tender woman! Ah, tenderness! More terrible and lovely than the death I died—"'[1]

The 'tender flame of healing'—I emphasize that sexual tenderness in *Lady Chatterley's Lover* is a *restorative* force because Lawrence is often misunderstood to be claiming in the novel that such tenderness can solve the problems of an industrial society.[2] All that it can do, as he despondently realizes ('There's a bad time coming', Mellors writes in the letter which concludes the book), is to mitigate them; but in so doing, it is the means, as in the scene with the chair, of preserving a hold on life. And Connie kisses Mellors' hand not only in denial of Clifford's inhumanity but in gratitude for the 'warm, flamy life' (p. 277) he has given her.

IV

It is immediately after she kisses Mellors' hand that Connie realizes 'for the first time' that she 'consciously and definitely' hates Clifford 'with vivid hate', and the thought that comes into her mind is: 'Now I've hated him, I shall never be able to go on living with him.' Hitherto she has had 'fugitive dreams of friendship' between the two men, 'one her husband, the other the father of her child', but she now becomes fully aware that 'the two males' are 'as hostile as fire and water' (p. 200). It has all along, of course, been Mellors' radical difference from Clifford that has drawn Connie to him in her repulsion from her husband.

The most obvious way in which this difference manifests itself is in

---

[1] *Tales*, p. 1125.

[2] Cf. 'William Tiverton' (Martin Jarrett-Kerr), who states that 'the little boat on which [Lawrence] sails this novel will not bear the weight of the world's future which is to be its cargo'. *D. H. Lawrence and Human Existence*, p. 95.

the physical aura of the two men. I say 'aura' because the difference is clearly so much more than a matter of Mellors' having the full use of his body. Mellors has 'a vital presence'–as Connie discovers when she one day comes upon him unawares:

'In the little yard two paces beyond her, the man was washing himself, utterly unaware. He was naked to the hips, his velveteen breeches slipping down over his slender loins. And his white slim back was curved over a big bowl of soapy water, in which he ducked his head, shaking his head with a queer, quick little motion, lifting his slender white arms, and pressing the soapy water from his ears, quick, subtle as a weasel playing with water, and utterly alone. Connie backed away round the corner of the house, and hurried away to the wood. In spite of herself, she had had a shock. After all, merely a man washing himself; commonplace enough, Heaven knows!

'Yet in some curious way it was a visionary experience: it had hit her in the middle of the body. She saw the clumsy breeches slipping down over the pure, delicate, white loins, the bones showing a little, and the sense of aloneness, of a creature purely alone, overwhelmed her. Perfect, white, solitary nudity of a creature that lives alone, and inwardly alone. And beyond that, a certain beauty of a pure creature. Not the stuff of beauty, not even the body of beauty, but a lambency, the warm, white flame of a single life, revealing itself in contours that one might touch: a body!

'Connie had received the shock of vision in her womb, and she knew it; it lay inside her. But with her mind she was inclined to ridicule. A man washing himself in a backyard! No doubt with evil-smelling yellow soap! She was rather annoyed; why should she be made to stumble on these vulgar privacies' (pp. 68–9).

'A vital presence', it will be recalled, is what the trees in the wood are said to possess,[1] and Mellors' body, we see, bears the same relation to the wood as Clifford's to Wragby; that is to say, it epitomizes the man by projecting the 'spirit of place' in which he has his being. It is for this reason that Mellors is referred to so often as 'a creature'; and he seems 'pure', I take it, because his body communicates a sense of a living wholeness, an aliveness, a 'quickness' such as is reflected in his movements, like that of a weasel playing with water. Like the trees in the wood, he too compels a recognition of his solitary 'inwardness': he seems to be 'utterly alone', 'purely alone', 'inwardly alone', and we remember that before Connie kisses his hand, she notices not only how

[1] See p. 269 above.

'alive' it is, but how 'still': 'It seemed so still, like him, with a curious inward stillness that made her want to clutch it . . .' And like that of the wood, his vitality is associated with a delicate tenderness: his loins are 'slender' and 'delicate', his back is 'slim', his arms are 'slender', and, most revealingly, for 'flamy life' is a crucial image in the novel, his whole body suggests 'a lambency, the warm, white flame of a single life'. This description recalls that of Morel in *Sons and Lovers*: 'Therefore the dusky, golden softness of this man's sensuous flame of life, that flowed off his flesh like the flame from a candle, not baffled and gripped into incandescence by thought and spirit as her life was, seemed to her something wonderful, beyond her.'[1] It is perhaps worth pointing out that some of the warmest scenes in *Sons and Lovers* are those in which Morel, like Mellors, is pictured washing himself, and that Morel also comes of a lower social class than his wife. The connections between the two novels prompt the thought that in *Lady Chatterley's Lover*, among other things, Lawrence was ultimately vindicating his father.

Mellors' vitality, again like that of the wood, is later on also associated with 'power', and Connie is at first both 'startled' and 'frightened' when she is made aware of the quality, but I shall discuss that in the last section of this chapter. I should like now to point out that Connie's reaction to Mellors in this scene is a direct illustration of the way in which 'the mental and nerve consciousness', to use an earlier formulation of Lawrence's, 'exerts a tyranny over the blood-consciousness'.[2] Like Louisa in 'Daughters of the Vicar', Connie has a 'visionary experience', registering the shock of its impact 'in her womb'; but unlike Louisa, she allows her mind to vulgarize it.[3] It is significant, however, that she thinks of Mellors as having a body 'one might touch'. It is, of course, when he touches her in the scene at the pheasant coops, when she actually makes contact with his tenderness, that she begins to value it.

Mellors draws out a 'faintly-peeping chick' from among the mother bird's feathers and hands it to Connie:

' "There!" he said, holding out his hand to her. She took the little drab thing between her hands, and there it stood, on its impossible little stalks of legs, its atom of balancing life trembling through its almost weightless feet into Connie's hands. But it lifted its handsome,

[1] See Chap. 2, pp. 61–2 above.
[2] Letter to Bertrand Russell (December 1915), *Collected Letters*, p. 393.
[3] See the description of a similar scene in *Tales*, p. 79. 'Daughters of the Vicar' was published in 1914.

clean-shaped little head boldly, and looked sharply round, and gave a little "peep". "So adorable! So cheeky!" she said softly.

'The keeper, squatting beside her, was also watching with an amused face the bold little bird in her hands. Suddenly he saw a tear fall on to her wrist.

'And he stood up, and stood away, moving to the other coop. For suddenly he was aware of the old flame shooting and leaping up in his loins, that he had hoped was quiescent for ever. He fought against it, turning his back to her. But it leapt, and leapt downwards, circling in his knees.

'He turned again to look at her. She was kneeling and holding her two hands slowly forward, blindly, so that the chicken should run in to the mother-hen again. And there was something so mute and forlorn in her, compassion flamed in his bowels for her.

'Without knowing, he came quickly towards her and crouched beside her again, taking the chick from her hands, because she was afraid of the hen, and putting it back in the coop. At the back of his loins the fire suddenly darted stronger.

'He glanced apprehensively at her. Her face was averted, and she was crying blindly, in all the anguish of her generation's forlornness. His heart melted suddenly, like a drop of fire, and he put out his hand and laid his fingers on her knee.

' "You shouldn't cry," he said softly.

'But then she put her hands over her face and felt that really her heart was broken and nothing mattered any more.

'He laid his hand on her shoulder, and softly, gently, it began to travel down the curve of her back, blindly, with a blind stroking motion, to the curve of her crouching loins. And there his hand softly, softly, stroked the curve of her flank, in the blind instinctive caress.

'She had found her scrap of handkerchief and was blindly trying to dry her face.

' "Shall you come to the hut?" he said, in a quiet, neutral voice' (pp. 119–20).

This, though it is regrettable to have to use the word again and again, must surely be the most tender scene in Lawrence. We are forced to use the word, for no other will do as well, and in a novel which he at one time proposed to call *Tenderness*,[1] this scene strikingly defines its

---

[1] Cf. the following extract from a letter to Dorothy Brett (January 1928): 'I've been re-writing my novel, for the third time. It's done, all but the last chapter. I think I shall re-christen it *Tenderness*.' *Letters*, p. 697.

meaning. The chicken, it is clear, stirs all the latent tenderness in Connie, affecting her with a sense of gentle, pulsating life in much the same way that the wood does; it is no accident that it is said to have 'little stalks of legs'. Its 'almost weightless feet' which tremble on her hands also, of course, touch her thwarted maternal instincts, pressing as if on an exposed nerve. And Connie weeps not only in the sadness of her own barrenness but 'in all the anguish of her generation's forlornness', in the anguish, that is, of the crippled life at Wragby. Her releasing of the chicken, indeed, the way in which she holds her hands 'slowly forward, blindly', is expressive of a mute recognition that her own hold on life is slipping, that she can no longer hold it in her hands, as it were.

Mellors, who '[held] out his hand to her' to give her the 'atom of balancing life', is again distinguished from Clifford in the nature of his response to her misery. Above all, he has here 'the courage of [his] own tenderness' (p. 290); courage, not only because he ignores the social and moral conventions which would enjoin a more distant form of sympathy towards the wife of his employer, but because he fights himself, fights his will to move away – he '[stands] up, and [stands] away', as soon as he sees she is crying – his will to avoid any further connection with women. But he allows his spontaneous feeling, his vital instincts, to triumph over his will; and when, 'without knowing', he goes 'quickly' towards her, when he softly and 'blindly' strokes her back with 'a blind stroking motion', he accepts the responsibility of his tenderness with a reckless generosity. We are reminded of the trees, 'round and vital', which throw off 'reckless limbs' – and we are reminded, too, of Clifford's insensate will and of his refusal of responsibility for the consequences of his own insentience, for the beetles of Tevershall.

If we understand what Lawrence is doing in this scene, it seems utterly insensitive to say:

'If Lawrence does not regard sex as an end in itself, he certainly endows it with priority not only over marriage but over love as well. For in *Lady Chatterley* the first sexual act between Connie and Mellors quite definitely precedes any love between them and, if love in any sense comes later, it cannot finally find expression in sex, because it is from sex that it first issued.'[1]

'The first sexual act', as is abundantly clear from the scene, is not a matter of 'sex', of promiscuous and indiscriminate lust. The 'old

[1] Colin Welch, 'Black Magic, White Lies', *Encounter*, 16 (February 1961), 75–6.

flame' which shoots up in Mellors and melts his heart rises from the bowels of his compassion, and if it is also a flame of desire, the desire he has for Connie is an expression of the tenderness he feels towards her. 'Sex', indeed, as Lawrence makes us see, is the tenderness of touch. 'Love' between them does grow later–in as full a 'sense' as any ever communicated in English literature–and, rooted in the tenderness of contact which is established before she goes to the hut with him, which is established when he lays his fingers on her knee, it continues to find a natural expression in the sexual connection.

It is not only their love that grows; with it there slowly comes the knowledge that an intimacy between the sexes *can* be 'perfected', to use Clifford's word, by a harmonious sexual relation. Their eventual achievement of a full reciprocity in that relation is the more precious in that both of them have previously had shattering sexual experiences. The record of those experiences reads, indeed, like an abstract of the typical sexual problems that emerge in the novels prior to *Lady Chatterley's Lover*, and makes it appear that Lawrence's last novel is truly a final testament in which he looks back on those problems with a certain tranquillity and serenely disposes of them. I might add, therefore, that it seems to me misguided to suggest that the earlier experiences of the lovers invalidate their relationship:

'A more valid criticism is that the relation of Connie and Mellors is so unlike a normal love relation. Both are deeply injured and unhappy people: what they find in each other is the almost desperate satisfaction of desires that have long been cramped and distorted. And that is not at all like the simple flowering of natural passion and tenderness which Lawrence wishes to recommend. . . .'[1]

I would not have the temerity, myself, to try to define what a 'normal love relation' is, let alone to invoke it as a criterion in judging that of Mellors and Connie. I believe, moreover, that what Lawrence can be taken to 'recommend' in the novel is what he presents us with, and that though the 'flowering of passion' may be 'natural', it is seldom 'simple', as Lawrence knew only too well, and as most of us, I should say, know too.

In her sexual relations with Mellors, Connie has to learn to overcome both her irreverence for the act of sex and her inclination to assert herself in it. When she has her youthful lovers in Germany, she regards 'the love-making' as 'a sort of primitive reversion and a bit of an anti-climax' to 'the impassioned interchange of talk' which alone

[1] Graham Hough, *The Dark Sun*, pp. 165–6.

is of significance, and she cannot help thinking that 'the sex thing' (we recall Clifford's later use of the phrase) is 'one of the most ancient, sordid connections and subjections' (p. 7). Her irreverence turns to bitterness after her disappointment in the affair with Michaelis, but the terms in which the bitterness is expressed reveal the persistence of her youthful attitudes: 'Sex and a cocktail: they both lasted about as long, had the same effect, and amounted to about the same thing' (p. 66). And even after she has gratefully responded to Mellors' sexual tenderness, which is unlike anything she has experienced either with the German youths or with Clifford or with Michaelis, her mental reservations about sex return to plague her:

'... she lay with her hands inert on his striving body, and do what she might, her spirit seemed to look on from the top of her head, and the butting of his haunches seemed ridiculous to her, and the sort of anxiety of his penis to come to its little evacuating crisis seemed farcical. Yes, this was love, this ridiculous bouncing of the buttocks, and the wilting of the poor insignificant, moist little penis. This was the divine love! After all, the moderns were right when they felt contempt for the performance; for it was a performance. It was quite true, as some poets said, that the God who created man must have had a sinister sense of humour, creating him a reasonable being, yet forcing him to take this ridiculous posture, and driving him with blind craving for this ridiculous performance. Even a Maupassant found it a humiliating anti-climax. Men despised the intercourse act, and yet did it' (pp. 178–9).

The 'humiliating anti-climax'–the mature woman, we see, is still in part the immature girl, and the mind which ridiculed her 'visionary experience' in Mellors' backyard functions here, with a cynical clarity, to make 'the intercourse act' ridiculous (the word recurs like a refrain). But by now her hands, which lie 'inert' on his body while her spirit looks on 'from the top of her head', know enough to make her regret that she has withdrawn them from him 'when he [has] finished':

'She wept bitterly, sobbing: "But I want to love you, and I can't. It only seems horrid."

'He laughed a little, half bitter, half amused.

' "It isna horrid," he said, "even if tha thinks it is. An' tha canna ma'e it horrid . . ." ' (p. 180).

That is the lesson Connie has to learn, and when he is about to rise, her sudden realization of the deprivation to which she has condemned herself, makes her cling to him in terror and cry out: 'Don't! Don't

go! Don't leave me! Don't be cross with me! Hold me! Hold me fast!'
He takes her in his arms again, and overcoming 'her own inward
anger and resistance', she begins 'to melt in a marvellous peace'
(p. 180).

In Germany Connie finds that she can yield to a man 'without
yielding her inner, free self', and that she can even 'use this sex thing
to have power over him'. She discovers that all she has to do is to let
the man 'finish and expend himself without herself coming to the
crisis' and then to 'prolong the connection and achieve her orgasm
and her crisis while he [is] merely her tool'. The interdependence of
her irreverence and her assertiveness is neatly revealed in a simile
when we are told she comes to appreciate this has 'a thrill of its own
too . . . a final spasm of self-assertion, like the last word' (p. 8). With
Michaelis she is forced to assert herself in this way because 'he [is]
always come and finished so quickly', and she soon learns 'to hold
him' and to achieve 'her own orgasmic satisfaction from his hard,
erect passivity'. Michaelis is at first quite content with this arrangement, and it gives Connie 'a subtle sort of self-assurance, something
blind and a little arrogant' (pp. 30–1). But one night, with a sudden
and sneering brutality, he tells her that he is 'darned if hanging on
waiting for a woman to go off is much of a game for a man'; Connie
is completely taken aback, and 'her whole sexual feeling for him, or
for any man, [collapses] that night' (p. 57).

Mellors, too, we discover, has been bitterly disillusioned in his sexual
experiences. It is significant, for this focuses attention on a crucial
sexual problem in the novel, that his wife has also attempted to assert
herself in the sex act in the same manner as Connie. One night Connie
asks him why he married Bertha Coutts, and he explains to her:

' "I'll tell you," he said. "The first girl I had, I began with when I was
sixteen. . . . She was the romantic sort that hated commonness. She
egged me on to poetry and reading: in a way, she made a man of me.
. . . And she adored me. The serpent in the grass was sex. She somehow
didn't have any; at least, not where it's supposed to be. I got thinner
and crazier. Then I said we'd got to be lovers. I talked her into it, as
usual. So she let me. I was excited, and she never wanted it. . . . She
adored me, she loved me to talk to her and kiss her: in that way she
had a passion for me. But the other, she just didn't want. . . . And it
was just the other that I *did* want. So there we split. I was cruel,
and left her. Then I took on with another girl, a teacher, who had
made a scandal by carrying on with a married man and driving him

nearly out of his mind. She was a soft, white-skinned, soft sort of a woman, older than me, and played the fiddle. And she was a demon. She loved everything about love, except the sex. Clinging, caressing, creeping into you in every way: but if you forced her to the sex itself, she just ground her teeth and sent out hate. I forced her to it, and she could simply numb me with hate because of it. So I was balked again. I loathed all that. I wanted a woman who wanted me, and wanted *it*.

' "Then came Bertha Coutts. . . . Well, I married her, and she wasn't bad. Those other 'pure' women had nearly taken all the balls out of me, but she was all right that way. She wanted me, and made no bones about it. . . . [But then] she got so's she'd never have me when I wanted her: never. Always put me off, brutal as you like. And then when she'd put me right off, and I didn't want her, she'd come all lovey-dovey, and get me. And I always went. But when I had her, she'd never come off when I did. Never! She'd just wait. If I kept back for half an hour, she'd keep back longer. And when I'd come and really finished, then she'd start on her own account, and I had to stop inside her till she brought herself off, wriggling and shouting, she'd clutch clutch with herself down there, an' then she'd come off, fair in ecstasy. And then she'd say: That was lovely! Gradually I got sick of it: and she got worse. She sort of got harder and harder to bring off, and she'd sort of tear at me down there, as if it was a beak tearing at me. By God, you think a woman's soft down there, like a fig. But I tell you the old rampers have beaks between their legs, and they tear at you with it [*sic*] till you're sick. Self! Self! Self! all self! tearing and shouting! They talk about men's selfishness, but I doubt if it can ever touch a woman's blind beakishness, once she's gone that way. . . . And she'd even try. She'd try to lie still and let *me* work the business. She'd try. But it was no good. She got no feeling off it, from my working. She had to work the thing herself, grind her own coffee. And it came back on her like a raving necessity, she had to let herself go, and tear, tear, tear, as if she had no sensation in her except in the top of her beak, the very outside top tip, that rubbed and tore. . . . Well in the end I couldn't stand it . . . " ' (pp. 208–11).

In what I shall have to say about the relation between this passage and the novels, I am indebted to John Middleton Murry, who was the first to draw attention to a connection between them.[1] Though Murry's work is productive of genuine critical insights, it is vitiated, as I

[1] See *Son of Woman*, pp. 361–4.

shall now have to point out in a particular instance, by an utter confusion of art and life. From what we know of the facts of Lawrence's life, it would seem to be true, as Murry says, that 'the sexual youth of Mellors is Lawrence's own youth: there is barely an effort at disguise' (p. 362); it is at least likely, therefore, that Bertha Coutts is a partial representation of Frieda, and that her relations with Mellors project one particular aspect of Lawrence's own relations with his wife. I grant, too, that it is important to realize the connection between Lawrence's work and his life, since the work so directly reflects the life, but a great deal depends both on the spirit and on the manner in which we make such a connection. When we consider that Lawrence started his life in a miner's cottage in Eastwood and ended it as the greatest English novelist of the century, that alone should induce us to approach the facts of his life with the utmost respect. But that is not all. If Lawrence, as I have tried to show in my discussion of the novels of the third period, fought out in his own person, as it were, the central battle of our times and recorded it, far in advance of the times, for our benefit, we should be moved not only to condemnation when we contemplate the ultimate position he took up, and certainly not to attach to him the easy label of fascist. And if in his sexual relations he had the sort of experiences that are recounted by Mellors, we should sympathize with his travail and wonder at the creative spirit that used the bare facts as impetus for an unmatched artistic statement of sexual problems. It ill becomes us to say, for instance, as Murry does, that 'she is the woman who made demands upon his masculinity which he could not satisfy, and his loathing for her is now uttered with a fearful nakedness of physical hatred' (p. 364). Though this analysis is ostensibly framed in terms of the novel, the context makes it clear enough whom Murry is talking about, the more especially since, in the sentence which follows, he says: 'Now, in Oliver Mellors the gamekeeper, Lawrence is physically reborn . . .' The perils of such criticism, moreover, are manifest. Murry is so concerned with his harrying of Lawrence that he forgets all about the novel; if we go by Mellors' account, and that is all we have to go by, it is clear that it is a complete misrepresentation to say that Bertha makes demands on Mellors' masculinity which he cannot satisfy. Bertha's 'demand' is that her sexual partner, no matter how 'masculine', should cease to be a man and submit to being her instrument: she deliberately 'keeps back longer'. Indeed, I take it that Lawrence carefully uses Michaelis, among other things, to point the difference between a kind of 'masculinity' that he shows to be deficient and that of Mellors.[1]

The importance of identifying Lawrence with Mellors in the passage quoted is that such an identification enables us to view the development of the novels from a fresh standpoint, for as Aldous Huxley long ago remarked of *Son of Woman*, Murry 'has written at great length about Lawrence–but about a Lawrence whom you would never suspect, from reading that curious essay in destructive hagiography, of being an artist'.[2] Mellors' description of his relationship with his 'first girl', then, suggests a likeness between it and that between Paul and Miriam in *Sons and Lovers*, and *their* relationship, it is clear, is a full and frank working out of that which is only hinted at in the relationship of Emily and the narrator in Lawrence's first novel, *The White Peacock*. The second woman with whom Mellors 'takes on', the one who 'plays the fiddle', closely resembles Helena of *The Trespasser*, the second novel. This much, I think, will be at once apparent to anyone acquainted with the early novels. What is not at once apparent is the close connection between Mellors' account of Bertha and Skrebensky's experience with Ursula in the second of the two strange scenes under the moon in *The Rainbow*.[3] Murry should be given full credit here for pointing out the connection, though I cannot agree with his unsubstantiated statement that there is also a relation, in this respect, between the 'sexual experience' of Will and Anna and that of Mellors and Bertha, and I have already indicated my objections to the sort of conclusion he comes to:

'To discover all that underlies this fearful encounter, we should have to go to *Lady Chatterley's Lover*, to Mellors' account of his sexual experience with Bertha Coutts. That is, in the present state of affairs, unquotable. But in that page and a half the curious will find not only the naked physical foundation–"the blind beakishness"–of this experience of Ursula and Anton, but also Lawrence's final account of the sexual experience from which both the sexual experience of Will and Anna, and of Anton and Ursula is derived. *The Rainbow* is, radically, the history of Lawrence's final sexual failure' (p. 88).

[1] Murry's procedure is the more suspect in that it has now been revealed that he was Frieda's lover during Lawrence's absence in America in 1923, and that he later contemplated asking her to leave Lawrence. See his letters to Frieda (December 1951 and November 1955), *Frieda Lawrence: The Memoirs and Correspondence*, ed. E. W. Tedlock (London, 1961), pp. 311, 367.

[2] Introduction to *Letters*, p. x.

[3] See Chap. 3, pp. 118–21 above.

I did not introduce Mellors and Bertha into my interpretation of the
scene under the moon because I wished, as now, to use the last novel
as a vantage point, so to speak, from which to view in retrospect the
subsidiary line of development that runs from *The Rainbow* to it. We do
not labour today under the restrictions that limited Murry, and the
striking recurrence of images of beaks in the passages under consideration enables us to establish with reasonable certainty just what
it was that Ursula did to Skrebensky, though it is impossible to determine this from the text of *The Rainbow* alone. Ursula, we recall, 'clinches
hold' of Skrebensky, kissing him with a 'fierce, beaked, harpy's kiss',
and 'pressing in her beaked mouth' till she has 'the heart of him'; in
the intercourse which follows, 'the fight, the struggle for consummation' is 'terrible' and lasts till it is 'agony to his soul' and he gives way
'as if dead'. Furthermore, the kiss which 'annihilates' Skrebensky in
the first scene under the moon is related to the later experience in a
way which makes it strikingly premonitory of it: 'a sudden lust' seizes
Ursula to 'tear' Skrebensky and 'make him into nothing', while he
hopes to be able to 'net' her body in the iron of his hands; in the kiss
she 'fastens' on him 'hard and fierce', and she '[holds] him there, the
victim, consumed, annihilated'.[1]

This reading of the two passages in *The Rainbow* helps, I think, to
explain what underlies the male resentment of a female sexual
assertiveness in the novels that follow, and it perhaps clarifies the
nature of the attempts made to counter it. It should be related, that is
to say, to three significant developments. In *Women in Love*, it might be
remembered, I suggested that the ultra-phallic sexual experience of
Birkin and Ursula appeared to be presented as a means of controlling
the 'old destructive fires' which he feared to kindle in her. In *Aaron's
Rod* the Marchesa, like Bertha, is a woman who never wants her husband when he wants her; but Aaron, with his overweening, male
eagle power is shown to overcome this resistance in her, and in the sex
act she is 'almost like a clinging child in his arms'. Finally, in *The
Plumed Serpent* Kate is made to forego her 'orgiastic "satisfaction"' altogether when Cipriano succeeds in inducing her to renounce 'the
beak-like friction of Aphrodite of the foam'.

The main purpose of this retrospective survey, however, is to make
clear the nature of Lawrence's achievement in *Lady Chatterley's Lover*.
If, in the aspect to which I have just referred, we can suppose his work
to have been influenced in a directly personal way by his sexual

[1] See Chap. 3, pp. 111–12 above.

experience with his wife, then in his last novel he triumphantly rises above himself; and it seems to me pernicious to attempt to dismiss it, as Murry does (p. 364), as an essay in wish-fulfilment. It has, indeed, been one of the aims of this study to show that, where there are elements of personal 'compensation' in the novels, the weakness, the lack of a true conviction or the sense of an imposed significance, invariably manifests itself in the text and can be exposed in a critical examination. It seems to me that, with one exception (to which I will refer in the next section), there are no such elements in *Lady Chatterley's Lover*. The particular sexual problem I have been discussing, moreover, is presented with an unflinching honesty and frankness and is convincingly resolved.

In her sexual relations with Mellors, Connie starts where Kate ended with Cipriano. When she goes to the hut with him after the scene at the coops and they have intercourse for the first time, she lies still, 'in a kind of sleep, always in a kind of sleep. The activity, the orgasm was his, all his; she could strive for herself no more' (pp. 120–1). We are to understand, I take it, that it is Michaelis who has cowed the frictional Aphrodite in her–she can strive 'no more'; but it is interesting to note that her passivity, unlike that of Kate, is not presented as providing all the 'satisfaction' that she needs or wants, but as a minimal gratification. When Mellors asks her whether it was 'good' for her too, she replies affirmatively, but 'a little untruthfully, for she had not been conscious of much' (p. 122), had not been conscious, that is, as she will be later, of the sense of fulfilment that a true reciprocity brings. Nevertheless, her union with Mellors clearly has a significance which transcends the question of sexual gratification. After her full realization, in the scene with the chicken, of the barrenness and futility of her life, the 'kind of sleep' Mellors gives her is a renewal; indeed, 'the intense movement of his body, and the springing of his seed in her, [is] a kind of sleep' (p. 121).

When they have intercourse for the second time, Connie again lies still: 'Even, when he had finished, she did not rouse herself to get a grip on her own satisfaction, as she had done with Michaelis; she lay still, and the tears slowly filled and ran from her eyes.' We are reminded here of the tears which fall from Ursula's eyes when she has 'annihilated' Skrebensky in *The Rainbow*, of the tear which runs 'with its burden of moonlight, into the darkness, to fall in the sand'. I suggested that Ursula's tears were a tacit admission of the vanity of her victory and of the limits of her assertiveness; Connie's tears spring from feeling 'left out'. They, too, represent an admission; she knows she is left out because it is 'partly . . . her own fault', because she '[wills] herself into this separateness' (pp. 130–1). The next time–I do not wish this to seem like a catalogue of their love-making, but each meeting is the occasion of a significant development–the next time, then, she does not cling to her separateness, and she discovers the joy of a full reciprocity: 'We came off together that time', Mellors tells her, and he adds: 'It's good when it's like that. Most folks live their lives through and they never know it' (p. 139). Connie also begins, at this stage, to understand herself, and the admission that she makes now is of fundamental importance in her relationship with Mellors:

'It was not the passion that was new to her, it was the yearning adoration. She knew that she had always feared it, for it left her help-less; she feared it still, lest if she adored him too much, then she would lose herself, become effaced, and she did not want to be effaced, a slave, like a savage woman . . .' (p. 141).

What she sees now, and what we see with sudden clarity, is that her previous assertiveness in the sexual relation has been a defence against her own fear, her fear of 'losing' herself. Connie, that is to say, has been running blindly within a closed circle: fear of losing herself in adoration of a man has led her to value her own separateness above all else; separateness carried over into the unavoidable physical union of the sexual relation has led to a destructive 'keeping back longer'; the holding back in the sex act has meant that the man must submit to being used as an instrument, and that has meant a dominating female assertiveness. It is a difficult admission for Connie to make, and 'in the flux of new awakening', the 'old hard passion' flames up and she sees Mellors as 'a contemptible object, the mere phallos-bearer, to be torn to pieces when his service [is] performed'. But her heart is heavy at the thought, and she realizes once and for all that she does not want to exercise that sort of power, for it is 'known and barren, birthless; the adoration [is] her treasure'. She decides to 'give up her hard bright female power' and to 'sink in the new bath of life' (p. 141). She is ready, that is, to 'lose' herself. And whereas it was Cipriano's superior power that made Kate abandon her sexual assertiveness, made her accept his 'recoil' from a 'beak-like friction', it is Mellors' tenderness that wins Connie's submission.

Connie's insight into herself is, in regard to the development of Lawrence's ideas, a turning-point in the novels. It is illuminating to relate that insight to what Dorothea Krook says about Lawrence:

'. . . when, as in Lawrence, an extraordinary capacity for love (and need of love) is combined with as extraordinary a capacity to resist and resent the necessary condition of love, that to find one's self one must lose it, it is indeed inevitable that he should suffer perpetually from the fear of a total loss of identity in the act of loving, which seems to have haunted Lawrence all his life and is one of the central experiences repeatedly enacted in his novels and stories. There are signs in his later works of a gradual weakening of this obsessive fear, resulting in a corresponding weakening of the destructive element in the sexual relation and a strengthening of the kind of tenderness that drives out all fear, pride and self-love (Mellors, we remember, was the man "who had the courage of his tenderness"); and *The Man Who Died* represents the most advanced point in Lawrence's development in this direction. . . .'[1]

Though I believe that it is clearly *Lady Chatterley's Lover*, and not 'The Man Who Died', which is of major significance in Lawrence's thinking about the self and love, and that the novel, as I shall try to show, represents a return and not an advance, this is a penetrating commentary, and taken together with Connie's discovery, it opens a new view of a central preoccupation in the novels from *The Rainbow* on. *The Rainbow* was the first novel in which Lawrence considered how separate identity could be preserved in a close union between a man and a woman, how a relationship that he characterized as the 'two in one' could be established. And in his portrayal of the relationship of Tom and Lydia he showed a distinct awareness of what Mrs Krook calls 'the necessary condition of love'; in my analysis of the difficult but crucial passage which describes the consolidation of their union, I suggested that we are shown how Tom 'loses' himself to 'find' himself. In his depiction of the next generation, however, Lawrence indicated how, in Will, a readiness to lose himself in the sexual relation, to fuse with Anna in an undistinguished oneness, represented a flight from the responsibility of singleness and resulted in the virtual extinction of his creative 'man-being'. It is a fear of the 'loss of identity' in this sense which can be said to become 'obsessive' in the novels that follow. It is this fear, as I pointed out, that lies behind Birkin's emphatic insistence on singleness in *Women in Love*, and that leads to his advocacy of a 'unison in separateness' rather than a relation which is 'two in one'. And we can suppose that it is a fear of a loss of identity that is behind Aaron's obsessive dread of 'giving' himself, for his 'intrinsic

[1] *Three Traditions of Moral Thought* (Cambridge, 1959), pp. 284–5.

and central aloneness' is said to be the 'very centre of his being', and he reflects that if he were to break his aloneness, he would 'break his being'.[1] It seems likely, moreover, that the development in *Aaron's Rod* of a concept of relations between the sexes that is concisely defined by the phrase 'one up, one down' is a reflection not only of a defensive attempt to assert a 'male' significance but of the same fear; if the woman 'loses' herself to a man who guards his separateness, that, clearly, can allay the man's fear of a loss of self, if not altogether remove it. And this is precisely what happens to Kate in *The Plumed Serpent*.

Where I must register disagreement with Mrs Krook is in her assumption that Lawrence never overcame this fear. Connie's self-analysis is evidence that he fully understood the sort of fear that could be masked by a sexual assertiveness, and the presentation of her sexual relations with Mellors shows conclusively, I think, that Lawrence could rise above it himself. For Mellors is no Cipriano. From the first, as I have tried to show, he gives generously of himself, despite his experiences with the previous women he has loved; and in the intercourse which prompts Connie to her self-revelation, they both '[lie] and [know] nothing, not even of each other, both lost' (p. 139). The phrase 'both lost' is important, for since the point of view in the descriptions of their relations is predominantly Connie's, we are given no more substantial proof than this that Mellors, too, is ready to lose himself in his love for her. But this is sufficient; the lovers are shown to be moving all the time to the attainment of a full reci-procity, and I think we can safely conclude that what is said of Connie in regard to the vital issue of selfhood applies to Mellors as well. We should remember, too, that it is Connie, after all, who starts by with-holding herself.

If this is so, then Lawrence shows with calm assurance how the fear of a loss of self can be overcome on both sides:

'And she felt him like a flame of desire, yet tender, and she felt herself melting in the flame. She let herself go. She felt his penis risen against her with silent amazing force and assertion, and she let herself go to him. She yielded with a quiver that was like death, she went all open to him. And oh, if he were not tender to her now, how cruel, for she was all open to him and helpless!

'She quivered again at the potent inexorable entry inside her, so strange and terrible. It might come with the thrust of a sword in her

[1] See Chap. 4, p. 194 above.

softly-opened body, and that would be death. She clung in a sudden anguish of terror. But it came with a strange slow thrust of peace, the dark thrust of peace and a ponderous, primordial tenderness, such as made the world in the beginning. And her terror subsided in her breast, her breast dared to be gone in peace, she held nothing. She dared to let go everything, all herself, and be gone in the flood.

'And it seemed she was like the sea, nothing but dark waves rising and heaving, heaving with a great swell, so that slowly her whole darkness was in motion, and she was ocean rolling its dark, dumb mass. Oh, and far down inside her the deeps parted and rolled asunder, in long, far-travelling billows, and ever, at the quick of her, the depths parted and rolled asunder, from the centre of soft plunging, as the plunger went deeper and deeper, touching lower, and she was deeper and deeper and deeper disclosed, the heavier the billows of her rolled away to some shore, uncovering her, and closer and closer plunged the palpable unknown, and further and further rolled the waves of herself away from herself, leaving her, till suddenly, in a soft, shuddering convulsion, the quick of all her plasm was touched, she knew herself touched, the consummation was upon her, and she was gone. She was gone, she was not, and she was born: a woman. . . .

' "It was so lovely!" she moaned. "It was so lovely!" But he said nothing, only softly kissed her, lying still above her. And she moaned with a sort of bliss, as a sacrifice, and a newborn thing' (pp. 180–2).

This remarkable passage is an instance of how the novel, 'properly handled', can 'reveal the most secret places of life', of how it can 'inform and lead into new places the flow of our sympathetic consciousness' (p. 104). We are made fully conscious here, in a way that we have not been before, of what usually remains half-conscious; in other words, there is a return in this passage to something like the method employed in *The Rainbow*, and we have accordingly to be prepared to respond to a similar use of language. The plangent rhythm of the prose is also reminiscent of passages in the earlier novel, but if it conveys to us the nature of the experience described with a direct, almost non-verbal immediacy, we should guard against allowing ourselves to be swept away by it, for the words demand a careful scrutiny and will be found, I think, to be used with precision.

The significance of the passage in respect of the theme of the self and love is clear. Lawrence here defines the prerequisites for a willing acceptance of a loss of self. The first condition is that there be a full assurance of the existence of a warm, tender love in the partner to whom the self is to be surrendered: Connie feels Mellors 'like a flame of desire, yet tender' (is made aware, that is, of both the warmth and the tenderness of his love), and it is this flame that 'melts' her, that melts the self in its hard isolation, and this knowledge that enables her to 'let herself go'. We remember the flame that melted Mellors' will to preserve his separateness in the scene at the coops. It is interesting to find that, whereas the actual moment of consummation in the sex act has often been thought of as a 'death', Lawrence believes the moment of 'death' to be anterior to that; it is the moment when the self is yielded, when there is a 'dying' to self: 'She yielded with a quiver that was like death, she went all open to him.' At such a moment, of course, with the protective casing of separateness removed, the self, in its 'death', is particularly vulnerable, and that is why Connie dreads the thought of Mellors not being 'tender' to her, for if he should come 'with the thrust of a sword in her softly-opened body', that would be a different kind of 'death'–the kind that Cipriano presumably inflicted on Kate. But Mellors comes to her with 'a strange slow thrust of peace, the dark thrust of peace and a ponderous, primordial tenderness, such as made the world in the beginning'; he comes to her, that is, with a tenderness that is creative as well as procreative, for it transforms a 'death' into a 'rebirth' and enables the lost self to find itself. When Connie is thus reassured of his tenderness, she dares 'to let go everything, all herself, and be gone in the flood', and in the consummation that follows, she is 'gone, she [is] not, and she [is] born: a woman'. Her moan of 'bliss' is a recognition that the 'sacrifice' of self is rewarded by a new birth; she is 'a newborn thing'.

With an enhanced sense of 'the wonder of life, and of being' (p. 184), Connie does not only 'find' herself; she awakes to the 'living universe': as she runs home in the twilight, the trees in the wood seem to be 'bulging and surging at anchor on a tide, and the heave of the slope to the house [is] alive' (p. 185). Her joy in a world that is alive and with which she has established a living connection is later given instinctive expression in her nude dance in the rain. She runs out into the rain 'with a wild little laugh, holding up her breasts to the heavy rain and spreading her arms, and running blurred in the rain with the eurhythmic dance-movements she had learned so long ago in Dresden'. We are reminded both of Kate's ritual marriage to Cipriano in the rain and of Gudrun's eurhythmic dancing and frenzied rush on Gerald's Highland bullocks. The difference between Connie and the other two women could not be more profound. She, we know, will not kneel before Mellors and kiss his feet; neither does she feel impelled to assert herself and make an aggressive bid for dominance. What she does, in fact, is to offer herself to Mellors in 'a wild obeisance' (p. 230); hers is the submission of a free self, freely offered in the knowledge that she commands a like homage.[1]

After a lacerating and exhaustive investigation of alternatives, Lawrence, we see, has realized again (for he first described the process in the case of Tom in *The Rainbow*) that a yielding of the self in the act of love need not lead to a rightly abhorred 'mingling and merging', to a loss of identity; he knows again, and conveys the knowledge to us through the conviction of his art, that if the self is yielded in and to tenderness, it is at once found, and found to be enhanced and undiminished. When we bear in mind both his struggle and his achievement, it is incredible to reflect that T. S. Eliot could have been so imperceptive as to say:

'[Lawrence's] vision is spiritual, but spiritually sick. . . . I cannot see much development in *Lady Chatterley's Lover*. Our old acquaintance, the gamekeeper, turns up again: the social obsession which makes his well-born–or almost well-born–ladies offer themselves to–or make use of–plebeians springs from the same morbidity which makes other of his female characters bestow their favours upon savages. The author of that book seems to me to have been a very sick man indeed.'[2] Lawrence's sane healthiness and the remarkable development between *The Plumed Serpent* and *Lady Chatterley's Lover* are surely manifest.

Connie and Mellors, then, the 'couple of battered warriors' (p. 213), as she remarks when she has heard his account of his previous experiences with women, meet in a mutual tenderness and find both healing and fulfilment. They meet, too, in a relationship of the same kind as that which Lawrence earlier symbolized by the rainbow, the

---

[1] Graham Hough lists Connie's dance in the rain as one of the 'lapses' he objects to in the novel. I agree that the other instances he mentions are regrettable weaknesses, but his placing of the dance in the same category seems to suggest he has not grasped its significance: 'There are a few other lapses [he has just discussed the obscene words], all, I believe, dictated by the extraneous passion against the spirit of censorship. They can be briefly dismissed. Connie's dancing in the rain, and her subsequent decoration of Mellors' person with forget-me-nots are bits of self-conscious nudism that fall heavily into the ridiculous. And there is a disastrous, impossibly vulgar conversation between Mellors and Connie's father which simply shows Lawrence hopelessly at sea, and failing unpleasantly in inventing a tone for a dialogue that he has not really felt.' *The Dark Sun*, p. 161.

[2] *After Strange Gods* (London, 1934), pp. 60-1.

'two in one'. Mellors, indeed, finds an equally vivid and illuminating symbol to epitomize the relationship by which he stands: in the letter to Connie which ends the novel he tells her he believes in 'the little flame' that is between them, and he goes on: 'It's my Pentecost, the forked flame between me and you' (p. 316). Lawrence's work, we see, has come full circle. His attempt to determine the basis of an abiding relation between the sexes is at last successfully concluded; his search for 'the third thing' between man and woman, for the Holy Ghost, is over. The rainbow is replaced by the Pentecostal forked flame, and the new image, defined by the novel as a whole, adds to the old the vital quality of tenderness. Mellors may say that the child which Connie is expecting is 'a side issue', for it is not the third thing, but we cannot help feeling that this evidence of the fruitfulness of the relationship is also in some measure a confirmation of its validity. *The Rainbow*, we remember, comes to a close with Ursula's miscarriage.

V

What, then, of that which I have tried to trace in this study, what of the conflict within Lawrence between male and female elements? Does the serenity with which he solves so many of the problems that agitated him for so long indicate that harmony is established in this respect too? Or does it at least indicate that Lawrence is finally reconciled to the predominantly 'female' quality of his vision? His last novel would seem to suggest that he did ultimately write in grudging, if camouflaged, acceptance of the 'female' view of things, for, as I have pointed out, his vindication of the 'phallic consciousness' is, in effect, if not in intention, a vindication of the female principle. Such a conclusion would certainly help to explain the sudden blaze of creative achievement which follows so unexpectedly on the decline that is plainly evident in the novels of the third period, the period in which he was apparently driven to write against his own deepest instincts. But such a conclusion would not convey the whole truth. *Lady Chatterley's Lover* forces us to conclude, rather, that, deep down, so deep, indeed, as radically to qualify the nature of what is offered us while barely disturbing the surface, Lawrence's self-division compels him to make a 'male' counter-assertion of a kind which it is impossible to reconcile with the overt 'female' statement of the novel.

On the face of it there is not much evidence of male assertion on

Lawrence's part. On the contrary, those obtrusive elements which so disfigure the novels of the leadership phase are pleasurably absent. Clifford, for instance, is, in terms of the Hardy essay, all 'man'. Committed both by mishap and by inclination to the spirit, not the flesh, he achieves 'utterance' in his writing and is eminently successful in his work in the 'man's world' of the mines. Yet I need not stress, at this stage, what sort of person he is shown to be, both futile as a writer and utterly inhuman as an industrialist. And the futility and the inhumanity are directly attributable, of course, to the paralysis of his emotional or 'female' self. To be all 'man', we see, and this is a strong refutation of Birkin's characteristic insistence in *Women in Love*, is to be only half a man, is to be, indeed, a 'half-corpse'. Clifford wins his 'man's victory', but at the same time he lets Mrs Bolton shave him and sponge him 'as if he were a child'; he also becomes 'almost a *creature*, with a hard, efficient shell of an exterior and a pulpy interior, one of the amazing crabs and lobsters of the modern, industrial and financial world', and when he is forced out of that world, when, for instance, he discusses the question of Connie's having a child, he speaks 'like a cornered dog' (pp. 113–15). Dog, lobster, crab, child – the indictment of the unadulterated male is vicious. The epithets, moreover, are shown to be not unjustified when Clifford has to face up to the emotional crisis of Connie's abandonment of him. After he has read the letter in which she breaks the news to him, he is 'like a hysterical child', and his face is 'yellow, blank, and like the face of an idiot'; the experienced Mrs Bolton realizes that his hysteria is a sign that 'his manhood [is] dead, temporarily if not finally'. When she comforts him, he clings to her and lets 'himself go altogether, at last'. Clifford's letting go, of course, has to be sharply distinguished from the way in which Connie and Mellors let go: his is a 'sheer relaxation . . . letting go all his manhood, and sinking back to a childish position that [is] really perverse'. In the end he gets into the habit of kissing Mrs. Bolton's breasts 'in exultation, the exultation of perversity, of being a child when he [is] a man' (pp. 302–5). His childish perversity is exhibited just as damagingly, and this is the last we see of him, in his refusal to grant Connie a divorce when he discovers it is Mellors she wishes to marry (pp. 310–12).

Mellors, on the other hand, with whom Lawrence is closely identified in several important respects, as I have indicated, clearly has (again in the sense in which the word is used in the Hardy essay) a preponderantly 'female' character. He even says of himself: 'They used to say I had too much of the woman in me', and though he adds, with justification, 'But it's not that. I'm not a woman because I don't want to shoot birds, neither because I don't want to make money, or get on' (p. 289), we know, nevertheless, that he is in fact presented as an exemplar of the 'phallic consciousness', that is, of the female principle. And we have seen that it is not merely a matter of his having no ambition to make money; he has totally rejected the 'man's world', and his occupation has symbolic undertones, for his task is to preserve the wild life of the wood. He would like, too, to 'try an' live [his] own life' (p. 230), simply to be. It is here that Lawrence is faced by what proves to be an insoluble problem in his fiction when the protagonist is not a writer–the difficulty of establishing a convincing 'male' meaning in such a life. (In his own life, of course, his writing was both his 'utterance' and his 'action', even though it has an unmistakable 'female' quality.) Mellors, indeed, is very much aware of this problem: 'A man must offer a woman *some* meaning in his life', he tells Connie, 'if it's going to be an isolated life, and if she's a genuine woman. I can't be just your male concubine' (p. 289).

The problem is of no consequence to Connie. She assures Mellors he has something that other men do not have, the courage of his own tenderness, and that it is this which will 'make the future' (p. 290); but though the novel has established the supreme importance of this kind of courage in a world in which the Cliffords have power, we remain aware that tenderness is not a 'male' quality. Nor does Mellors in any way modify his rejection of the outer world: he hopes that ultimately he and Connie will be able to have 'some small farm of their own', into which he can 'put his energy' (p. 312), and he writes to her that 'the little flame' between them is for him 'the only thing in the world' (p. 316). He seems set, that is to say, to live the kind of life lived by the Brangwen forebears in *The Rainbow*, a life based on a close connection with the earth and with a woman, a life that is characterized by 'the drowse of blood-intimacy'. It was from that drowse that Tom Brangwen stirred, we remember, girding himself to face the task of establishing his 'man-being'; and it was with an unsatisfied bitterness that he many years later recognized the limitations, as well as the value, of a life which had in fact 'amounted' to nothing but 'the long marital embrace with his wife'.[1] Mellors, in the end, is not conscious of a similar sense of dissatisfaction both because he is more confident of his priorities and because he believes he has found

[1] See Chap. 3, p. 90 above.

the 'male' meaning he is seeking when he conceives of opposing his faith in tenderness to the insentience of the 'man's world':

' "I stand for the touch of bodily awareness between human beings," he said to himself, "and the touch of tenderness. And she is my mate. And it is a battle against the money, and the machine, and the insentient ideal monkeyishness of the world. And she will stand behind me there. Thank God I've got a woman! Thank God I've got a woman who is with me, and tender and aware of me . . ." ' (p. 292).

That Lawrence can permit Mellors this triumphant confidence in the value of tenderness and sexual love is a measure of the distance he has travelled between *The Rainbow* and *Lady Chatterley's Lover*; but when he also allows Mellors to believe that to stand by his tenderness in the isolation of his life with Connie will indeed constitute 'a battle' against the world he hates, he merely evades the point at issue–for Mellors' battle, it is clear, is to be fought outside that world, not from within it, and does not commit him to any characteristic 'male' activity. Lawrence himself, of course, fought such a battle courageously and magnificently in the writing of *Lady Chatterley's Lover*; Mellors cannot respond in a similar way to a challenge he is no doubt ready to take up. If we never feel that he is merely Connie's 'male concubine', we are nevertheless not convinced that he *has* found a genuine male meaning in his life.

I believe it is Lawrence's own uncertainty, in this regard, that makes him feel the need of asserting Mellors' 'manhood' in some other manner:

'It was a night of sensual passion, in which she was a little startled and almost unwilling: yet pierced again with piercing thrills of sensuality, different, sharper, more terrible than the thrills of tenderness, but, at the moment, more desirable. Though a little frightened, she let him have his way, and the reckless, shameless sensuality shook her to her foundations, stripped her to the very last, and made a different woman of her. It was not really love. It was not voluptuousness. It was sensuality sharp and searing as fire, burning the soul to tinder.

'Burning out the shames, the deepest, oldest shames, in the most secret places. It cost her an effort to let him have his way and his will of her. She had to be a passive, consenting thing, like a slave, a physical slave. Yet the passion licked round her, consuming, and when the sensual flame of it pressed through her bowels and breast, she really thought she was dying: yet a poignant, marvellous death.

'She had often wondered what Abélard meant, when he said that in their year of love he and Héloïse had passed through all the stages and refinements of passion. The same thing, a thousand years ago: ten thousand years ago! The same on the Greek vases, everywhere! The refinements of passion, the extravagances of sensuality! And necessary, forever necessary, to burn out false shames and smelt out the heaviest ore of the body into purity. With the fire of sheer sensuality.

'In the short summer night she learnt so much. She would have thought a woman would have died of shame. Instead of which, the shame died. Shame, which is fear: the deep organic shame, the old, old physical fear which crouches in the bodily roots of us, and can only be chased away by the sensual fire, at last it was roused up and routed by the phallic hunt of the man, and she came to the very heart of the jungle of herself. She felt, now, she had come to the real bed-rock of her nature, and was essentially shameless. She was her sensual self, naked and unashamed. She felt a triumph, almost a vainglory. So! That was how it was! That was life! That was how oneself really was! There was nothing left to disguise or be ashamed of. She shared her ultimate nakedness with a man, another being.

'And what a reckless devil the man was! really like a devil! One had to be strong to bear him. But it took some getting at, the core of the physical jungle, the last and deepest recess of organic shame. The phallos alone could explore it. And how he had pressed in on her!' (pp. 258–9).

This passage has been the object of considerable critical attention, and there is no need to repeat in detail the arguments with which certain critics have established the meaning of the allusions to Abélard and the Greek vases. These allusions, which by themselves are inconclusive, link up, as Eliseo Vivas was the first to point out,[1] with others to Mellors' sexual practices with his wife and, in particular, with Clifford's reference (in a letter to Connie) to Mellors' apparent liking for using his wife, 'as Benvenuto Cellini says, "in the Italian way" ' (p. 280). They should also be related to Connie's immediate understanding of Mrs Bolton's vague report of 'the low, beastly things' Mellors is alleged to have done to his wife: 'Connie remembered the last night she had spent with him, and shivered. He had known all that sensuality, even with a Bertha Coutts!' (p. 276). I think, there-

---

[1] *D. H. Lawrence* (1960), pp. 133–5. Cf. Andrew Shonfield, 'Lawrence's Other Censor', *Encounter*, 17 (September 1961), 63–4; G. Wilson Knight, 'Lawrence, Joyce and Powys', *Essays in Criticism*, 11 (October 1961), 403–17; and John Sparrow, 'Regina v. Penguin Books Ltd.', *Encounter*, 18 (February 1962), 35–43.

fore, that we can now take it as established beyond doubt that the 'night of sensual passion' is a night on which Mellors has anal intercourse with Connie; but what needs to be investigated is the significance of the experience.

The experience is overtly presented as a necessary purification: the 'sensual fire', and we note how fire images recur throughout the passage, burns out 'false shames' and smelts out 'the heaviest ore of the body into purity'. It is as if Connie must be made to realize, despite conventional revulsion and disgust, that nothing to do with the body is 'low' and 'beastly', that where there is love between a man and a woman, everything is permissible. It seems that the fire is intended to consume the shame associated with 'the most secret places' and with the practice of what is usually regarded as a sexual 'perversion' in much the same way that Lawrence's use of the 'obscene' words is meant to startle us out of a different, but related, shame. Lawrence, says G. Wilson Knight, is trying to 'blast through . . . degradation to a new health. . . . So the deathly is found to be the source of some higher order of being; contact with a basic materiality liberates the person.'[1]

If this is what Lawrence is trying to do in the passage, it strikes me that we have to face two objections to the way in which he presents the experience. In the first place, if it is love that can be deemed to give the practice an individual moral sanction in defiance of convention, it is clear that Mellors, on this night, does not come to Connie in love. It is not only that we are told that his sensual passion is 'not really love'; it seems to spring directly from his anger with Hilda. Immediately before, he has had a fierce altercation with Connie's sister, and when Connie remonstrates with him, he replies: 'She should ha' been slapped in time.' Though Connie cannot help being aware of how 'outwardly angry' he is even when they are alone together, she is sure that his anger is not directed to her. Nevertheless, he takes 'no notice of her', and when he asks her to go up to the bedroom, 'the anger still [sits] firm' on his brows (p. 257). Mellors' 'sensuality', therefore, would appear to be an expression of his anger, a release of the violence that is coiled within him; the man who cannot bring himself to shoot birds, we note, here lends himself with gusto to 'the phallic hunt'. Is it, we wonder, and I shall return to this point later, that Lawrence cannot reconcile the experience he describes with the kind of love he has previously shown to exist between

[1] *Ibid.,* p. 408.

Connie and Mellors, and that he consequently feels compelled to provide a context of anger and violence for it? That, at all events, *is* the context of Mellors' 'sensuality'–just as the scene at the coops defines the meaning of his 'tenderness'.

Second, I think we cannot help noticing that there is something peculiarly one-sided about the way in which the experience is presented. I have remarked earlier, in regard to the important question of the 'losing' and 'finding' of the self in the sex act, that we are left in no doubt that what is shown to happen to Connie applies to Mellors as well. Here, though we are told that the shame and fear crouch 'in the bodily roots of us', of all of us, that is, it is only Connie, apparently, who needs to be subjected to the purifying fire. If it is maintained that, in the nature of things, it is only Connie who can be so subjected, then Wilson Knight has pointed out that, in *Women in Love*, there are hints of an analogous practice in which 'the implements are fingers'.[1] If this is so, and I find Wilson Knight's argument convincing in its broad outline, though not always in detail, then it is most noticeable that in *Women in Love* Birkin wishes to share in the same experience:

'And he too waited in the magical steadfastness of suspense, for her to take this knowledge of him as he had taken it of her. He knew her darkly, with the fullness of dark knowledge. Now she would know him, and he too would be liberated . . .' (p. 360).

In *Lady Chatterley's Lover* there is no indication that Mellors wishes Connie to take this liberating knowledge of him; and though it is said to be 'forever necessary' to burn out a shame that is twice referred to as 'organic', he shows no desire to be purified of *his* shame and fear.

I suggest the experience is shown to be one-sided because its covert significance is the aggrandizement of the male. The vitality of the trees in the wood, we recall, was associated with power as well as with tenderness, and it seems to me that in the quoted passage Mellors, the keeper of the wood and the man who has the courage of his tenderness, is celebrated as a man of power. Indeed, the Mellors who is presented to us in this passage bears a distinct resemblance to Cipriano of *The Plumed Serpent*. He has both 'his way' and 'his will' of Connie, and she has to be 'a passive, consenting thing, like a slave, a physical slave'. I have already indicated that I believe it is Lawrence's uncertainty about the 'male' meaning in Mellors' life that leads him to present this kind of evidence of his manhood. Connie's reaction to Mellors on this night would seem to confirm the analysis: she reflects what 'a

[1] See Chap. 3, p. 179 above.

reckless devil the man' is, 'really like a devil'; she contrasts Mellors' manhood with that of men like Clifford and Michaelis, whom she thinks of as 'so doggy', and she realizes 'how rare a thing a man is' when most men, it seems, are 'dogs that trot and sniff and copulate'; finally, she looks appreciatively at Mellors, who is 'sleeping so like a wild animal asleep' (p. 259). Mellors, we see, is a wild animal where other men are tame dogs; he is a devil who dares everything where other men only copulate; he is a 'man'.

Two further objections to the passage now present themselves. First, it seems to me that Lawrence is guilty of forcing Connie's reaction to the experience in much the same way that he forces Kate's responses to Cipriano. For Lawrence to say flatly that Connie was a 'little' startled and 'almost' unwilling, but that 'at the moment' the 'thrills of sensuality' were 'more desirable' than the 'thrills of tenderness', for him to say that she was a 'little' frightened, but that 'she let him have his way' seems to me to be a wanton denial of the scrupulous and penetrating presentation of her previous reactions to Mellors. We remember that her fear of 'losing' herself was a fear of becoming 'effaced', and that 'she did not want to be effaced, a slave, like a savage woman'.[1] It was tenderness alone which broke down her resistance to even orthodox intercourse, and induced her to accept her effacement. Nevertheless, she dreaded 'the thrust of a sword in her softly-opened body', fearing that it 'would be death'.[2] Her fear, then, was allayed by Mellors' tenderness, and, allowing herself to 'die', she was 'reborn'; here, his passion 'consumes', and she 'really [thinks] she [is] dying'. The desirability of such a 'death' is not established merely by saying that it is 'poignant' and 'marvellous', for we have just been told that Mellors' sensuality '[burns] the soul to tinder'.

Second, it has struck several critics as significant that, in a book as determinedly frank as *Lady Chatterley's Lover*, Lawrence should be reticent and oblique in his description of the 'night of sensual passion'. I think this is an important consideration, but it seems to me absurd to say, as Andrew Shonfield does, that the reticence and obliquity are 'cowardly',[3] or to maintain, as John Sparrow does, that the method betrays a 'fundamental dishonesty'.[4] We can hardly think of the man who wrote *Lady Chatterley's Lover*, when he wrote it, as a coward; and if Lawrence expressed his meaning obliquely in the passage under

---

[1] See p. 294 above.   [2] See pp. 296–7 above.
[3] 'Lawrence's Other Censor', *loc. cit.*, p. 64.
[4] 'Regina v. Penguin Books Ltd.', *loc cit.*, p. 41.

discussion, he was not dishonest about it, for he carefully added a sufficient number of clues elsewhere to make it quite unambiguous. Sparrow has himself shown the pains that Lawrence took to make his meaning clear, and if Shonfield, writing before Sparrow, could only make 'a reasonable guess' at it, that is attributable to his own failure to follow up all the clues, not to Lawrence's cowardice. Nor do I believe it is justified to say that Lawrence is 'completely reticent about the sensuality' because he 'cannot achieve any sort of innocence about it . . . It is evil, because he believes it to be evil.'[1] Whatever the covert meaning of the scene may be, I have already indicated, in discussing its overt significance, that Lawrence assuredly did not believe the practice itself to be evil, that he was, indeed, fighting against those who would automatically assume it to be so. I think it more likely that he is reticent because he does not know how to present the experience directly in such a way that it will not appear to be 'unnatural' or disgusting or degrading–though he is convinced it is none of these. And he does not know how to say directly what he wants to say because he is uncertain of the value of what he is offering, uncertain that the liberation of which Wilson Knight writes can be achieved in this way, uncertain–and these are the points that I should like to stress–that he can really reconcile this kind of sensuality with love and tenderness, and that it is a legitimate means of asserting manhood.

It is scarcely surprising that Lawrence is uncertain. If he is trying to blast through to a new health, as Wilson Knight says he is, it is perhaps only to be expected that he should be tentative about this method of doing so, for he is exploring an experience of an unusual kind at a level far removed from ordinary understanding. If, moreover, he is also using the experience as a means of asserting Mellors' manhood, he must be uneasily aware that this represents a reversion to the ethos of *The Plumed Serpent*, an ethos which he tacitly repudiated in undertaking to write *Lady Chatterley's Lover* and from which he later explicitly dissociated himself in his letters.[2] Finally, if he is trying to reconcile the sensuality with love and tenderness, he must also be uneasily aware that he is negating a great deal of what he has so profoundly established in the book. We have been shown that there is no need for tenderness to be balanced by power; it has its own power, a revivifying

[1] John Middleton Murry, *Son of Woman*, p. 365.
[2] See, for instance, the letter to Witter Bynner, quoted in part in Chap. 4 pp. 256–7 above.

power, and we cannot reconcile the flame that melts and heals with the fire that sears and consumes. Lawrence, it seems, is trying to suggest that love between a man and a woman must be both 'sensual' and 'tender', in the sense in which these words are defined by their contexts in the novel. It is not a convincing position because he has not been able to establish that the 'sensuality' is a manifestation of love. We can see clearly enough that the same man can be both 'tender' and 'sensual'; we are not convinced that he can be both with the woman he loves. I submit that Lawrence cannot convince us because, in effect, he is also trying to reconcile a 'male' sensuality with a 'female' tenderness; and though the two are perhaps not intrinsically irreconcilable, he–at any rate–was temperamentally incapable of effecting such a reconciliation.

In discussing *Women in Love*, I suggested that Birkin, who is a most Lawrence-like figure, felt free to express his desire for 'oneness' in the wrestling bout with Gerald because he was under no defensive compulsion, as he apparently was in regard to a woman, to realize the man's 'otherness'. To the extent that we can identify Lawrence with Birkin in this respect, I think we can say that Lawrence, who had a predominantly 'female' disposition, laboured under a similar compulsion; we may add that his characteristic insistence that the man should not 'lose' himself in the sex act sprang, to follow Mrs Krook, from the fear of a loss of identity, of his male identity, and that the presence in *Women in Love* of hints of an unorthodox sexual practice indulged in by Birkin and Ursula should be related to the same fear. Inasmuch as Lawrence can be identified with Mellors on the 'night of sensual passion', therefore, I would suggest that the sensuality represents not only a reversion to a desire for male domination, but also a recrudescence of the old fear of a loss of identity, which, as we have seen, is the fundamental cause of a sexual assertiveness. Mellors' tenderness has taught Connie to overcome this fear, but it would seem that, in this instance, a similar fear on his part is responsible for his departure from the more usual form of intercourse; there is no fear of a 'loss' of self in this kind of contact because there is no tenderness to melt the separateness of the self. Indeed, the repeated emphases on the fact that Mellors is 'a man', to which I have already referred in another connection, take on further significance when we interpret them in this light, and we become aware of a deeper level of meaning when we are told that Connie 'shared her ultimate nakedness with a man, another being'.

The passage which I have discussed at such length does, I think, impair the quality of the novel both because it introduces an alien element into the vision of tenderness which is otherwise so superbly rendered, and because, on a small scale, in the forcing of Connie's response, it represents a failure of artistic integrity. But we should not over-emphasize the failure here. Mellors, after all, puts his faith, in the end, in the little flame of tenderness, not in the searing fire of sensuality, and we are left with the forked flame burning gently and unalloyed.

The passage is also an indication, however, of Lawrence's failure to reconcile his 'male' and 'female' impulses. I believe that this failure, as I have tried to show throughout this study, was the fundamental determinant of the direction he took in the large enterprise of the novels. *Sons and Lovers* gave him both the knowledge and the confidence of his power as a writer, and was the fullest expression in his early work of that opposition between the spirit and the flesh which was to continue to be of prime concern to him. The opposition, of course, is a basic instance of the male and female principles, of which he was to write at length in the Hardy essay; and it was of such concern to him not only because it was externalized in the conflict between his mother and father and in his own relations with Jessie Chambers, but also because it projected a violent clash within himself. In *The Rainbow* Lawrence made his most strenuous effort to show how the male and female principles could be reconciled both within the individual psyche and within marriage. I think that this is Lawrence's finest novel, less flawed than *Women in Love*, if not more profound; and I do not believe it is coincidental that in it he succeeded in depicting an individual who was able to achieve a full reconciliation between the two principles. It is perhaps not without significance that the individual should have been a woman, that the task, as it were, was to balance an inherently female disposition with 'male' qualities. In *The Rainbow*, however, no man was found to match Ursula's achievement, and in *Women in Love*–the most remarkable of the novels in its scope–her marriage to Birkin proved to be a marriage on essentially 'female' terms. In it, moreover, Birkin persuaded Ursula to withdraw with him from the 'man's world', and this withdrawal, I believe, necessitated the ensuing effort to redefine the meaning of 'man-being' and to explore alternative ways of effecting a return to the world of men. This effort led to the compensatory male assertion, of which there was already some evidence in *Women in Love*, that characterized the novels of the third period, and that drove Lawrence through *Aaron's Rod* and *Kangaroo* to the cul-de-sac of *The Plumed Serpent.* These novels are the worst of Lawrence's mature work. The decline in artistic achievement, in comparison with *Women in Love,* which preceded them, is marked; and it would seem that, in trying to establish a new kind of 'male' significance and to assert a desire for male domination, Lawrence wrote so badly because he was writing against his own deepest values. In *Lady Chatterley's Lover* he succeeded in giving full and vivid expression to those values and in producing a novel that is only a little inferior to *The Rainbow* and *Women in Love.* To the end, however, he could not reconcile the male and female elements in himself; and his attempt to balance the overt 'female' tendency of the novel by asserting a covert 'male' significance resulted in its major blemish.

Appendix: The Bathing Scene in *The White Peacock*

IN MY PREFACE I REMARKED THAT *The White Peacock* DEALS tentatively with themes that are fully developed in the later novels; I find it of special interest, in this respect, in its treatment of the theme of male friendship. The bathing scene in particular is anticipatory of the wrestling bout in *Women in Love*, of the sick-room scene in *Aaron's Rod*, and of Cipriano's initiation into godhood in *The Plumed Serpent*.

In *The White Peacock* the most vivid relationship is that between George and Cyril, the narrator and the character with whom Lawrence is obviously identified. Cyril's general attitude to George is one of sympathetic, if often irritated, understanding; but on occasion his feeling is transformed into a powerful love:

'[George] knew how I admired the noble, white fruitfulness of his form. As I watched him, he stood in white relief against the mass of green. He polished his arm, holding it out straight and solid; he rubbed his hair into curls, while I watched the deep muscles of his shoulders, and the bands stand out in his neck as he held it firm; I remembered the story of Annable.

'He saw I had forgotten to continue my rubbing, and laughing he took hold of me and began to rub me briskly, as if I were a child, or rather, a woman he loved and did not fear. I left myself quite limply in his hands, and, to get a better grip of me, he put his arm round me and pressed me against him, and the sweetness of the touch of our naked bodies one against the other was superb. It satisfied in some measure the vague, indecipherable yearning of my soul; and it was the same with him. When he had rubbed me all warm, he let me go, and we looked at each other with eyes of still laughter, and our love was perfect for a moment, more perfect than any love I have known since, either for man or woman' (p. 292).

The direct observation and simple, unimpeded sincerity of this description give it a remarkable emotional force. It is perhaps the best known and most widely referred to passage in *The White Peacock*, but I should like to discuss some points that have gone unnoticed.

Harry T. Moore has stated that George is based on Jessie Chambers' brother Alan.[1] The crucial fact, however, of the squalid drunken extinction of George's potentially bright physical being accords with what we know of the decline of Lawrence's father; and the sentence with which the book ends strikingly anticipates the plight of Walter Morel in *Sons and Lovers*: '[George] sat apart and obscure among us, like a condemned man.' I would suggest, therefore, that it is more rewarding to view George as an unconscious projection of Lawrence's father, and that the quoted passage is expressive of a passionate love for the disguised father-figure. The disguise, moreover, slips for an instant: George is said to hold and rub Cyril 'as if [he] were a child'–'or rather' (it is immediately added), 'a woman he loved and did not fear' (I shall comment on this amendment later). That the comparison which first comes to Lawrence's mind is not a casual one but springs from a deeply felt wish is disclosed by an incident which immediately precedes this scene. Cyril is out walking in the fields when he becomes aware of 'two tiny larks' in a nest in the grass:

'I gently put down my fingers to touch them; they were warm; gratifying to find them warm, in the midst of so much cold and wet. . . . When one fledgling moved uneasily, shifting his soft ball, I was quite excited; but he nestled down again, with his head close to his brother's. In my heart of hearts, I longed for someone to nestle against, someone who would come between me and the coldness and wetness of the surroundings. I envied the two little miracles exposed to

[1] *The Intelligent Heart*, p. 66.

any tread, yet so serene. It seemed as if I were always wandering, looking for something which they had found even before the light broke into their shell. I was cold . . . I ran with my heavy clogs and my heart heavy with vague longing, down to the Mill . . .' (p. 289).

Though the baby larks nestle against each other, what really comes between them and the coldness and wetness of the surroundings is the warmth and security of the parental nest, which is presumably what they had found even before the light broke into their shell. The 'someone' whom Cyril wishes to nestle against is surely a protective parent, and the 'vague longing' of this passage is the same 'vague, indecipherable yearning of [his] soul' which is in some measure appeased when he nestles, like a child, against George and is rubbed 'all warm'.

Cyril's reference to Annable ('I remembered the story of Annable') as he watches George drying himself is also revealing. The reference should be linked to the recurrence, in relation to Annable, of one of the comparisons that immediately follows mention of his name in the bathing passage:

'With all this, [Annable] was fundamentally very unhappy – and he made me also wretched. It was this power to communicate his unhappiness that made me somewhat dear to him, I think. He treated me as an affectionate father treats a delicate son; I noticed he liked to put his hand on my shoulder or my knee as we talked; yet withal, he asked me questions, and saved his thoughts to tell me, and believed in my knowledge like any acolyte' (p. 196).

Annable, it would seem, is – like George – a projection of Lawrence's father. For even apart from the suggested relation between the quoted passages, the reference to the mature, Cambridge-educated man's believing in Cyril's knowledge 'like any acolyte' becomes intelligible only if it is traced back to Lawrence's miner-father. Some of the attributes of the gamekeeper, moreover, are not unlike those of Walter Morel in *Sons and Lovers*: '[Annable] had a great attraction for me; his magnificent physique, his great vigour and vitality, and his swarthy, gloomy face drew me' (p. 195).

This interpretation of the bathing scene deals with only one aspect of its meaning. If the scene suggests a strong, unconscious yearning and love for a father-figure, it is overtly concerned with the theme of male friendship. Whether there is a connection between the two motifs is a matter for conjecture, but I should think that their interlinking in a crucial passage in Lawrence's first book is not coincidental.

Even if we regard the scene as unambiguously and innocently descriptive of the intense friendship between Cyril and George, we cannot help noticing the significant amendment of the comparison first used to amplify the nature of the relationship: '. . . he took hold of me and began to rub me briskly, as if I were a child, or rather, a woman he loved and did not fear'. The simile seems to be intended to suggest the free and unrestrained quality of the naked intimacy of the two men as distinguished from the restrictive hesitations which a man might be supposed to feel in a similar situation with a woman – the male friend, we are told, is loved but not feared. If this is Lawrence's intention, the comparison is in fact a decisive indication of the 'effeminacy' that is attributed to Cyril throughout the novel. The description of the drying is clearly suggestive of a homosexual situation in which Cyril plays the female role; and the passage affords an early instance of the unconscious homosexual tendency in Lawrence's work that is exhibited, again and again, on those occasions when he describes a physical intimacy between men with one of whom he is identified.

Index